## DATE DUE

Alfred R Wallace

# A NARRATIVE OF TRAVELS

ON THE

# AMAZON AND RIO NEGRO,

## WITH AN ACCOUNT OF THE NATIVE TRIBES,

### AND OBSERVATIONS ON THE CLIMATE, GEOLOGY, AND NATURAL HISTORY OF THE AMAZON VALLEY.

BY

## ALFRED RUSSEL WALLACE, LL.D.

WITH A BIOGRAPHICAL INTRODUCTION BY THE EDITOR.

## GREENWOOD PRESS, PUBLISHERS
### NEW YORK

Originally published in 1895
by Ward, Lock & Bowden Ltd., London

First Greenwood Reprinting 1969

Library of Congress Catalogue Card Number 68-55226

SBN 8371-1641-4

PRINTED IN UNITED STATES OF AMERICA

# BIOGRAPHICAL INTRODUCTION.

(*BY THE EDITOR.*)

M R. ALFRED RUSSEL WALLACE, the co-discoverer with Mr. Darwin of the principle of natural selection as the main agent in the evolution of species, has in his published works travelled over a much more diversified range of subjects than Mr. Darwin. To books of travel, of philosophical and of systematic natural history, he has added others dealing with the causes of depression of trade, proposing land nationalisation, defending belief in miracles and in modern spiritualism, and attacking vaccination. Although it would not be right here to enter into a criticism of such controversial works, enough may be said to indicate that their author, admittedly a master-mind in regard to the philosophy and the details of evolution, is widely qualified in regard to political and social questions.

Born at Usk in Monmouthshire on the 8th of January, 1823, and educated at Hertford Grammar School, the future adventurous traveller early became a voyager on a small scale, during his residence with an elder brother, a land surveyor and architect. From 1836 to 1848 while so occupied he resided in various parts of England and Wales, and acquired some knowledge of agriculture and of the social and economic conditions of the labouring classes. While living in South Wales, about 1840, he first turned his attention to natural history, devoting all his spare time to collecting and preserving the native plants, and eagerly reading books of travel. While residing at Leicester in 1844-5 (as an English master in the Collegiate School), he made the acquaintance of Mr. H. W. Bates, an ardent entomologist, and when, some years later, the desire to visit tropical countries became too strong to be resisted, he proposed to Mr. Bates a joint expedition to the Amazons, one of the objects, in addition to the collection of natural history specimens, being to gather facts, as Mr. Wallace expressed it in one of his letters to Mr. Bates, "towards solving the problem of the origin of species," a subject on which they had already conversed and corresponded extensively. The two friends met in London early in 1848 to study the collections of South American animals and plants already there; and they embarked at Liverpool in a small trading vessel on the 20th of April, 1848, reaching the mouth of the Amazons just a month later. From this date the present volume speaks for itself. We will merely note that Mr. Bates took a different route of exploration from Mr. Wallace from March 1850; he remained seven years longer in the country, and in 1863 published his most attractive "Naturalist on the Amazons."

Mr. Wallace's travels on the Rio Negro and to the upper waters of the Orinoco, his adventurous ascent of the rapid river Uaupés, his observations on the natural history and the native tribes of the Amazon valley, are simply and naturally recorded in this volume. His assemblage of facts will be seen to form a broad basis for induction as to causes and modes of transformation of species. His return voyage bade fair to be his last, for the vessel in which he sailed took fire, and was completely destroyed, with a large proportion of Mr. Wallace's live animals and valuable specimens. Ten anxious days had to be spent in boats, tortured not only by shortness of food but by remembrances of the dangers encountered in obtaining valued specimens, now irretrievably lost. It was only after an eighty days' voyage that Mr. Wallace landed at Deal on the 18th of October, 1852. His "Travels on the Amazon and Rio Negro," published in the autumn of 1853, had an excellent reception, and after disposing of the collections which had been sent home previous to his return Mr. Wallace started for another tropical region, the Malay archipelago.

From July 1854, when he arrived in Singapore, to the early part of 1862, Mr. Wallace travelled many thousand miles, mostly in regions little explored before, especially for natural history purposes. Borneo, Java, Sumatra, Timor, Celebes, the Moluccas, the Aru and Ké Islands, and even New Guinea were visited, some more than once, and long sojourns were made in the most interesting regions. Even those who have read his delightful " Malay Archipelago," first published in 1869, cannot know all the treasures given to science by Mr. Wallace's eight years' expatriation, for before writing his travels he had contributed no fewer than eighteen papers to the transactions or journals of the Linnean, Zoological, and Entomological Societies, and twelve articles to various scientific periodicals, while in his subsequent volumes on "Natural Selection," 1871, his monumental work on the " Geographical Distribution of Animals," 1876, on "Tropical Nature," 1878, and on "Island Life," 1880, he laid open still more fully his accumulations of travel and thought in both hemispheres. One of the most valuable results of his travels in Malaysia was the establishment of a line dividing the archipelago into two main groups, Indo-Malaysia and Austro-Malaysia, marked by peculiar species and groups of animals. This line, now everywhere known as Wallace's line, is marked by a deep sea belt between Celebes and Borneo, and Lombok and Bali respectively ; and it is curious that a similar line, but somewhat further east, divides on the whole the Malay from the Papuan races of man. The new facts on butterflies, on birds of paradise, on mimicry between various animals and plants, and on the Malay and Papuan races are only a few of the subjects of intense interest illuminated by Mr. Wallace as the result of his travels in Malaysia.

In a paper in the *Annals and Magazine of Natural History* for September, 1855, " On the Law that has regulated the Introduction of New Species," Mr. Wallace had already drawn the conclusion that every species has come into existence coincident both in space and time with a pre-existing closely allied species. In the same paper is a brief expression of the idea which Mr. Darwin expanded into one of his fine passages comparing all members of the same class of beings to a great tree. The varied facts of the distribution of animal and plant life, set forth and explained in this paper, foreshadow the author's future great work on the subject. Mr. Darwin, already an observer and student of long standing on the question of the origin of species, had noted this paper and agreed to the truth of almost every word of it. In October 1856, Mr. Wallace wrote to Mr. Darwin from Celebes, and in replying to his letter Mr. Darwin, on May 1st, 1857, said he could plainly see that they had thought much alike, and had to a certain extent come to similar conclusions ; and later in the same year he wrote to Mr. Wallace, "I infinitely admire and honour your zeal and courage in the good cause of Natural Science."

In February 1858 Mr. Wallace wrote an essay at Ternate, "On the Tendency of Varieties to depart indefinitely from the original Type," which proved to be the proximate cause of the publication of Mr. Darwin's "Origin of Species." The manuscript of this paper was sent to Mr. Darwin, and reached him on June 18th, 1858, and the views it expressed coincided remarkably with those developed in Mr. Darwin's mind by many different lines of investigation. He proposed to get Mr. Wallace's consent to publish it as soon as possible ; but on the urgent persuasion of Sir Joseph Hooker and Sir Charles Lyell, a joint communication of some extracts from a manuscript written by Mr. Darwin in 1839—1844, and a letter written by him to Professor Asa Gray of Boston, U.S., in 1857, together with Mr. Wallace's paper, was made to the Linnean Society on July 1st, 1858. As Sir Joseph Hooker wrote, "The interest excited was intense, but the subject was too novel and too ominous for the old school to enter the lists before armouring ;" and there was no attempt at discussion. The further history of the "Origin of Species" controversy is well known, and has previously been sketched in the first volume of this library. What deserves repeating and emphasizing is that Mr. Wallace must rank as a completely independent and original discoverer of the essential feature of the "Origin of Species." Mr. Wallace originally termed his view one of progression and continued divergence. "This progression," he wrote in the Linnean essay, "by minute steps, in various directions, but always checked and balanced by the necessary conditions, subject to which alone existence can be preserved, may, it is believed, be followed out so as to agree with all the phenomena presented by organized beings, their extinction and succession in past ages, and all the extraordinary modifications of form, instinct, and habits which they exhibit." Nothing in scientific history is more interesting or more admirable than the way in which the two great discoverers in biological evolution fully admired and recognized each other's independent work ; and continued their intercourse through life untinged by any shadow of un- worthy feeling. Mr. Darwin wrote to Mr Wallace on January 25th, 1859, "Most cordially do I wish you health and entire success in all your pursuits, and, God knows, if admirable zeal and energy deserve success, most amply do you deserve it;" and in 1876 he wrote to him, "You have paid me the highest conceivable compliment by what you say of your work in relation to my chapters on distribution in the 'Origin,' and I heartily thank you for it."

In one important point Mr. Wallace early found himself in divergence from Mr. Darwin. This was as to the limits of natural selection as applied to man. Mr. Darwin saw no reason to imagine a break or a new force or kind of action in regard to the development of man, and especially of his brain and mind; while Mr. Wallace, from the belief that savage man possesses a brain too large for his actual requirements, from the absence of a general hairy covering in lower men, from the difficulty of conceiving the origin of some of man's physical and mental faculties by natural selection, and from the nature of the moral sense, came to the conclusion that a superior intelligence, acting nevertheless through natural and universal laws, has guided the development of man in a definite direction and for a special purpose.

This divergence of view from that of Darwinism pure and simple may be interestingly illustrated from an autobiographical passage in Mr. Wallace's Essays "On Miracles and Modern Spiritualism," 1881. He says: "From the age of fourteen I lived with an elder brother, of advanced liberal and philosophical opinions, and I soon lost (and have never since regained) all capacity of being affected in my judgments, either by clerical influence or religious prejudice. Up to the time when I first became acquainted with the facts of spiritualism, I was a confirmed philosophical sceptic, rejoicing in the works of Voltaire, Strauss, and Carl Vogt, and an ardent admirer (as I am still) of Herbert Spencer. I was so thorough and confirmed a materialist that I could not at that time find a place in my mind for the conception of spiritual existence, or for any other agencies in the universe than matter and force. Facts, however, are stubborn things. My curiosity was at first excited by some slight but inexplicable phenomena occurring in a friend's family, and my desire for knowledge and love of truth forced me to continue the inquiry. The facts became more and more assured, more and more varied, more and more removed from anything that modern science taught, or modern philosophy speculated on. The facts beat me." By slow degrees he came to believe in the existence of a number of preterhuman intelligences of various grades, and that some of these, though invisible and intangible to us, can and do act on matter and influence our minds. He was thus led to attack the *à priori* arguments against miracles, and to believe that many of the so-called spiritualistic phenomena are genuine and occasioned by unseen beings. He further championed spiritualism as teaching valuable moral lessons, and leading to moral and spiritual improvement, when rightly followed out. Here he claims that he does not depart in any way from scientific principle. "The cardinal maxim of spiritualism," he says, "is that every one must find out the truth for himself. It makes no claim to be received on hearsay evidence; but on the other hand it demands that it be not rejected without patient, honest, and fearless inquiry."

In yet another field Mr. Wallace has proved himself a bold originator. His early gained knowledge of land-tenure and the condition of tenants and labourers gave him an experience which with riper years produced the conviction that there was no way to remedy the evils resulting from landlordism but the adoption of a properly guarded system of occupying owner-ship under the State as landlord. He has endeavoured to show the necessity and the practicability of his views in his work entitled "Land Nationalisation, its Necessity and its Aims," first published in 1882. In a third edition he has added an appendix on the nationalisation of house property, the State being destined, he believes, to become sole ground landlord. A later work of his on "Bad Times," 1885, is an essay on the then existing depression of trade, tracing it to the evils caused by great foreign loans, excessive war expenditure, the increase of speculation, and of millionaires, and the depopulation of the rural districts. Among other remedies he is strongly in favour of the increase of labourers' allotments, and of personal culture of the land by the occupier. In the same year his zeal and fearlessness in championing causes which he identifies with that of liberty, were exhibited in a pamphlet entitled "Forty-five Years of Registration Statistics," in which he sought to prove vaccination both useless and dangerous. Beside all this, Mr. Wallace has been a frequent contributor to scientific trans-actions, and to the leading magazines and reviews. Finally, this year he has produced a standard work on "Darwinism," which is the most perfect as well as the most readable form in which the subject has yet been presented.

Such worthy work has not been without recognition. Mr. Wallace was awarded in 1868 the Royal Medal of the Royal Society for his many contributions to theoretical and practical zoology, among which his discussion of the conditions which have determined the distribution of animals in the Malay archipelago, as well as his writings on the origin of species, found prominent mention. In 1870, he received the Gold Medal of the *Société de Géographie* of Paris. In 1876 he was President of the Biological Section at the Glasgow meeting of the British Association. After the publication of his work on land nationalisation a Land Nationalisation Society was formed, of which Mr. Wallace is President. In 1881 he was awarded a Civil List pension of £200 a year, in recognition of the amount and value of his scientific work; and in 1882 the University of Dublin conferred upon him the honorary degree of LL.D.

On all occasions Mr. Wallace has persistently exalted Mr. Darwin's work, and, comparatively speaking, made light of his own. Full well may we say with Mr. Darwin, "You are the only man I ever heard of who persistently does himself an injustice, and never demands justice. But you cannot burke yourself, however much you may try." The intelligent minds which honour the name of Darwin, will not forget to honour that of his fellow-discoverer, Alfred Russel Wallace.

G. T. B.

# PREFACE.

A N earnest desire to visit a tropical country, to behold the luxuriance of animal and vegetable life said to exist there, and to see with my own eyes all those wonders which I had so much delighted to read of in the narratives of travellers, were the motives that induced me to break through the trammels of business and the ties of home, and start for

" Some far land where endless summer reigns."

My attention was directed to Pará and the Amazon by Mr. Edwards's little book, " A Voyage up the Amazon," and I decided upon going there, both on account of its easiness of access and the little that was known of it compared with most other parts of South America.

I proposed to pay my expenses by making collections in Natural History, and I have been enabled to do so ; and the pleasures I have found in the contemplation of the strange and beautiful objects continually met with, and the deep interest arising from the study in their native wilds of the varied races of mankind, have been such as to determine my continuing in the pursuit I have entered upon, and to cause me to look forward with pleasure to again visiting the wild and luxuriant scenery and the sparkling life of the tropics.

In the following pages I have given a narrative of my journeys and of the impressions excited at the time. The first and last portions are from my journals, with little altera- tion ; but all the notes made during two years, with the greater part of my collections and sketches, were lost by the burning of the ship on my homeward voyage. From the fragmentary notes and papers which I have saved I have written the intermediate portion, and the four last chapters on the Natural History of the country and on the Indian tribes, which, had I saved all my materials, were intended to form a separate work on the Physical History of the Amazon.

In conclusion, I trust that the great loss of materials which I have suffered, and which every naturalist and traveller will fully appreciate, may be taken into consideration, to explain the inequalities and imperfections of the narrative, and the meagreness of the other part of the work, so little proportionate to what might be expected from a four years' residence in such an interesting and little-known country.

LONDON, *October,* 1853.

## PREFACE TO NEW EDITION.

THIS issue is substantially a reprint of the original work, but the proof sheets have been carefully revised and many verbal corrections made. A few notes have been added, and English names have in many cases been substituted for the local terms which were used too freely in the first edition. The only omissions are the vocabularies of Indian languages and Dr. Latham's observations on them, which were thought to be unsuitable to the general reader. The publishers have supplied a few additional woodcuts which give a fair idea of Amazonian scenery. A. R. W.

PARKSTONE, DORSET, *October,* 1889.

# CONTENTS.

## CHAPTER I.
### PARÁ.

Arrival at Pará—Appearance of the city and its environs—The inhabitants and their costumes—Vegetation—Sensitive plants —Lizards—Ants and other insects—Birds —Climate—Food of the inhabitants...... 1

## CHAPTER II.
### PARÁ.

Festas—Portuguese and Brazilian currency —M. Borlaz' estate—Walk to the rice-mills—The virgin forest, its plants and insects—Milk-tree—Saw and rice-mills— Caripé or pottery-tree—India-rubber-tree —Flowers and trees in blossom—Saûba ants, wasps, and chegoes—Journey by water to Magoary—The monkeys—The commandante at Laranjeiras—Vampire bats—The timber-trade—Boa constrictor and sloth ......................................... 13

## CHAPTER III.
### THE TOCANTÍNS.

Canoe, stores, and crew—River Mojú— Igaripé Miri—Cametá—Senhor Gomez and his establishment—Search for a din-ner—Jambouassú—Polite letter — Baião and its inhabitants—A swarm of wasps— Enter the rocky district—The Mutuca— Difficulty of getting men—A village with-out houses—Catching an alligator—Duck-shooting—Aroyas, and the Falls—A noc-turnal concert—Blue macaws—Turtles' eggs—A slight accident—Capabilities of the country—Return to Pará ............ 35

## CHAPTER IV.
### MEXIANA AND MARAJÓ.

Visit to Olería—Habits of birds—Voyage to Mexiana—Arrival—Birds—Description of the island—Population—Slaves, their treatment and habits—Journey to the Lake—Beautiful stream—Fish and birds at the lake — Catching alligators — Strange sounds, and abundance of ani-mal life—Walk back—Jaguar meat—Visit to Jungcal in Marajó—Embarking cattle —Ilha das Frechas ......................... 57

## CHAPTER V.
### THE GUAMÁ AND CAPIM RIVERS.

Natterer's hunter, Luiz—Birds and insects —Prepare for a journey—First sight of the Piroróco—St. Domingo—Senhor Calistro—Slaves and slavery—Anecdote —Cane-field—Journey into the forest— Game—Explanation of the Piroróco— Return to Pará—Bell-birds and yellow parrots ............................................. 77

## CHAPTER VI.
### SANTAREM AND MONTEALEGRE.

Leave Pará—Enter the Amazon—Its pecu-liar features—Arrive at Santarem—The town and its inhabitants—Voyage to Mon-tealegre—Mosquito plague and its remedy —Journey to the Serras—A cattle estate— Rocks, picture writings, and cave—The *Victoria regia*—Mandiocca fields—A festa —Return to Santarem—Beautiful insects —Curious tidal phenomenon — Leave Santarem—Obydos—Villa Nova—A kind priest—Serpa—Christmas Day on the Amazon ............................................. 92

## CHAPTER VII.
### BARRA DO RIO NEGRO AND THE SOLIMÕES.

Appearance of the Rio Negro—The city of Barra, its trade and its inhabitants— Journey up the Rio Negro—The Lingoa Geral—The umbrella bird—Mode of life of the Indians — Return to Barra— Strangers in the city—Visit to the Solimões — The Gapó — Manaquery —

Country life — Curl-crested Araçaris—
Vultures and Onças—Tobacco growing
and manufacture—The Cow-fish—Senhor
Brandão—A fishing party with Senhor
Henrique—Letters from England ...  112

## CHAPTER VIII.

### THE UPPER RIO NEGRO.

Quit Barra for the Upper Rio Negro—
Canoe and cargo—Great width of the
river—Carvoeiro and Barcellos—Granite
rocks—Castanheiro—A polite old gentleman—São Jozé—A new language—The
cataracts—São Gabriel—Nossa Senhora
da Guía—Senhor L. and his family—
Visit to the river Cobati—An Indian
village—The Serra—Cocks of the rock—
Return to Guía—Frei Jozé dos Santos
Innocentos .....................................  133

## CHAPTER IX.

### JAVITA.

Leave Guía—Marabitánas—Serra de Cocoi
—Enter Venezuela—São Carlos—Pass
the Cassiquiare—Antonio Dias—Indian
shipbuilders—Feather-work—Maróa and
Pimichín—A black jaguar—Poisonous
serpents—Fishing—Walk to Javíta—Residence there—Indian road-makers—Language and customs—A description of
Javíta—Runaway Indians—Collections at
Javíta—Return to Tómo—A domestic
broil—Marabitánas and its inhabitants—
Reach Guía ...................................  159

## CHAPTER X.

### FIRST ASCENT OF THE RIVER UAUPÉS.

Rapid current—An Indian Malccca—The
Inmates—A Festival—Paint and ornaments—Illness—São Jeronymo—Passing
the cataracts—Jauarité—The Tushaúa
Calistro—Singular palm—Birds—Cheap
provisions— Edible ants, and earth-
worms—A grand dance—Feather ornaments—The snake-dance—The Capí—A

State cigar — Ananárapicóma — Fish —
Chegoes—Pass down the falls—Tame
birds—Orchids—Piums—Eating dirt—
Poisoning — Return to Guía — Manoel
Joaquim—Annoying delays ............  188

## CHAPTER XI.

### ON THE RIO NEGRO.

Difficulties of starting—Descending the
falls — Catching an alligator — Tame
parrots—A fortnight in Barra—Frei
Jozé's diplomacy—Pickling a cow-fish—
A river storm—Brazilian veracity—Wana-
wáca—Productiveness of the country—
A large snake—São Gabriel—São Joaquim
—Fever and ague .........................  218

## CHAPTER XII.

### THE CATARACTS OF THE UAUPÉS.

Start for the Uaupés—São Jeronymo and
Jauarité—Indians run away—Numerous
cataracts—Reach Carurú—Difficult passage—Painted Malocca—Devil music—
More falls — Ocokí — Curious rocks —
Reach Uarucapurí — Cobeu Indians—
Reach Mucúra—An Indian's house and
family—Height above the sea—Tenente
Jesuino—Return to Uarucapurí—Indian
prisoners—Voyage to Jauarité—Correcting the calendar—Delay at São Jeronymo
236

## CHAPTER XIII.

### SÃO JERONYMO TO THE DOWNS.

Voyage down the Rio Negro—Arrive at
Barra—Obtaining a passport—State of
the city—Portuguese and Brazilian enterprise—System of credit—Trade—Immorality, and its causes—Leave Barra—A
storm on the Amazon—Salsaparilha—A
tale about Death—Pará—The yellow fever
—Sail for England—Ship takes fire—Ten
days in the boats—Get picked up—Heavy
gales—Short of provisions—Storm in the
Channel—Arrive at Deal .............  256

PAGE

## CHAPTER XIV.

THE PHYSICAL GEOGRAPHY AND GEOLOGY OF THE AMAZON VALLEY .........................  280

## CHAPTER XV.

VEGETATION OF THE AMAZON VALLEY .................................................................  300

## CHAPTER XVI.

OBSERVATIONS ON THE ZOOLOGY OF THE AMAZON DISTRICT ......................................  310

## CHAPTER XVII.

ON THE ABORIGINES OF THE AMAZON ..................................................................  331

# LIST OF FULL-PAGE ILLUSTRATIONS.

1.—PORTRAIT OF MR. WALLACE . . . . *Facing Title*

2.—MAP OF THE AMAZON AND PARTS OF ITS
    BASIN VISITED BY MR. WALLACE . . Facing page   1

3.—CHAPEL AT NAZARÉ NEAR PARÁ . . .   ,,    ,,    14

4.—A BRAZILIAN PLANTATION ON THE LOWER
    AMAZONS . . . . . . . .   ,,    ,,    95

5.—ON THE RIO NEGRO . . . . .   ,,    ,,    136

6.—A VILLAGE ON THE RIO NEGRO . . .   ,,    ,,    138

7.—A STREAM IN THE FOREST . . . .   ,,    ,,    199

8.—AN INDIAN VILLAGE ON THE RIO NEGRO .   ,,    ,,    232

9.—GRANITE ROCKS AND VEINS, ETC. . .   ,,    ,,    293

10.—FORMS OF GRANITE ROCKS . . . .   ,,    ,,    294

11.—COMPARATIVE CURVES OF TEMPERATURE,
    PARÁ AND LONDON . . . . .   ,,    ,,    297

12.—CURVES OF PRESSURE AND RAIN AT PARÁ .   ,,    ,,    298

13.—INDIAN IMPLEMENTS AND DOMESTIC ARTICLES   ,,    ,,    350

14.—    ,,      ,,      ,,      ,,    ,,    ,,    352

15.—FIGURES ON THE GRANITE ROCKS, RIVER
    UAUPÉS . . . . . . .   ,,    ,,    360

16.—FIGURES ON THE GRANITE ROCKS, RIVER
    UAUPÉS . . . . . . .   ,,    ,,    362

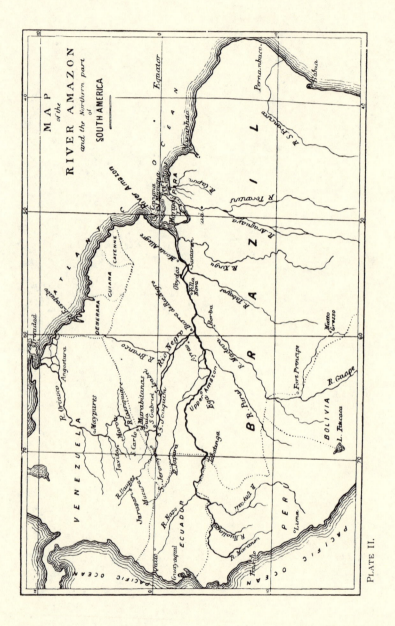

MAP
of the
RIVER AMAZON
and the Northern part
of
SOUTH AMERICA

PLATE II.

# TRAVELS

ON THE

# AMAZON AND RIO NEGRO.

---

## CHAPTER I.

### PARÁ.

Arrival at Pará—Appearance of the City and its Environs—The Inhabitants and their Costume—Vegetation—Sensitive Plants—Lizards—Ants and other Insects—Birds—Climate—Food of the Inhabitants.

T was on the morning of the 26th of May, 1848, that after a short passage of twenty-nine days from Liverpool, we came to anchor opposite the southern entrance to the River Amazon, and obtained our first view of South America. In the afternoon the pilot came on board, and the next morning we sailed with a fair wind up the river, which for fifty miles could only be distinguished from the ocean by its calmness and discoloured water, the northern shore being invisible, and the southern at a distance of ten or twelve miles. Early on the morning of the 28th we again anchored; and when the sun rose in a cloudless sky, the city of Pará, surrounded by the dense forest, and overtopped by palms and plantains, greeted our sight, appearing doubly beautiful from the presence of those luxuriant tropical productions in a state of nature, which we had so often admired in the conservatories of Kew and Chatsworth. The canoes

I

passing with their motley crews of Negroes and Indians, the vultures soaring overhead or walking lazily about the beach, and the crowds of swallows on the churches and house-tops, all served to occupy our attention till the Custom-house officers visited us, and we were allowed to go on shore.

Pará contains about 15,000 inhabitants, and does not cover a great extent of ground; yet it is the largest city on the greatest river in the world, the Amazon, and is the capital of a province equal in extent to all Western Europe. It is the residence of a President appointed by the Emperor of Brazil, and of a Bishop whose see extends two thousand miles into the interior, over a country peopled by countless tribes of unconverted Indians. The province of Pará is the most northern portion of Brazil, and though it is naturally the richest part of that vast empire, it is the least known, and at present of the least commercial importance.

The appearance of the city from the river, which is the best view that can be obtained of it, is not more foreign than that of Calais or Boulogne. The houses are generally white, and several handsome churches and public buildings raise their towers and domes above them. The vigour of vegetation is everywhere apparent. The ledges and mouldings support a growth of small plants, and from the wall-tops and window-openings of the churches often spring luxuriant weeds and sometimes small trees. Above and below and behind the city, as far as the eye can reach, extends the unbroken forest; all the small islands in the river are wooded to the water's edge, and many sandbanks flooded at high-water are covered with shrubs and small trees, whose tops only now appeared above the surface. The general aspect of the trees was not different from those of Europe, except where the " feathery palm-trees " raised their graceful forms; but our imaginations were busy picturing the wonderful scenes to be beheld in their dark recesses, and we longed for the time when we should be at liberty to explore them.

On landing, we proceeded to the house of Mr. Miller, the consignee of our vessel, by whom we were most kindly received, and invited to remain till we could settle ourselves as we should find most convenient. We were here introduced to most of the English and American residents, who are all engaged in trade, and are few in number. For the four

following days we were occupied in walking in the neighbourhood of the city, presenting our passports and obtaining license
to reside, familiarising ourselves with the people and the
vegetation, and endeavouring to obtain a residence fitted for
our pursuits. Finding that this could not be immediately
done, we removed to Mr. Miller's "rosinha," or country-house,
situated about half a mile from the city, which he kindly gave
us the use of till we could find more convenient quarters.
Beds and bedsteads are not wanted here, as cotton woven
hammocks are universally used for sleeping in, and are very
convenient on account of their portability. These, with a few
chairs and tables and our boxes, are all the furniture we had
or required. We hired an old Negro man named Isidora for
a cook and servant of all work, and regularly commenced
house-keeping, learning Portuguese, and investigating the
natural productions of the country.

My previous wanderings had been confined to England and
a short trip on the Continent, so that everything here had the
charm of perfect novelty. Nevertheless, on the whole I was
disappointed. The weather was not so hot, the people were
not so peculiar, the vegetation was not so striking, as the
glowing picture I had conjured up in my imagination, and had
been brooding over during the tedium of a sea-voyage. And
this is almost always the case with everything but a single view
of some one definite object. A piece of fine scenery, as
beheld from a given point, can scarcely be overdrawn; and
there are many such, which will not disappoint even the most
expectant beholder. It is the general effect that strikes at
once and commands the whole attention : the beauties have
not to be sought, they are all before you. With a district or
a country the case is very different. There are individual
objects of interest, which have to be sought out and observed
and appreciated. The charms of a district grow upon one in
proportion as the several parts come successively into view,
and in proportion as our education and habits lead us to
understand and admire them. This is particularly the case
with tropical countries. Some such places will no doubt strike
at once as altogether unequalled, but in the majority of cases
it is only in time that the various peculiarities, the costume of
the people, the strange forms of vegetation, and the novelty of
the animal world, will present themselves so as to form a con-

nected and definite impression on the mind.  Thus it is that
travellers who crowd into one description all the wonders and
novelties which it took them weeks and months to observe, must
produce an erroneous impression on the reader, and cause him,
when he visits the spot, to experience much disappointment.
As one instance of what is meant, it may be mentioned that
during the first week of our residence in Pará, though constantly
in the forest in the neighbourhood of the city, I did not see a
single humming-bird, parrot, or monkey.   And yet, as I
afterwards found, humming-birds, parrots, and monkeys are
plentiful enough in the neighbourhood of Pará ; but they
require looking for, and a certain amount of acquaintance
with them is necessary in order to discover their haunts, and
some practice is required to see them in the thick forest, even
when you hear them close by you.

But still Pará has quite enough to redeem it from the
imputations we may be supposed to have cast upon it.   Every
day showed us something fresh to admire, some new wonder
we had been taught to expect as the invariable accompaniment
of a luxuriant country within a degree of the equator.   Even
now, while writing by the last glimmer of twilight, the vampire
bat is fluttering about the room, hovering among the timbers
of the roof (for there are no ceilings), and now and then
whizzing past my ears with a most spectral noise."

The city has been laid out on a most extensive plan ; many
of the churches and public buildings are very handsome, but
decay and incongruous repairs have injured some of them,
and bits of gardens and waste ground intervening between the
houses, fenced in with rotten palings, and filled with rank
weeds and a few banana-plants, look strange and unsightly to
a European eye.   The squares and public places are picturesque, either from the churches and pretty houses which
surround them, or from the elegant palms of various species,
which with the plantain and banana everywhere occur ; but
they bear more resemblance to village-greens than to parts
of a great city.   A few paths lead across them in different
directions through a tangled vegetation of weedy cassias,
shrubby convolvuli, and the pretty orange-flowered *Asclepias
curassavica*,—plants which here take the place of the rushes,
docks, and nettles of England.   The principal street, the
"Rua dos Mercadores" (Street of Merchants), contains almost

the only good shops in the city. The houses are many of them only one storey high, but the shops, which are often completely open in front, are very neatly and attractively furnished, though with rather a miscellaneous assortment of articles. Here are seen at intervals a few yards of foot-paving, though so little as only to render the rest of your walk over rough stones or deep sand more unpleasant by comparison. The other streets are all very narrow. They consist either of very rough stones, apparently the remains of the original paving, which has never been repaired, or of deep sand and mud-holes. The houses are irregular and low, mostly built of a coarse ferruginous sandstone, common in the neighbourhood, and plastered over. The windows, which have no glass, have the lower part filled with lattice, hung above, so that the bottom may be pushed out and a peep obtained sideways in either direction, and from these many dark eyes glanced at us as we passed. Yellow and blue wash are liberally used about most of the houses and churches in decorating the pilasters and door and window openings, which are in a debased but picturesque style of Italian architecture. The building now used as custom-house and barracks, formerly a convent, is handsome and very extensive.

Beyond the actual streets of the city is a large extent of ground covered with roads and lanes intersecting each other at right angles. In the spaces formed by these are the "rosinhas," or country-houses, one, two, or more on each block. They are of one storey, with several spacious rooms and a large verandah, which is generally the dining-room and most pleasant sitting and working apartment. The ground attached is usually a swamp or a wilderness of weeds or fruit-trees. Sometimes a portion is formed into a flower-garden, but seldom with much care or taste, and the plants and flowers of Europe are preferred to the splendid and ornamental productions of the country. The general impression of the city to a person fresh from England is not very favourable. There is such a want of neatness and order, such an appearance of neglect and decay, such evidences of apathy and indolence, as to be at first absolutely painful. But this soon wears off, and some of these peculiarities are seen to be dependent on the climate. The large and lofty rooms, with boarded floors and scanty furniture, and with half-a-dozen doors and windows in each, look at first comfortless, but are nevertheless exactly adapted to a tropical country, in which a carpeted, curtained, and cushioned room would be unbearable.

The inhabitants of Pará present a most varied and interesting mixture of races.    There is the fresh-coloured Englishman, who seems to thrive as well here as in the cooler climate of his native country, the sallow American, the swarthy Portuguese, the more corpulent Brazilian, the merry Negro, and the apathetic but finely formed Indian ; and between these a hundred shades and mixtures, which it requires an experienced eye to detect.   The white inhabitants generally dress with great neatness in linen clothes of spotless purity.   Some adhere to the black cloth coat and cravat, and look most uncomfortably clad with the thermometer from 85° to 90° in the shade.   The men's dress, whether Negro or Indian, is simply a pair of striped or white cotton trousers, to which they sometimes add a shirt of the same material.   The women and girls on most gala occasions dress in pure white, which, contrasting with their glossy black or brown skins, has a very pleasing effect ; and it is then that the stranger is astonished to behold the massy gold chains and ornaments worn by these women, many of whom are slaves.   Children are seen in every degree of clothing, down to perfect nudity, which is the general condition of all the male coloured population under eight or ten years of age.   Indians fresh from the interior are sometimes seen looking very mild and mannerly, and, except for holes in their ears large enough to put a cart-rope through, and a peculiar wildness with which they gaze at all around them, they would hardly be noticed among the motley crowd of regular inhabitants.

I have already stated that the natural productions of the tropics did not at first realise my expectations.   This is principally owing to the accounts of picture-drawing travellers, who, by only describing the beautiful, the picturesque, and the magnificent, would almost lead a person to believe that nothing of a different character could exist under a tropical sun.   Our having arrived at Pará at the end of the wet season, may also explain why we did not at first see all the glories of the vegetation.   The beauty of the palm-trees can scarcely be too highly drawn ; they are peculiarly characteristic of the tropics, and their varied and elegant forms, their beautiful foliage, and their fruits, often useful to man, give them a never-failing interest to the naturalist, and to all who are familiar with descriptions of the countries where they most abound. The rest of the vegetation was hardly what I expected. We found many beautiful flowers and climbing plants, but there are also many places which are just as weedy in their appearance as in our own bleak climate. But very few of the forest-trees were in flower, and most of them had nothing very peculiar in their appearance. The eye of the botanist, indeed, detects numerous tropical forms in the structure of the stems, and the form and arrangement of the leaves; but most of them produce an effect in the landscape remarkably similar to that of our own oaks, elms, and beeches. These remarks apply only to the immediate vicinity of the city, where the whole surface has been cleared, and the present vegetation is a second growth. On proceeding a few miles out of the town into the forest which everywhere surrounds it, a very different scene is beheld. Trees of an enormous height rise on every side. The foliage varies from the most light and airy to the darkest and most massive. Climbing and parasitic plants, with large shining leaves, run up the trunks, and often mount even to the highest branches, while others, with fantastic stems, hang like ropes and cables from their summits. Many curious seeds and fruits are here seen scattered on the ground; and there is enough to engage the wonder and admiration of every lover of nature. But even here there is something wanting that we expected to find. The splendid Orchideous plants, so much sought after in Europe, we had thought must abound in every luxuriant tropical forest; yet here are none but a few small species with dull brown or yellow flowers. Most of the parasitic plants which clothe the stems of every old or fallen tree with verdure, are of quite a different character, being ferns, *Tillandsias*, and species of *Pothos* and *Caladium*, plants resembling the Ethiopian lily so commonly cultivated in houses. Among the shrubs near the city that immediately attracted our attention were several *Solanums*, which are allied to our potato. One of these grows from eight to twelve feet high, with large woolly leaves, spines on both leaves and stem, and handsome purple flowers larger than those of the potato. Some other species have white flowers, and one much resembles our bitter-sweet (*Solanum Dulcamara*). Many handsome convolvuluses climb over the hedges, as well as several most beautiful *Bignonias* or trumpet-flowers, with yellow, orange, or purple blossoms. But most striking of all are the passion-flowers, which are abundant on the skirts of the forest, and are of various colours,—purple, scarlet, or pale pink : the purple ones have an exquisite perfume, and they all produce an agreeable fruit—the grenadilla of the West Indies. There are besides many other elegant flowers, and numbers of less conspicuous ones. The papilionaceous flowers, or peas, are common ; cassias are very numerous, some being mere weeds, others handsome trees, having a profusion of bright yellow blossoms. Then there are the curious sensitive plants (*Mimosa*), looked upon with such interest in our greenhouses, but which here abound as common wayside weeds. Most of them have purple or white globular heads of flowers. Some are very sensitive, a gentle touch causing many leaves to drop and fold up; others require a ruder hand to make them exhibit their peculiar properties ; while others again will scarcely show any signs of feeling, though ever so roughly treated. They are all more or less armed with sharp prickles, which may partly answer the purpose of guarding their delicate frames from some of the numerous shocks they would otherwise receive.

The immense number of orange-trees about the city is an interesting feature, and renders that delicious fruit always abundant and cheap. Many of the public roads are lined with them, and every garden is well stocked, so that the cost is merely the trouble of gathering and taking to market. The mango is also abundant, and in some of the public avenues is planted alternately with the Mangabeira, or silk cotton-tree, which grows to a great size, though, as its leaves are deciduous, it is not so well adapted to produce the shade so much required as some evergreen trees. On almost every roadside, thicket, or waste, the coffee-tree is seen growing, and generally with flower or fruit, and often both ; yet such is the scarcity of labour or indolence of the people, that none is gathered but a little for private consumption, while the city is almost entirely supplied with coffee grown in other parts of Brazil.

Turning our attention to the world of animal life, what first attract notice are the lizards. They abound everywhere. In the city they are seen running along the walls and palings, sunning themselves on logs of wood, or creeping up to the eaves of the lower houses. In every garden, road, and dry sandy situation they are scampering out of the way as we walk along. Now they crawl round the trunk of a tree, watching us as we pass, and keeping carefully out of sight, just as a squirrel will do under similar circumstances; now they walk up a smooth wall or paling as composedly and securely as if they had the plain earth beneath them. Some are of a dark coppery colour, some with backs of the most brilliant silky green and blue, and others marked with delicate shades and lines of yellow and brown. On this sandy soil, and beneath this bright sunshine, they seem to enjoy every moment of their existence, basking in the hot sun with the most indolent satisfaction, then scampering off as if every ray had lent vivacity and vigour to their chilly constitutions. Far different from the little lizards with us, which cannot raise their body from the ground, and drag their long tails like an encumbrance after them, these denizens of a happier clime carry their tails stuck out in the air, and gallop away on their four legs with as much freedom and muscular power as a warm-blooded quadruped. To catch such lively creatures was of course no easy matter, and all our attempts utterly failed; but we soon got the little Negro and Indian boys to shoot them for us with their bows and arrows, and thus obtained many specimens.

Next to the lizards, the ants cannot fail to be noticed. They startle you with the apparition of scraps of paper, dead leaves, and feathers, endued with locomotive powers; processions engaged in some abstruse engineering operations stretch across the public paths; the flowers you gather or the fruit you pluck is covered with them, and they spread over your hand in such swarms as to make you hastily drop your prize. At meals they make themselves quite at home upon the tablecloth, in your plate, and in the sugar-basin, though not in such numbers as to offer any serious obstruction to your meal. In these situations, and in many others, you will find them, and in each situation it will be a distinct kind. Many plants have ants peculiar to them. Their nests are seen forming huge black masses, several feet in diameter, on the branches of trees. In paths in woods and gardens we often see a gigantic black species wandering about singly or in pairs, measuring near an inch and a half long; while some of the species that frequent

houses are so small as to require a box-lid to fit very closely in
order to keep them out.  They are great enemies to any dead
animal matter, especially insects and small birds.  In drying
the specimens of insects we procured, we found it necessary to
hang up the boxes containing them to the roof of the verandah;
but even then a party got possession by descending the string,
as we caught them in the act, and found that in a few hours
they had destroyed several fine insects.  We were then informed that the Andiroba oil of the country, which is very
bitter, would keep them away, and by well soaking the suspend-
ing string we have since been free from their incursions.

Having at first employed ourselves principally in collecting
insects, I am enabled to say something about the other families
of that numerous class.  None of the orders of insects were so
numerous as I expected, with the exception of the diurnal
*Lepidoptera*, or butterflies; and even these, though the number
of different species was very great, did not abound in individuals to the extent I had been led to anticipate.  In about
three weeks Mr. B. and myself had captured upwards of a
hundred and fifty distinct species of butterflies.  Among them
were eight species of the handsome genus *Papilio*, and three
*Morphos*, those splendid large metallic-blue butterflies which
are always first noticed by travellers in South America, in
which country alone they are found, and where, flying lazily
along the paths in the forest, alternately in deep shade and
bright sunshine, they present one of the most striking sights
the insect world can produce.  Among the smaller species the
exquisite colouring and variety of marking is wonderful.  The
species seem inexhaustible, and probably not one-half of those
which exist in this country are yet discovered.  We did not
fall in with any of the large and remarkable insects of South
America, such as the rhinoceros or harlequin beetles, but saw
numerous specimens of a large *Mantis*, or praying insect, and
also several of the large *Mygale*, or bird-catching spiders,
which are here improperly called "tarantulas," and are said to be
very venomous.  We found one which had a nest on a silk
cotton-tree, formed like the web of some of our house-spiders,
as a place of concealment, but of a very strong texture, almost
like silk.  Other species live in holes in the ground.  Beetles
and flies were generally very scarce, and, with few exceptions,
of small size, but bees and wasps were abundant, and many of

them very large and handsome. Mosquitoes, in the low parts
of the city and on shipboard, are very annoying, but on the
higher grounds and in the suburbs there are none. The
moqueen, a small red tick, scarcely visible—the " bête rouge "
of Cayenne—abounds in the grass, and, getting on the legs, is
very irritating ; but these are trifles which one soon gets used
to, and in fact would hardly think oneself in the tropics without them.

Of birds we at first saw but few, and those not very remarkable ones. The only brilliant-coloured bird common about
the city is the yellow troupial (*Cassicus icteronotus*), which
builds its nests in colonies, suspended from the ends of the
branches of trees. A tree is sometimes covered with their
long purse-like nests, and the brilliant black and yellow birds
flying in and out have a pretty effect. This bird has a variety
of loud clear notes, and has an extraordinary power of imitating
the song of other birds, so as to render it worthy of the title of
the South American mocking-bird. Besides this, the common
silver-beak tanager (*Rhamphocœlus jacapa*), some pale blue
tanagers, called here " Sayis," and the yellow-breasted tyrant
flycatchers are the only conspicuous birds common in the
suburbs of Pará. In the forest are constantly heard the curious
notes of the bush-shrikes, tooo-too-to-to-t-t-t, each succeeding
sound quicker and quicker, like the successive reboundings of
a hammer from an anvil. In the dusk of the evening many
goat-suckers fly about and utter their singular and melancholy
cries. One says " Whip-poor-will," just like the North American
bird so called, and another with remarkable distinctness keeps
asking, " Who are *you* ? " and as their voices often alternate,
an interesting though rather monotonous conversation takes
place between them.

The climate, so far as we had yet experienced, was delightful.
The thermometer did not rise above 87° in the afternoon, nor
sink below 74° during the night. The mornings and evenings
were most agreeably cool, and we had generally a shower and
a fine breeze in the afternoon, which was very refreshing, and
purified the air. On moonlight evenings till eight o'clock
ladies walk about the streets and suburbs without any head-
dress and in ball-room attire, and the Brazilians, in their
rosinhas, sit outside their houses bareheaded and in their
shirt-sleeves till nine or ten o'clock, quite unmindful of the

night airs and heavy dews of the tropics, which we have been accustomed to consider so deadly.

We will now add a few words on the food of the people. Beef is almost the only meat used. The cattle are kept on estates some days' journey across and up the river, whence they are brought in canoes; they refuse food during the voyage, and so lose most of their fat, and arrive in very poor condition. They are killed in the morning for the day's consumption, and are cut up with axes and cutlasses, with a total disregard to appearance, the blood being allowed to run all over the meat. About six every morning a number of loaded carts may be seen going to the different butchers' shops, the contents bearing such a resemblance to horse-flesh going to a kennel of hounds, as to make a person of delicate stomach rather uneasy when he sees nothing but beef on the table at dinner-time. Fish is sometimes obtained, but it is very dear, and pork is killed only on Sundays. Bread made from United States flour, Irish and American butter, and other foreign products, are in general use among the white population; but farinha, rice, salt-fish, and fruits are the principal food of the Indians and Negroes. Farinha is a preparation from the root of the mandiocca or cassava plant, of which tapioca is also made; it looks something like coarsely ground peas, or perhaps more like sawdust, and when soaked in water or broth is rather glutinous, and is a very nutritious article of food. This, with a little salt-fish, chili peppers, bananas, oranges, and assai (a preparation from a palm fruit), forms almost the entire subsistence of a great part of the population of the city. Our own bill of fare comprised coffee, tea, bread, butter, beef, rice, farinha, pumpkins, bananas, and oranges. Isidora was a good cook, and made all sorts of roasts and stews out of our daily lump of tough beef; and the bananas and oranges were such a luxury to us, that, with the good appetite which our walks in the forest always gave us, we had nothing to complain of.

# CHAPTER II.

## PARÁ.

Festas—Portuguese and Brazilian Currency—M. Borlaz' Estate—Walk to the Rice-mills—The Virgin Forest, its Plants and Insects—Milk-tree—Saw and Rice Mills—Caripé or Pottery-tree—India-rubber-tree —Flowers and Trees in Blossom—Saüba Ants, Wasps, and Chegoes—Journey by Water to Magoary—The Monkeys—The Commandante at Laranjeiras—Vampire Bats—The Timber-tradè—Boa Constrictor and Sloth.

ABOUT a fortnight after our arrival at Pará there were several holidays, or "festas," as they are called. Those of the "Espirito Santo" and the "Trinidade" lasted each nine days. The former was held at the cathedral, the latter at one of the smaller churches in the suburbs. The general character of these festas is the same, some being more celebrated and more attractive than others. They consist of fireworks every night before the church; Negro girls selling "doces," or sweetmeats, cakes, and fruit; processions of saints and crucifixes; the church open, with regular services; kissing of images and relics; and a miscellaneous crowd of Negroes and Indians, all dressed in white, thoroughly enjoying the fun, and the women in all the glory of their massive gold chains and earrings. Besides these, a number of the higher classes and foreign residents grace the scene with their presence; showy processions are got up at the commencement and termination, and on the last evening a grand display of fireworks takes place, which is generally provided by some person who is chosen or volunteers to be "Juiz da festa," or governor of the feast,—a rather expensive honour among people who, not content with an unlimited supply of rockets at night, amuse themselves by firing off great quantities during the day for the sake of the whiz and the bang that accompany them. The rockets are looked upon as quite a part of the religious ceremony: on asking an old Negro why they were let off in the morning, he looked up to the sky and answered very gravely, "Por Deos" (for God). Music, noise, and fireworks are the three essentials to please a Brazilian populace ; and for a fortnight we had enough of them, for besides the above-mentioned amusements, they fire off guns, pistols, and cannon from morning to night.

After many inquiries, we at last succeeded in procuring a house to suit us. It was situated at Nazaré, about a mile and a half south of the city, just opposite a pretty little chapel. Close behind, the forest commences, and there are many good localities for birds, insects, and plants in the neighbourhood. The house consisted of a ground-floor of four rooms, with a verandah extending completely round it, affording a rather extensive and very pleasant promenade. The grounds contained oranges and bananas, and a great many forest and fruit trees, with coffee and mandiocca plantations. We were to pay twenty milreis a month rent (equal to £2 5s.), which is very dear for Pará, but we could get no other house so convenient. Isidora took possession of an old mud-walled shed as the domain of his culinary operations ; we worked and took our meals in the verandah, and seldom used the inner rooms but as sleeping apartments.

We now found much less difficulty in mustering up sufficient Portuguese to explain our various wants. We were some time getting into the use of the Portuguese, or rather Brazilian, money, which is peculiar and puzzling. It consists of paper, silver, and copper. The rey is the unit or standard, but the milrey, or thousand reis, is the value of the lowest note, and serves as the unit in which accounts are kept; so that the system is a decimal one, and very easy, were it not complicated by several other coins, which are used in reckoning; as the vintem, which is twenty reis, the patac, three hundred and twenty, and the crusado, four hundred, in all of which coins sums of money are often reckoned, which is puzzling to a beginner, because the patac is not an integral part of the milrey (three patacs and two vintems making a milrey), and the Spanish dollars which are current here are worth six patacs. The milrey was originally worth 5s. 7½d., but now fluctuates from 2s. 1d. to 2s. 4d., or not quite half, owing probably to the

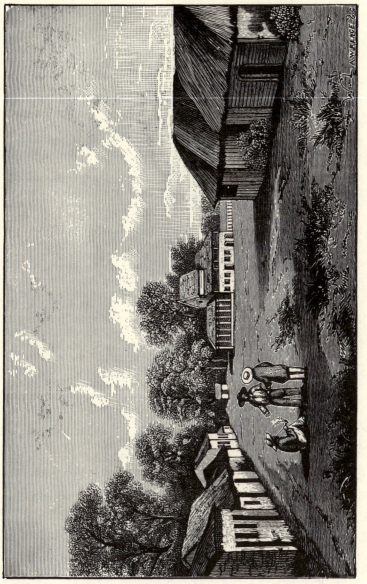

PLATE III.

CHAPEL AT NAZARÉ, NEAR PARA.

over-issue of paper and its inconvertibility into coin. The metallic currency, being then of less nominal than real value, would soon have been melted down, so it became necessary to increase its value. This was done by restamping it and making it pass for double. Thus a vintem restamped is two vintems; a patac with one hundred and sixty on it counts for three hundred and twenty reis; a two-vintem piece counts for four. The newer coinage also having been diminished in size with the depreciation of the currency, there has arisen such a confusion, that the size of the coin is scarcely any index to its value, and when two pieces are of exactly the same size one may be double the value of the other. An accurate examination of each coin is therefore necessary, which renders the making up of a large sum a matter requiring much practice and attention.

There were living on the premises three Negroes, who had the care of the coffee- and fruit-trees, and of the mandiocca field. The principal one, named Vincente, was a fine stout handsome Negro, who was celebrated as a catcher of " bichos," as they here call all insects, reptiles, and small animals. He soon brought us in several insects. One was a gigantic hairy spider, a *Mygale*, which he skilfully dug out of its hole in the earth, and caught in a leaf. He told us he was once bitten by one, and was bad some time. When questioned on the matter, he said the " bicho " was " muito mal " (very bad), and concluded with an expressive " whew-w-w," which just answers to a schoolboy's " Ain't it though ? " and intimates that there can be no doubt at all about the matter. It seems probable therefore that this insect is not armed in vain with such powerful fangs, but **is** capable of inflicting with them an envenomed wound.

During one of our exploratory rambles we came upon the country-house of a French gentleman, M. Borlaz, who is Swiss Consul in Pará. Much to our surprise he addressed us in English, and then showed us round his grounds, and pointed out to us the paths in the woods we should find most practicable. The vegetation here on the banks of the river, a mile below Pará, was very rich. The Miriti (*Mauritia flexuosa*), a fine fan-palm, and a slender species, the Marajá (*Bactris Maraja*), a small prickly tree which bears a fruit with a thin outer pulp, of a pleasant subacid taste, were both abundant.

A mass of cactus, thirty feet high, grew near the house, having a most tropical aspect, but this was planted. The thickets were full of curious *Bromeliaceæ* and *Arums,* and many singular trees and shrubs, and in their shady recesses we captured some very fine insects. The splendid blue and orange butterflies (*Epicalia ancea*) were abundant, settling on the leaves ; and they would repeatedly return to the same tree, and even to the same leaf, so that, though very difficult to capture, five specimens were taken without removing from the spot.

On our return to the house M. Borlaz treated us to some fine fruits,—the berribee, a species of *Anona,* with a pleasant acid custard-like pulp, the nuts of the bread-fruit roasted, very similar to Spanish chestnuts, and plantains dried in the sun, and much resembling figs. The situation of the house was delightful, looking over the river to the opposite islands, yet sufficiently elevated to be dry and healthy. The moist woods along the bank of the river were so productive that we often afterwards availed ourselves of M. Borlaz' kind invitation to visit his grounds whenever we felt disposed. As an instance of the voracity of the ants, I may mention that, having laid down my collecting-box in the verandah during half-an-hour's conversation, I was horrified to find, on opening it to put in a fresh capture, that it swarmed with small red ants, who had already separated the wings from near a dozen insects, and were dragging them in different directions about the box ; others were at the process of dismemberment, while some had buried themselves in the plumpest bodies, where they were enjoying a delicious repast. I had great difficulty in making them quit their prey, and gained some useful experience at the expense of half a successful day's captures, including some of the splendid *Epicalias* which I so much prized.

On the morning of the 23rd of June we started early to walk to the rice-mills at Magoary, which we had been invited to visit by the proprietor, Mr. Upton, and the manager, Mr. Leavens, both American gentlemen. At about two miles from the city we entered the virgin forest, which the increased height of the trees and the deeper shade had some time told us we were approaching. Its striking characteristics were, the great number and variety of the forest-trees, their trunks rising frequently for sixty or eighty feet without a branch, and perfectly straight; the huge creepers, which climb about them, sometimes stretching obliquely from their summits like the stays of a mast, sometimes winding around their trunks like immense serpents waiting for their prey. Here, two or three together, twisting spirally round each other, form a complete living cable, as if to bind securely these monarchs of the forest; there, they form tangled festoons, and, covered themselves with smaller creepers and parasitic plants, hide the parent stem from sight.

Among the trees the various kinds that have buttresses projecting around their base are the most striking and peculiar. Some of these buttresses are much longer than they are high, springing from a distance of eight or ten feet from the base, and reaching only four or five feet high on the trunk, while others rise to the height of twenty or thirty feet, and can even be distinguished as ribs on the stem to forty or fifty. They are complete wooden walls, from six inches to a foot thick, sometimes branching into two or three, and extending straight out to such a distance as to afford room for a comfortable hut in the angle between them. Large square pieces are often cut out of them to make paddles, and for other uses, the wood being generally very light and soft.

Other trees, again, appear as if they were formed by a number of slender stems growing together. They are deeply furrowed and ribbed for their whole height, and in places these furrows reach quite through them, like windows in a narrow tower, yet they run up as high as the loftiest trees of the forest, with a straight stem of uniform diameter. Another most curious form is presented by those which have many of their roots high above the surface of the ground, appearing to stand on many legs, and often forming archways large enough for a man to walk beneath.

The stems of all these trees, and the climbers that wind or wave around them, support a multitude of dependants. *Tillandsias* and other *Bromeliaceæ*, resembling wild pine-apples, large climbing *Arums*, with their dark green arrowhead-shaped leaves, peppers in great variety, and large-leaved ferns, shoot out at intervals all up the stem, to the very topmost branches. Between these, creeping ferns and delicate little species like our *Hymenophyllum* abound, and in moist dark places the leaves of these are again covered with minute creeping mosses and *Hepaticæ,*—so that we have parasites on parasites, and on these parasites again. On looking upwards, the finely-divided foliage, strongly defined against the clear sky, is a striking characteristic of the tropical forests, as is repeatedly remarked by Humboldt. Many of the largest forest-trees have leaves as delicate as those of the trembling *Mimosa,* belonging like them to the extensive family of the *Leguminosæ,* while the huge palmate leaves of the *Cecropias,* the oval glossy leaves of the *Clusias,* and a hundred others of intermediate forms, afford sufficient variety ; and the bright sunshine lighting up all above while a sombre gloom reigns below, adds to the grandeur and solemnity of the scene.

Flowers were very few and far between, a few small *Orchideæ* and inconspicuous wayside weeds, with now and then a white- or green-blossomed shrub, being all that we met with. On the ground many varieties of fruits lay decaying : curiously twisted legumes like peas a yard long, huge broad beans, nuts of various sizes and forms, and large fruits of the pot-trees, which have lids like the utensil from which they derive their name. The herbage consisted principally of ferns, *Scitamineæ,* a few grasses and small creeping plants ; but dead leaves and rotten wood occupied the greater part of the surface.

We found very few insects, but almost all that we met with were new to us. Our greatest treasure was the beautiful clear-winged butterfly, with a bright violet patch on its lower wings, the *Hætera esmeralda,* which we now saw and caught for the first time. Many other rare insects were also obtained, and the gigantic blue *Morphos* frequently passed us, but their undulating flight baffled all our efforts at capturing them. Of quadrupeds we saw none, and of birds but few, though we heard enough of the latter to assure us that they were not altogether wanting. We are inclined to think that the general statement, that the birds of the tropics have a deficiency of song proportionate to their brilliancy of plumage, requires to be modified. Many of the brilliant birds of the tropics belong to families or groups which have no song ; but our most brilliantly coloured birds, as the goldfinch and canary, are not the less musical, and there are many beautiful little birds here which are equally so. We heard notes resembling those of the blackbird and the robin, and one bird gave forth three or four sweet plaintive tones that particularly attracted our attention; while many have peculiar cries, in which words may easily be traced by the fanciful, and which in the stillness of the forest have a very pleasing effect.

On reaching the mills we found it was one o'clock, the interesting objects on the road having caused us to linger for six hours on a distance of scarcely twelve miles. We were kindly welcomed by Mr. Leavens, who soon set before us substantial fare. After dinner we strolled round the premises, and saw for the first time toucans and paroquets in their native haunts. They frequent certain wild fruit-trees, and Mr. Leavens has many specimens which he has shot, and preserved in a manner seldom equalled. There are three mills— a saw-mill and two for cleaning rice. One rice-mill is driven by steam, the other two by water-power, which is obtained by damming up two or three small streams, and thus forming extensive mill-pools. The saw-mill was recently erected by Mr. Leavens, who is a practical millwright. It is of the kind commonly used in the United States, and the manner of applying the water is rather different from which we generally see in England. There is a fall of water of about ten feet, which, instead of being applied to an overshot or breast-wheel, is allowed to rush out of a longitudinal aperture at the bottom, against the narrow floats of a wheel only twenty inches in diameter, which thus revolves with great velocity, and communicates motion by means of a crank and connecting-rod directly to the saw, which of course makes a double stroke to each revolution of the wheel. The expense of a large slow-motion wheel is thus saved, as well as all the gearing necessary for producing a sufficiently rapid motion of the saws; and the whole having a smaller number of working parts, is much less liable to get out of order, and requires few repairs. The platform carrying the log is propelled on against the saw in the usual manner, but the method of carrying it back at the end of the cut is ingenious. The water is shut off from the main wheel, and let on at another shoot against a vertical wheel, on the top of the upright shaft of which is a cog-wheel working into a rack on the frame, which runs it back with great rapidity, and in the simplest manner. One saw only is used, the various thicknesses into which the trees are cut rendering more inconvenient.

We here saw the different kinds of timber used, both in the

log and in boards, and were told their various uses by Mr. Leavens. Some are very hard woods resembling oak, and others lighter and less durable. What most interested us, however, were several large logs of the Masseranduba, or Milk-tree. On our way through the forest we had seen some trunks much notched by persons who had been extracting the milk. It is one of the noblest trees of the forest, rising with a straight stem to an enormous height. The timber is very hard, fine-grained, and durable, and is valuable for works which are much exposed to the weather. The fruit is eatable and very good, the size of a small apple, and full of a rich and very juicy pulp. But strangest of all is the vegetable milk, which exudes in abundance when the bark is cut : it has about the consistence of thick cream, and but for a very slight peculiar taste could scarcely be distinguished from the genuine product of the cow. Mr. Leavens ordered a man to tap some logs that had lain nearly a month in the yard. He cut several notches in the bark with an axe, and in a minute the rich sap was running out in great quantities. It was collected in a basin, diluted with water, strained, and brought up at teatime and at breakfast next morning. The peculiar flavour of the milk seemed rather to improve the quality of the tea, and gave it as good a colour as rich cream ; in coffee it is equally good. Mr. Leavens informed us that he had made a custard of it, and that, though it had a curious dark colour, it was very well tasted. The milk is also used for glue, and is said to be as durable as that made use of by carpenters. As a specimen of its capabilities in this line, Mr. Leavens showed us a violin he had made, the belly-board of which, formed of two pieces, he had glued together with it applied fresh from the tree without any preparation. It had been done two years ; the instrument had been in constant use, and the joint was now perfectly good and sound throughout its whole length. As the milk hardens by exposure to air, it becomes a very tough, slightly elastic substance, much resembling gutta-percha ; but, not having the property of being softened by hot water, is not likely to become so extensively useful as that article.

After leaving the wood-yard, we next visited the rice-mills, and inspected the process by which the rice is freed from its husk. There are several operations to effect this. The grain first passes between two mill-stones, not cut as for grinding flour, but worked flat, and by them the outer husk is rubbed off. It is then conveyed between two boards of similar size and shape to the stones, set all over with stiff iron wires about three-eighths of an inch long, so close together that a grain of rice can just be pushed in between them. The two surfaces very nearly touch one another, so that the rice is forced through the spaces of the wires, which rub off the rest of the husk and polish the grain. A quantity, however, is broken by this operation, so it is next shaken through sifters of different degrees of fineness, which separate the dust from the broken rice. The whole rice is then fanned, to blow off the remaining dust, and finally passes between rubbers covered with sheep-skin with the wool on, which clean it thoroughly, and render it fit for the market. The Pará rice is remarkably fine, being equal in quality to that of Carolina, but, owing to the careless-ness with which it is cultivated, it seldom shows so good a sample. No care is taken in choosing seed or in preparing the ground ; and in harvesting, a portion is cut green, because there are not hands enough to get it in quickly when it is ripe, and rice is a grain which rapidly falls out of the ear and is wasted. It is therefore seldom cultivated on a large scale, the greater portion being the produce of Indians and small land-holders, who bring it to the mills to sell.

In the morning, after a refreshing shower-bath under the mill-feeder, we shouldered our guns, insect-nets, and pouches, and, accompanied by Mr. Leavens, took a walk into the forest. On our way we saw the long-toed jacanas on the river-side, Bemteví* flycatchers on the branches of every bare tree, and toucans flying with out-stretched bills to their morning repast. Their peculiar creaking note was often heard, with now and then the loud tapping of the great woodpeckers, and the extraordinary sounds uttered by the howling monkeys, all telling us plainly that we were in the vast forests of tropical America. We were not successful in shooting, but returned with a good appetite to our coffee and masseranduba milk, pirarucú, and eggs. The pirarucú is the dried fish which, with farinha, forms the chief subsistence of the native population, and in the interior is often the only thing to be obtained, so we thought it as well to get used to it at once. It resembles in appearance nothing eatable, looking as much like a dry cowhide

---

* "Bemteví" (I saw you well) ; the bird's note resembles this word,

grated up into fibres and pressed into cakes, as anything I can compare it with. When eaten, it is boiled or slightly roasted, pulled to pieces, and mixed with vinegar, oil, pepper, onions, and farinha, and altogether forms a very savoury mess for a person with a good appetite and a strong stomach.

After breakfast, we loaded our old Negro (who had come with us to show the way) with plants that we had collected, and a basket to hold anything interesting we might meet with on the road, and set out to walk home, promising soon to make a longer visit. We reached Nazaré with boxes full of insects, and heads full of the many interesting things we had seen, among which the milk-giving tree, supplying us with a necessary of life from so new and strange a source, held a prominent place.

Wishing to obtain specimens of a tree called Caripé, the bark of which is used in the manufacture of the pottery of the country, we inquired of Isidora if he knew such a tree, and where it grew. He replied that he knew the tree very well, but that it grew in the forest a long way off. So one fine morning after breakfast we told him to shoulder his axe and come with us in search of the Caripé,—he in his usual dishabille of a pair of trousers,—shirt, hat, and shoes being altogether dispensed with in this fine climate ; and we in our shirt-sleeves, and with our hunting apparatus across our shoulders. Our old conductor, though now following the domestic occupation of cook and servant of all work to two foreign gentlemen, had worked much in the forest, and was well acquainted with the various trees, could tell their names, and was learned in their uses and properties. He was of rather a taciturn disposition, except when excited by our exceeding dulness in understanding what he wanted, when he would gesticulate with a vehemence and perform dumb-show with a minuteness worthy of a more extensive audience ; yet he was rather fond of displaying his knowledge on a subject of which we were in a state of the most benighted ignorance, and at the same time quite willing to learn. His method of instruction was by a series of parenthetical remarks on the trees as he passed them, appearing to speak rather to them than to us, unless we elicited by questions further information.

"This," he would say, "is Ocööba, very good medicine, good for sore-throat," which he explained by going through the action of gargling, and showed us that a watery sap issued freely on the bark being cut. The tree, like many others, was notched all over by the number of patients who came for the healing juice. "This," said he, glancing at a magnificent tall straight tree, "is good wood for houses, good for floors; call it Quaróóba." "This," pointing to one of the curious furrowed trees that look as if a bundle of enormously long sticks had grown into one mass, "is wood for making paddles;" and, as we did not understand this in Portuguese, he imitated rowing in a canoe; the name of this was Pootiéka. "This," pointing to another large forest-tree, "is good wood for burning, to make charcoal; good hard wood for everything,—makes the best charcoal for forges," which he explained by intimating that the wood made the fire to make the iron of the axe he held in his hand. This tree rejoiced in the name of Nowará. Next came the Caripé itself, but it was a young tree with neither fruit nor flowers, so we had to content ourselves with specimens of the wood and bark only; it grew on the edge of a swamp filled with splendid palm-trees. Here the Assai Palm, so common about the city, reached an enormous height. With a smooth stem only four inches in diameter, some specimens were eighty feet high. Sometimes they are perfectly straight, sometimes gently curved, and, with the drooping crowns of foliage, are most beautiful. Here also grew the Inajá, a fine thick-stemmed species, with a very large dense head of foliage. The undeveloped leaves of this as well as many other kinds form an excellent vegetable, called here *palmeto*, and probably very similar to that produced by the cabbage-palm of the West Indies. A prickly-stemmed fan-leaved palm, which we had observed at the mills, was also growing here. But the most striking and curious of all was the Paxiuba, a tall, straight, perfectly smooth-stemmed palm, with a most elegant head, formed of a few large curiously-cut leaves. Its great singularity is, that the greater part of its roots are above ground, and they successively die away, fresh ones springing out of the stem higher up, so that the whole tree is supported on three or four stout straight roots, sometimes so high that a person can stand between them with the lofty tree growing over his head. The main roots often diverge again before they reach the ground, each into three or more smaller ones, not an inch each in diameter. Though the stem of the tree is quite smooth, the roots are thickly covered with large tuberculous prickles. Numbers of small trees of a few feet high grow all around, each standing on spreading legs, a miniature copy of its parent. Isidora cut down an Assai palm, to get some *palmeto* for our dinner; it forms an agreeable vegetable of a sweetish flavour. Just as we were returning, we were startled by a quiet remark that the tree close by us was the Seringa, or India-rubber-tree. We rushed to it, axe in hand, cut off a piece of bark, and had the satisfaction to see the extraordinary juice come out. Catching a little in a box I had with me, I next day found it genuine india-rubber, of a yellowish colour, but possessing all its peculiar properties.

It being some saint's day, in the evening a fire was lit in the road in front of our house, and going out we found Isidora and Vincente keeping it up. Several others were visible in the street, and there appeared to be a line of them reaching to the city. They seemed to be made quite as a matter of business, being a mark of respect to certain of the more illustrious saints, and, with rockets and processions, form the greater part of the religion here. The glorious southern constellations, with their crowded nebulæ, were shining brilliantly in the heavens as the fire expired, and we turned into our hammocks well satisfied with all that we had seen during the day.

*July 4th.*—The vegetation now improved in appearance as the dry season advanced. Plants were successively budding and bursting their blossoms, and bright green leaves displaced the half-withered ones of the past season. The climbers were particularly remarkable, as much for the beauty of·their foliage as for their flowers. Often two or three climb over one tree or shrub, mingling in the most perplexing though elegant confusion, so that it is a matter of much difficulty to decide to which plant the different blossoms belong, and should they be high up it is impossible. A delicate white and a fine yellow convolvulus were now plentiful ; the purple and yellow trumpet-flowers were still among the most showy; and some noble thick-leaved climbers mounted to the tops of trees, and sent aloft bright spikes of scarlet flowers. Among the plants not in flower, the twin-leaved *Bauhinias* of various forms were most frequently noticed. The species are very numerous : some are shrubs, others delicate climbers, and one is the most extraordinary among the extraordinary climbers of the forest, its broad flattened woody stems being twisted in and out in a most singular manner, mounting to the summits of the very loftiest forest-trees, and hanging from their branches in gigantic festoons, many hundred feet in length.  A handsome pink and white *Clusia* was now abundant, with large shining leaves, and flowers having a powerful and very fragrant odour.  It grows not only as a good-sized tree out of the ground, but is also parasitical on almost every other forest-tree.  Its large round whitish fruits are called " cebola braba" (wild onion), by the natives, and are much eaten by birds, which thus probably convey the seeds into the forks of lofty trees, where it seems most readily to take root in any little decaying vegetable matter, dung of birds, etc., that may be there ; and when it arrives at such a size as to require more nourishment than it can there obtain, it sends down long shoots to the ground, which take root, and grow into a new stem.  At Nazaré there is a tree by the road-side, out of the fork of which grows a large Mucujá palm, and on the palm are three or four young *Clusia* trees, which no doubt have, or will have, *Orchideæ* and ferns again growing upon them.  A few forest-trees were also in blossom ; and it was truly a magnificent sight to behold a great tree covered with one mass of flowers, and to hear the deep distant hum of millions of insects gathered together to enjoy the honeyed feast.  But all is out of reach of the curious and admiring naturalist.  It is only over the outside of the great dome of verdure exposed to the vertical rays of the sun that flowers are produced, and on many of these trees there is not a single blossom to be found at a less height than a hundred feet.  The whole glory of these forests could only be seen by sailing gently in a balloon over the undulating flowery surface above : such a treat is perhaps reserved for the traveller of a future age.

A jararáca, said to be one of the most deadly serpents in Brazil, was killed by a Negro in our garden.  It was small, and not brightly coloured.  A fine coral snake was also brought in ; it was about a yard long, and beautifully marked with black, red, and yellow bands. Having, perhaps, had some experience of the lavish manner in which foreigners pay for such things, the man had the coolness to ask two milreis, or 4s. 6d. for it, so he had to throw it away, and got nothing.  A

penny or twopence is enough to give for such things, which
are of no value to the natives; and though they will not search
much after them for such a price, yet they will bring you all
that come in their way when they know you will purchase
them.  Snakes were unpleasantly abundant at this time.  I
nearly trod on one about ten feet long, which rather startled
me, and it, too, to judge by the rapid manner in which it
glided away.  I caught also a small *Amphisbena* under the
coffee-trees in our garden.  Though it is known to have no
poison-fangs, the Negroes declared it was very dangerous, and
that its bite could not be cured.  It is commonly known as
the two-headed snake, from the tail being blunt and the head
scarcely visible; and they believe that if it is cut in two, and
the two parts thrown some yards apart, they will come together
again, and join into an entire animal.

Among the curious things we meet with in the woods are
large heaps of earth and sand, sometimes by the roadside, and
sometimes extending quite across the path, making the pedes-
trian ascend and descend (a pleasing variety in this flat
country), and looking just as if some " Pará and Peru direct
Railway Company " had commenced operations.  These
mounds are often thirty or forty feet long, by ten or fifteen
wide, and about three or four feet high; but instead of being
the work of a lot of railway labourers, we find it is all due to
the industry of a native insect, the much-dreaded Saüba ant.
This insect is of a light-red colour, about the size of our largest
English species, the wood-ant, but with much more powerful
jaws.  It does great injury to young trees, and will sometimes
strip them of their leaves in a single night.  We often see,
hurrying across the pathways, rows of small green leaves; these
are the Saübas, each with a piece of leaf cut as smoothly as
with scissors, and completely hiding the body from sight.  The
orange-tree is very subject to their attacks, and in our garden
the young trees were each planted in the centre of a ring-shaped
earthen vessel, which being filled with water completely surrounded the stem, preventing the ants from reaching it.  Some
places are so infested by them that it is useless planting anything.  No means of destroying them are known, their numbers
being so immense, as may readily be seen from the great
quantities of earth they remove.

Many different kinds of wasps' and bees' nests are constantly met with; but we were rather shy of meddling with them. They are generally attached to the undersides of leaves, especially of the young Tucumá palm, which are broad, and offer a good shelter. Some are little flat domes, with a single small opening ; others have the cells all exposed. Some have only two or three cells, others a great number. These are all of a delicate papery substance; but some have large cylindrical nests, on high trees, of a material like thick cardboard. Then again there are nests in hollow trees, and others among their roots in the earth, while the solitary species make little holes in the paths, and pierce the mud-walls of the houses, till they appear as if riddled with shot. Many of these insects sting very painfully ; and some are so fierce, that on their nests being approached, they will fly out and attack the unwary passer-by. The larger kinds of wasps have very long stings, and can so greatly extend their bodies that we were often stung when endeavouring to secure them for our collections.

I also suffered a little from another of our insect enemies : the celebrated *chigoe* at length paid us a visit. I found a tender pimple on the side of my foot, which Isidora pronounced to be a "bicho do pé," or chigoe ; so preferring to extract it myself, I set to work with a needle, but not being used to the operation, could not get it out entire. I then rubbed a little snuff in the wound, and afterwards felt no more of it. The insect is a minute flea, which burrows into the skin of the toes, where it grows into a large bag of eggs as big as a pea, the insect being just distinguishable as a black speck on one side of it. When it first enters it causes a slight irritation, and if found may then be easily extracted ; but when it grows large it is very painful, and if neglected may produce a serious wound. With care and attention, however, this dreaded insect is not so annoying as the mosquito or our own domestic flea.

Having made arrangements for another and a longer visit to Magoary, we packed up our hammocks, nets, and boxes, and went on board a canoe which trades regularly to the mills, bringing the rice and timber, and taking whatever is required there. We left Pará about nine at night, when the tide served, and at five the next morning found the vessel lying at anchor, waiting for the flood. We were to proceed on to the mills in a montaria, or small Indian canoe, and as we were five with the Negroes who were to paddle, I felt rather nervous on finding that we sank the little boat to within two inches of the water's edge, and that a slight motion of any one of the party would be enough to swamp us altogether.  However, there was no help for it, so off we went, but soon found that with its unusual load our boat leaked so much that we had to keep baling by turns with a calabash all the time.  This was not very agreeable; but after a few miles we got used to it, and looked to the safe termination of our voyage as not altogether improbable.

The picturesque and novel appearance of the river's banks, as the sun rose, attracted all our attention.  The stream, though but an insignificant tributary of the Amazon, was wider than the Thames.  The banks were everywhere clothed with a dense forest.  In places were numerous mangroves, their roots descending from the branches into the water, having a curious appearance; on some we saw the fruit germinating on the tree, sending out a shoot which would descend to the water, and form another root to the parent.  Behind these rose large forest-trees, mingled with the Assai, Miriti, and other palms while passion-flowers and convolvuluses hung their festoons to the water's edge.

As we advanced the river became narrower, and about seven o'clock we landed, to stretch our cramped limbs, at a sitio, where there was a tree covered with the hanging nests of the yellow troupial, with numbers of the birds continually flying in and out.  In an hour more we passed Larangeiras, a pretty spot, where there are a few huts, and the residence of Senhor C., the Commandante of the district.  Further on we turned into a narrow igaripé, which wound about in the forest for a mile or two, when a sudden turn at length brought us the welcome sight of the mills.  Here a hearty welcome from Mr. Leavens, and a good breakfast, quite compensated for our four hours' cramping in the montaria, and prepared us for an exploring expedition among the woods, paths, and lakes in the vicinity.

Our daily routine during our stay at the mills was as follows: —We rose at half-past five, when whoever pleased took a bath at the mill-stream.  We then started, generally with our guns, into the forest, as early in the morning is the best time for shooting, and Mr. Leavens often accompanied us, to show us the best feeding-trees.  At eight we returned to breakfast, and then again started off in search of insects and plants till

dinner-time. After dinner we generally had another walk for
an hour or two ; and the rest of the evening was occupied in
preparing and drying our captures, and in conversation.
Sometimes we would start down the igaripé in the montaria, not
returning till late in the afternoon; but it was in my early
expeditions into the forest that I had my curiosity most
gratified by the sight of many strange birds and other animals.
Toucans and parrots were abundant, and the splendid blue
and purple chatterers were also sometimes met with. Humming-
birds would dart by us, and disappear in the depths of the
forest, and woodpeckers and creepers of various sizes and
colours were running up the trunks and along the branches.
The little red-headed and puff-throated manakins were also
seen, and heard making a loud clapping noise with their wings
which it seemed hardly possible for so small a bird to produce.

But to me the greatest treat was making my first acquaintance
with the monkeys. One morning, when walking alone in the
forest, I heard a rustling of the leaves and branches, as if a
man were walking quickly among them, and expected every
minute to see some Indian hunter make his appearance, when
all at once the sounds appeared to be in the branches above,
and turning up my eyes there, I saw a large monkey looking
down at me, and seeming as much astonished as I was myself.
I should have liked to have had a good look at him, but he
thought it safer to retreat. The next day, being out with Mr.
Leavens, near the same place, we heard a similar sound, and it
was soon evident that a whole troop of monkeys were
approaching. We therefore hid ourselves under some trees,
and, with guns cocked, waited their coming. Presently we
caught a glimpse of them skipping about among the trees,
leaping from branch to branch, and passing from one tree to
another with the greatest ease. At last one approached too
near for its safety. Mr. Leavens fired, and it fell, the rest
making off with all possible speed. The poor little animal was
not quite dead, and its cries, its innocent-looking countenance,
and delicate little hands were quite childlike. Having often
heard how good monkey was, I took it home, and had it cut
up and fried for breakfast : there was about as much of it as a
fowl, and the meat something resembled rabbit, without any
very peculiar or unpleasant flavour. Another new dish was
the Cotia or Agouti, a little animal, something between a

guinea-pig and a hare, but with longer legs. It is abundant, and considered good eating, but the meat is rather dry and tasteless.

One day we took the montaria and started to pay a visit to the Commandante at Larangeiras. The morning was beautiful ; swallows and kingfishers flew before us, but the beautiful *pavon* (*Eurypygia helias*), which I most wanted, wisely kept out of the way. The banks of the igaripé were covered with a species of *Inga*, in flower, from which Mr. B. obtained some fine floral beetles. Among the roots of the mangroves numbers of "calling crabs" were running about; their one large claw held up, as if beckoning, having a very grotesque appearance. At Larangeiras the Commandante welcomed us with much politeness in his palace of posts and clay, and offered us wine and bananas. He then produced a large bean, very thick and hard, on breaking which, with a hammer, the whole interior was seen to be filled with a farinaceous yellow substance enveloping the seeds : it has a sweet taste, and is eaten by the Indians with much relish. On our expressing a wish to go into the forest, he kindly volunteered to accompany us. We soon reached a lofty forest-tree, under which lay many of the legumes, of which we collected some fine specimens. The old gentleman then took us along several paths, showing us the various trees, some useful as timber, others as "remedios" for all the ills of life. One tree, which is very plentiful, produces a substance intermediate between camphor and turpentine. It is called here white pitch, and is extensively collected, and when melted up with oil, is used for pitching boats. Its strong camphor-like odour might, perhaps, render it useful in some other way.

In the grounds around the house were a breadfruit-tree, some cotton-plants, and a fine castanha, or Brazil-nut tree, on which were several large fruits, and many nests of the yellow troupial, which seems to prefer the vicinity of houses. Finding in Mr. Edwards's book a mention of his having obtained some good shells from Larangeiras, we spoke to Senhor C. about them, when he immediately went to a box and produced two or three tolerable specimens ; so we engaged his son, a boy of eleven or twelve, to get us a lot at a vintem (halfpenny) each, and send them to Mr. Leavens at the mill, which, however, he never did.

During our makeshift conversation, carried on with our very slender Portuguese vocabulary, Senhor C. would frequently ask us what such and such a word was in "Americano" (for so the English language is here called), and appeared highly amused at the absurd and incomprehensible terms used by us in ordinary conversation. Among other things we told him that we called "rapaz" in Americano "boy," which word (*boi*) in Portuguese means an ox. This was to him a complete climax of absurdity, and tickled him into roars of laughter, and he made us repeat it to him several times, that he might not forget so good a joke ; even when we were pulling away into the middle of the stream, and waving our "adeos," his last words were, as loud as he could bawl, "O que se chama rapaz ? " (What do you call *rapaz*?)

A day or two before we left the mills we had an opportunity of seeing the effects of the vampire's* operations on a young horse Mr. Leavens had just purchased. The first morning after its arrival the poor animal presented a most pitiable appearance, large streams of clotted blood running down from several wounds on its back and sides. The appearance was, however, I daresay, worse than the reality, as the bats have the skill to bleed without giving pain, and it is quite possible the horse, like a patient under the influence of chloroform, may have known nothing of the matter. The danger is in the attacks being repeated every night till the loss of blood becomes serious. To prevent this, red peppers are usually rubbed on the parts wounded, and on all likely places ; and this will partly check the sanguinivorous appetite of the bats, but not entirely, as in spite of this application the poor animal was again bitten the next night in fresh places.

Mr. Leavens is a native of Canada, and has been much engaged in the timber-trade of that country, and we had many conversations on the possibility of obtaining a good supply of timber from the Amazons. It seems somewhat extraordinary that the greater part of our timber should be brought from countries where the navigation is stopped nearly half the year by ice, and where the rivers are at all times obstructed by rapids and subject to storms, which render the bringing down the rafts a business of great danger ; where, too, there is little

* This is a blood-sucking bat (Phyllostoma sp.), nisnamed "vampyre," while the bats of the genus Vampyrus are fruit-eaters.

variety of timber, and much of it of such poor quality as only
to be used on account of its cheapness.  On the other hand
the valley of the Amazon and its countless tributary streams,
offers a country where the rivers are open all the year, and are
for hundreds and even thousands of miles unobstructed by
rapids, and where violent storms at any season seldom occur.
The banks of all these streams are clothed with virgin forests,
containing timber-trees in inexhaustible quantities, and of such
countless varieties that there seems no purpose for which wood
is required but one of a fitting quality may be found.  In
particular, there is cedar, said to be so abundant in some
localities, that it could, on account of the advantages before
mentioned, be sent to England at a less price than even the
Canada white pine.  It is a wood which works nearly as easy
as pine, has a fine aromatic odour, and is equal in appearance
to common mahogany, and is therefore well adapted for doors
and all internal finishings of houses ; yet, owing to the want
of a regular supply, the merchants here are obliged to have pine
from the States to make their packing-cases.  For centuries
the woodman's axe has been the pioneer of civilisation in the
gloomy forests of Canada, while the treasures of this great and
fertile country are still unknown.

Mr. Leavens had been informed that plenty of cedar is to
be found on the Tocantíns, the first great tributary of the
Amazon from the south, and much wished to make a trip to
examine it, and, if practicable, bring a raft of the timber down
to Pará ; in which case we agreed to go with him, for the
purpose of investigating the natural history of that almost
unknown district.  We determined to start, if at all, in a few
weeks ; so having been nearly a fortnight at the mills, we
returned to Pará on foot, sending our luggage and collections
by the canoe.

Vessels had arrived from the States and from Rio.  A law
had been lately passed by the Imperial Government, which
was expected to produce a very beneficial effect on the
commerce and tranquillity of the province.  It had hitherto
been the custom to obtain almost all the recruits for the
Brazilian army from this province.  Indians, who came down
the rivers with produce, were forcibly seized and carried off
for soldiers.  This was called voluntary enlistment, and had
gone on for many years, till the fear of it kept the natives from

coming down to Pará, and thus seriously checked the trade of
the province.   A law had now been passed (in consequence
of the repeated complaints of the authorities here, frightening
the Government with the prospect of another revolution),
forbidding enlistment in the province of Pará for fifteen years ;
so we may now hope to be free from any disturbances which
might have arisen from this cause.

Nothing impressed me more than the quiet and orderly
state of the city and neighbourhood.   No class of people carry
knives or other weapons, and there is less noise, fighting, or
drunkenness in the streets both day and night, than in any
town in England of equal population.   When it is remembered
that the population is mostly uneducated, that it consists of
slaves, Indians, Brazilians, Portuguese, and foreigners, and
that rum is sold at every corner at about twopence per pint, it
says much for the good-nature and pacific disposition of the
people.

*August 3rd.*—We received a fresh inmate into our verandah
in the person of a fine young boa constrictor.   A man who
had caught it in the forest left it for our inspection.   It was
tightly tied round the neck to a good-sized stick, which
hindered the freedom of its movements, and appeared nearly
to stop respiration.   It was about ten feet long, and very
large, being as thick as a man's thigh.   Here it lay writhing
about for two or three days, dragging its clog along with it,
sometimes stretching its mouth open with a most suspicious
yawn, and twisting up the end of its tail into a very tight curl.
At length we agreed with the man to purchase it for two
milreis (4s. 6d.), and having fitted up a box with bars at the
top, got the seller to put it into the cage.   It immediately
began making up for lost time by breathing most violently, the
expirations sounding like high-pressure steam escaping from a
Great Western locomotive.   This it continued for some hours,
making about four and a half inspirations per minute, and
then settled down into silence, which it afterwards maintained,
unless when disturbed or irritated.

Though it was without food for more than a week, the
birds we gave it were refused, even when alive.   Rats are
said to be their favourite food, but these we could not procure.
These serpents are not at all uncommon, even close to the
city, and are considered quite harmless.   They are caught by

pushing a large stick under them, when they twist round it, and their head being then cautiously seized and tied to the stick, they are easily carried home.  Another interesting little animal was a young sloth, which Antonio, an Indian boy, who had enlisted himself in our service, brought alive from the forest.  It was not larger than a rabbit, was covered with coarse grey and brown hair, and had a little round head and face resembling the human countenance quite as much as a monkey's, but with a very sad and melancholy expression.  It could scarcely crawl along the ground, but appeared quite at home on a chair, hanging on the back, legs, or rails.  It was a most quiet, harmless little animal, submitting to any kind of examination with no other manifestation of displeasure than a melancholy whine.  It slept hanging with its back downwards and its head between its fore-feet.  Its favourite food is the leaf of the *Cecropia peltata*, of which it sometimes ate a little from a branch we furnished it with.  After remaining with us three days, we found it dead in the garden, whither it had wandered, hoping no doubt to reach its forest home.  It had eaten scarcely anything with us, and appeared to have died of hunger.

We were now busy packing up our first collection of insects to send to England.  In just two months we had taken the large number of 553 species of *Lepidoptera* of which more than 400 were butterflies, 450 beetles, and 400 of other orders, making in all 1,300 species of insects.

Mr. Leavens decided on making the Tocantíns trip, and we agreed to start in a week, looking forward with much pleasure to visiting a new and unexplored district.

# CHAPTER III.

## THE TOCANTÍNS.

Canoe, Stores, and Crew—River Mojú—Igaripé Miri—Cametá—Senhor Gomez and his Establishment—Search for a Dinner—Jambouassú—Polite Letter—Baião and its Inhabitants—A Swarm of Wasps—Enter the Rocky District—The Mutuca—Difficulty of getting Men—A Village without Houses—Catching an Alligator—Duck-shooting—Aroyas, and the Falls—A Nocturnal Concert—Blue Macaws—Turtles' Eggs—A Slight Accident—Capabilities of the Country—Return to Pará.

On the afternoon of the 26th of August we left Pará for the Tocantíns. Mr. Leavens had undertaken to arrange all the details of the voyage. He had hired one of the country canoes, roughly made, but in some respects convenient, having a tolda, or palm-thatched roof, like a gipsy's tent, over the stern, which formed our cabin; and in the forepart a similar one, but lower, under which most of our provisions and baggage were stowed. Over this was a rough deck of cedar-boards, where the men rowed, and where we could take our meals when the sun was not too hot. The canoe had two masts and fore and aft sails, and was about twenty-four feet long and eight wide.

Besides our guns, ammunition, and boxes to preserve our collections in, we had a three months' stock of provisions, consisting of farinha, fish, and caxaça for the men; with the addition of tea, coffee, biscuits, sugar, rice, salt beef, and cheese, for ourselves. This, with clothes, crockery, and about a bushel sack of copper money—the only coin current in the interior—pretty well loaded our little craft. Our crew consisted of old Isidora, as cook; Alexander, an Indian from the mills, who was named Captain; Domingo, who had been up the river, and was therefore to be our pilot; and Antonio, the boy before mentioned. Another Indian deserted when we were about to leave, so we started without him, trusting to get two or three more as we went along.

Though in such a small boat, and going up a river in the same province, we were not allowed to leave Pará without passports and clearances from the custom-house, and as much difficulty and delay as if we had been taking a two hundred ton ship into a foreign country. But such is the rule here, even the internal trade of the province, carried on by Brazilian subjects, not being exempt from it. The forms to be filled up, the signing and countersigning at different offices, the applications to be made and formalities to be observed, are so numerous and complicated, that it is quite impossible for a stranger to go through them; and had not Mr. Leavens managed all this part of the business, we should probably have been obliged, from this cause alone, to have given up our projected journey.

Soon after leaving the city night came on, and the tide turning against us, we had to anchor. We were up at five the next morning, and found that we were in the Mojú, up which our way lay, and which enters the Pará river from the south. The morning was delightful; the Suacuras, a kind of rail, were tuning their melancholy notes, which are always to be heard on the river-banks night and morning; lofty palms rose on either side, and when the sun appeared all was fresh and beautiful. About eight, we passed Jaguararí, an estate belonging to Count Brisson, where there are a hundred and fifty slaves engaged principally in cultivating mandiocca. We breakfasted on board, and about two in the afternoon reached Jighery, a very pretty spot, with steep grassy banks, cocoa and other palms, and oranges in profusion. Here we stayed for the tide, and dined on shore, and Mr. B. and myself went in search of insects. We found them rather abundant, and immediately took two species of butterflies we had never seen at Pará. We had not expected to find, in so short a distance, such a difference in the insects; though, as the same thing takes place in England, why should it not here? I saw a very long and slender snake, of a brown colour, twining among the bushes, so that till it moved it was hardly distinguishable from the stem of a climbing plant. Our men had caught a sloth in the morning, as it was swimming across the river, which was about half a mile wide; it was different from the species we had had alive at Pará, having a patch of short yellow and black fur on the back. The Indians stewed it for their dinner, and as they consider the meat a great delicacy, I tasted it, and found it tender and very palatable.

In the evening, at sunset, the scene was lovely. The groups of elegant palms, the large cotton-trees relieved against the golden sky, the Negro houses surrounded with orange and mango trees, the grassy bank, the noble river, and the background of eternal forest, all softened by the mellowed light of the magical half-hour after sunset, formed a picture indescribably beautiful.

At nine A.M., on the 28th, we entered the Igaripé Mirí, which is a cut made for about half a mile, connecting the Mojú river with a stream flowing into the Tocantíns, nearly opposite Cametá; thus forming an inner passage, safer than the navigation by the Pará river, where vessels are at times exposed to a heavy swell and violent gales, and where there are rocky shoals, very dangerous for the small canoes by which the Cametá trade is principally carried on. When about halfway through, we found the tide running against us, and the water very shallow, and were obliged to wait, fastening the canoe to a tree. In a short time the rope by which we were moored broke, and we were drifted broadside down the stream, and should have been upset by coming against a shoal, but were luckily able to turn into a little bay where the water was still. On getting out of the canal, we sailed and rowed along a winding river, often completely walled in with a luxuriant vegetation of trees and climbing plants. A handsome tree with a mass of purple blossoms was not uncommon, and a large aquatic *Arum*, with its fine white flowers and curious fruits, grew on all the mudbanks along the shores. The Miriti palm here covered extensive tracts of ground, and often reached an enormous height.

At five P.M. we arrived at Santa Anna, a village with a pretty church in the picturesque Italian architecture usual in Pará. We had anticipated some delay here with our passports; but finding there was no official to examine them we continued our journey.

The 29th was spent in progressing slowly among intricate channels and shoals, on which we several times got aground, till we at last reached the main stream of the Tocantíns, studded with innumerable palm-covered islands.

On the 30th, at daylight, we crossed over the river, which is five or six miles wide, to Cametá, one of the principal towns in the province. Its trade is in Brazil-nuts, cacao, india-rubber, and cotton, which are produced in abundance by the surrounding district. It is a small straggling place, and though there are several shops, such a thing as a watch-key, which I required, was not to be obtained. It has a picturesque appearance, being situated on a bank thirty or. forty feet high ; and the view from it, of the river studded with island beyond island, as far as the eye can reach, is very fine. We breakfasted here with Senhor Le Roque, a merchant with whom Mr. Leavens is acquainted, and who showed us round the place, and then offered to accompany us in his boat to the sitio of Senhor Gomez, about thirty miles up the river, to whom we had an introduction, and who we hoped would be able to furnish us with some more men.

On going to our canoe, however, one of our men, Domingo, the pilot, was absent ; but the tide serving, Senhor Le Roque set off, and we promised to follow as soon as we could find our pilot, who was, no doubt, hidden in some *taverna*, or liquor-shop, in the town. But after making every inquiry and search for him in vain, waiting till the tide was almost gone, we determined to start without him, and send back word by Senhor Le Roque, that he was to come on in a montaria the next day. If we had had more experience of the Indian character, we should have waited patiently till the following morning, when we should, no doubt, have found him. As it was, we never saw him during the rest of the voyage, though he had left clothes and several other articles in the canoe.

In consequence of our delay we lost the wind, and our remaining man and boy had to row almost all the way, which put them rather out of humour ; and before we arrived, we met Senhor Le Roque returning. Senhor Gomez received us kindly, and we stayed with him two days, waiting for men he was trying to procure for us. We amused ourselves very well, shooting and entomologising. Near the house was a large leguminous tree loaded with yellow blossoms, which were frequented by paroquets and humming-birds. Up the igaripé were numbers of the curious and handsome birds, called "Ciganos," or Gipsies (*Opisthocomus cristatus*). They are as large as a fowl, have an elegant movable crest on their head, and a varied brown and white plumage. I shot two, but they were not in good condition; and as they are plentiful on all these streams, though not found at Pará, it was with less regret that I threw them away. They keep in flocks on low trees and bushes on the banks of the river, feeding on the fruits and leaves of the large *Arum* before mentioned. They never descend to the ground, and have a slow and unsteady flight.

In the Campos, about a mile through the forest, I found wax-bills, pigeons, toucans, and white-winged and blue chatterers. In the forest we found some fine new *Heliconias* and *Erycinidæ*, and I took two *Cicadas* sitting on the trunk of a tree: when caught they make a noise almost deafening; they generally rest high up on the trees, and though daily and hourly heard, are seldom seen or captured. As I was returning to the house, I met a little Indian boy, and at the same time a large iguana at least three feet long, with crested back and hanging dewlap, looking very fierce, ran across the path. The boy immediately rushed after it, and seizing the tail with both hands, dashed the creature's head against a tree, killing it on the spot, and then carried it home, where it no doubt made a very savoury supper.

We here had an opportunity of seeing something of the arrangements and customs of a Brazilian country-house. The whole edifice in this case was raised four or five feet on piles, to keep it above water at the high spring tides. Running out to low-water mark was a substantial wooden pier, terminated by a flight of steps. This leads from a verandah, opening out of which is a room where guests are received and business transacted, and close by is the sugar-mill and distillery. Quite detached is the house where the mistress, children, and servants reside, the approach to it being through the verandah, and along a raised causeway forty or fifty feet in length. We took our meals in the verandah with Senhor Gomez, never once being honoured by the presence of the lady or her grown-up daughters. At six A.M. we had coffee; at nine, breakfast, consisting of beef and dried fish, with farinha, which supplies the place of bread; and, to finish, coffee and farinha cakes, and the rather unusual luxury of butter. We dined at three, and had rice or shrimp soup, a variety of meat, game or fresh fish, terminating with fruit, principally pine-apples and oranges, cut up in slices and served in saucers; and at eight in the evening we had tea and farinha cakes. Two or three Negro and Indian boys wait at table, constantly changing the plates, which, as soon as empty, are whipped off the table, and re-placed by clean ones, a woman just behind being constantly at work washing them.

Our boy Antonio had here turned lazy, disobeyed orders, and was discharged on the spot, going off with a party who were proceeding up the Amazon after pirarucú. We now had but one man left, and with two that Senhor Gomez lent us to go as far as Baião, we left Vista Alegre on the morning of the 2nd of September. The river presented the same appearance as below,—innumerable islands, most of them several miles long, and the two shores never to be seen at once. As we had nothing for dinner, I went with Mr. Leavens in the montaria, which our Indians were to return in, to a house up an igaripé, to see what we could buy. Cattle and sheep, fowls and ducks were in plenty, and we thought we had come to the right place; but we were mistaken, for the following conversation took place between Mr. Leavens and a Negro woman, the only person we saw:—" Have you any fowls to sell ? "—" No." " Any ducks ? "—" No." " Any meat ? "—" No." " What do you do here then ? "—" Nothing." " Have you any eggs to sell ? "—" No, the hens don't lay eggs." And notwithstanding our declaration that we had nothing to eat, we were obliged to go away as empty as we came, because her master was not at home, and nothing was hers to sell. At another house we were lucky enough to buy a small turtle, which made us an excellent meal.

We were to call at Jambouassú, a sitio about fifteen miles below Baião, where Senhor Seixus, to whom we had a letter, sometimes resided. The house is situated up a narrow igaripé, the entrance to which even our Indians had much difficulty in discovering, as it was night when we reached the place. Mr. Leavens and myself then went in the montaria up the narrow stream, which the tall trees, almost meeting overhead, made intensely dark and gloomy. It was but a few hundred yards to the house, where we found Senhor Seixus, and delivered the letter from his partner in Pará; and as it is a very good speci-men of Portuguese composition and politeness, I will here give a literal translation of it.

" *Senhor Jozé Antonio Correio Seixus & Co., Baião.*

"FRIENDS AND GENTLEMEN,—

"Knowing that it is always agreeable for you to have an opportunity of showing your hospitable and generous feelings towards strangers in general, and more particularly to those who visit our country for the purpose of making discoveries and extending the sphere of their knowledge ; I do not hesitate to take advantage of the opportunity which the journey of Mr. Charles Leavens and his two worthy companions presents, to recommend them to your friendship and protection in the scientific enterprise which they have undertaken, in order to obtain those natural productions which render our province a classic land in the history of animals and plants.

"In this laborious enterprise, which the illustrious (*elites*) travellers have undertaken, I much wish that they may find in you all that the limited resources of the place allows, not only that whatever difficulties they encounter may be removed, but that you may render less irksome the labours and privations they must necessarily endure ; and for men like them, devoted to science, and whose very aliment is Natural History, in a country like ours abounding in the most exquisite productions, it is easy to find means to gratify them.

"I therefore hope, and above all pray you to fulfil my wishes in the attentions you pay to Senhor Leavens and his companions, and thus give me another proof of your esteem and friendship.

"Your friend and obedient servant,

"JOÃO AUGUSTO CORREIO."

After reading the letter Senhor Seixus told us that he was going to Baião in two or three days, and that we could either remain here, or have the use of his house there till he arrived. We determined to proceed, as we wished to send back the men Senhor Gomez had lent us, and therefore returned to our canoe to be ready to start the next tide. In the morning I went on ahead in the montaria, with Alexander, to shoot some birds. We saw numbers of kingfishers and small green-backed swallows, and some pretty red-headed finches (*Tanagra gularis*), called here "marinheiros," or sailors : they are always found near the water, on low trees and bushes.  We landed on an extensive sandy beach, where many terns and gulls were flying about, of which, after a good many ineffectual attempts, we shot two.  We reached the canoe again as she came to anchor at Baião, under a very steep bank about a hundred feet high, which commences a few miles below.  Here we had about a hundred and twenty irregular steps to ascend, when we found the village on level ground, and the house of Senhor Seixus close at hand, which, though the floors and walls were of mud, was neatly whitewashed.  As the house was quite empty, we had to bring a great many necessaries up from the canoe, which was very laborious work in the hot sun.  We did not see a floored house in the village, which is not to be wondered at when it is considered that there is not such a thing as a sawn board in this part of the country.  A tree is cut longitudinally down the middle with an axe, and the outside then hewn away, and the surface finished off with an adze, so that a tree makes but two boards.  All the boarded floors at Cametá, and many at Pará, have been thus formed, without the use of either saw or plane.

We remained here some days, and had very good sport.  Birds were tolerably plentiful, and I obtained a brown jacamar, a purple-headed parrot, and some fine pigeons.  All round the village, for some miles, on the dry high land, are coffee-plantations and second-growth forest, which produced many butterflies new to us, particularly the whites and yellows, of which we obtained six or seven species we had not before met with.  While preparing insects or skinning birds in the house, the window which opened into the street was generally crowded with boys and men, who would wait for hours, watching my operations with the most untiring curiosity.  The constantly-repeated remark, on seeing a bird skinned, was, " Oh, the patience of the whites ! "  Then one would whisper to another, " Does he take all the meat out ? "   " Well, I never ! "   " Look, he makes eyes of cotton ! "  And then would come a little conversation as to what they could possibly be wanted for.  " Para mostrar " (to show) was the general solution ; but they seemed to think it rather unsatisfactory, and that the English could hardly be such fools as to want to see a few parrot and pigeon skins.  The butterflies they settled much to their own satisfaction, deciding that they were for the purpose of obtaining new patterns for printed calicoes and other goods, while the ugly insects were supposed to be valuable for " remedios," or medicine. We found it best quietly to assent to this, as it saved us a deal of questioning, and no other explanation that we could give would be at all intelligible to them.

One day, while I was in the woods pursuing some insects, I was suddenly attacked by a whole swarm of small wasps, whose nest, hanging from a leaf, I had inadvertently disturbed. They covered my face and neck, stinging me severely, while in my haste to escape, and free myself from them, I knocked off my spectacles, which I did not perceive till I was at some distance from the spot, and as I was quite out of any path, and had not noticed where I was, it was useless to seek them. The pain of the stings, which was at first very severe, went off altogether in about an hour ; and as I had several more glasses with me, I did not suffer any inconvenience from my loss.

The soil here is red clay, in some places of so bright a colour as to be used for painting earthenware. Igaripés are much rarer than they were lower down, and where they occur form little valleys or ravines in the high bank. When Senhor Seixus arrived, he insisted on our all taking our meals with him, and was in every way very obliging to us. His son, a little boy of six or seven, ran about the house completely naked.

The neighbours would drop in once or twice a day to see how the *brancos* (white people) got on, and have a little conversation, mostly with Mr. Leavens, who spoke Portuguese fluently. One inquired if in America (meaning in the United States) there was any *terra firma*, appearing to have an idea that it was all a cluster of islands. Another asked if there were campos, and if the people had mandiocca and seringa. On being told they had neither, he asked why they did not plant them, and said he thought it would answer well to plant seringa-trees, and so have fresh milk every day to make india-rubber shoes. When told that the climate was too cold for mandiocca or seringa to grow if planted, he was quite astonished, and wondered how people could live in a country where such necessaries of life could not be grown ; and he no doubt felt a kind of superiority over us, on account of our coming to his country to buy india-rubber and cocoa, just as the inhabitants of the Celestial Empire think that we must be very poor miserable barbarians, indeed, to be obliged to come so far to buy their tea.

Even Senhor Seixus himself, an educated Brazilian and the Commandante of the district, inquired if the government of England were constitutional or despotic, and was surprised to hear that our Sovereign was a woman.

We at length procured two men, and proceeded on our journey up the river, having spent four days very pleasantly at Baião. As we went slowly along the shore, we saw on a tree an iguana, called here a chameleon, which Mr. Leavens shot, and our men cooked for their supper. In the evening, we anchored under a fine bank, where a large leguminous tree was covered with clusters of pink and white flowers and large pale green flat pods. Venus and the moon were shining brilliantly, and the air was deliciously cool, when, at nine o'clock, we turned in under our tolda, but mosquitoes and sand-flies would not allow us to sleep for some hours. The next day we had a good wind and went along briskly; the river was narrower and had fewer islands; palms were less abundant than below, but the vegetation of the banks was equally luxuriant. Here were plenty of porpoises, and we saw some handsome birds like golden orioles.

On the 9th, early in the morning, we arrived at Jutahí, a cattle estate, where we expected to get more men; but the owner of the place being out, we had to wait till he returned. We obtained here about a gallon of delicious new milk, a great treat for us. We shot a few birds, and found some small shells in the river, but none of any size or beauty, and could see scarcely any insects.

As the man we wanted did not arrive, we left on the 10th, hoping to meet him up the river. I walked across an extensive sandbank, where, about noon, it was decidedly hot. There were numerous little Carabideous beetles on the sand, very active, and of a pale colour with dark markings, reminding me of insects that frequent similar situations in England. In the afternoon we reached a house, and made a fire on the beach to cook our dinner. Here were a number of men and women, and naked children. The house was a mere open shed,—a roof of palm-thatch supported on posts, between which the *rédés* (hammocks) are hung, which serve the purpose of bed and chair. At one end was a small platform, raised about three feet above the floor, ascended by deep notches cut in a post, instead of a ladder. This seemed to be a sort of boudoir, or ladies' room, as they alone occupied it; and it was useful to keep clothes and food out of the way of the fowls, ducks, pigs, and dogs, which freely ranged below. The head of the establishment was a Brazilian, who had come down from the mines. He had in cultivation cotton, tobacco, cacao, mandiocca, and abundance of bananas. He wanted powder and shot, which Mr. Leavens furnished him with in exchange for tobacco. He said they had not had any rain for three months, and that the crops were much injured in consequence. At Pará, from which we were not distant more than one hundred and fifty miles, there had never been more than three days without rain. The proximity to the great body of water of the Amazon and the ocean, together with the greater extent of lowland and dense forest about the city, are probably the causes of this great difference of climate in so short a distance.

Proceeding on our way, we still passed innumerable islands, the river being four or five miles wide. About four in the afternoon, we came in sight of the first rocks we met with on the river, on a projecting point, rugged and volcanic in appearance, with little detached islands in the stream, and great blocks lying along the shore. After so much flat alluvial country, it had quite a picturesque effect. A mile further, we reached Patos, a small village, were we hoped to get men, and anchored for the night. I took a walk along the shore to examine the rocks, and found them to be decidedly volcanic, of a dark colour, and often as rugged as the scoriæ of an iron-furnace. There was also a coarse conglomerate, containing blackened quartz pebbles, and in the hollows a very fine white quartz sand.

We remained here two days; Mr. Leavens going up the igaripé to look for cedar, while we remained hunting for birds, insects, and shells. I shot several pretty birds, and saw, for the first time, the beautiful blue macaws, which we had been told we should meet with up the Tocantíns. They are entirely of a fine indigo-blue, with a whitish beak; but they flew very high, and we could not find their feeding-place. The insects most abundant were the yellow butterflies, which often settled in great numbers on the beach, and when disturbed rose in a body, forming a complete yellow and orange fluttering cloud.    Shells were tolerably plentiful, and we added some new ones to our small stock.    Since leaving Baião, a small fly, with curiously marked black and white wings, had much annoyed us, setting on our hands and faces in the quietest manner, and then suddenly piercing them like the prick of a needle.    The people call it the Mutúca, and say it is one of the torments of the interior, being in many parts much more abundant than it is here.

Mr. Leavens having ascertained that there was no cedar within a mile of the water, we arranged to proceed the next day, when a pilot and two men from Patos had agreed to accompany us to the Falls.    In the morning we waited till eight o'clock, and no one making their appearance, we sent to them, when they replied, they could not come; so after having waited a day, we were at last obliged to go on without them, hoping to be able to get as far as the Falls, and then return.    Cedar was quite out of the question, as men could not be got to work the canoe, much less to cut timber.    We had now altogether been delayed nine or ten days waiting for men, and in only one instance had got them after all.    This is one of the greatest difficulties travellers here have to encounter. All the men you want must be taken from Pará, and if they choose to run away, as they are almost sure to do, others cannot be procured.

At ten in the morning we reached Troquera, on the west bank of the river, where there is a small igaripé, on which there are some falls.    There were several families living here, yet they had not a house among them, but had chosen a nice clear space under some trees, between the trunks and from the branches of which they hung their *rédés*.    Numbers of children were rolling about naked in the sand, while the women and some of the men were lounging in their hammocks. Their canoes were pulled up on the beach, their guns were leaning against the trees, a couple of large earthen pots were on the fire, and they seemed to possess, in their own estimation, every luxury that man can desire.    As in the winter the place is all under water, it is only a summer encampment; during which season they collect seringa, grow a little cotton, mandiocca, and maize, catch fish and hunt.    All they wanted of us was ammunition and caxaça (rum), which Mr. Leavens supplied them with, taking rubber in exchange.

We walked about a mile through the forest to the Falls on the igaripé. Black slaty rocks rose up at a high angle in the bed of the brook, in irregular stratified masses, among which the water foams and dashes for about a quarter of a mile: "a splendid place for a sawmill," said Mr. Leavens. There were no palms here, or any striking forms of tropical vegetation; the mosses and small plants had nothing peculiar in them; and, altogether, the place was very like many I have seen at home. The depths of the virgin forest are solemn and grand, but there is nothing in this country to surpass the beauty of our river and woodland scenery. Here and there some exquisite clump of plants covered with blossoms, or a huge tree overrun with flowering climbers, strikes us as really tropical; but this is not the general character of the scenery. In the second-growth woods, in the campos, and in many other places, there is nothing to tell any one but a naturalist that he is out of Europe.

Before leaving Troquera, I shot some goat-suckers, which were flying about and settling upon the rocks in the hot sunshine. We went on to Panajá, where there is a house occupied by some seringa-gatherers, and stayed there for the night. All along the sandy shore, from Baião to this place, are trailing prickly cassias, frequently forming an impenetrable barrier; and, in places, there is a large shrubby species, also prickly. The large-stemmed arums had now disappeared, and with them the ciganos. The next morning I went with our Indian, Alexander, to visit a lake, about a mile through the woods. There was a small montaria, which would just hold two, in which we embarked to explore it, and shoot some birds. Alligators were very abundant, showing their heads every now and then above water. Alexander fired at one, which immediately disappeared, but soon came up again, half turned over, and with one leg out of water; so we thought he was quite dead, and paddled up to secure him. I seized hold of the elevated claw, when—dash! splash!—over he turned, and dived down under our little boat, which he had half filled with water and nearly upset. Again he appeared at the surface, and this time we poked him with a long stick, to see if he were really dead or shamming, when he again dived down and appeared no more.

We went to the end of the lake, which was about a mile long, and then returned to the place where we had embarked. I had shot a kingfisher, and was loading my gun, when Alexander shot at a small coot or rail, and having a large charge, the shock threw me off my balance, and to save myself I dropped my gun into the water and very nearly swamped the canoe. I thought my shooting for this voyage was all over; but, luckily, the water was only three or four feet deep, and we soon hooked the gun up. I employed the rest of the morning in taking off the locks, and by careful cleaning and oiling got all right again.

We went on with a fair wind for a few hours, when two of our men proposed taking the montaria to go and shoot ducks at a place near, where they abounded; so Mr. B. and myself agreed to go with them, while Mr. Leavens proceeded a mile or two on, to get dinner ready and wait for us. We had about half a mile of paddling to reach the shore, then half a mile of walking over a sandy beach, when our Indians plunged into the forest along a narrow path, we following in silence. About a mile more brought us to some open ground, where there was abundance of fine grass and scattered clumps of low trees and shrubs, among which were many pretty flowers. We walked for a mile through this kind of country, along a track which was often quite imperceptible to us, till at length we reached an extensive morass covered with aquatic plants, with some clumps of bushes and blackened clumps of trees.

Our Indians, without saying a word, plunged in up to their knees, and waded after the ducks, which we could see at a distance, with egrets and other aquatic birds. As we could do nothing on shore, we followed them, floundering about in mud and water, among immersed trees and shrubs, and tangled roots of aquatic plants, feeling warm and slimy, as if tenanted by all sorts of creeping things. The ducks were far from easy to get at, being very wild and shy. After one or two ineffectual long shots, I saw one sitting on the top of a stump, and by creeping cautiously along under cover of some bushes, got within shot and fired. The bird flew away, I thought unhurt, but soon fell into the water, where I picked it up dead. It had been shot through the head, and flown, I suppose, in the same manner that fowls will run after being decapitated.

I then came out on to dry land, and waited for the Indians, who soon appeared, but all empty-handed. A pale yellow water-lily and some pretty buttercups and bladder-worts were abundant in the lake. We had a long row to reach the canoe, which we found at Jucahipuá, where Senhor Joaquim resided, who, we had been told, would pilot us up to the Falls. After a good dinner of turtle I skinned my birds, and then took a walk along the beach: here were fine crystalline sandstone rocks, in regularly stratified beds. In the evening a small *Ephemera* was so abundant about the candle as to fall on the paper like rain, and get into our hair and down our necks in such abundance as to be very annoying.

In the morning we passed the locality of the old settlement of Alcobaza, where there was once a fort and a considerable village, but now no signs of any habitation. The inhabitants were murdered by the Indians about fifty years ago, and since then it has never been re-settled. The river was now about a mile wide, and had fewer islands. There was a fine flat-bedded sandstone here, very suitable for building. We were shown a stone on which is said to be writing which no man can read, being circular and pothook marks, almost as much like the work of nature as of art. The water was here beautifully transparent, and there were many pretty fishes variously marked and spotted.

About noon we reached the "Ilha dos Santos," a small sandy island in the middle of the river, where there was a house, the inhabitants of which continually asked us for caxaça. We had a land-tortoise for dinner to-day, which was as good as turtle. Two hours further we landed for the night. The river was now very full of rocks and eddies, and we were unable to go in our large canoe. The next morning, having put our *rédés* and some provisions into the montaria, we started with two of our men and Senhor Joaquim, leaving one man and old Isidora in charge of the canoe till we returned. In about an hour we all had to get out of the boat for the men to pull it up a little rapid over some rocks. The whole river is here full of small rocky islands and masses of rock above and under water. In the wet season the water is fifteen to twenty feet higher than it was now, and this part is then safe for large canoes. We passed the mouth of an igaripé on the west bank, and another on the opposite side, in both of which gold is said to exist. Large silk-cotton-trees appear at intervals, raising their semi-globular heads above the rest of the forest, and the castanha, or Brazil-nut, grows on the river-banks, where we saw many of the trees covered with fruit.

We passed the Ilha das Pacas, which is completely covered with wood, and very abrupt and rocky. The rocks in the river were now thicker than ever, and we frequently scraped against them; but as the bottoms of the montarins are hollowed out of the trunks of trees and left very thick, they do not readily receive any injury. At three P.M. we reached Aroyas, a mile below the Falls. Here the bank of the river slopes up to a height of about three hundred feet, and is thickly wooded. There was a house near the river, with numerous orange-trees, and on the top of the hill were mandiocca and coffee plantations. We dined here; and when we had finished, the mistress handed round a basin of water and a clean napkin to wash our hands,—a refinement we had hardly expected in a room without walls, and at such a distance from civilisation.

After dinner we went on to see the Falls. The river was still about a mile wide, and more wild and rocky than before. Near the Falls are vast masses of volcanic rock; one in particular, which we passed close under in the montaria is of a cubical form, thirty feet on the side and twenty feet high. There are also small islands composed entirely of scoria-like rocks, heaped up and containing caves and hollows of a most picturesque appearance, affording evident proofs of violent volcanic action at some former period. On both sides of the river, and as far as the sight extends, is an undulating country, from four to five hundred feet high, covered with forest, the commencement of the elevated plains of central Brazil.

On arriving at the Falls we found the central channel about a quarter of a mile wide, bounded by rocks, with a deep and very powerful stream rushing down in an unbroken sweep of dark green waters, and producing eddies and whirlpools below more dangerous to canoes than the Fall itself. When the river is full they are much more perilous, the force of the current being almost irresistible, and much skill is required to avoid the eddies and sunken rocks. The great cubical block I have mentioned is then just under water, and has caused the loss of many canoes. The strata were much twisted and confused, dipping in various directions about 12°, with volcanic masses rising up among them. As nearly as we could judge by the distances we had come, these rapids must be in about 4° of south latitude, where a considerable bend in the river occurs. Above are numerous falls and rapids, and after a time the forest ceases, and open undulating plains are found. From the point we reached, the country becomes very interesting, and we much regretted that we were unable to explore it further.

On our return to Aroyas, our men, while descending the various smaller rapids, shouted and sang in the most wild and excited manner, and appeared to enjoy it amazingly. They had had a hard day's work, having paddled and poled about twenty miles against a powerful current, in some places so strong as to require all their exertions to keep the boat's head up the stream. At Aroyas we took some coffee, and then turned into our *rédés* in an open shed about twelve feet square, at the back part of the house, where six or eight other members of the family also found room for themselves. We were kept awake some time by our pilot, who had got drunk on caxaça, and was very violent and abusive, so to quiet him we administered another glass or two, which soon had the desired sedative effect. The next morning he looked very dull and sheepish ; in fact, most of the Tapuyas, or half-civilised Indians, consider it disgraceful to get drunk, and seem ashamed afterwards.

After paying our hostess in biscuit, tea, and sugar, which were great luxuries to her, we started on our return to the canoe, which we reached about noon, having stayed an hour to explore the igaripé for gold, but without the smallest success. At the canoe we found that Isidora had some turtle stew ready, to which we did ample justice, and, finding the man we had left with him very ill, went on immediately to Jucahipuah, where he could have some "remedios" given him by the women. We found there a canoe going to Baião, and sent him by it, as he would thus get home sooner than if he remained with us.

While walking on the beach I saw a tall, narrow-leaved, white-flowered *Polygonum*, so like some of our British species as to call up thoughts of home and of my botanical rambles there. Many curious land-shells were found, but all dead and bleached, and though we searched repeatedly we could find no living specimens. The feathers of the blue macaw were lying about the ground where the people had been feasting off their flesh, but we could not succeed in obtaining any specimens.

Every night, while in the upper part of the river, we had a concert of frogs, which made most extraordinary noises. There are three kinds, which can frequently be all heard at once. One of these makes a noise something like what one would expect a frog to make, namely a dismal croak, but the sounds uttered by the others were like no animal noise that I ever heard before. A distant railway-train approaching, and a blacksmith hammering on his anvil, are what they exactly resemble. They are such true imitations, that when lying half-dozing in the canoe I have often fancied myself at home, hearing the familiar sounds of the approaching mail-train, and the hammering of the boiler-makers at the iron-works. Then we often had the " guarhibas," or howling monkeys, with their terrific noises, the shrill grating whistle of the cicadas and locusts, and the peculiar notes of the suacúras and other aquatic birds ; add to these the loud unpleasant hum of the mosquito in your immediate vicinity, and you have a pretty good idea of our nightly concert on the Tocantíns.

On the morning of the 19th, at Panajá, where we had passed the night, I took my gun and went into the forest, but found nothing. I saw, however, an immense silk-cotton-tree, one of the buttresses of which ran out twenty feet from the trunk. On the beach was a pretty yellow *Œnothera*, which is common all along this part of the river, as well as a small white passion-flower. Mr. Leavens here bought some rubber, and we then rowed or sailed on for the rest of the day. In the afternoon I took the montaria, with Isidora, to try and shoot some of the pretty yellow orioles. I killed one, but it stuck in a thick prickly tree, and we were obliged to come away without it. We passed Patos in the afternoon ; near it was a tree covered with a mass of bright yellow blossoms, more brilliant than laburnum, and a really gorgeous sight.

The next day we left the land of the blue macaw without a single specimen. From this place to the Falls we had seen them every day, morning and evening, flying high over the river. At almost every house feathers were on the ground, showing that this splendid bird is often shot for food. Alexander once had a chance at them, but his gun missed fire, and they immediately flew off. Lower down the river they are scarcely ever seen, and never below Baião, while from this place up they are very abundant. What can be the causes which so exactly limit the range of such a strongly-flying bird? It appears with the rock, and with this there is no doubt a corresponding change in the fruits on which the birds feed.

Our Indians seeing a likely place on the beach for turtles' eggs, went on shore in the montaria, and were fortunate enough to find a hundred and twenty-three buried in the sand. They are oily and very savoury, and we had an immense omelet for dinner. The shell is leathery, and the white never coagulates, but is thrown away, and the yolk only eaten. The Indians eat them also raw, mixed with farinha. We dined on the beach, where there was abundance of a plant much resembling chamomile. The sands were very hot, so that it was almost impossible to walk over them barefooted. The Indians, in crossing extensive beaches, stop and dig holes in the sand to cool their feet in. We now got on very slowly, having to tack across and across the river, the wind blowing up it, as it always does at this season.

Where we stopped for breakfast on the 21st, I shot a very prettily-marked small hawk. Insects were also rather abundant, and we captured some fine *Papilios*, and two or three new species of clear-winged *Heliconia*. Alexander found a bees'-nest in a hole in a tree, and got about two quarts of honey, which when strained was very sweet, but with a hot waxy taste. The comb consists of oval cells of black wax, very irregular in shape and size, and displaying little of the skill of our bees at home. The next night, rather late, we arrived at Jambouassu, the sitio of Senhor Seixus, where we were kindly received, and, about nine o'clock, turned into our *rédés* in his verandah.

The next morning I walked out to examine the premises. The whole of the forest, for some miles round the house, is a cacao plantation, there being about sixty thousand trees, which have all been planted; the small trees and brush having been cleared from the forest, but all the seringa and other large forest-trees left for shade, which the cacao requires. The milk from the seringa-trees is collected every morning in large univalve shells, which are stuck with clay to the tree, and a small incision made in the bark above. It is formed into shoes or bottles, on moulds of clay, or into flat cakes. It hardens in a few hours, and is blackened with a smoke produced by burning the nuts of the Urucurí palm, and is then india-rudder. Just before leaving this place I met with an accident, which might have been very serious. My gun was lying loaded on the top of the canoe, and wishing to shoot some small birds near the house, I drew it towards me by the muzzle, which, standing on the steps of the landing-place, was the only part I could reach. The hammer, however, lay in a joint of the boards, and as I drew the gun towards me it was raised up, and let fall on the cap, firing off the gun, the charge carrying off a small piece of the under-side of my hand near the wrist, and, passing under my arm within a few inches of my body luckily missed a number of people who were behind me. I felt my hand violently blown away, and looking at it, saw a stream of blood, but felt no pain for some minutes. As we had nothing to put to it, I tied it up with a quantity of cotton ; and about twelve o'clock, the tide serving, we bade adieu to Senhor Seixus, who had treated us very kindly both here and at Baião.

On the 24th we stayed for the tide, at a house on an island abounding in cacao and seringa. The water of the river had become muddy, but not ill-tasted. On the 25th we stayed at a sugar estate, where there was a tree full of the hanging nests of the japims, or yellow troupials. Seeing a number of the large frigate-bird pelican over the river, I went out with Alexander in the montaria to try and shoot one, and, after a few ineffectual shots, Alexander succeeded in doing so. It measured seven feet from wing to wing; the feet were very small and webbed, and the bill long and hooked at the end. They appear almost to live upon the wing, going in small flocks over the river, and darting down to seize any fish which may appear near the surface. The neck is partly bare, and very extensible, like that of the true pelicans. There are two kinds, which fly together, one with the body entirely black, the other with the head and neck white, which are said to be the male and female of the same species.

On the 26th we stayed for the tide at a low island covered with palms and underwood. Just as we were going to step on shore we saw a large snake twisted on a branch overhead, so we hung back a little till Mr. Leavens shot it. It was about ten feet long, and very handsomely marked with yellow and black slanting lines. In the wood we got some assai, and made a quantity of the drink so much liked by the people here, and which is very good when you are used to it. The fruit grows in large bunches on the summit of a graceful palm, and is about the size and colour of a sloe. On examining it, a person would think that it contained nothing eatable, as immediately under the skin is a hard stone. The very thin, hardly perceptible pulp, between the skin and the stone, is what is used. To prepare it, the fruit is soaked half an hour in water, just warm enough to bear the hand in. It is next rubbed and kneaded with the hands, till all the skin and pulp is worn off the stones. The liquid is then poured off, and strained, and is of the consistence of cream, and of a fine purple colour. It is eaten with sugar and farinha; with use it becomes very agreeable to the taste, something resembling nuts and cream, and is no doubt very nourishing; it is much used in Pará, where it is constantly sold in the streets, and, owing to the fruit ripening at different seasons, according to the locality, is to be had there all the year round.

On the east side of the river, along which we had kept in our descent, there was more cultivation than on the side we went up. A short distance from the shore the land rises, and most of the houses are situated on the slope, with the ground cleared down to the river. Some of the places are kept in tolerable order, but there are numbers' of houses and cottages unoccupied and in ruins, with land once cultivated, overgrown with weeds and brushwood. Rubber-making and gathering cacao and Brazil-nuts are better liked than the regular cultivation of the soil.

In the districts we passed through, sugar, cotton, coffee, and rice might be grown in any quantity and of the finest quality. The navigation is always safe and uninterrupted, and the whole country is so intersected by igaripés and rivers that every estate has water-carriage for its productions. But the indolent disposition of the people, and the scarcity of labour, will prevent the capabilities of this fine country from being developed till European or North American colonies are formed. There is no country in the world where people can produce for themselves so many of the necessaries and luxuries of life. Indian corn, rice, mandiocca, sugar, coffee, and cotton, beef, poultry, and pork, with oranges, bananas, and abundance of other fruits and vegetables, thrive with little care. With these articles in abundance, a house of wood, calabashes, cups and pottery of the country, they may live in plenty without a single exotic production. And then what advantages there are in a country where there is no stoppage of agricultural operations during winter, but where crops may be had, and poultry be reared, all the year round ; where the least possible amount of clothing is the most comfortable, and where a hundred little necessaries of a cold region are altogether superfluous. With regard to the climate I have said enough already ; and I repeat, that a man can work as well here as in the hot summer months in England, and that if he will only work three hours in the morning and three in the evening, he will produce more of the necessaries and comforts of life than by twelve hours' daily labour at home.

Nothing more of importance occurred, and we arrived safely at Pará on the 30th of September, just five weeks from the day we left. We had not had a wet day the whole voyage, yet found to our surprise that it had been there the same as usual—a shower and a thunderstorm every second or third day.

# CHAPTER IV.

## MEXIANA AND MARAJÓ.

Visit to Olería—Habits of Birds—Voyage to Mexiana—Arrival—Birds—
Description of the Island—Population—Slaves, their Treatment and
Habits—Journey to the Lake—Beautiful Stream—Fish and Birds at
the Lake—Catching Alligators—Strange Sounds, and Abundance of
Animal Life—Walk back—Jaguar Meat—Visit to Jungcal in Marajó
—Embarking Cattle—Ilha das Frechas.

SOON after our return to Pará, my hand became so much
inflamed, that I was obliged to put my arm in a sling, and
go to a doctor, under whose treatment I remained a fortnight,
unable to do anything, not even pin an insect, and consequently rather miserable. As I intended, as soon as possible,
going to the great island of Marajó, in search of some of the
curious and rare water-birds which abound there, I obtained
permission from Mr. C., an English gentleman, to visit his
cattle estates ; but as there was no canoe going there for some
weeks, I spent the interim at Olería, where M. Borlaz kindly
offered me a room and a place at his table.

I found plenty of occupation in procuring specimens of the
various small birds, and making myself acquainted with their
habits. None were more abundant, both in species and
individuals, than the bush-shrikes, which are all remarkable
for the same kind of falling note I have already alluded to,
though each one has some slight peculiarity by which it may
be distinguished. They generally hide themselves in the very
thickest and most impenetrable bushes, where it is impossible
to see them except by creeping up within a distance of two
yards, when it is difficult to shoot without blowing them to
pieces. They are small birds with very loose, long, silky
feathers, prettily banded or spotted with black and white, and

are constantly hopping about the bushes and twigs, picking off whatever small insects they fall in with.

The ant-thrushes are another closely allied group, which are equally abundant. They have stronger legs and very short tails, and walk more on the ground, picking up insects, especially ants, very much after the manner of poultry. When one is shot, it is often a dangerous matter to go and fetch it, for the ground generally swarms with ants, which attack an intruder most unmercifully both with stings and jaws. Many times, after a fruitless attempt, have I been obliged to leave the dead body on the field, and beat an inglorious retreat.

In all works on Natural History, we constantly find details of the marvellous adaptation of animals to their food, their habits, and the localities in which they are found. But naturalists are now beginning to look beyond this, and to see that there must be some other principle regulating the infinitely varied forms of animal life. It must strike every one, that the numbers of birds and insects of different groups, having scarcely any resemblance to each other, which yet feed on the same food and inhabit the same localities, cannot have been so differently constructed and adorned for that purpose alone. Thus the goat-suckers, the swallows, the tyrant fly-catchers, and the jacamars, all use the same kind of food, and procure it in the same manner : they all capture insects on the wing, yet how entirely different is the structure and the whole appearance of these birds ! The swallows, with their powerful wings, are almost entirely inhabitants of the air ; the goat-suckers, nearly allied to them, but of a much weaker structure, and with largely developed eyes, are semi-nocturnal birds, sometimes flying in the evening in company with the swallows, but most frequently settling on the ground, seizing their prey by short flights from it, and then returning to the same spot. The fly-catchers are strong-legged, but short-winged birds, which can perch, but cannot fly with the ease of the swallows : they generally seat themselves on a bare tree, and from it watch for any insects which may come within reach of a short swoop, and which their broad bills and wide gape enable them to seize. But with the jacamars this is not the case : their bills are long and pointed—in fact, a weak kingfisher's bill—yet they have similar habits to the preceding : they sit on branches in open parts of the forest, from thence flying after insects, which they catch on the wing, and then return to their former station to devour them. Then there are the trogons, with a strong serrated bill, which have similar habits; and the little humming-birds, though they generally procure insects from the flowers, often take them on the wing, like any other fissi-rostral bird.

What birds can have their bills more peculiarly formed than the ibis, the spoonbill, and the heron? Yet they may be seen side by side, picking up the same food from the shallow water on the beach; and on opening their stomachs, we find the same little crustacea and shell-fish in them all. Then among the fruit-eating birds, there are pigeons, parrots, toucans, and chatterers,—families as distinct and widely separated as possible,—which yet may be often seen feeding all together on the same tree; for in the forests of South America, certain fruits are favourites with almost every kind of fruit-eating bird. It has been assumed by some writers on Natural History, that every wild fruit is the food of some bird or animal, and that the varied forms and structure of their mouths may be neces-sitated by the peculiar character of the fruits they are to feed on; but there is more of imagination than fact in this statement: the number of wild fruits furnishing food for birds is very limited, and birds of the most varied structure and of every size will be found visiting the same tree.

Insects were now more abundant than ever, and new kinds were met with almost every day. Lovely little butterflies, spangled with gold, or glittering with the most splendid metallic tints, hid themselves under leaves or expanded their wings in the morning sun; while the larger and more majestic kinds flew lazily along the shaded forest paths. The more sombre *Hesperidæ* were the most abundant, and it would often happen that, of a dozen specimens taken in a day's excursion, no two were alike.

At length the canoe, for which I had been waiting, was ready to sail; and on the 3rd of November we left Pará for the island of Mexiana, situated in the main stream of the Amazon, between the great island of Marajó and the northern shore. We had to go down the Pará river, and round the eastern point of Marajó, where we were quite exposed to the ocean; and, though most of the time in fresh water, I was very sea-sick all the voyage, which lasted four days. The canoe was intended for the conveyance of cattle, and therefore had no particular accommodation for human passengers. There was certainly a little cabin, with two berths just five feet long, but not at all suitable for me (I am six feet two inches high), so I preferred the hold. Our crew consisted of eight young Tapuyas,—fine active fellows, from fifteen to twenty years of age. Each wore a tight-fitting pair of trousers and a very short shirt, so that six inches of red skin appeared between the two garments. The shrouds of the canoe consisted of the stay-ropes only, without any rattlins or cross-steps, yet up these they would run like monkeys, holding on with their toes.

The island of Mexiana is about twenty-five miles long by twelve broad, of a regular oval shape, and is situated exactly on the equator. It is quite flat, and is all *campo*, or open ground, but dotted with scattered trees and bushes, and with a little forest at the water's edge. It is celebrated for its birds, alligators, and onças, and is used as a cattle estate by the proprietor. The alligators abound in a lake in the centre of the island, where they are killed in great numbers for their fat, which is made into oil.

I was accompanied by Mr. Yates, a collector of Orchids, who, after a few weeks' stay, not finding much variety of those plants, returned to Pará. On our arrival we were received by Senhor Leonardo, a German, who is the overseer, to whom we presented our letter from Mr. C. We were then shown the rooms we were to occupy in the house, which is spacious and has an upper story; and having got our luggage on shore, we soon made ourselves at home. Round the house are a good many orange and mango trees, behind which is a row of cottages, where reside the *vaqueiros* or herdsmen, who are mostly Negroes and slaves; and beyond, as far as the eye can reach, is the flat campo, dotted over with cattle and horses.

On inquiring about the best localities for insects, birds, and plants, we were rather alarmed by being told that onças were very numerous, even near the house, and that it was dangerous to walk out alone or unarmed. We soon found, however, that no one had been actually attacked by them; though they, poor animals, are by no means unmolested, as numerous handsome skins drying in the sun, and teeth and skulls lying about, sufficiently proved. There is no doubt but they are unpleasant animals to encounter, and their teeth and claws are so fearfully adapted to destroy whatever may come within their reach, that it is much better to be a little cautious, than to run any risk : I therefore put half-a-dozen bullets in my game-bag, in case of an encounter.

Some of the horses and cattle were miserable-looking objects, from wounds inflicted by the bats, which cause them to lose much blood, and sometimes, by successive attacks, kill them. Senhor Leonardo informed us that they particularly abounded in some parts of the island, and that he often has bat-hunts, when several thousands are killed. It is a large species, of coffee-brown colour, probably the *Phyllostoma hastatum*.

The morning after my arrival I took my gun, and walked out to see what sport the island afforded. First going to a tree near the house, which Senhor Leonardo pointed out to me, I found numerous humming-birds fluttering about the leaves (which were still wet with dew), and seeming to wash and cool themselves with the moisture: they were of a blue and green colour, with a long forked tail (*Campylopterus hirundinaceus*). Walking on in the campo, I found abundance of Bemteví fly-catchers, cuckoos, and tanagers, and also shot a buzzard and a black eagle different from any I had seen at Pará. Insects were very scarce, owing to the dryness of the season and the absence of forest; so I soon gave up collecting them, and attended entirely to birds, which were rather plentiful, though not very rare or handsome. In ten days I obtained seventy specimens, among which were fourteen hawks and eagles, several herons, egrets, paroquets, woodpeckers, and one of the large yellow-billed toucans (*Rhamphastos Toco*), which are not found at Pará.

Having made several excursions for some miles into the interior of the island and along the coast, I obtained a tolerable idea of its geography. It is everywhere a perfect flat, the greatest elevations being a very few feet. Along the shore in most places, and extending along the banks of the creeks inland, is a belt of forest, varying in width from a hundred yards to half a mile, containing a few palms and lofty trees, and abundance of bamboos and climbers, rendering it almost impassable. The whole of the interior is campo, or open plain, covered with a coarse herbage, and in places sprinkled with round-headed palms, and with low branching trees bearing a profusion of yellow flowers. Scattered about, at intervals of a few miles, are clumps of trees and bushes, some very small, but others sufficiently extensive to form little forests. These are generally known as "ilhas," or islands, and many of them have separate names, as, "Ilha do São Pedro," "Ilha dos Urubus." In the wet season a great part of the island appears to be flooded, and dead crabs and fresh-water shells are found a long way inland : these groves are then probably real islands, though not perceptibly above the general level.

A phenomenon, which is seen on the banks of the Mississippi and most other rivers which overflow their banks, also occurs here. The land is highest near the water's edge, and gradually falls inland, caused by the heavier sediment being deposited during floods at the shortest distance, while the lighter matter only is carried inland, and spread over a larger area. The surface of the campos is very uneven for walking, being in little clumps or hillocks, so that it is equally tiresome and fatiguing to walk on their summits or between them. The stems of the palms were all covered with orchideous plants, but they had now generally neither leaves nor flowers, and seemed to be of very little variety of species. In the marshy places shrubby convolvuli are abundant, and in others are large beds of cassias and mimosas, while scattered among them are many delicate little flowers.

Long-tailed, light-coloured cuckoos were continually flying about from tree to tree, uttering their peculiar note, not at all like that of our cuckoo, but more like the creaking of a rusty hinge, which the name given to them, *Careru,* is intended to resemble. Equally abundant are the black hornbill cuckoos, called Anús ; and on almost every tree may be seen sitting a hawk or buzzard, the variety of which is very great, as in a few weeks I obtained eight different kinds. Pretty paroquets, with white and orange bands on their wings, and others with an orange-coloured crown, were very plentiful, and it was amusing to watch the activity with which they climbed about over the trees, and how suddenly and simultaneously they flew away when alarmed. Their plumage is so near the colour of the foliage, that it is sometimes impossible to see them, though you may have watched a whole flock enter a tree, and can hear them twittering overhead, when, after gazing until your patience is exhausted they will suddenly fly off with a scream of triumph.

Then among the bushes there were flocks of the beautiful red-breasted oriole, *Icterus militaris ;* but they were unfortunately not in good plumage at the time of my visit. The common black vulture is generally to be seen sailing overhead, or seated on some dead tree ; and great Muscovy ducks fly past with a rushing sound, like some great aërial machine beating the air violently to support its ponderous body, and offering a striking contrast to the great wood-ibis, which sails along with noiseless wings in flocks of ten or a dozen. In the skirts of forest and in the larger " ilhas," black and spotted jaguars are often found, while pacas, cotias, tatus or armadillos, deer, and other small game are plentiful.

The whole population of the island consists of about forty persons, of whom twenty are slaves, and the remainder free Indians and Negroes in the employ of the proprietors. These are all engaged in attending to the cattle and horses on the island, which vary in number, and were much more numerous three or four years ago ; the horses in particular having been almost exterminated by a disease which suddenly appeared among them. There were now about fifteen hundred head of cattle, besides a great number of wild ones, which keep in the remote parts of the island, and four hundred horses. The slaves and labourers are allowed farinha only ; but they can cultivate Indian corn and vegetables for themselves, and have powder and shot given them for hunting, so that they do not fare so badly. They also have tobacco allowed them, and most of them earn money by making baskets or other trifles, or by killing onças, the skin being worth from five to ten shillings. Besides attending to the cattle and horses, they have to build houses and corrals, to hunt alligators for oil, and kill bats, which do great injury to the cattle by sucking their blood night after night. The bats live in holes in trees, where they are killed in considerable numbers, Senhor Leonardo informing me that they had destroyed about seven thousand during the last six months. Many hundreds of cattle are said to have been killed by them in a few years.

The slaves appeared contented and happy, as slaves generally do. Every evening at sunset they came to bid good-night to Senhor Leonardo and myself, a similar salutation taking place when they first met us in the morning. If a negro goes out for the day to any distance, he bids adieu to all he may meet, as if he were parting from his dearest friends on the eve of a long journey; contrasting strongly with the apathy of the Indian, who scarcely ever exhibits any feelings of regret on parting, or of pleasure on his return. In the evening they play and sing in their own houses: their instrument is a home-made guitar, from which they obtain three or four notes, which are repeated for hours with the most wearisome monotony. To this music they join an extempore song, generally relating to some events of the day; and the doings of the " brancos," or white people, have often a considerable share in it. Many of them keep fowls and ducks, which they sell, to buy any little luxuries they may require, and they often go fishing to supply the house, when they have a share for themselves.

Every Saturday evening they meet for Divine service, which is performed in a room fitted up as a chapel, with an altar gaily decorated with figures of the Virgin and Child, and several saints painted and gilt in a most brilliant manner. Some of these figures are the work of Senhor Leonardo, who is an excellent self-taught carver; and when the candles are lit, and all is in order, the effect is equal to that of many village churches. Two of the oldest Negroes conduct the service, kneeling at the altar; the rest kneel or stand about the room. What they chant is, I believe, part of the vesper service of the Roman Catholic Church, and all join in the responses with much fervour, though without understanding a word. Sunday is their own day, for working in their gardens, hunting, or idleness, as they choose; and in the evening they often assemble in the verandah to dance, and sometimes keep it up all night.

While I was on the island a child of a few weeks old was to be baptized. This they consider a most important ceremony; so the father and mother, with godfathers and godmothers, set out in a canoe for Chaves, on the island of Marajó, the nearest place where there is a priest. They were absent three days, and then returned with the news that the Padre was ill, and could not perform the ceremony; so they were obliged to bring back the poor little unsanctified creature, liable, according to their ideas, should it die, to eternal perdition. The same evening they sang for three hours to their usual music the whole history of their journey, judging from the portions which were here and there intelligible.

They made every fact into a verse, which was several times
repeated. Thus one would suddenly burst out,—

> " The Padre was ill, and could not come,
> The Padre was ill, and could not come."

#### CHORUS.

> " The Padre was ill, and could not come."

Then for a time the music continued without the voices, while
they were trying to find another fact to found a verse upon.
At length some one continued the subject :—

> " He told us to come the next day,
> To see if he was better."

#### CHORUS.

> " He told us to come the next day,
> To see if he was better."

And so on to the end of the history, which struck me as being
probably very similar to the unwritten lays of the ancient bards,
who could thus make well-known facts interesting by being
sung to music in an appropriate and enthusiastic manner. In
a warlike nation, what more would at first be necessary than to
relate the bold deeds of the warriors, the discomfiture of the
enemy, and the trophies of victory, in order to raise the enthu-
siasm of the audience to the highest pitch ? Some of these
would be handed down from generation to generation, the
language improved, and when they came to be reduced to
writing, rhyme would be added, and a regular poem constructed.

Having now arrived at the height of the dry season, and the
waters of the lake before mentioned being sufficiently low, the
German steward informed me that he should make an excursion
there to kill alligators, and I determined to accompany him.
There are two ways to reach the place—overland in nearly a
direct line, or round to the other side of the island in a boat
and up a stream, which can be ascended to within a few miles
of the lake, with which indeed in the wet season it communicates. The tide served for the boat to start about midnight,
and I decided on going in it, as I thought I should thus see
more of the island. The overseer was to go by land in the
morning. Being roused up at midnight, I got into the canoe
with three Negroes, and tried to compose myself for a nap as
well as I could upon the baskets of farinha and salt with which

it was loaded.  It was a large clumsy canoe, and with a sail and the tide we went on pretty well; but as morning dawned we got out rather far from land into the ocean-like river, and the swell beginning to be disagreeable, I arose from my uneven couch very qualmish and uncomfortable.

However, about ten o'clock we reached the mouth of the igaripé, or small stream we were to ascend, and I was very glad to get into still water.  We stayed for breakfast in a little clear space under a fine tree, and I enjoyed a cup of coffee and a little biscuit, while the men luxuriated on fish and farinha. We then proceeded up the stream, which was at its commence- ment about two hundred yards wide, but soon narrowed to fifty or eighty.  I was much delighted with the beauty of the vege- tation, which surpassed anything I had seen before : at every bend of the stream some new object presented itself,—now a huge cedar hanging over the water, or a great silk-cotton-tree standing like a giant above the rest of the forest.  The graceful assaí palms occurred continually, in clumps of various sizes, sometimes raising their stems a hundred feet into the air, or bending in graceful curves till they almost met from the opposite banks.  The majestic murutí palm was also abundant, its straight and cylindrical stems like Grecian columns, and with its immense fan-shaped leaves and gigantic bunches of fruit, produced an imposing spectacle.  Some of these bunches were larger than any I had before seen, being eight or ten feet in length, weighing probably two or three hundredweight : each consisted of several bushels of a large reticulated fruit.  These palms were often clothed with creepers, which ran up to the summits, and there put forth their blossoms.  Lower down, on the water's edge, were numerous flowering shrubs, often com- pletely covered with convolvuluses, passion-flowers, or bignonias. Every dead or half-rotten tree was clothed with parasites of singular forms or bearing beautiful flowers, while smaller palms, curiously-shaped stems, and twisting climbers, formed a back- ground in the interior of the forest.

Nor were there wanting animated figures to complete the picture.  Brilliant scarlet and yellow macaws flew continually overhead, while screaming parrots and paroquets were passing from tree to tree in search of food.  Sometimes from a branch over the water were suspended the hanging nests of the black and yellow troupial (*Cassicus icteronotus*), into which those

handsome birds were continually entering. The effect of the
scene was much heightened by the river often curving to one
side or the other, so as to bring to view a constant variety of
objects. At every bend we would see before us a flock of the
elegant white heron, seated on some dead tree overhanging the
water ; but as soon as we came in sight of them, they would
take flight, and on passing another bend we would find them
again perched in front of us, and so on for a considerable distance. On many of the flowering shrubs gay butterflies were
settled, and sometimes on a muddy bank a young alligator
would be seen comfortably reposing in the sun.

We continued our journey thus for several hours, the men
rowing vigorously for fear of the tide turning against us before
we reached our destination : this, however, happened just as
we entered a narrower part of the stream. The scenery was
now much more gloomy ; the tall trees closed overhead so as
to keep out every sunbeam. The palms twisted and bent in
various contortions, so that we sometimes could hardly pass
beneath, and sunken logs often lay across from bank to bank,
compelling us to get out of the canoe, and use all our exertions
to force it over. Our progress was therefore very slow, and
the stream was every minute running stronger against us.
Here was a building-place for various aquatic birds : the wood-
ibis and numerous cranes and herons had their nests on the
summits of the lofty trees over the water, while lower down
was the station chosen by the boat-bill. There was a continual
rustle and flapping of wings as these long-legged, clumsy birds
flew about, startled at our approach ; and when I shot one
of the large wood-ibises, the confusion was at its height.
Numerous kingfishers were continually passing up and down, or
darting from some dead stick into the water to seize their prey.

After about two hours of very hard and disagreeable work,
we reached the landing-place, where there was an old deserted
cottage, and the overseer and several Negroes with horses were
waiting to convey the provisions we had brought to the Lake.
We immediately set off on foot over an extensive plain, which
was in places completely bare, and in others thinly clothed
with low trees. There could not be a greater contrast than
between the scene we had just left, and that which we now
entered upon. The one was all luxuriance and verdure, the
other as brown and barren as could be,—a dreary waste of

marsh, now parched up by the burning sun, and covered with tufts of a wiry grass, with here and there rushes and prickly sensitive plants, and a few pretty little flowers occasionally growing up among them. The trees, which in some places were abundant, did not much diminish the general dreariness of the prospect, for many of the leaves had fallen off owing to the continued drought, and those that were left were brown and half-shrivelled. The ground was very disagreeable for walking, being composed of numerous little clumps and ridges, placed so closely together that you could neither step securely upon nor between them : they appeared to be caused by the rains and floods in the wet season washing away the earth from between the roots of the grass-tufts, the whole being afterwards hardened by the excessive heat of the sun, and the grass almost entirely burnt away.

After walking over four or five miles of such ground, we arrived at the Lake just as it was getting dark. The only building there was a small shed without any walls, under which we hung our hammocks, while the Negroes used the neighbouring trees and bushes for the same purpose. A large fire was blazing, and round it were numerous wooden spits, containing pieces of fresh fish and alligator's tail for our supper. While it was getting ready, we went to look at some fish which had just been caught, and lay ready for salting and drying the next day : they were the pirarucú (*Sudis gigas*), a splendid species, five or six feet long, with large scales of more than an inch in diameter, and beautifully marked and spotted with red. The Lake contains great quantities of them, and they are salted and dried for the Pará market. It is a very fine-flavoured fish, the belly in particular being so fat and rich that it cannot be cured, and is therefore generally eaten fresh. This, with farinha and some coffee, made us an excellent supper, and the alligator's tail, which I now tasted for the first time, was by no means to be despised. We soon turned into our hammocks, and slept soundly after the fatigue of the day. Jaguars were abundant, and had carried off some fish a night or two before; the alligators too were plunging and snorting within twenty yards of us : but we did not suffer such trifles to disturb our slumbers.

Before daybreak I had my gun upon my shoulder, eager to make an attack upon the ducks and other aquatic birds which swarmed about the lake.  I soon found plenty of them, and, my gun being loaded with small shot, I killed seven or eight at the first fire.  They were very pretty little birds, with metallic-green and white wings, and besides forming good specimens, provided us with an excellent breakfast.  After the first discharge, however, they became remarkably shy, so I went after the roseate spoonbills, white herons, and long-legged plovers, which I saw on the other side : they also seemed to have taken warning by the fate of their companions, for I could not get near enough for a shot, as there was no means of concealing my approach.

What is called the Lake is a long, winding piece of water, from thirty to fifty yards wide and of little depth.  It is bordered with aquatic plants and shrubs, and in some parts is thickly covered with floating grass and duckweed.  It is inhabited by immense numbers of the fish already mentioned, and alligators, which are so thick that there is scarcely any place where you may not stir one up.  There are also great quantities of very small fish about two inches long, which I suppose serve as food for the larger ones, which in their turn are probably sometimes devoured by the alligators ; though it appears almost a mystery how so many large animals can find a subsistence, crowded together in such a small space.

After breakfast the overseer commenced the alligator-hunt. A number of Negroes went into the water with long poles, driving the animals to the side, where others awaited them with harpoons and lassos.

Sometimes the lasso was at once thrown over their heads, or, if first harpooned, a lasso was then secured to them, either over the head or the tail ; and they were easily dragged to the shore by the united force of ten or twelve men.  Another lasso was fixed, if necessary, so as to fasten them at both ends, and on being pulled out of the water a Negro cautiously approached with an axe, and cut a deep gash across the root of the tail, rendering that formidable weapon useless ; another blow across the neck disabled the head, and the animal was then left, and pursuit of another commenced, which was speedily reduced to the same condition.  Sometimes the cord would break, or the harpoon get loose, and the Negroes had often to wade into the water among the ferocious animals in a very hazardous manner.  They were from ten to eighteen feet long, sometimes even twenty, with enormous mis-shapen heads, and fearful rows of long sharp teeth.  When a number were out on the land, dead or dying, they were cut open, and the fat which accumulates in considerable quantities about the intestines was taken out, and made up into packets in the skins of the smaller ones, taken off for the purpose.  There is another smaller kind, here called Jacaré-tinga, which is the one eaten, the flesh being more delicate than in the larger species.  After killing twelve or fifteen, the overseer and his party went off to another lake at a short distance, where the alligators were more plentiful, and by night had killed near fifty.  The next day they killed twenty or thirty more, and got out the fat from the others.

I amused myself very well with my gun, creeping among the long grass, to get a shot at the shy aquatic birds, and sometimes wandering about the campo, where a woodpecker or a macaw rewarded my perseverance.  I was much pleased when I first brought down a splendid blue and yellow macaw, but it gave me some hours of hard work to skin and prepare it, for the head is so fleshy and muscular, that it is no trifling matter to clean it thoroughly.  The great tuyuyú (*Mycteria Americana*) was often seen stalking about; but, with every precaution, I could not get within gunshot of it.  The large and small white herons were abundant, as well as black and grey ibises, boat-bills, blue storks, and ducks of several species; there were also many black and yellow orioles, and a glossy starling,—of all of which I procured specimens.

I had an opportunity of seeing the manner of curing fish practised here.  They are partially skinned, and a large piece of meat cut out from each side, leaving the backbone with the head and skin attached.  Each piece of meat is then cut lengthways, so as to unfold into a large flat slab, which is then slightly sprinkled with salt and laid upon a board.  Other slices are laid on this, and, when the salt has penetrated sufficiently, they are hung upon poles or laid upon the ground in the sun to dry, which does not occupy more than two or three days.  They are then packed up in bundles of about a hundred pounds each, and are ready for market.  The bones and heads furnish a fine feast for the vultures, and sometimes a jaguar will carry them away in the night, but he prefers an entire fish if one is left in his way.

Immediately on the fish being cut up, every part of it is blackened by thousand of flies, which keep up a continual hum the whole day.   In fact, the sound of animal life never ceases. Directly after sunset, the herons, bitterns, and cranes begin their discordant cries, and the boat-bills and frogs set up a dismal croaking.   The note of one frog deserves a better name : it is an agreeable whistle, and, could it be brought into civilised society, would doubtless have as many admirers as the singing mouse, or the still more marvellous whistling oyster described by *Punch*.   All night long, the alligators and fish keep up a continual plunging ; but, with the grey of morning, commence the most extraordinary noises.   All of a sudden ten thousand white-winged paroquets begin their morning song with such a confusion of piercing shrieks as it is quite impossible to describe : a hundred knife-grinders at full work would give but a faint idea of it.   A little later, and another noise is heard : the flies, which had weighed down every blade of grass, now wake up, and, with a sounding hum, commence their attack upon the fish : every piece that has lain a few hours upon the ground has deposited around it masses of their eggs as large as walnuts.   In fact, the abundance of every kind of animal life crowded into a small space was here very striking, compared with the sparing manner in which it is scattered in the virgin forests.   It seems to force us to the conclusion, that the luxuriance of tropical vegetation is not favourable to the production and support of animal life.   The plains are always more thickly peopled than the forest ; and a temperate zone, as has been pointed out by Mr. Darwin, seems better adapted to the support of large land-animals than the tropics.

In this lake the overseer informed me he had killed as many as a hundred alligators in a few days, whereas in the Amazon or Pará rivers it would be difficult to procure as many in a year.   Geologists, judging from the number of large reptiles, the remains of which are found in considerable quantities in certain strata, tell us of a time when the whole world was peopled by such animals, before a sufficient quantity of dry land had been formed to support land quadrupeds.   But, as it is evident that the remains of these alligators would be found accumulated together should any revolution of the earth cause their death, it would appear that such descriptions are founded upon insufficient data, and that considerable portions of the earth might have been as much elevated as they are at present, notwithstanding the numerous remains of aquatic reptiles, which would seem to indicate a great extent of shallow water for their abode.

The alligator fat and a quantity of fish were now ready, so we prepared to return home. I determined this time to walk overland, so as to see the character of the interior of the island. I returned with the two Negrðes to the ruined cottage before mentioned, so as to be ready to start the next morning for a walk of some ten or twelve miles across the campo. On our way to the hut we passed over a part which was burning, and saw the curious phenomenon of the fire proceeding in two opposite directions at once. The wind carried the fire rapidly in a westerly direction, while, at the same time, by causing the tall grass to bend over into the flames, they progressed, though at a slower rate, towards the east. The campos are set on fire purposely every summer, as the coarse grass being burnt down, leaves room for a fine crop to spring up afresh with the first rains. Near the hut I shot a large grey heron, which made us a very good supper ; and we then hung up our hammocks for the night in the little dirty ruined hut, from which a short time before a jaguar had carried away a large bundle of fish.

In the morning the canoe was loaded to return, and I proceeded along a faint track homewards. The scene was generally very desolate and barren. Sometimes there was not a blade of grass for miles. Then would come a wide bed of gigantic rushes, which extends across the island nearly from one side to the other. In other places were large beds of prickly mimosas, and, at intervals, considerable tracts covered with leafless trees about which numbers of woodpeckers were busily at work. Hawks and vultures were also seen, and the great red-billed toucan (*Rhamphastos Toco*) flew by in an undulating course in parties of three or four. It was cloudy, and there was a good deal of wind ; but at this time of the year no rain ever falls here, so I did not hurry myself on that account, and, early in the afternoon, reached the house, rather tired, but much interested with my walk. I forgot to mention that in the evening, after the alligator-hunt, the Negroes sang several hymns, as a thanksgiving for having escaped their jaws.

The next day all were busily employed boiling the fat into oil,

which supplies the lamps on all Mr. C.'s estates.  It has rather
a disagreeable smell, but not worse than train-oil.  I now went
out every day with my gun about the campo, or to the clumps
of wood called islands, on the banks of the small streams.
The principal birds I procured were toucans, parrots, hawks,
and buzzards, the red-headed manakin, and numerous small
finches and fly-catchers.  The mango-trees were loaded with
ripe fruit, and attracted many small tanagers and paroquets.
I now ate the mango for the first time, and soon got to like it
very much.  It is not generally eaten in Pará except by the
Negroes, who seem very fond of it, to judge by the certainty
with which every fruit disappeared the moment it became
ripe.  There seems to be scarcely an animal that is not fond
of it,—cattle, sheep, pigs, ducks, and fowls, all rush to secure
every fruit that falls.

Soon after Christmas we had a few showers at intervals, and
the grass began to grow more greenly—a sign that the summer
was nearly at an end.  Some butterflies and moths now made
their appearance, and the skirts of the forest were covered
with passion-flowers, convolvuluses, and many other flowers.
Bees and wasps also began to abound, and several aquatic birds
I had not before seen made their appearance.  In January,
Mr. C. and his family and some visitors arrived to spend a few
weeks on the island, and the time passed more pleasantly.
Several of the Negroes were sent hunting, and wild ducks of
various species, deer, armadillos, and fish, with beef and
mutton, gave us plenty for our table.  Several jaguars were
killed, as Mr. C. pays about eight shillings each for their skins :
one day we had some steaks at the table, and found the meat
very white, and without any bad taste.

It appears evident to me that the common idea of the
food of an animal determining the quality of its meat is quite
erroneous.  Domestic poultry and pigs are the most unclean
animals in their food, yet their flesh is very highly esteemed,
while rats and squirrels, which eat only vegetable food, are in
general disrepute.  Carnivorous fish are not less delicate eating
than herbivorous ones, and there appears no reason why some
carnivorous animals should not furnish wholesome and palatable
food.  Venison, so highly esteemed at home, is here the most
dry and tasteless meat that can be had, as it must be cooked
within twelve hours after it is killed.

A great deal more rain now fell, and small pools were formed in some parts of the campos. About these, plovers and other birds were to be seen wading, and a small flock of the elegant long-legged plover (*Himantopus*). After much difficulty I succeeded in killing three or four of them. The curious razor-bill was also often seen skimming over the water, and the great tuyuyú occasionally approached near the house, but always kept out of gunshot, and although I crawled along prostrate to get within reach of him, he always found me out in time for his own safety.

As I was getting scarcely any insects here, and the birds were not very valuable, I determined to return to Pará with Mr. C., who was going to pass a week at his other estate on the island of Marajó by the way.

The journey across in Mr. C.'s schooner occupied but a few hours, and we then entered a river which leads up to the estate called Jungcal. On arriving we found a mud-walled house not quite finished, which was to be our abode while we stayed. At the back of the house stretched out, as far as the eye could reach, a perfectly flat plain or campo, on which fed numerous herds of cattle. Round about were "corrals" fenced in for collecting the cattle, and huts for the "vaqueiros," or cowherds ; and along the banks of the river were patches of wood, and thickets of a great prickly bamboo. About the campo were numerous marshes and narrow streams or ditches, which contained many curious and pretty aquatic plants. Mosquitoes were plentiful, and annoyed us much in the evenings, when we wished to enjoy the cool air in the verandah.

The Negroes and Mulattoes employed about the estate were mostly fine young men, and led a life of alternate idleness and excitement, which they seemed to enjoy very much. All their work is done on horseback, where they showed to great advantage, only wearing a pair of trousers and a cap with a tassel, displaying the fine symmetry of their bodies. We were much amused by seeing them bring in the cattle, driving them into the corral, or using the lasso when one was to be slaughtered. For this purpose they generally get two lassos on the head or legs of the animal, the end of each of which is held by a horseman. The "matador" then goes up and hamstrings the poor animal with a cutlass. This quite disables

him : in vain he tries to rise on his legs and run at his
merciless assailants, till the cutlass is thrust into his neck and
deep down into his chest.    He is hardly dead when he is
skinned and cut up, and the dogs and vultures rush to feast
upon the pool of blood and entrails which mark the spot.
The sight was a sickening one, and I did not care to witness
it more than once.

There were few birds or insects worth catching, and it was
not the time of the year for the spoonbills and ibises, which
have a building-place near, and arrive in immense numbers in
the month of June.

After spending about a week at Jungcal we embarked to
return to Pará.    A cattle-canoe was to accompany us, and we
were to take some of the animals on board our schooner.    We
started early in the morning, and in about an hour arrived at a
corral on the river-side, where the cattle were.    The boat was
anchored about twenty yards from the shore, and a block and
fall rigged to haul them up on deck.    In the corral were
twenty or thirty wild cattle, which had been kicking and plunging
about till they had filled the place with mud knee-deep.
Several men with lassos were trying to secure them, by
throwing the loops over their horns.    The cattle used all their
endeavours to avoid being caught, by shaking their heads and
throwing the cords off before they could be pulled tight.    Each
man kept his attention directed to one animal, following it
about to every part of the corral.    After a few attempts he
generally succeeded in getting the loop fixed over the horns,
and then half a dozen came to his assistance, to get the ox out
of the corral into the water.    This was done by some pulling
at the lassos, while others poked and beat the animal with long
poles, which would so irritate it that it would roll itself
on the ground and rush at the men with all its force.    At this
they did not seem to be much alarmed, but jumped on one
side or sprang on to the rails of the corral, and then immediately returned to the attack.    At length the creature would
be either pulled or driven into the water, and the end of the
rope being quickly thrown on board the canoe, the ox was
towed up to the vessel's side.    A strong rope was then noosed
over its horns, by which it was lifted into the air, struggling as
helplessly as a kitten held by the skin of its neck ; it was then
lowered into the hold, where, after a little disturbance, it soon

became quiet. One after another were put on board in this manner, each offering something interesting, arising from the fury of the animal or the great skill and coolness of the vaqueiros. Once or twice the lasso, which is made of twisted hide, was thrown short of the canoe, and I then admired the rapidity with which an Indian plunged head foremost after it, not stopping even to take the cap from his head; he then gave the rope to those on board, and mounting on the back of the swimming ox, rode in triumph to the canoe.

We did not get them all on board without an accident. The principal herdsman, a strong and active Mulatto, was in the corral, driving the cattle to one end of it, when a furious ox rushed at him, and with the rapidity of lightning he was stretched, apparently dead, upon the ground. The other men immediately carried him out, and Mr. and Mrs. C. went on shore to attend to him. In about half an hour he revived a little. He appeared to have been struck in the chest by the animal's head, the horns not having injured him. In a very short time he was in the corral again, as if nothing had happened, and when all were embarked he came on board and made a hearty dinner, his appetite not having suffered by the accident.

We then proceeded on our voyage, and as soon as we got into the Amazon I again experienced the uncomfortable sensation of sea-sickness, though in fresh-water. The next night we had a very strong wind, which split our mainsail all to pieces. The following day we landed at a little island called Ilha das Frechas (the Isle of Arrows), on account of the quantity of a peculiar kind of reed, used by the Indians for making their arrows, which grows there. We stayed nearly the whole day, dining under the shade of the trees, and roaming about, picking a wild fruit, like a small plum, which grew there in abundance; there were also many curious fruits and handsome flowers which attracted our attention. Some years ago the island is said to have swarmed with wild hogs, but they are now nearly exterminated. The next day we passed the eastern point of the island of Marajó, where there is a sudden change from the waters of the Amazon to those of the Pará river, the former being yellow and fresh, the latter green and salt: they mix but little at the junction, so that we passed in a moment from one kind of water to the other. In two days more we reached Pará.

# CHAPTER V.

## THE GUAMÁ AND CAPIM RIVERS.

Natterer's Hunter, Luiz—Birds and Insects—Prepare for a Journey—
First Sight of the Piroróco—St. Domingo—Senhor Calistro—Slaves
and Slavery—Anecdote—Cane-field—Journey into the Forest—
Game—Explanation of the Piroróco—Return to Pará—Bell-birds
and Yellow Parrots.

I HAD written to Mr. Miller to get me a small house at Nazaré,
and I now at once moved into it, and set regularly to work in
the forest, as much as the showery and changeable weather
would allow me. An old Portuguese, who kept a kind of
tavern next door, supplied my meals, and I was thus enabled
to do without a servant. The boys in the neighbourhood soon
got to know of my arrival, and that I was a purchaser of all
kinds of "bichos." Snakes were now rather abundant, and
almost every day I had some brought me, which I preserved
in spirits.

As insects were not very plentiful at this season, I wished to
get a hunter to shoot birds for me, and came to an arrangement with a Negro named Luiz, who had had much experience.
He had been with Dr. Natterer during the whole of his
seventeen years' residence in Brazil, having been purchased by
him in Rio de Janeiro when a boy ; and when the doctor left
Pará, in 1835, he gave him his freedom. His whole occupation
while with Dr. Natterer was shooting and assisting to skin birds
and animals. He had now a little land, and had saved enough
to purchase a couple of slaves himself,—a degree of providence
that the less careful Indian seldom attains to. He is a native
of Congo, and a very tall and handsome man. I agreed to
give him a milrei (2s. 3d.) a day and his living. He used to
amuse me much by his accounts of his travels with the doctor,
as he always called Natterer. He said he treated him very

well, and gave him a small present whenever he brought a new bird.

Luiz was an excellent hunter. He would wander in the woods from morning to night, going a great distance, and generally bringing home some handsome bird. He soon got me several fine cardinal chatterers, red-breasted trogons, toucans, etc. He knew the haunts and habits of almost every bird, and could imitate their several notes so as to call them to him.

In this showery weather the pretty little esmeralda butterfly (*Hætera Esmeralda*) seemed to delight, for almost every wet day I got one or two specimens in a certain narrow gloomy path in the forest, though I never found but one in any other place. Once or twice I walked over to tne rice-mills, to see my friend Mr. Leavens, and get some of the curious insects which were seldom met with near the city. Several young men in Pará were now making collections, and it is a proof of the immense abundance and luxuriance of insect life in this country, that in every collection, however small, I almost always saw something new to me.

Having heard much of the " Piroróco," or bore, that occurs in the Guamá River at spring-tides, I determined to take a little trip in order to see it, and make some variation from my rather monotonous life at Pará. I wished to go in a canoe of my own, so as to be able to stop where and when I liked, and I also thought it would be useful afterwards in ascending the Amazon. I therefore agreed to purchase one that I thought would suit me, of a Frenchman in Pará, and having paid part of the purchase-money, got it fitted up and laid in a stock of requisites for the voyage. I took a barrel and a quantity of spirits for preserving fish, and everything necessary for collecting and preparing birds and insects. As the canoe was small, I did not want many men, for whom there would not indeed have been room, so determined to manage with only a pilot, and one man or boy besides Luiz.

I soon found a boy who lived near, and had been accustomed to bring me insects. To all appearance he was an Indian, but his mother had Negro blood in her, and was a slave, so her son of course shared her fate. I had, therefore, to hire him of his master, an officer, and agreed for three milreis (about seven shillings) a month. People said that the boy's master was his father, which, as he certainly resembled him, might have been the case. He generally had a large chain round his body and leg as a punishment, and to prevent his running away ; he wore it concealed under his trousers, and it clanked very disagreeably at every step he took. Of course this was taken off when he was delivered over to me, and he promised to be very faithful and industrious if I took him with me. I also agreed with a lame Spaniard to go as pilot, because he said he knew the river, and some little experience is required at the time of the Piroróco. He begged for a few milreis beforehand to purchase some clothes ; and when I wanted him to assist me in loading the canoe he was feasting on biscuit and cheese, with oil, vinegar, and garlic, washing it down so plentifully with caxaça that he was quite intoxicated, so I was obliged to wait till the next day, when, having spent all his money and got a little sober, he was very quiet and submissive.

At length, all being ready, we started, rowing along quietly with the flood-tide, as there was no wind, and at night, when the tide turned, anchoring a few miles up the Guamá. This is a fine stream, about half a mile wide in the lower part. A short distance up, the banks are rather undulating, with many pretty sitios. During ebb-tide we managed generally to anchor near some house or cottage, where we could get on shore and make a fire under a tree to cook our dinner or supper. Luiz would then take his gun and I my insect-net, and start off into the forest to make the most of our time till the tide turned again, when we would continue our voyage, and I generally had occupation skinning birds or setting out insects till the evening. About thirty miles above Pará the Piroróco commences. There was formerly an island in the river at this point, but it is said to have been completely washed away by the continual action of the bore, which, after passing this place, we rather expected to see, now being the time of the highest tides, though at this season (May) they are not generally high enough to produce it with any great force. It came, however, with a sudden rush, a wave travelling rapidly up the stream, and breaking in foam all along the shore and on the shallows. It lifted our canoe just as a great rolling ocean-wave would do, but, being deep water, did no harm, and was past in an instant, the tide then continuing to flow up with very great velocity. The highest tide was now past, so at the next we had no wave, but the flood began running up, instantaneously, and not gradually, as is generally the case.

The next day we arrived at São Domingo, a little village at the junction of the Guamá and Capim rivers. I had a letter of introduction to a Brazilian trader residing here, on presenting which he placed his house at my disposal. I took him at his word, and said I should stay a few days. Luiz went into the woods every day, generally bringing home some birds, and I wandered about in search of insects, which I did not find very abundant, the dry season having scarcely begun; there were, however, plenty of pleasant paths about the woods to the rice and mandiocca-fields, and abundance of oranges and other fruit. Our food was principally fish from the river and some jerked beef, with beans and rice. The house was little better than a mud hovel, with a bench, a rickety table, and a few hammocks for furniture; but in this country the people away from the towns never think of expending any great labour or going to any expense to make a comfortable house.

After staying nearly a week, with not much success in my collections, I proceeded up the west branch of the river, called the Capim. My canoe was a very unsteady and top-heavy one, and soon after leaving the village a sudden squall nearly upset us, the water pouring in over the side, and it was with some difficulty we got the sail down and secured the boat to a bush on the river's bank till the storm had passed over. We went pleasantly along for two or three days, the country being prettily diversified with cane-fields, rice-grounds, and houses built by the early Portuguese settlers, with elegant little chapels attached, and cottages for the Negroes and Indians around, all much superior in appearance and taste to anything erected now. At length we reached São Jozé, the estate of Senhor Calistro, to whom I brought letters of introduction. He received me very kindly, and on my telling him the purpose of my visit he invited me to stay with him as long as I liked, and promised to do all he could to assist me. He was a stout, good-humoured looking man, of not much more than thirty. He had recently built a rice-mill and warehouses, one of the best modern buildings I had seen in the country. It was entirely of stone; the mill was approached by arches in the centre, and the warehouses, offices, and dwelling apartments were at the sides. There was a gallery or verandah on the first floor connecting the two ends of the building, and looking down upon the mill, with its great water-wheel in the centre, and out through the windows on to the river, and a handsome stone quay which ran along the whole front of the building. It was all substantially constructed, and had cost him several thousand pounds.

He had about fifty slaves of all ages, and about as many Indians, employed in his cane- and rice-fields, and in the mills, and on board his canoes. He made sugar and caxaça, but most of the latter as it paid best. Every kind of work was done on the premises : he had shoemakers, tailors, carpenters, smiths, boat-builders, and masons, either slaves or Indians, some of whom could make good locks for doors and boxes, and tin and copper articles of all kinds. He told me that by having slaves and Indians working together he was enabled to get more work out of the latter than by any other system. Indians will not submit to strict rules when working by themselves, but when with slaves, who have regular hours to commence and leave off work, and stated tasks to perform, they submit to the same regulations and cheerfully do the same work. Every evening at sunset all the workpeople come up to Senhor Calistro to say good-night or ask his blessing. He was seated in an easy chair in the verandah, and each passed by with a salutation suited to his age or station. The Indians would generally be content with " Boa noite " (good-night) ; the younger ones, and most of the women and children, both Indians and slaves, would hold out their hand, saying, " Sua benção " (your blessing), to which he would reply, " Deos te bençoe " (God bless you), making at the same time the sign of the Cross. Others—and these were mostly the old Negroes —would gravely repeat, " Louvado seja o nome do Senhor Jesu Christo " (blessed be the name of the Lord Jesus Christ), to which he would reply, with equal gravity, " Para sempre " (for ever).

Children of all classes never meet their parents in the morning or leave them at night without in the same manner asking their blessing, and they do the same invariably of every stranger who enters the house. In fact, it is the common salutation of children and inferiors, and has a very pleasing effect.

The slaves here were treated remarkably well. Senhor

Calistro assured me he buys slaves, but never sells any, except as the last punishment for incorrigibly bad conduct.  They have holidays on all the principal saints' days and festivals, which are pretty often, and on these occasions an ox is killed for them, and a quantity of rum given, to make themselves merry.  Every evening, as they come round, they prefer their several petitions : one wants a little coffee and sugar for his wife, who is unwell ; another requires a new pair of trousers or a shirt; a third is going with a canoe to Pará, and asks for a milrei to buy something.  These requests are invariably granted, and Senhor Calistro told me that he never had cause for refusal, because the slaves never begged for anything unreasonable, nor asked favours when from bad conduct they did not deserve them.  In fact, all seemed to regard him in quite a patriarchal view, at the same time he was not to be trifled with, and was pretty severe against absolute idleness. When picking rice, all had a regular quantity to bring in, and any who were considerably deficient several times, from idleness alone, were punished with a moderate flogging.  He told me of one Negro he had bought, who was incorrigibly lazy, though quite strong and healthy.  The first day he was set a moderate task, and did not near complete it, and received a moderate flogging.  The next day he was set a much larger task, with the promise of a severe flogging if he did not get through it : he failed, saying it was quite beyond his ability, and received the flogging.  The third day he was set a still larger amount of work, with the promise of a much severer flogging if he failed to finish it ; and so, finding that the two former promises had been strictly kept, and that he was likely to gain nothing by carrying out his plan any longer, he completed the work with ease, and had ever since done the same quantity, which was after all only what every good workman did on the estate. Every Sunday morning and evening, though they do not work, they are required to appear before their master, unless they have special leave to be absent : this, Senhor Calistro told me, was to prevent their going to a great distance to other plantations to steal, as, if they could go off after work on Saturday evening, and not return till Monday morning, they might go to such a distance to commit robbery as to be quite free from suspicion.

In fact, Senhor Calistro attends to his slaves just as he

would to a large family of children. He gives them amusement, relaxation, and punishment in the same way, and takes
the same precautions to keep them out of mischief. The
consequence is, they are perhaps as happy as children : they
have no care and no wants, they are provided for in sickness
and old age, their children are never separated from them, nor
are husbands separated from their wives, except under such
circumstances as would render them liable to the same separation, were they free, by the laws of the country. Here, then,
slavery is perhaps seen under its most favourable aspect, and, in
a mere physical point of view, the slave may be said to be better
off than many a freeman. This, however, is merely one particular case,—it is by no means a necessary consequence of
slavery, and from what we know of human nature, can be but
a rare occurrence.

But looking at it in this, its most favourable light, can we
say that slavery is good or justifiable? Can it be right to
keep a number of our fellow-creatures in a state of adult
infancy,—of unthinking childhood? It is the responsibility
and self-dependence of manhood that calls forth the highest
powers and energies of our race. It is the struggle for existence,
the "battle of life," which exercises the moral faculties and
calls forth the latent sparks of genius. The hope of gain, the
love of power, the desire of fame and approbation, excite to
noble deeds, and call into action all those faculties which are
the distinctive attributes of man.

Childhood is the animal part of man's existence, manhood
the intellectual; and when the weakness and imbecility of
childhood remain, without its simplicity and pureness, its grace
and beauty, how degrading is the spectacle ! And this is the
state of the slave when slavery is the best that it can be. He
has no care of providing food for his family, no provision to
make for old age. He has nothing to incite him to labour but
the fear of punishment, no hope of bettering his condition, no
future to look forward to of a brighter aspect. Everything
he receives is a favour ; he has no rights,—what can he know
therefore of duties? Every desire beyond the narrow circle
of his daily labours is shut out from his acquisition. He has
no intellectual pleasures, and, could he have education and
taste them, they would assuredly embitter his life; for what
hope of increased knowledge, what chance of any further

acquaintance with the wonders of nature or the triumphs of art, than the mere hearing of them, can exist for one who is the property of another, and can never hope for the liberty of working for his own living in the manner that may be most agreeable to him ?

But such views as these are of course too refined for a Brazilian slaveholder, who can see nothing beyond the physical wants of the slave. And as the teetotalers have declared that the example of the moderate drinker is more pernicious than that of the drunkard, so may the philanthropist consider that a good and kind slave-master does an injury to the cause of freedom, by rendering people generally unable to perceive the false principles inherent in the system, and which, whenever they find a suitable soil in the bad passions of man, are ready to spring up and produce effects so vile and degrading as to make honest men blush for disgraced human nature.

Senhor C. was as kind and good-tempered a man as I have ever met with. I had but to mention anything I should like, and, if it was in his power, it was immediately got for me. He altered his dinner-hour to suit my excursions in the forest, and made every arrangement he could for my accommodation. A Jewish gentleman called when I was there : he was going up the river to collect some debts, and brought a letter for Senhor C. He stayed with us some days, and, as he would not eat any meat, because it had not been killed according to the rules of his religion, nor any fish that had not scales, which include some of the best these rivers produce, he hardly found anything at table the first day that he could partake of. Every day afterwards, however, while he was with us, there was a variety of scaled fish provided, boiled and roasted, stewed and fried, with eggs, rice, and vegetables in abundance, so that he could always make an excellent meal. Senhor C. was much amused at his scruples, though perfectly polite about them, and delighted to ask him about the rites of his religion, and me about mine, and would then tell us the Catholic doctrine on the same questions. He related to us many anecdotes, of which the following is a specimen, serving to illustrate the credulity of the Negroes. "There was a Negro," said he, "who had a pretty wife, to whom another Negro was rather attentive when he had the chance. One day the husband went out to hunt, and the other party thought it a good opportunity to pay a visit to the lady. The husband, however, returned rather unexpectedly, and the visitor climbed up on the rafters to be out of sight among the old boards and baskets that were stowed away there. The husband put his gun by in a corner, and called to his wife to get his supper, and then sat down in his hammock. Casting his eyes up to the rafters, he saw a leg protruding from among the baskets, and, thinking it something supernatural, crossed himself, and said, 'Lord, deliver us from the legs appearing overhead!' The other, hearing this, attempted to draw up his legs out of sight, but, losing his balance, came down suddenly on the floor in front of the astonished husband, who, half frightened, asked, 'Where do you come from?' 'I have just come from heaven,' said the other, 'and have brought you news of your little daughter Maria.' 'Oh! wife, wife! come and see a man who has brought us news of our little daughter Maria;' then, turning to the visitor, continued, 'And what was my little daughter doing when you left?' 'Oh! she was sitting at the feet of the Virgin, with a golden crown on her head, and smoking a golden pipe a yard long.' 'And did she not send any message to us?' 'Oh yes, she sent many remembrances, and begged you to send her two pounds of your tobacco from the little rhossa, they have not got any half so good up there.' 'Oh! wife, wife! bring two pounds of our tobacco from the little rhossa, for our daughter Maria is in heaven, and she says they have not any half so good up there.' So the tobacco was brought, and the visitor was departing, when he was asked, 'Are there many white men up there?' 'Very few,' he replied; 'they are all down below with the *diabo.*' 'I thought so,' the other replied, apparently quite satisfied; 'good-night!'"

Senhor Calistro had a beautiful canoe made of a single piece of wood, without a nail, the benches being all notched in. He often went in it to Pará, near two hundred miles, and, with twelve good Indians to paddle, and plenty of caxaça, reached the city, without stopping, in twenty-four hours. We sometimes went out to inspect the cane-fields in this canoe, with eight little Negro and Indian boys to paddle, who were always ready for such service. I then took my gun and net, and shot some birds or caught any insects that we met with, while Senhor Calistro would send the boys to climb after any handsome flowers I admired, or to gather the fruit of the passion-flowers, which hung like golden apples in the thickets on the banks. His cane-field this year was a mile and a half long and a quarter of a mile wide, and very luxuriant; across it were eight roads, all planted on each side with bananas and pine-apples. He informed me that when the fruit was in full season all the slaves and Indians had as much as they liked to take, and could never finish them all; but, said he, "It is not much trouble planting them when setting the cane-field, and I always do it, for I like to have plenty." It was altogether a noble sight,—a sample of the over-flowing abundance produced by a fertile soil and a tropical sun. Having mentioned that I much wished to get a collection of fish to preserve in spirits, he set several Indians to work stopping up igaripés to poison the water, and others to fish at night with line and bow and arrow; all that they procured being brought to me to select from, and the rest sent to the kitchen. The best way of catching a variety was, however, with a large drag-net fifty or sixty yards long. We went out one day in two canoes, and with about twenty Negroes and Indians, who swam with the net in the water, making a circuit, and then drew it out on to a beach. We had not very good fortune, but soon filled two half-bushel baskets with a great variety of fish, large and small, from which I selected a number of species to increase my collection.

Senhor Calistro was now going to send several Indian hunters up a small stream into the deep forest to hunt for him, and salt and dry game, and bring home live tortoises, of which there are great numbers in the forest. I particularly wanted a large and handsome species of *Tinamus*, or Brazilian partridge, which is found in these forests, but which I have not yet met with since I saw one being plucked for supper on the Tocantíns; I was also anxious to procure the hyacinthine macaw: so he kindly offered to let me go with them, and to lend me a small canoe and another Indian, to return when I liked, as they were going to stay two or three months. All the Indians took was farinha and salt, with powder and shot; but my kind host loaded my canoe with fowls, roast meat, eggs, plantains, pine-apples, and cocoa-nuts, so that I went well provided. It was about half-a-day's journey further up the river, to the mouth of the narrow stream or igaripé we were to enter; after going up which a short distance we stayed at the cottage of some acquaint-ances of our men for the night. The next morning early we proceeded on our journey, and soon passed the last house, and entered upon the wild, unbroken and uninhabited virgin forest. The stream was very narrow and very winding, running with great rapidity round the bends, and often much obstructed by bushes and fallen trees. The branches almost met overhead, and it was as dark and gloomy and silent as can be imagined. In these sombre shades a flower was scarcely ever to be found. A few of the large blue butterflies (*Morphos*) were occasionally seen flitting over the water or seated upon a leaf on the banks, and numerous green-backed kingfishers darted along before us. Early in the afternoon we found a little cleared place where hunters were accustomed to stay, and here we hung up our hammocks, lit our fire, and prepared to pass the night. After an excellent supper and some coffee, I lay down in my hammock, gazing up through the leafy canopy overhead, to the skies spangled with brightly shining stars, from which the fire-flies, flitting among the foliage, could often hardly be distinguished. They were a species of *Pyrophorus*, larger than any I had seen in Pará. They seemed attracted by the fire, to which they came in numbers; by moving one over the lines of a newspaper I was enabled easily to read it. The Indians amused themselves by recounting their hunting adventures, their escapes from jaguars and serpents, or of their being lost in the forest. One told how he had been lost for ten days, and all that time had eaten nothing, for he had no farinha, and though he could have killed game he would not eat it alone, and seemed quite surprised that I should think him capable of such an action, though I should certainly have imagined a week's fast would have overcome any scruples of that sort.

The next day the Indians went hunting, proposing to return early in the afternoon to proceed on, and I searched the woods after insects ; but in these gloomy forests, and without any paths along which I could walk with confidence, I met with little success. In the afternoon some of them returned with two trumpeters (*Psophia viridis*) and a monkey, which I skinned; but as one Indian did not arrive till late, we could not continue our voyage till the next day. This night we were not so fortunate as the last, for just about dusk it began to rain, and our canoes were so small and so loaded with articles that must be kept dry, that we had little chance of making ourselves comfortable in them. I managed to crowd in somehow, terribly cramped, hoping the shower would soon pass over; but as it did not, and we had turned in without our suppers, I began to feel very hungry. It was pitch-dark, but I groped my way out, fumbled about for some wood, and with an Indian's assistance made up the fire, by which I sat with some palm-leaves over my head, and made a hearty meal of Jacu (a species of *Penelope*), which had been stewed in the afternoon. When I had finished, I was pretty well soaked; but to find or put on dry clothes was out of the question, so I again rolled myself up uncomfortably into a ball, and slept pretty well till daybreak, when it had just ceased raining, and a cup of hot coffee set me all right. We then resumed our journey, and this day had great difficulties to encounter: several sunken logs were passed over with great labour but at last there was a tree fallen over the stream, which the canoe could not possibly pass under, so we had to spend more than an hour cutting it through with axes which we carried for the purpose. About three in the afternoon we reached another stopping-place, and as we did not wish to have a repetition of last night's enjoyment, the Indians set to work making a little sleeping-hut. They had a long way to go for thatch, as there was only one palm-tree about a mile off, and this they cut down to supply us with a roof.

However, as we took the trouble to make a house, we had fine weather the three days we stayed, and did not want it. While here we had not much success. The hunters killed some deer, large birds, and monkeys, but did not meet with either of those I particularly wanted. Insects also, as at the former station, were very scarce, and though I got several curious small birds, I was not very well satisfied with the success of my expedition.

Accordingly, after three days, I set out on my return, the rest of the party proceeding further up into the forest in search of a better hunting-ground. On the second day we again reached the open river, and I much enjoyed the change from the dark forest, the damp foliage and decaying leaves and branches, to the bright sunshine and the blue sky, with the chirping birds and the gay flowers on the banks. Passing an estate of Senhor Calistro's on the opposite side of the river, I went on shore to shoot a large goat-sucker which was sitting on the ground in the sunshine, and succeeded in killing two, which I skinned on our way to São Jozé, where we arrived just in time for supper, and were heartily received by Senhor Calistro. After a few days more I left his hospitable roof, loaded with luxuries: eggs, tapioca, a roast pig, pine-apples, and sweets were sent to my canoe; and I bade adieu with regret to my kind host.

On our way down I again encountered the "piroróco" when I hardly expected it. We had gone in shore at a sugar estate to wait for the tide, when the agent told us we had better put out further into the stream, as the piroróco beat there. Though thinking he only wished to frighten us, we judged it prudent to do as he advised; and while we were expecting the tide to turn, a great wave came suddenly rushing along, and breaking on the place where our canoe had been at first moored. The wave having passed, the water was as quiet as before, but flowing up with great rapidity. As we proceeded down the river, we saw everywhere signs of its devastations in the uprooted trees which lined the shores all along, and the high mud-banks where the earth had been washed away. In winter, when the spring-tides are highest, the "piroróco" breaks with terrific force, and often sinks and dashes to pieces boats left incautiously in too shallow water. The ordinary explanations given of this phenomenon are evidently incorrect. Here there is no meeting of salt and fresh water, neither is the stream remarkably narrowed where it commences. I collected all the information I could respecting the depth of the river, and the shoals that occur in it. Where the bore first appears there is a shoal across the river, and below that, the stream is somewhat contracted. The tide flows up past Pará with great velocity, and entering the Guamá river comes to the narrow part of the channel. Here the body of tidal water will be deeper and flow faster, and coming suddenly on to the shoal will form a wave, in the same manner that in a swift brook a large stone at the bottom will cause an undulation, while a slow-flowing stream will keep its smooth surface. This wave will be of great size, and, as there is a large body of water in motion, will be propagated onwards unbroken. Wherever there are shallows, either in the bed or on the margin of the river, it will break, or as it passes over slight shoals will be increased, and, as the river narrows, will go on with greater rapidity. When the tides are low, they rise less rapidly, and at the commencement a much less body of water is put in motion : the depth of the moving water is less, and does not come in contact with the bottom in passing over the shoal, and so no wave is formed.  It is only when the body of water in motion, as the tide first flows in, is of sufficient depth, that it comes in contact with the shoal, and is, as it were, lifted up by it, forming a great rolling wave.

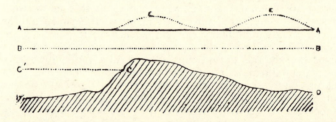

The above diagram will show more clearly the manner in which I suppose the wave to the formed.  A A represents the level of the water when the tide is out; D D the bottom of the river; B B the depth to which the water is put in motion at low tides, not reaching so deep as the bottom of the river at the shoal C, at which time no wave, but a swift current only, is formed; C′ C the depth to which the water is set in motion at spring-tides, when the mass, coming in contact with the bottom at C, is lifted up, and forms a wave at E, which is propagated up the river.  It appears, therefore, that there must exist some peculiar formation of the bottom, and not merely a narrowing and widening in a tidal river to produce a bore, otherwise it would occur much more frequently than it does. In the Mojú and Acarrá the same phenomenon is said to take place; and, as these rivers all run parallel to each other, it is probable that the same bed of rock running across produces a somewhat similar shoal in all of them.  It may also easily be seen why there is only one wave, not a succession of them ; for, when the first wave has passed, the water has risen so much that the stream now flows clear over the shoal, and is therefore not affected by it.

On arriving at Pará I again took up my abode at Nazaré. I had found in this voyage that my canoe was far too unsteady and confined to think of going up the Amazon in it, so I returned it to the owner, who had warranted it steady and adapted for my purpose, but, after much trouble and annoyance, I was obliged to lose the £10 I had given in part payment. In the beginning of July my younger brother H. came out to Pará to assist me; and by the return of the vessel in which he arrived, I sent off my collections of fish and insects up to this time.

We had the good fortune one day to fall in with a small flock of the rare and curious bell-bird (*Chasmorhynchus carunculatus*), but they were on a very thick lofty tree, and took flight before we could get a shot at them. Though it was about four miles off in the forest, we went again the next day, and found them feeding on the same tree, but had no better success. On the third day we went to the same spot, but from that time saw them no more. The bird is of a pure white colour, the size of a blackbird, has a broad bill, and feeds on fruits. From the base of the bill above grows a fleshy tubercle, two to three inches long, and as thick as a quill, sparingly clothed with minute feathers: it is quite lax, and hangs down on one side of the bird's head, not stuck up like a horn, as we see it placed in some stuffed specimens. This bird is remarkable for its loud clear ringing note, like a bell, which it utters at midday, when most other birds are silent.

A few days after, we found feeding on the same tree some beautiful yellow parrots. They are called here imperial parrots, and are much esteemed because their colours are those of the Brazilian flag—yellow and green. I had long been seeking them, and was much pleased when my brother shot one. It is the *Conurus Carolineæ*, and is figured by Spix in his expensive work on the birds of Brazil.

# CHAPTER VI.

## SANTAREM AND MONTEALEGRE.

Leave Pará—Enter the Amazon—Its Peculiar Features—Arrive at San-
tarem—The Town and its Inhabitants—Voyage to Montealegre—
Mosquito Plague and its Remedy—Journey to the Serras—A Cattle
Estate—Rocks, Picture Writings, and Cave—The *Victoria regia*—
Mandiocca Fields—A Festa—Return to Santarem—Beautiful Insects
—Curious Tidal Phenomenon—Leave Santarem—Obydos—Villa
Nova—A Kind Priest—Serpa—Christmas Day on the Amazon.

WE now prepared for our voyage up the Amazon ; and, from
information we obtained of the country, determined first to go
as far as Santarem, a town about five hundred miles up the
river, and the seat of a considerable trade. We had to wait a
long time to procure a passage, but at length with some
difficulty agreed to go in a small empty canoe returning to
Santarem.

We were to have the hold to ourselves, and found it very
redolent of salt-fish, and some hides which still remained in *it*
did not improve the odour. But voyagers on the Amazon
must not be fastidious, so we got our things on board, and
hung up our hammocks as conveniently as we could for the
journey.

Our canoe had a very uneven deck, and, we soon found, a
very leaky one, which annoyed us much by wetting our clothes
and hammocks ; and there were no bulwarks, which, in the
quiet waters of the Amazon, are not necessary. We laid in a
good stock of provisions for the voyage, and borrowed some
books from our English and American friends, to help to pass
away the time ; and in the beginning of August, left Pará with
a fine wind, which soon carried us beyond the islands opposite
the city into the wide river beyond. The next day we crossed

the little sea formed opposite the mouth of the Tocantíns, and sailed up a fine stream till we entered again among islands, and soon got into the narrow channel which forms the communication between the Pará and Amazon rivers.  We passed the little village of Breves, the trade of which consists principally of india-rubber, and painted basins and earthenware, very brilliantly coloured.   Some of our Indians went on shore while we stayed for the tide, and returned rather tipsy, and with several little clay teapot-looking doves, much valued higher up the country.

We proceeded for several days in those narrow channels, which form a network of water—a labyrinth quite unknown, except to the inhabitants of the district.   We had to wait daily for the tide, and then to help ourselves on by warping along shore, there being no wind.   A small montaria was sent on ahead, with a long rope, which the Indians fastened to some projecting tree or bush, and then returned with the other end to the large canoe, which was pulled up by it.   The rope was then taken on again, and the operation repeated continually till the tide turned, when we could not make way against the current.   In many parts of the channel I was much pleased with the bright colours of the leaves, which displayed all the variety of autumnal tints in England.   The cause, however, was different : the leaves were here budding, instead of falling.   On first opening they were pale reddish, then bright red, brown, and lastly green ; some were yellow, some ochre, and some copper-colour, which, together with various shades of green, produced a most beautiful appearance.

It was about ten days after we left Pará that the stream began to widen out and the tide to flow into the Amazon instead of into the Pará river, giving us the longer ebb to make way with.   In about two days more we were in the Amazon itself, and it was with emotions of admiration and awe that we gazed upon the stream of this mighty and far-famed river. Our imagination wandered to its sources in the distant Andes, to the Peruvian Incas of old, to the silver mountains of Potosi, and the gold-seeking Spaniards and wild Indians who now inhabit the country about its thousand sources.   What a grand idea it was to think that we now saw the accumulated waters of a course of three thousand miles ; that all the streams that for a length of twelve hundred miles drained from the snow-clad Andes were here congregated in the wide extent of ochre-coloured water spread out before us! Venezuela, Columbia, Ecuador, Peru, Bolivia, and Brazil—six mighty states, spreading over a country far larger than Europe—had each contributed to form the flood which bore us so peacefully on its bosom.

We now felt the influence of the easterly wind, which during the whole of the summer months blows pretty steadily up the Amazon, and enables vessels to make way against its powerful current. Sometimes we had thunder-storms, with violent squalls, which, as they were generally in the right direction, helped us along the faster; and twice we ran aground on shoals, which caused us some trouble and delay. We had partly to unload the canoe into the montaria, and then, by getting out anchors in the deep water, managed after some hard pulling to extricate ourselves. Sometimes we caught fish, which were a great luxury for us, or went on shore to purchase fruit at some Indian's cottage.

The most striking features of the Amazon are—its vast expanse of smooth water, generally from three to six miles wide; its pale yellowish-olive colour; the great beds of aquatic grass which line its shores, large masses of which are often detached, and form floating islands; the quantity of fruits and leaves and great trunks of trees which it carries down, and its level banks clad with lofty unbroken forest. In places the white stems and leaves of the *Cecropias* give a peculiar aspect, and in others the straight dark trunks of lofty forest-trees form a living wall along the water's edge. There is much animation, too, on this giant stream. Numerous flocks of parrots, and the great red and yellow macaws, fly across every morning and evening, uttering their hoarse cries. Many kinds of herons and rails frequent the marshes on its banks, and the large handsome duck (*Chenalopex jubata*) is often seen swimming about the bays and inlets. But perhaps the most characteristic birds of the Amazon are the gulls and terns, which are in great abundance: all night long their cries are heard over the sand-banks, where they deposit their eggs, and during the day they constantly attracted our attention by their habit of sitting in a row on a floating log, sometimes a dozen or twenty side by side, and going for miles down the stream as grave and motionless as if they were on some very important business. These

PLATE IV.

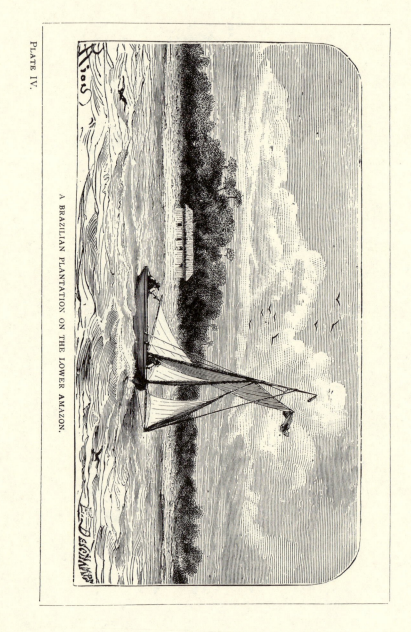

A BRAZILIAN PLANTATION ON THE LOWER AMAZON.

birds deposit their eggs in little hollows in the sand, and the Indians say that during the heat of the day they carry water in their beaks to moisten them and prevent their being roasted by the glowing rays of the sun. Besides these there are divers and darters in abundance, porpoises are constantly blowing in every direction, and alligators are often seen slowly swimming across the river.

On the north bank of the Amazon, for about two hundred miles, are ranges of low hills, which, as well as the country between them, are partly bare and partly covered with brush and thickets. They vary from three hundred to one thousand feet high, and extend inland, being probably connected with the mountains of Cayenne and Guiana. After passing them there are no more hills visible from the river for more than two thousand miles, till we reach the lowest ranges of the Andes : they are called the Serras de Paru, and terminate in the Serras de Montealegre, near the little village of Montealegre, about one hundred miles below Santarem. A few other small villages were passed, and here and there some Brazilian's country-house or Indian's cottage, often completely buried in the forest. Fishermen were sometimes seen in their canoes, and now and then a large schooner passing down the middle of the river, while often for a whole day we would not pass a house or see a human being. The wind, too, was seldom enough for us to make way against the stream, and then we had to proceed by the laborious and tedious method of warping already described.

At length, after a prolonged voyage of twenty-eight days, we reached Santarem, at the mouth of the river Tapajoz, whose blue, transparent waters formed a most pleasing contrast to the turbid stream of the Amazon. We brought letters of introduction to Captain Hislop, an old Scotchman settled here many years. He immediately sent a servant to get a house for us, which after some difficulty was done, and hospitably invited us to take our meals at his table as long as we should find it convenient. Our house was by no means an elegant one, having mud walls and floors, and an open tiled roof, and all very dusty and ruinous ; but it was the best we could get, so we made ourselves contented. As we thought of going to Montealegre, three days' voyage down the river, before settling ourselves for any time at Santarem, we accepted Captain

Hislop's kind invitation as far as regarded dinner, but managed to provide breakfast and tea for ourselves.

The town of Santarem is pleasantly situated on a slope at the mouth of the Tapajoz, with a fine sandy beach, and a little hill at one end, where a mud fort commands the approach from the Amazon. The houses are neat and the streets regular, but, owing to there being no wheeled vehicles and but few horses, they are overgrown with grass. The church is a handsome building with two towers, and the houses are mostly coloured white or yellow, with the doors and windows painted bright green. There is no quay or wharf of any kind, everything being landed in montarias, so that you can seldom get on shore without a wet shoe and stocking. There is a fine beach extending for some miles above and below the town, where all the washing of the place is done, the linen being beautifully bleached on the hot sand. At all hours of the day are plenty of bathers, and the Negro and Indian children are quite amphibious animals. At the back of the town are extensive sandy campos, scattered over with myrtles, cashews, and many other trees and bushes, and beyond are low hills, some bare, and others covered with thick forest.

The trade here is principally in Brazil-nuts, sarsaparilla— which is the best on the Amazon,— farinha, and salt-fish,— some of which articles are obtained from the Mundrucús, an industrious tribe of Indians inhabiting the Tapajoz. There are here, as in Pará, many persons who live an idle life, entirely supported by the labours of a few slaves which they have inherited. The local executive government consists of a " Commandante Militar," who has charge of the fort and a dozen or two of soldiers ; the " Commandante dos trabalha-dores," who superintends the Indians engaged in any public service ; the " Juiz de direito," or civil and criminal judge of the district ; the " Delegardo de policia," who has the management of the passport office, the police, etc., the " Vicario," or priest, and a few subordinate officers. In the evening some of these, and a few of the principal traders, used generally to meet in front of Captain Hislop's house, which was in an airy situation overlooking the river, where they would sit and smoke, take snuff, and talk politics and law for an hour or two.

Besides the Captain, there were two Englishmen in Santarem, who had resided there many years, and were married to Brazilian women. A day or two after our arrival they invited us to take a trip up to a pretty stream which forms a small lake a mile or two above the town. We went in a neat canoe, with several Indians and Negros, and plenty of provisions, to make an agreeable picnic. The place was very picturesque, with dry sands, old trees, and shady thickets, where we amused ourselves shooting birds, catching insects, and examining the new forms of vegetation which were everywhere abundant. The clear, cool water invited us to a refreshing bathe, after which we dined, and returned home by moonlight in the evening.

I was acquainted with the "Juiz de direito," having met him in Pará, and he now very kindly offered to lend me an excellent canoe to go to Montealegre, and to give me introductions to his friends there; but he had no men to spare, so these I had to obtain as I could. This was, as is always the case here, a difficult matter. Captain H. went with me to the Commandante, who promised to give me three Indians, but after waiting a whole week we got only two; the Juiz, however, kindly lent me one with his canoe, and with these we started. The first night we stayed at a cacao-plantation, where we got some excellent fresh fish. In the morning we took a walk among the cacao-trees, and caught numbers of a butterfly (*Didonis biblis*), which, though a common South American species, we had never found either at Santarem or Pará; nor did I ever after see it until I reached Javíta, near the sources of the Rio Negro. As another instance of the peculiar distribution of these insects, I may mention that during four years' collecting I saw the beautiful *Epicalia Numilius* only twice,—once at Pará, and once at Javíta, stations two thousand miles apart.

In the afternoon, just as we reached the mouth of the little river that flows by Montealegre, a violent storm came on suddenly, producing a heavy sea, and nearly capsizing our boat, which the men did not very well know how to manage; but, after being some time in considerable danger, we got safely into smooth water, and, after about two hours' rowing up a winding stream, reached the village. The banks were mostly open, grassy, and half-flooded, with clumps of trees at intervals. Near the village was a range of high rocks, of a fine red and yellow colour, which we afterwards found to be merely indurated clay, in some places very hard, in others soft and friable : they were clothed with wood to their summits, and had a very picturesque appearance.

The village of Montealegre is situated on a hill about a quarter of a mile from the water's edge. The ascent to it is up a shallow ravine, and the path is entirely covered with deep, loose sand, which makes the walk a very laborious one. On each side are numbers of large cactus-plants, of the branched candelabrum form, and twenty to thirty feet high : they grow in immense masses, having great woody stems as thick as a man's body, and were quite a novel feature in the landscape. The village itself forms a spacious square, in which the most conspicuous object is the skeleton of a large and handsome church of dark sandstone, which was commenced about twenty years ago, when the place was more populous and thriving, and before the revolutions which did so much injury to the province ; but there is little prospect of its ever being finished. The present church is a low, thatched, barn-like edifice, and most of the houses are equally poor in their appearance. There are no neat enclosures or gardens,—nothing but weeds and rubbish on every side, with sometimes a few rotten palings round a corral for cattle.

The trade of this place is in cacao, fish, calabashes, and cattle. The cacao is grown on the low lands along the banks of the rivers. It is here planted on cleared ground fully exposed to the sun, and does not seem to thrive so well as when in the shade of the partially cleared forest, which is the plan we had seen adopted in the Tocantíns. When an Indian can get a few thousand cacao-trees planted, he passes an idle, quiet, contented life : all he has to do is to weed under the trees two or three times in the year, and to gather and dry the seeds. The fruit of the cacao-tree is of an oblong shape, about five inches long, and with faint longitudinal ribs. It is of a green colour, but turns yellow as it ripens, and it grows on the stem and larger branches by a short strong stalk, never on the smaller twigs ; it grows so firmly, that it will never fall off, but, if left, will entirely rot away on the tree. The outer covering is hard and rather woody. Within is a mass of seeds, which are the cacao-nuts, covered with a pure white pulp, which has a pleasant sub-acid taste, and when rubbed off in water and sweetened, forms an agreeable and favourite drink. In preparing the cacao, this pulp is not washed off, but the whole is laid in the sun to dry. This requires some care, for if wetted by rain or dew it moulds and is spoilt : on large cacao plantations they have a drying-frame running on rollers, so that it can be pushed under a shed every night or on the approach of rain. The price of good cacao is about 3*s.* for an arroba (thirty-two pounds).

The fish are the pirarucú, which abound in all the lakes here, and give plenty of employment to the Indians in the dry season. The cattle estates are situated at the base of the adjacent serras, where there is a scanty pasture, but in the dry season the marshes which extend to the Amazon afford abundance of herbage. The calabashes, or "cuyas," are made in great quantities, and exported to Pará and all parts of the Amazon. They are very neatly finished, scraped thin, and either stained of a shining black or painted in brilliant colours and gilt. The designs are fanciful, with sometimes figures of birds and animals, and are filled up with much taste and regularity. The Indian women make the colours themselves from various vegetable juices or from the yellow earth, and they are so permanent that the vessels may be constantly wetted for a long time without injury. There is no other place on the whole Amazon where painted calabashes are made with such taste and brilliancy of colour.

We brought a letter of introduction to Senhor Nunez, a Frenchman from Cayenne, who has a small shop in the village ; and he soon procured us an empty house, to which we had our things carried. It consisted of two good parlours, several small sleeping-rooms, a large verandah, and a closed yard behind. We were warned that the mosquitoes were here very annoying, and we soon found them so, for immediately after sunset they poured in upon us in swarms, so that we found them unbearable, and were obliged to rush into our sleeping-rooms, which we had kept carefully closed. Here we had some respite for a time, but they soon found their way in at the cracks and keyholes, and made us very restless and uncomfortable all the rest of the night.

After a few days' residence we found them more tormenting than ever, rendering it quite impossible for us to sit down to read or write after sunset. The people here all use cow-dung burnt at their doors to keep away the "praga," or plague, as they very truly call them, it being the only thing that has any effect.   Having now got an Indian to cook for us, we every afternoon sent him to gather a basket of this necessary article, and just before sunset we lighted an old earthen pan full of it at our bedroom door, in the verandah, so as to get as much smoke as possible, by means of which we could, by walking about, pass an hour pretty comfortably.   In the evening every house and cottage has its pan of burning dung, which gives rather an agreeable odour ; and as there are plenty of cows and cattle about, this necessary of life is always to be procured.

We found the country here an undulating, sandy plain, in some places thickly covered with bushes, in others with larger scattered trees.   Along the banks of the streams were some flat places and steep banks, all thickly clothed with wood, while at a distance of ten or twelve miles were several fine rocky mountains, on one of which was a curious and conspicuous pillar of rock, with a flat overhanging cap, something like a tall mushroom.   The cactus before mentioned was everywhere abundant, and  often in the most magnificent and lofty masses. Pine-apples were found growing wild in large beds in the thickets, and the cashew was also general.   On the rocky slopes above the river were numerous springs gushing out, where on the moistened rock grew curious ferns and mosses and pretty creeping plants.   These shady groves formed our best collecting-ground for insects.   Here we first found the beautiful indigo-blue butterfly, the *Callithea Leprieurii*, sitting on leaves in the shade, and afterwards more abundantly on stems from which a black gummy sap was exuding.   Here were also many trogons and jacamars, and a curious creeper, with a long sickle-shaped bill (*Dendrocolaptes* sp.).

We much wished to visit the serras, which daily seemed more inviting; and the account we had heard of the Indian picture-writings which exist there increased our curiosity.   We accordingly borrowed a small montaria of Senhor Nunez, as we had to go five or six miles by water to a cattle estate situated at the foot of the mountain.   Our canoe was furnished with a mat sail, made of strips of the bark of a large water-plant, and as soon as we got away from the village we hoisted it and were carried briskly along : it was rather nervous work at times, as the sail was far too heavy for the canoe, and rendered it very unsteady whenever there came a little extra puff of wind.  Numerous divers and darters were swimming in the river or seated upon trees on its banks.  We tried to shoot some, but without effect, as these birds are so active in the water that even when wounded they dive and swim beneath it so rapidly as to render all attempt to capture them fruitless. We then entered a narrower branch of the stream, which we soon found to be much impeded by water-plants growing in large floating masses.  We had now no wind, and had to paddle, till the weeds blocked up the channel so completely that we could get on no further.  Our Indian then went ashore, and cut two long poles with forked ends, and with these we commenced pushing on the canoe by means of the great masses of weeds, which were so thick and solid as to afford a tolerable hold to the fork.  Now and then we would emerge into clear water, and could row a little among pretty *Utricularias* and *Pontederias*.  Then, again, we would enter into a mass of weeds and tall grass, completely filling up the channel and rising above our heads, through which we almost despaired to make our way ; the grass, too, cut the hands severely if it merely brushed against them.  On the banks was now to be seen a vast extent of flat, grassy campo, half water and half land, which in the rainy season is a complete lake.  After forcing our way with great labour for several miles, we at length reached the cattle estate, where we were kindly received by the owner, to whom we had a note of introduction.

The house was situated close to the great marsh which extends from the Amazon to the serras.  It was built of mud, with two or three rooms, and an open shed adjoining, used as kitchen and sleeping-place for the Indians.  A corral—a square enclosed yard for the cattle—was near, and at the back rose the sloping ground towards the mountain.  All around were interspersed thickets and open ground, and the picturesque masses of cactus rose in every direction.  We strolled about a little before dark, and shot a couple of pretty green purple-shouldered paroquets, one of the smallest species that inhabits the country.  When we returned to the house we were offered some new milk, and then sat outside the door looking at the strange accoutrements of some of the herdsmen, who were going on horseback to some distant part of the estate.  Their curious and clumsy-looking wooden saddles, huge stirrups, long lassos, and leather ammunition-bags, with long guns and powder-horns of formidable dimensions, made them striking figures, and the more picturesque from their being dusky mulattoes. As soon as the sun set the mosquitoes made their appearance, and the doors of the house were shut, a pan of cow-dung lighted outside, and a lamp within. After a short time supper was announced, and we sat down on a mat on the floor to an excellent repast of turtle, which had been recently brought from the Amazon. We then turned into our hammocks, which were hung across the room in every direction. In fact, the house was pretty well occupied before we came, so that we were now rather crowded ; but a Brazilian thinks nothing of that, and is used to sleep in company. The doors and windows were well closed, and though rather warm we did not suffer from the mosquitoes, an annoyance to which any other is preferable.

The next morning we prepared for our expedition to the mountain, and as we did not know whether we should have to stay the night, we provided ourselves with sufficient provisions, and a large gourd to carry water. We walked some miles along the side of the marsh, on which were many curious aquatic birds, till we arrived at a deserted cottage, where we made our breakfast, and then turned off by a path through a wood. On passing this we found ourselves at the foot of a steep slope, covered with huge blocks of stone, in the greatest confusion, overgrown with coarse sedges and shrubs, rendering any ascent among them extremely difficult. Just above was the curious pillar we had seen from the village, and which we determined to reach. After a most fatiguing scramble over the rocks and among innumerable chasms, we found ourselves on the platform below the columnar mass, which rises perpendicularly thirty or forty feet, and then hangs over at the top all round in a most curious and fearful manner. Its origin is very plainly to be seen. The pillar is of friable stone, in horizontal layers, and is constantly decaying away by the action of the weather. The top is formed by a stratum of hard crystalline rock, which resists the rain and sun, and is apparently now of the same diameter that the pillar which supports it originally was.

We had thought, looking from below, that we could have proceeded along the ridge of the mountain to the further end, where the cave and picture-writings were to be found.  Now, however, we saw the whole summit completely covered with the same gigantic masses of rock and the same coarse rigid vegetation which had rendered our ascent so difficult, and made our proceeding for miles along similar ground quite out of the question.  Our only remedy was to descend on the other side into the sandy plain which extended along its base. We first took a good view of the prospect which spread out before us,—a wide undulating plain covered with scattered trees and shrubs, with a yellow sandy soil and a brownish vegetation.  Beyond this were seen, stretching out to the horizon, a succession of low conical and oblong hills, studding the distant plain in every direction.  Not a house was to be seen, and the picture was one little calculated to impress the mind with a favourable idea of the fertility of the country or the beauty of tropical scenery.  Our descent was very precipitous.  Winding round chasms, creeping under overhanging rocks, clinging by roots and branches, we at length reached the bottom, and had level ground to walk on.

We now saw the whole side of the mountain, along its summit, split vertically into numerous rude columns, in all of which the action of the atmosphere on the different strata of which they were composed was more or less discernible. They diminished and increased in thickness as the soft and hard beds alternated, and in some places appeared like globes standing on pedestals, or the heads and bodies of huge giants. They did not seem to be prismatic, but to be the result of successive earthquake shocks, producing vertical cracks in cross directions, the action of the sun and rains then widening the fissures and forming completely detached columns.

As we proceeded along the sands we found the heat very oppressive.  We had finished the water in our gourd, and knew not where to get more.  Our Indian told us there was a spring halfway up the mountain, a little further on, but it might now have failed, as it was the height of the dry season.

We soon came in sight of the spot, and a group of Mauritia palms, which always grow in damp places, as well as some patches of brilliant green herbage, gave us hope.  On reaching the palms we found a moist, boggy soil, but such a slow filtering of water among the weeds that it took nearly half an hour to fill our gourd.  Seeing a mass of green at the very base of the perpendicular rocks higher up, where the spring appeared to issue, we proceeded there, and found, to our great joy, a little trickle of pure and delightfully cool water, and a shady place where we could rest and eat our lunch in comfort.

We then went on till we arrived where our guide said the cave was situated; but having been there only once he could not find it again, among the confused mass of rock which in several places appeared to present openings, but which on searching the spot deceived us. After various clamberings we gave up the search, and determined to return home and get a better guide another day.

On our way back we passed by a high cliff, on which were some of the picture-writings I had so much wished to see. They were executed in a red tint, produced apparently by rubbing them in with pieces of the rock, which in places is of that colour. They looked quite fresh, and were not at all obliterated by the weather, though no one knows their antiquity. They consisted of various figures, rudely executed, some representing animals, as the alligator and birds, others like some household utensils, and others again circles and mathematical figures, while there were some very complicated and fantastic forms: all were scattered irregularly over the rock to the height of eight or ten feet. The size of most of the figures was from one to two feet.

I took a general sketch of the whole, and some accurate tracings of the more curious single figures, which have unfortunately been since lost. The night felt chilly and damp, and we had nothing to cover ourselves with, or should have slept on the mountain. As it was, we arrived home very tired about eight o'clock, and were soon glad to turn into our hammocks.

The next day Senhor Nunez determined to go with us himself to show us the cave and some more picture-writings, situated in another part of the mountain. We now went on horseback, but could no more find the cave than before, and were forced to send our Indian for an old man who lived a couple of miles off, and who knew the place well. While he was gone, Senhor Nunez went with me to find the picture-writings, which we did after a fatiguing walk. They were situated on a perpendicular rock, rising from the top of a steep, stony slope, which almost deterred me from getting up to them, as I was very tired and thirsty, and there was no water. How-

ever, having come on purpose to see them, I was determined
to persevere, and soon reached the place. They were much
larger than the others, and extended higher up the rock ; the
figures, too, were all different, consisting principally of large
concentric circles, called by the natives the sun and moon, and
several others more complicated and three or four feet high.
Among them were two dates of years about 1770, in very
neat well-formed figures, which I have no doubt were the work
of some travellers who wished to show that they knew how the
others were executed, and to record the date of their visit.
Near some of the higher figures were two or three impressions
of hands in the same colour, showing the palm and all the
fingers very distinctly, as if the person executing the upper
figures had stood on another's shoulders and supported himself
with one hand (smeared with the red colour) while he drew with
the other. I also took copies of the figures at this place,
which, being large and exposed, are visible from a considerable
distance round, and are more generally known than the others,
which are in a secluded and out-of-the-way situation, and were
probably not visited by any European traveller before myself.

We walked some distance further, to get some water, before
returning towards the cave. There we found that our guides
had arrived, and they soon led us up a steep path to its mouth,
which is so well concealed by trees and bushes that our failing
to discover it was not to be wondered at. The entrance is a
rude archway, fifteen or twenty feet high ; but what is most
curious is a thin piece of rock which runs completely across
the opening, about five feet from the ground, like an irregular
flat board. This stone has not fallen into its present position,
but is a portion of the solid rock harder than the rest, so that
it has resisted the force which cleared away the material above
and below it. Inside there is a large irregularly arched
chamber, with a smooth sandy floor, and at the end there are
openings into other chambers ; but as we had not brought
candles we could not explore them. There was nothing about
the cave at all remarkable, except the flat transverse rock at
its mouth. The vegetation around it was by no means
luxuriant or beautiful, nor were there any flowers worth noticing.
In fact, many of our caves in the limestone districts of
England are in every way more picturesque and interesting.

I had heard of a plant growing in the pools in the marsh,

which I was convinced must be the *Victoria regia*.   Senhor
Nunez told me there were plenty near his house, and early
the next morning he sent an Indian to try and get me one.
After some search the man found one, with a half-opened
flower, and brought it to me.   The leaf was about four feet
in diameter, and I was much pleased at length to see this
celebrated plant ; but as it has now become comparatively
common in England, it is not necessary for me to describe it.
It is found all over the Amazon district, but rarely or never
in the river itself.   It seems to delight in still waters, growing
in inlets, lakes, or very quiet branches of the river, fully exposed
to the sun.   Here it grew in the pools left in the bog ; but in
June the water would be twenty or thirty feet deeper, so its
leaf and flower-stalks must increase in length rapidly while the
water rises, as they did not seem to be very long now.   I took
the leaf home, in order to dry some portions of it.   It is called
by the Indians " Uaupé Japóna " (the Jacana's oven), from the
resemblance of the leaf, with its deep rim, to the clay ovens
used for making farinha.

As we wished to get home that day, we took leave of our
kind host, and again had to pole our way over the grass and
weeds in the small stream.   It did not, however, now seem so
tedious as on our ascent, and we soon got into the open river.

Passing along a sandy shore, our Indian saw signs of turtles'
eggs, and immediately jumped out and commenced scraping
away the sand, in a very short time turning up a hatful of eggs
of the small turtle called "Tracaxá."   A little lower down
there was an old tree giving a tempting shade, so we made a
fire under it, boiled our eggs, made some coffee, and with some
farinha and beef we had brought with us made an excellent
breakfast.   Proceeding on, we fell in with a great number of
alligators, of a large size, swimming about in all directions.
We fired at some of them, but only succeeded in making them
dive rapidly to the bottom.   They are much feared by the
natives, who never venture far into the water when bathing.
In a place where we had bathed a few days previously, we saw
one close in shore, and resolved to be more careful for the
future, as every year some lives are lost by incautiousness.

After a few days more at the village, we paid a visit to a
mandiocca plantation some miles in the interior, where there
is a considerable extent of forest-land, and where we therefore

expected to find more insects. We went on foot, carrying our *rédés*, guns, boxes, nets, and other necessaries for a week's stay. On arriving, we found the only accommodation to consist of a little low thatched hut, just large enough to hang our hammocks in, and the only inhabitants four or five Negroes belonging to the place.

However, we soon made ourselves at home, and our little coffee-pot supplied us with an unfailing and refreshing luxury. We found in the forest several scarce butterflies pretty abundant, and among them a new species of *Catagramma*, which we had only met with very rarely at Pará; trogons and jacamars were also plentiful, but there was not any great variety either of birds or insects. There was no running stream here, but a kind of moist, marshy flat, in which shallow holes were dug and soon became filled with water, whence the only supply of this necessary was obtained.

On returning to the village my brother sprained his leg, which swelled and formed an abscess above the knee, quite preventing him from going out for a fortnight. After some trouble I purchased a small canoe here, in which I intended to return to Santarem, and afterwards proceed up the Amazon to Barra, on the Rio Negro.

A festa took place before we left. The church was decorated with leaves and flowers, and sweetmeats were provided for all visitors. Dancing and drinking then went on all night and during the following day, and we were left to cook our own meals, as our Indian was a performer on the violin, and did not think it at all necessary to ask us in order to absent himself two days. The Indians now came in from all the country round, and I bought a number of the pretty painted calabashes for which this place is celebrated.

Soon after we returned to Santarem, where we found our house occupied, but got another, consisting of two small mud-floored rooms and a yard at the back, situated at the further end of the town. We here engaged an old Negro woman to cook for us, and soon got into a regular routine of living. We rose at six, got ready our collecting-boxes, nets, etc., while our old cook was preparing breakfast, which we took at seven; and having given her money to buy meat and vegetables for dinner, started at eight for a walk of about three miles, to a good collecting-ground we had found below the town.

We continued hard at work till about two or three in the afternoon, generally procuring some new and interesting insects, Here was the haunt of the beautiful *Callithea sapphira*, one of the most lovely of butterflies, and of numerous curious and brilliant little *Erycinidæ*. As we returned we stayed to bathe in the Tapajoz, and on arriving at home immediately ate a water-melon, which was always ready for us, and which at that time we found most grateful and refreshing. We then changed our clothes, dined, set out our insects, and in the cool of the evening took tea, and called on or received visits from our Brazilian or English friends—among whom was now Mr. Spruce, the botanist, who arrived here from Pará shortly after we had returned from Montealegre.

The constant hard exercise, pure air, and good living, not-withstanding the intense heat, kept us in the most perfect health, and I have never altogether enjoyed myself so much. In Santarem there is an abundance of beef, fish, milk, and fruits, a dry soil, and clear water,—a conjunction of advantages seldom to be met with in this country. There were some boggy meadows here, more like those of Europe than one often sees so near the equator, on which were growing pretty small *Melastomas* and other flowers. The paths and campos were covered with flowering myrtles, tall *Melastomas*, and numbers of passion-flowers, convolvuluses, and bignonias. At the back of the town, a mile or two off, were some bare conical hills, to which I paid some visits. They were entirely formed of scoriæ, and were as barren and uninviting as can possibly be imagined. A curious tidal phenomenon was to be seen here : the tide *rises* in the Amazon to considerably above Santarem, but it never *flows up*, the water merely rising and falling. The river Tapajoz had now very little water, and its surface was below the level of the Amazon at high water, so that the tide was every day seen to flow up the Tapajoz, while a hundred yards out in the stream of the Amazon it was still flowing rapidly down.

It was now November, and as some rain had fallen, and gloomy weather had set in, we determined to start for the Rio Negro as soon as we could. Our canoe was at length ready, having taken us a long time to repair the bottom, which was quite rotten. After much delay the Commandante had pro-cured us three Indians, who were to go with us only to Obydos,

about three days up the Amazon, and had given us a letter to
the authorities there, to furnish us with more.  Mr. Spruce
had set out for Obydos just a week before us, in a large canoe,
the owner of which had offered him a passage.  On our
arrival we found him unpacking his things, and he told us he
had only got there the night previous, having been ten days on
a journey which is frequently performed in a day and a night :
want of wind was the cause, and the owner of the canoe, who
was with them, would not move at night.  But to such delays
the unfortunate traveller who ventures on the Amazon must
make up his mind patiently to submit.  Captain Hislop had
written to a friend of his to lend us an unoccupied house,
where we had to remain several days quite alone, for our
Indians, after unloading the canoe, went off immediately, and
we could not get others till the Commandante had sent to
fetch them from a considerable distance.

We amused ourselves in the forest, where we found insects
very abundant, but mostly of species we had before obtained.
As our canoe had leaked so much in coming here that we
were almost afraid to venture in it, we had it pulled up on the
beach, and discovered some of the cracks, which we stopped
as well as we could by plugging in cotton dipped in hot pitch.
At length we set off again with two Indians, who were to go
with us only to Villa Nova, the next town, about four days'
voyage from Obydos.  As we had only two, we could not do
much with the paddles, one being required at the helm ; but
luckily the wind was strong and steady, and we went on day
and night very briskly.  We had to cross the river several
times, generally at night.  The wind created a great swell,
and as we dashed along furiously through it, I was rather
doubtful of our rotten boat holding together.  In four days,
however, we reached Villa Nova in safety, and I was very glad
to have got so far on our way.  We were kindly received on
the beach by the priest of the village, Padre Torquato, who
invited us in such a pressing manner to stay in his house till
we should get men to go on, that we could not refuse.  The
Commandante, to whom we brought letters, to give us more
men, was out at his sitio ; they therefore had to be sent after
him, and it would probably be several days before we had an
answer, and perhaps much longer before the men were
procured.

The Padre was a very well-educated and gentlemanly man, and made us as comfortable as he could, though, as he had only two small rooms to share with us, he was putting himself to much inconvenience on our account. He is already known to the English reader from having accompanied Prince Adalbert of Prussia up the Xingu, and he well deserves all the encomiums the Prince has bestowed upon him. He was very fond of enigmas, which he amused himself and his friends by inventing and solving. I much delighted him by turning such of our best as would bear the process into Portuguese; and I also translated for him the old puzzle on the word "tobacco" —in Portuguese, "tabaco," which did just as well—and much pleased him. I took here some fine insects, but it was too late in the season : from July to October Villa Nova would, I have no doubt, be a fine locality for an entomologist.

A week passed away, and the men came not, and as I was very anxious to be off, the Padre agreed with a trader to let me have three of his Indians, he taking instead those that the Commandante would probably soon send for me. One of the Indians, however, did not choose to come, and was driven to the canoe by severe lashes, and at the point of the bayonet. He was very furious and sullen when he came on board, vowing that he would not go with me, and would take vengeance on those who had forced him on board. He complained bitterly of being treated like a slave, and I could not much blame him. I tried what I could to pacify him, offering him good pay and plenty to eat and drink, but to no purpose; he declared he would go back from the first place we stopped at, and kill the man who had struck him. At the same time he was very civil, assuring me that he felt no ill-will against me, as I had had nothing to do with it. It was afternoon when we started, and about sunset we stayed to make supper; and then the ill-used Indian politely wished me good-bye, and taking his bundle of clothes returned through the forest to the village. As I could not go on with two only, I sent one of them back early in the morning to get another in the place of the one who had run away, which he did, and returning about ten o'clock, we pursued our journey.

We went along slowly, now and then sailing, but generally rowing, and suffering much annoyance from the rain, which was almost incessant. The mosquitoes, too, were a great torture: night after night we were kept in a state of feverish irritation, unable to close our eyes for a moment. Our Indians suffered quite as much as ourselves: it is a great mistake to suppose that the mosquitoes do not bite them. You hear them, all night long, slapping on their bare bodies to drive their tormentors off; or they will completely roll themselves up in the sail, suffering the pangs of semi-suffocation to escape from the irritating bites. There are particular spots along the banks of the river where there are no mosquitoes; and no inducement would make our men paddle so hard as the probability of reaching one of these places before midnight, and being enabled to enjoy the comforts of sleep till morning.

Towards the end of December, we reached the little village of Serpa, where we found a festa or procession going on,—a number of women and girls, with ribands and flowers, dancing along to the church with the priest at their head, in a most ludicrous manner. In the evening we went to the house where the dancing took place, and had some wine and sweetmeats. We bought here some coffee and a large basket of plantains. On Christmas day we reached a house where they had just caught a quantity of fish, and we wanted to buy some, which was refused, but they gave us a fine fat piece for our dinner. We bought some eggs, and when we stopped for the day concocted a farinha pudding, and so, with our fish and coffee, made a very tolerable Christmas dinner, while eating which our thoughts turned to our distant home, and to dear friends who at their more luxurious tables would think of us far away upon the Amazon.

# CHAPTER VII.

## BARRA DO RIO NEGRO AND THE SOLIMÕES.

Appearance of the Rio Negro—The City of Barra, its Trade and its Inhabitants—Journey up the Rio Negro—The Lingoa Geral—The Umbrella Bird—Mode of Life of the Indians—Return to Barra—Strangers in the City—Visit to the Solimões—The Gapó—Manaquery—Country Life—Curl-crested Araçaris—Vultures and Onças—Tobacco Growing and Manufacture—The Cow-Fish—Senhor Brandão—A Fishing Party with Senhor Henrique—Letters from England.

ON the 31st of December, 1849, we arrived at the city of Barra on the Rio Negro. On the evening of the 30th the sun had set on the yellow Amazon, but we continued rowing till late at night, when we reached some rocks at the mouth of the Rio Negro, and caught some fine fish in the shallows. In the morning we looked with surprise at the wonderful change in the water around us. We might have fancied ourselves on the river Styx, for it was black as ink in every direction, except where the white sand, seen at the depth of a few feet through its dusky wave, appeared of a golden hue. The water itself is of a pale brown colour, the tinge being just perceptible in a glass, while in deep water it appears jet black, and well deserves its name of Rio Negro—"black river."

We brought letters to Senhor Henrique Antony, an Italian gentleman settled here many years, and the principal merchant in the city; who received us with such hearty hospitality as at once to make us feel at home. He gave us the use of two large rooms in a new house of his own not quite finished, and invited us to take our meals at his table.

The city of Barra do Rio Negro is situated on the east bank of that river, about twelve miles above its junction with the Amazon. It is on uneven ground, about thirty feet above the

high-water level, and there are two small streams or gullies
running through it, where during the wet season the water
rises to a considerable height, and across which are two
wooden bridges.   The streets are regularly laid out, but quite
unpaved, much undulating, and full of holes, so that walking
about at night is very unpleasant.   The houses are generally
of one story, with red-tiled roofs, brick floors, white- and yellow-
washed walls, and green doors and shutters ; and, when the
sun shines, are pretty enough.   The " Barra," or fort, is now
represented by a fragment of wall and a mound of earth, and
there are two churches, but both very poor and far inferior to
that of Santarem.   The population is five or six thousand, of
which the greater part are Indians and half-breeds ; in fact,
there is probably not a single person born in the place of pure
European blood, so completely have the Portuguese amalga-
mated with the Indians.   The trade is chiefly in Brazil-nuts,
salsaparilha, and fish ; and the imports are European cotton-
goods of inferior quality, and quantities of coarse cutlery,
beads, mirrors, and other trinkets for the trade with the Indian
tribes, of which this is the head-quarters.   The distance from
Pará is about a thousand miles, and the voyage up in the wet
season often takes from two to three months, so that flour,
cheese, wine, and other necessaries, are always very dear, and
often not to be obtained.   The more civilised inhabitants of
Barra are all engaged in trade, and have literally no amusements whatever, unless drinking and gambling on a small
scale can be so considered : most of them never open a book,
or have any mental occupation.

As might be expected, therefore, etiquette in dress is much
attended to, and on Sunday at mass all are in full costume.
The ladies dress very elegantly in a variety of French muslins
and gauzes ; they all have fine hair, which they arrange carefully, and ornament with flowers, and never hide it or their
faces under caps or bonnets.   The gentlemen, who pass all
the week in dirty warehouses, in their shirt-sleeves and slippers,
are then seen in suits of the finest black, with beaver hats,
satin cravats, and patent-leather boots of the smallest dimensions ; and then is the fashionable visiting time, when every
one goes to see everybody, to talk over the accumulated
scandal of the week.   Morals in Barra are perhaps at the
lowest ebb possible in any civilised community : you will every

day hear things commonly talked of, about the most respectable families in the place, which would hardly be credited of the inhabitants of the worst parts of St. Giles's.

The wet season had now set in, and we soon found there was little to be done in collecting birds or insects at Barra.  I had been informed that this was the time to find the celebrated umbrella chatterers in plumage, and that they were plentiful in the islands about three days' voyage up the Rio Negro.  On communicating to Senhor Henrique my wish to go there, he applied to some of the authorities to furnish me with Indians to make the voyage.  When they came, which was after three or four days, I started in my own canoe, leaving my brother H. to pay a visit to an estate in another direction.  My voyage occupied three days, and I had a good opportunity of observing the striking difference between this river and the Amazon. Here were no islands of floating grass, no logs and uprooted trees, with their cargoes of gulls, scarcely any stream, and few signs of life in the black and sluggish waters.  Yet when there is a storm, there are greater and more dangerous waves than on the Amazon.  When the dark clouds above cause the water to appear of a yet more inky blackness, and the rising waves break in white foam over the vast expanse, the scene is gloomy in the extreme.

At Barra the river is about a mile and a half wide.  A few miles up it widens considerably, in many places forming deep bays eight or ten miles across.  Further on, again, it separates into several channels, divided by innumerable islands, and the total width is probably not less than twenty miles.  We crossed where it is four or five miles wide, and then keeping up the left bank we entered among the islands, when the opposite shore was no more seen.  We passed many sandy and pebbly beaches, with occasional masses of sandstone and volcanic rock, and a long extent of high and steep gravelly banks, everywhere, except in the most precipitous places, covered with a luxuriant vegetation of shrubs and forest-trees. We saw several cottages, and a village prettily situated on a high, grassy slope, and at length reached Castanheiro, the residence of Senhor Balbino, to whom I brought a letter.  After reading it he asked me my intentions, and then promised to get me a good hunter to kill birds and any other animals I wanted.

The house of Senhor Balbino is generally known as the

"Sobrado," or upper-storied house, being the only one of the kind out of Barra. It was, however, in rather a dilapidated condition, the ladder which served for stairs wanting two steps, and requiring a great exertion of the muscles of the leg to ascend it. This, Senhor Henrique afterwards informed me, had been in the same state for several years, though Balbino has always a carpenter at work making canoes, who might put in a couple of boards in an hour.

An Indian living near now arrived, and we accompanied him to his house, where I was to find a lodging. It was about half a mile further up the river, at the mouth of a small stream, where there was a little settlement of two or three families. The part which it was proposed I should occupy was a small room with a very steep hill for a floor, and three doorways, two with palm-leaf mats and the other doing duty as a window. No choice being offered me, I at once accepted the use of this apartment, and, my men having now brought on my canoe, I ordered my boxes on shore, hung up my hammock, and at once took possession. The Indians then left me; but a boy lent me by Senhor Henrique remained with me to light a fire and boil my coffee, and prepare dinner when we were so fortunate as to get any. I borrowed a table to work at, but, owing to the great inclination of the ground, nothing that had not a very broad base would stay upon it. The houses here were imbedded in the forest, so that although there were four not twenty yards apart, they were not visible from each other, the space where the forest had been cut down being planted with fruit-trees.

Only one of the men here could speak Portuguese, all the rest using the Indian language, called Lingoa Geral, which I found very difficult to get hold of without any books, though it is an easy and simple language. The word *igaripé*, applied to all small streams, means "path of the canoe"; *tatatinga*, smoke, is literally "white fire." Many of the words sound like Greek, as *sapucaia*, a fowl; *apegáua*, a man. In the names of animals the same vowel is often repeated, producing a very euphonious effect; as *parawá*, a parrot; *maracajá*, a tiger-cat; *sucurujú*, a poisonous snake. My Indian boy spoke Lingoa Geral and Portuguese, and so with his assistance I got on very well.

The next morning my hunter arrived, and immediately went out in his canoe among the islands, where the umbrella-birds are found.   In the evening after dark he returned, bringing one fine specimen.   This singular bird is about the size of a raven, and is of a similar colour, but its feathers have a more scaly appearance, from being margined with a different shade of glossy blue.   It is also allied to the crows in its structure, being very similar to them in its feet and bill.   On its head it bears a crest, different from that of any other bird. It is formed of feathers more than two inches long, very thickly set, and with hairy plumes curving over at the end.   These can be laid back so as to be hardly visible, or can be erected and spread out on every side, forming a hemispherical, or rather a hemi-ellipsoidal dome, completely covering the head, and even reaching beyond the point of the beak : the individual feathers then stand out something like the down-bearing seeds of the dandelion.   Besides this, there is another ornamental appendage on the breast, formed by a fleshy tubercle, as thick as a quill and an inch and a half long, which hangs down from the neck, and is thickly covered with glossy feathers, forming a large pendent plume or tassel.   This also the bird can either press to its breast, so as to be scarcely visible, or can swell out, so as almost to conceal the forepart of its body.   In the female the crest and the neck-plume are less developed, and she is altogether a smaller and much less handsome bird.   It inhabits the flooded islands of the Rio Negro and the Solimões, never appearing on the mainland.   It feeds on fruits, and utters a loud, hoarse cry, like some deep musical instrument ; whence its Indian name, *Ueramimbé*, "trumpet-bird."   The whole of the neck, where the plume of feathers springs from, is covered internally with a thick coat of hard, muscular fat, very difficult to be cleaned away,—which, in preparing the skins, must be done, as it would putrefy, and cause the feathers to drop off. The birds are tolerably abundant, but are shy, and perch on the highest trees, and, being very muscular, will not fall unless severely wounded.   My hunter worked very perseveringly to get them, going out before daylight and often not returning till nine or ten at night, yet he never brought me more than two at a time, generally only one, and sometimes none.

The only other birds found in the islands were the beautiful and rare little bristle-tailed manakin, and two species of curassowbird.   On the mainland, the white bell-bird was found on the loftiest trees of the forest, almost out of gunshot.   Three were brought me, much disfigured with blood, having been shot at four or five times each before they fell. The beautiful trumpeter (*Psophia crepitans*), a different species from that found at Pará, was plentiful here. A rare little toucan (*Pteroglossus Azaræ*), and a few parrots, hawks, and Brazilian partridges, were the only other birds we met with.

Insects were by no means abundant, there being few paths in the woods in which to hunt for them or to cause them to accumulate together; for I have invariably found that in an open path through the forest the chequered light and shade causes a variety of plants to spring up and flowers to blow, which in their turn attract a great variety of insects. An open pathway seems to have similar attractions for many kinds of insects to what it has for ourselves. The great blue butterflies, and many smaller ones, will course along it for miles, and if driven into the forest will generally soon return to it again. The gleams of sunshine and the free current of air attract some; others seek the blossoms which there abound; while every particle of animal matter in the pathway is sure to be visited by a number of different species : so that upon the number and extent of the paths and roads which traverse the forest will depend in a great measure the success of the entomologist in these parts of South America.

There were two other rooms in the house where I lived, inhabited by three families. The men generally wore nothing but a pair of trousers, the women only a petticoat, and the children nothing at all. They all lived in the poorest manner, and at first I was quite puzzled to find out when they had their meals. In the morning early they would each have a cuya of mingau * ; then about mid-day they would eat some dry farinha cake or a roasted yam ; and in the evening some more mingau of farinha or plantains. I could not imagine that they really had nothing else to eat, but at last was obliged to come to the conclusion that various preparations of mandiocca and water formed their only food. About once a week they would get a few small fish or a bird, but then it would be divided among so many as only to serve as a relish to the cassava bread. My hunter never took anything out with him but a bag of dry farinha, and after being away fourteen hours in his canoe would come home and sit down in his hammock, and converse as if

* Mingau is a kind of porridge made either of farinha or of the large plantain called pacova.

his thoughts were far from eating, and then, when a cuya of mingau was offered him, would quite contentedly drink it, and be ready to start off before daybreak the next morning. Yet he was as stout and jolly-looking as John Bull himself, fed daily on fat beef and mutton.

Most of the wild fruits—which are great favourites with these people, especially the women and children—are of an acrid or bitter taste, to which long practice only can reconcile a foreigner. Often, when seeing a little child gnawing away at some strange fruit, I have asked to taste it, thinking that it must be sweet to please at that lollipop-loving age, and have found a flavour like aloes or quassia, that I could not get out of my mouth for an hour ; others equally relished are like yellow soap, and some as sour as verjuice.

These people almost always seem at work, but have very little to show for it. The women go to dig up mandiocca or yams, or they have weeding or planting to do, and at other times have earthen pots to make, and their scanty clothing to mend and wash. The men are always busy, either clearing the forest or cutting down timber for a canoe or for paddles, or to make a board for some purpose or other ; and their houses always want mending, and then there is thatch to be brought from a long distance ; or they want baskets, or bows and arrows, or some other thing which occupies nearly their whole time, and yet does not produce them the bare necessaries of life, or allow them leisure to hunt the game that abounds in the forest around them. This is principally the result of everybody doing everything for himself, slowly and with much unnecessary labour, instead of occupying himself with one kind of industry, and exchanging its produce for the articles he requires. An Indian spends a week in cutting down a tree in the forest, and fashioning an article which, by the division of labour, can be made for sixpence : the consequence is, that his work produces but sixpence a week, and he is therefore all his life earning a scanty supply of clothing, in a country where food may be had almost for nothing.

Having remained here a month, and obtained twenty-five specimens of the umbrella-bird, I prepared to return to Barra. On the last day my hunter went out he brought me a fine male bird alive. It had been wounded slightly on the head, just behind the eye, and had fallen to the ground stunned, for in a short time it became very active, and when he brought it me was as strong and fierce as if it was quite uninjured. I put it in a large wicker basket, but as it would take no food during two days I fed it by thrusting pieces of banana down its throat; this I continued for several days, with much difficulty, as its claws were very sharp and powerful. On our way to Barra I found by the river-side a small fruit which it ate readily; this fruit was about the size of a cherry, of an acid taste, and was swallowed whole. The bird arrived safely in the city, and lived a fortnight; when one day it suddenly fell off its perch and died. On skinning it, I found the shot had broken the skull and entered to the brain, though it seems surprising that it should have remained so long apparently in perfect health. I had had, however, an excellent opportunity of observing its habits, and its method of expanding and closing its beautiful crest and neck-plume.

I had now a dull time of it in Barra. The wet season had regularly set in; a day hardly ever passed without rain, and on many days it was incessant. We seized every opportunity for a walk in the forest, but scarcely anything was to be found when we got there, and what we did get was with the greatest difficulty preserved; for the atmosphere was so saturated with moisture that insects moulded, and the feathers and hair dropped from the skins of birds and animals so as to render them quite unserviceable. Luckily, however, there were a good number of foreigners in Barra, so we had a little company. Two traders on the Amazon, an American and an Irishman, had arrived. Mr. Bates had reached Barra a few weeks after me, and was now here, unwilling, like myself, to go further up the country in such uninviting weather. There were also three Germans, one of whom spoke English well and was a bit of a naturalist, and all were good singers, and contributed a little amusement.

There was also a deaf and dumb American, named Baker, a very humorous and intelligent fellow, who was a constant fund of amusement both for the Brazilians and ourselves. He had been educated in the same institution with Laura Bridgman, as a teacher of the deaf and dumb. He seemed to have a passion for travelling, probably as the only means of furnishing through his one sense the necessary amount of exercise and stimulus to his mind. He had travelled alone through Peru and Chile, across to Brazil, through Pará to Barra, and now proposed going by the Rio Branco to Demerara, and so to the United States. He supported himself by selling the deaf and dumb alphabet, with explanations in Spanish and Portuguese. He carried a little slate, on which he could write anything in English or French, and also a good deal in Spanish, so that he could always make his wants known. He made himself at home in every house in Barra, walking in and out as he liked, and asking by signs for whatever he wanted. He was very merry, fond of practical jokes, and of making strange gesticulations. He pretended to be a phrenologist; and on feeling the head of a Portuguese or Brazilian would always write down on his slate, " Very fond of the ladies ; " which on being translated would invariably elicit, " He verdade" (that's very true), and signs of astonishment at his penetration. He was a great smoker, and would drink wine and spirits so freely as sometimes to make him carry his antics to a great length ; still he was much liked, and will be long remembered by the people of Barra. But, poor fellow ! he was never to see his native land again : he died a few months after, at the fortress of São Joaquim, on the Rio Branco,—it was said, of jaundice.

Notwithstanding all this, the time passed heavily enough ; and though Mr. Hauxwell soon after arrived to add to our party, still nothing could make up for the desolation and death which the incessant rains appeared to have produced in all animated nature. Between two and three months passed away in this unexciting monotony, when, the river having nearly risen to its height, and there being some appearance of the weather improving, I determined on taking a journey to the Solimões (as the Amazon is called above the entrance of the Rio Negro), to the estate of Senhor Brandão, my kind host's father-in-law.

The river was now so high that a great portion of the lowlands between the Rio Negro and the Amazon was flooded, being what is called " Gapó." This is one of the most singular features of the Amazon. It extends from a little above Santarem up to the confines of Peru—a distance of about seventeen hundred miles—and varies in width on each side of the river from one to ten or twenty miles. From Santarem to Coarí, a little town on the Solimões, a person may go by canoe in the wet season without once entering into the main river.

He will pass through small streams, lakes, and swamps, and everywhere around him will stretch out an illimitable waste of waters, but all covered with a lofty virgin forest. For days he will travel through this forest, scraping against tree-trunks, and stooping to pass beneath the leaves of prickly palms, now level with the water, though raised on stems forty feet high. In this trackless maze the Indian finds his way with unerring certainty, and by slight indications of broken twigs or scraped bark, goes on day by day as if travelling on a beaten road. In the Gapó peculiar animals are found, attracted by the fruits of trees which grow only there. In fact, the Indians assert that every tree that grows in the Gapó is distinct from all those found in other districts; and when we consider the extraordinary conditions under which these plants exist, being submerged for six months of the year till they are sufficiently lofty to rise above the highest water-level, it does not seem improbable that such may be the case. Many species of trogons are peculiar to the Gapó, others to the dry virgin forest. The umbrella chatterer is entirely confined to it, as is also the little bristle-tailed manakin. Some monkeys are found there only in the wet season, and whole tribes of Indians, such as the Purupurús and Múras, entirely inhabit it, building small, easily-removable huts on the sandy shores in the dry season, and on rafts in the wet; spending a great part of their lives in canoes, sleeping suspended in rude hammocks from trees over the deep water, cultivating no vegetables, but subsisting entirely on the fish, turtle, and cow-fish which they obtain from the river.

On crossing the Rio Negro from the city of Barra, we entered into a tract of this description. Our canoe was forced under branches and among dense bushes, till we got into a part where the trees were loftier, and a deep gloom prevailed. Here the lowest branches of the trees were level with the surface of the water, and were many of them putting forth flowers. As we proceeded we sometimes came to a grove of small palms, the leaves being now only a few feet above us, and among them was the marajá, bearing bunches of agreeable fruit, which, as we passed, the Indians cut off with their long knives. Sometimes the rustling of leaves overhead told us that monkeys were near, and we would soon perhaps discover them peeping down from among the thick foliage, and then bounding rapidly away as soon as we had caught a glimpse of them.  Presently we came out into the sunshine, in a grassy lake filled with lilies and beautiful water-plants, little yellow bladder-worts (*Utricularia*), and the bright-blue flowers and curious leaves with swollen stalks of the *Pontederias*.  Again in the gloom of the forest, among the lofty cylindrical trunks rising like columns out of the deep water : now a splashing of falling fruit around us would announce that birds were feeding overhead, and we could discover a flock of paroquets, or some bright-blue chatterers, or the lovely pompadour, with its delicate white wings and claret-coloured plumage ; now with a whirr a trogon would seize a fruit on the wing, or some clumsy toucan make the branches shake as he alighted.

But what lovely yellow flower is that suspended in the air between two trunks, yet far from either ?  It shines in the gloom as if its petals were of gold.  Now we pass close by it, and see its stalk, like a slender wire a yard and a half long, springing from a cluster of thick leaves on the bark of a tree. It is an *Oncidium*, one of the lovely orchis tribe, making these gloomy shades gay with its airy and brilliant flowers.  Presently there are more of them, and then others appear, with white and spotted and purple blossoms, some growing on rotten logs floating in the water, but most on moss and decaying bark just above it.  There is one magnificent species, four inches across, called by the natives St. Ann's flower (Flor de Santa Anna), of a brilliant purple colour, and emitting a most delightful odour ; it is a new species, and the most magnificent flower of its kind in these regions ; even the natives will sometimes deign to admire it, and to wonder how such a beautiful flower grows "atóa" (uselessly) in the Gapó.

At length, after about eight hours' paddling, we came out again into the broad waters of the Solimões.  How bright shone the sun ! how gay flowed the stream ! how pleasant it was again to see the floating grass islands, and the huge logs and trees, with their cargoes of gulls sitting gravely upon them ! These, with the white-leaved and straggling umboöbas (*Cecropia*), give an aspect to the Amazon quite distinct from that of the, Rio Negro, independently of their differently-coloured waters.  Now, however, there was no land to be reached, and we feared we should have to sup on farinha and water, but luckily found a huge floating trunk fast moored amongst some grass near the side, and on it, with the assistance of a few dead twigs, we soon made a fire, roasted our fish, and boiled some coffee.  But we had intruded on a colony of stinging ants, who, not liking the vicinity of fire, and not choosing to take to the water, swarmed into our canoe and made us pay for our supper in a very unpleasant manner.  Dusk soon came on, and we had to stay for the night ; but the mosquitoes made their presence known, and we lay uncomfortable and feverish till the morning.  By the next night we had reached the mouth of the small stream that leads us to Manaquery, and had few mosquitoes to annoy us.  In the morning we went on, and soon plunged again into the Gapó, passing through some small lakes so choked up with grass that the canoe could hardly be forced over it.  Again we emerged into the igaripé—here about a quarter of a mile wide—and at ten in the morning reached Manaquery.

The estate is situated on the south side of the Solimões, about a hundred miles above its junction with the Rio Negro. The whole tract of country round it consists of igaripés, or small streams, lakes, gapó, and patches of high and dry land, so scattered and mixed together that it is very difficult to tell whether any particular portion is an island or not.  The land, for a short distance on the banks of the stream, rises in an abrupt, rocky cliff, thirty or forty feet above high-water mark : the rocks are of a volcanic nature, being a coarse and often vitreous scoria.  On ascending by some rude steps, I found myself in a flat grassy meadow, scattered over with orange-trees, mangoes, and some noble tamarind and calabash trees, and at the back a thicket of guavas.

Cattle and sheep were grazing about, and pigs and poultry were seen nearer the house.  This was a large thatched shed, half of which contained the cane-mill, and was only enclosed by a railing instead of a wall ; the other half had coarse mud walls, with small windows and thatch shutters.  The floor was of earth only, and very uneven, yet here resided Senhor Brandão and his daughter, whom I had met at Barra.  The fact was that some ten or twelve years before, during the Revolution, a party of Indians burnt down his house, and completely destroyed his garden and fruit-trees, killing several of his servants and cattle, and would have killed his wife and children, had they not, at a moment's notice, escaped to the forest, where they remained three days, living on Indian corn and wild fruits. Senhor B. was at the time in the city, and while the Revolution lasted, which was several years, he was glad to have his family with him in safety, and could not think of rebuilding his house. Afterwards he was engaged as Delegarde de Policia for some years, and he had now only just returned to live on his estate with one unmarried daughter, and of course had plenty to do to get things a little in order. His wife being dead, he did not feel the pleasure he had formerly done in improving his place, and it is, I think, not improbable that, after having lived here a few years, he will get so used to it that he will think it quite unnecessary to go to the expense of rebuilding his house. Still it seemed rather strange to see a nicely-dressed young lady sitting on a mat on a very mountainous mud-floor, and with half-a-dozen Indian girls around her engaged in making lace and in needlework. She introduced me to an elder married sister who was staying with them, and soon Senhor B. came in from his cane-field, and heartily welcomed me. About twelve we sat down to dinner, consisting of tambakí, the most delicious of fish, with rice, beans, and Indian-meal bread, and afterwards oranges *ad libitum.*

I stayed here nearly two months, enjoying a regular country life, and getting together a tolerable collection of birds and insects.

In a few days a hunter I had engaged in Barra arrived, and forthwith commenced operations. In the afternoon he generally brought me some birds or monkeys, which were very plentiful. We rose about half-past five, and by six had a cup of hot coffee ; I then sat down to skin birds, if any had been brought late over-night, or, if not, took my gun and walked out in search of some. At seven or half-past we had a basin of Indian-meal porridge, or chocolate, with new milk, as a sort of breakfast. At twelve punctually we dined, the standing dish being tambakí, varied occasionally with fowl, cow-fish, deer, or other game. At four we had another cup of coffee, with biscuit or fruit, and at seven we took supper of fish like our dinner, if the fisherman had arrived. In the morning, for a couple of hours, I generally went with my net in search of insects. Several rare butterflies were found sitting on the river's side, on the margin of mud left by the retiring waters. Small toucans or araçaris of several species were very abundant the rarest and most beautiful being the "curl-crested," whose head is covered with little glossy curls of a hard substance, more like quill or metallic shavings than feathers. These are at times plentiful, but did not appear till some weeks later than the other species, when I was at last rewarded for my patience by obtaining several beautiful specimens.

The common black vultures were abundant, but were rather put to it for food, being obliged to eat palm-fruits in the forest when they could find nothing else. Every morning it was an amusing sight to see them run after the pigs the moment they got up, three or four following close at the heels of each animal, for the purpose of devouring its dung the moment it was dropped. The pigs seemed to be very much annoyed at such indecent behaviour, and would frequently turn round and take a run at the birds, who would hop out of the way or fly a short distance, but immediately resume their positions as soon as the pig continued his walk.

I am convinced, from repeated observations, that the vultures depend entirely on sight, and not at all on smell, in seeking out their food. While skinning a bird, a dozen of them used to be always waiting attendance at a moderate distance. The moment I threw away a piece of meat they would all run up to seize it; but it frequently happened to fall in a little hollow of the ground or among some grass, and then they would hop about, searching within a foot of it, and very often go away without finding it at all. A piece of stick or paper would bring them down just as rapidly, and after seeing what it was they would quietly go back to their former places. They always choose elevated stations, evidently to see what food they can discover; and when soaring at an immense height in the air, they will descend into the forest where a cow has died or been killed, long before it becomes putrid or emits any strong smell. I have often wrapped a piece of half-putrid meat in paper and thrown it to them, and even then, after hopping up to it, they will retire quite satisfied that it is only paper, and nothing at all eatable.

Senhor B. had two fine sows, very fat, and each was expected to bring forth a litter of pigs in a few days. There were no pig-sties or sheds of any kind; and all animals retire into the forest on such occasions, and in a few days return with their young family, just as cats do with us. These sows had both disappeared for some days, and had not returned, and we began to be afraid that a jaguar which had been heard near the house, and whose track had been seen, had destroyed them. A search was accordingly made, and the remains of a sow were discovered in a thicket not far from the house. The next night we heard the jaguar roaring within fifty yards of us, as we lay in our hammocks in the open shed ; but there being plenty of cattle, pigs, and dogs about, we did not feel much alarmed. Presently we heard a report of a gun from an Indian's cottage near, and made sure the animal was dead. The next morning we found that it had passed within sight of the door, but the man was so frightened that he had fired at random and missed, for there are some Indians who are as much cowards in this respect as any one else. For two or three days more we heard reports of the animal at different parts of the estate, so my hunter went out at night to lie in wait for it, and succeeded in killing it with a bullet. It was an onça of the largest size, and was believed to have killed, besides the sow, a cow which had disappeared some weeks previously.

The weather was now very dry : no rain had fallen for some time ; the oranges were fully ripe, and the grass, so green and fresh when I arrived, was beginning to assume a brownish-yellow tinge. Tobacco-picking had begun, and I saw the process of the manufacture as carried on here. Tobacco is sown thickly on a small patch of ground, and the young plants are then set in rows, just as we do cabbages. They are much attacked by the caterpillar of a sphinx moth, which grows to a large size, and would completely devour the crop unless carefully picked off. Old men, and women, and children are therefore constantly employed going over a part of the field every day, and carefully examining the plants leaf by leaf till the insects are completely exterminated. When they show any inclination to flower, the buds are nipped off ; and as soon as the leaves have reached their full size, they are gathered in strong wicker baskets, and are laid out in the house or a shed, on poles supported by uprights from the floor to the ceiling. In a few days they dry, and during the hot days become quite crisp ; but the moisture of the night softens them, and early in the morning they are flaccid. When they are judged sufficiently dry, every leaf must have the strong fibrous midrib taken out of it. For this purpose all the household—men, women, and children—are called up at four in the morning, and are set to work tearing out the midrib, before the heat of the day makes the leaves too brittle to allow of the operation. A few of the best leaves are sometimes selected to make cigars, but the whole is generally manufactured into rolls of two or four pounds each. The proper quantity is weighed out, and placed regularly in layers on a table in a row about a yard long, rather thicker in the middle. Beginning at one end, this is carefully rolled up and wound round with a cord as tightly as possible. In a few days these rolls are opened out, to see if there is any tendency to heat or mould, and if all is right they are again made up with greater care. Every day they are rebound tighter and tighter, the operator sitting on the ground with the cord twisted round a post, and winding and tightening with all his strength, till at length the roll has become compressed into a solid mass about an inch in diameter, and gradually tapering towards each end. It is then wound closely from end to end with a neat strip of the rind of the Uarumá (a water-rush), and tied up in bundles of an arroba and half an arroba (thirty-two and sixteen pounds), and is ready for sale. When the tobacco is good, or has, as they term it, "much honey in it," it will cut as smooth and solid as a piece of Spanish liquorice, and can be bent double without cracking. The price varies according to the quality and the supply, from 4*d*. to 1*s*. per pound.

One day the fisherman brought us in a fine "peixe boi," or cow-fish, a species of *Manatus*, which inhabits the Amazon, and is particularly abundant in the lakes in this part of the river. It was a female, about six feet long, and near five in circumference in the thickest part. The body is perfectly smooth, and without any projections or inequalities, gradually changing into a horizontal semicircular flat tail, with no appearance whatever of hind limbs. There is no distinct neck; the head is not very large, and is terminated by a large mouth and fleshy lips, somewhat resembling those of a cow. There are stiff bristles on the lips, and a few distantly scattered hairs over the body. Behind the head are two powerful oval fins, and just beneath them are the breasts, from which, on pressure being applied, flows a stream of beautiful white milk. The ears are minute holes, and the eyes very small. The dung resembles that of a horse. The colour is a dusky lead, with some large pinkish-white marbled blotches on the belly.  The skin is about an inch thick on the back, and a quarter of an inch on the belly.  Beneath the skin is a layer of fat of a greater or less thickness, generally about an inch, which is boiled down to make an oil used for light and for cooking. The intestines are very voluminous, the heart about the size of a sheep's, and the lungs about two feet long, and six or seven inches wide, very cellular and spongy, and can be blown out like a bladder.  The skull is large and solid, with no front teeth; the vertebræ extend to the very tip of the tail, but show no rudiments of posterior limbs ; the fore limbs, on the contrary, are very highly developed, the bones exactly corresponding to those of the human arm, having even the five fingers, with every joint distinct, yet enclosed in a stiff inflexible skin, where not a joint can have any motion.

The cow-fish feeds on grass at the borders of the rivers and lakes, and swims quickly with the tail and paddles ; and though the external organs of sight and hearing are so imperfect, these senses are said by the hunters to be remarkably acute, and to render necessary all their caution and skill to capture the animals.  They bring forth one, or rarely two, young ones, which they clasp in their arms or paddles while giving suck.  They are harpooned, or caught in a strong net, at the narrow entrance of a lake or stream, and are killed by driving a wooden plug with a mallet up their nostrils.  Each yields from five to twenty-five gallons of oil.  The flesh is very good, being something between beef and pork, and this one furnished us with several meals, and was an agreeable change from our fish diet.

As I now expected a canoe shortly to arrive, bringing me letters and remittances from England, after which I was anxious to set off for the Upper Rio Negro as soon as possible, I determined to return to Barra, and having agreed for a passage in a canoe going there, I took leave of my kind host. I must, however, first say a few words about him.  Senhor José Antonio Brandão had come over from Portugal when very young, and had married early and settled, with the intention of spending his life here.  Very singularly for a Portuguese, he entirely devoted himself to agriculture.  He built himself a country-house at Manaquery, on a lake near the main river, brought Indians from a distance to settle with him, cleared the forest, planted orange, tamarind, mango, and many other fruit-bearing trees, made pleasant avenues, gardens, and pastures, stocked them well with cattle, sheep, pigs, and poultry, and set himself down to the full enjoyment of a country life. But about twenty years ago, while his family were yet young, disturbances and revolutions broke out, and he, as well as all natives of Portugal, though he had signed the constitution of the Empire, and was in heart a true Brazilian, became an object of dislike and suspicion to many of the more violent of the revolutionists. A tribe of Indians who resided near him, and to whom he had shown constant kindness, were incited to burn down his house and destroy his property. This they did effectually, rooting up his fruit-trees, burning his crops, killing his cattle and his servants, and his wife and family only escaped from their murderous arrows by timely flight to the forest. During the long years of anarchy and confusion which followed, he was appointed a magistrate in Barra, and was unable to look after his estate. His wife died, his children married, and he of course felt then little interest in restoring things to their former state.

He is a remarkably intelligent man, fond of reading, but without books, and with a most tenacious memory. He has taught himself French, which he now reads with ease, and through it he has got much information, though of course rather tinged with French prejudice. He has several huge quarto volumes of Ecclesiastical History, and is quite learned in all the details of the Councils, and in the history of the Reformation. He can tell you, from an old work on geography, without maps, the length and breadth of every country in Europe, and the main particulars respecting it. He is about seventy years of age, thirsting for information, and has never seen a map ! Think of this, ye who roll in intellectual luxury. In this land of mechanics' institutions and cheap literature few have an idea of the real pursuit of knowledge under difficulties, —of the longing thirst for information which there is no fountain to satisfy. In his conversation there was something racy and refreshing : such an absence of information, but such a fertility of ideas. He had read the Bible in Portuguese, as a forbidden book, though the priests make no very great objection to it here ; and it was something new to hear a man's opinions of it who had first read it at a mature age, and solely from a desire for information. The idea had not entered his mind that it was all inspired, so he made objections to any parts which he thought incredible, or which appeared to him to be capable of a simple explanation; and, as might have been expected, he found of his own accord confirmation of the doctrines of the religion in which he had been brought up from childhood.

On arriving at Barra, the expected canoe had not arrived, and many weeks passed wearily away. The weather was fine, but Barra is a very poor locality for making collections. Insects were remarkably scarce and uninteresting, and I looked forward anxiously to the time when I could start for some distant and more promising district. The season was very dry and hot: the thermometer, at two, every afternoon, reaching 94° and 95° in the shade, and not often sinking below 75° during the night. The lowest which I observed, just before sunrise, was 70°, and the highest in the afternoon, 96°. There was scarcely any rain during the months of July and August, so the grass about the city was completely burnt up. The river was now falling rapidly, and the sandbanks in the Amazon were, some of them, just rising above the water.

One day, Senhor Henrique made a party to go fishing, with a large drag-net, in the Solimões. We started in the afternoon in a good canoe, with a party of about a dozen, and eight or ten Indian rowers; and just before sunset, reached the mouth of the Rio Negro, and turned up into the strong and turbid waters of the Solimões. There was a bright moon, and we kept on talking and singing, while passing the narrow channels and green islands on the north side of the river which looked most picturesquely wild and solitary by the pale silvery moon-light, and amid the solemn silence of the forest. By about midnight, we reached a large sandbank, just rising out of the water. Most of the party turned up their trousers, and waded though the shallows, till they reached the bank, where they began searching for small turtles' eggs, and those of gulls and other water-birds, which lay them in little hollows scraped in the sand. Gulls, divers, ducks, and sandpipers flew screaming about as we landed, and the splash of fish in the shallow water told us that there was abundance of sport for us. Senhor Henrique soon ordered the Indians to get out the net, and commenced dragging. Every time the net was drawn on shore we nearly filled a basket with numerous small fishes, and a few of larger size. There were quantities of little ones armed with spines, which inflict a serious wound if trodden on, so we had to be cautious with our bare feet. I was much interested in the great variety and the curious forms that every basketful contained. There were numbers of a little fish, peculiar to the Amazon, which inflates the fore part of the body into a complete ball, and when stamped upon explodes with a noise similar to that produced by the bursting of an inflated paper bag.

After two or three hours, we felt rather tired, so we made a fire, and cooked some of our fish for a meal,—which we might call supper or breakfast, as we pleased, for dawn was now appearing. We then again went on fishing, while others got their guns, and endeavoured to shoot some of the wild ducks. One gentleman, with a rifle, made an extraordinary shot, bringing down a single duck flying, at a long distance, with a bullet. Now it was daylight, I endeavoured to sketch some of the curious fish, but they were so numerous, and the sun was so hot, that I could do but little; and as they became putrid in a few hours, I could not keep them for the purpose till we returned home. About ten in the morning we left off fishing, and began cooking. We had roasted, broiled, and stewed fish, and with oil and vinegar, and plenty of pepper and salt, made a very excellent breakfast. We also had wine, bread, and farinha, and coffee for those who preferred it. While we were at breakfast, our Indians lay down on the sand, in the sun, to take a nap, as they had been hard at work for two days without sleep. In about an hour they were roused to breakfast, and then at noon we started on our way home.

At five in the afternoon we reached a place at the mouth of the Rio Negro, where there are some flat rocks, and generally abundance of fish. Here most of the party began fishing again with rod and line, and were pretty successful; and a fisherman coming in with a fine pirarucú, weighing thirty or forty pounds, Senhor Henrique bought it of him, in order to have something worth showing from our excursion.

We then proceeded homewards, many of us dozing; and our Indians rowing hard, but hardly able to keep their eyes open. Now and then, one would regularly drop off to sleep, but keep on paddling mechanically, without pulling very hard.

One of his companions would then tickle his nose, and rouse him up, and his look of astonishment to find he had been sleeping would set all in a roar of laughter at his expense. It was midnight when we reached Barra, and we were all pretty glad to seek our hammocks.

Several weeks more passed wearily, till at length we had news of the long-expected canoe ; one of the owners, having arrived beforehand in a montaria, informing us that it would be up in two days more. There was at this time in the city a trader from the upper Rio Negro, a Portuguese, and generally considered a very good sort of fellow. He was to start the next day, but on Senhor Henrique's representation, he agreed to stay till Senhor Neill Bradley's canoe arrived, and then give me a passage up to the Falls of the Rio Negro, or to any other place I might wish to go to. The next afternoon the expected vessel reached Barra ; about six in the evening I got a long arrear of letters from Pará, from England, from California, and Australia, some twenty in number, and several dated more than a year back. I sat up till two in the morning reading them, lay down, but slept little till five in the morning ; I then commenced answering the most important of them,— packing up— buying forgotten necessaries for the voyage—making up a box for England—giving instructions to my brother H., who was to stay in Barra, and, in six months, return to England,—and by noon was ready to start on a voyage of seven hundred miles, and, probably, for a year's absence. The Juiz de Direito, or Judge of the district, had kindly sent me a turkey and a sucking-pig ; the former of which I took alive, and the latter roasted ; so I had a stock of provisions to commence the voyage.

# CHAPTER VIII.

## THE UPPER RIO NEGRO.

Quit Barra for the Upper Rio Negro—Canoe and Cargo—Great Width of the River—Carvoeiro and Barcellos—Granite Rocks—Castanheiro —A Polite Old Gentleman—S. Jozé—A New Language—The Cataracts —S. Gabriel—Nossa Senhora da Guía—Senhor L. and his Family— ' Visit to the River Cobati—An Indian Village—The Serra—Cocks of the Rock—Return to Guia—Frei Jozé dos Santos Innocentos.

It was on the last day of August, 1850, at about two o'clock on a fine bright afternoon, that I bade adieu to Barra, looking forward with hope and expectation to the distant and little-known regions I was now going to visit. I found our canoe a tolerably roomy one, it being about thirty-five feet long and seven broad. The after-part had a rough deck, made of split palm-stems, covered with a tolda, or semicircular roof, high enough to sit up comfortably within it, and well thatched with palm-leaves. A part of the front opening was stopped up on each side, leaving a doorway about three feet wide. The forepart was covered with a similar tolda, but much lower, and above it was a flat deck, formed like the other, and supported by upright poles along the sides. This is called the jangáda, or raft, and serves for the Indians to stand on, while rowing with oars formed of paddle-blades fixed to long poles. The canoe was well loaded with all the articles most desired by the semi-civilised and savage inhabitants of the Upper Rio Negro. There were bales of coarse cotton cloth and of the commonest calico, of flimsy but brilliantly-coloured prints, of checked and striped cottons, and of blue or red handkerchiefs. Then there were axes and cutlasses, and coarse pointed knives in great profusion, fish-hooks by thousands, flints and steels, gunpowder, shot, quantities of blue,

black, and white beads, and countless little looking-glasses ;
needles and thread, and buttons and tape were not forgotten.
There was plenty of caxaça (the rum of the country), and wine
for the trader's own use, as well as a little brandy for
"medicine," and tea, coffee, sugar, vinegar, oil for cooking and
for light, biscuits, butter, garlic, black pepper, and other little
household luxuries, sufficient to last the family for at least
six months, and supply the pressing wants of any famishing
traveller.

My host, Senhor João Antonio de Lima, was a middle-sized,
grizzly man, with a face something like that of the banished lord
in the National Gallery. He had, however, all the politeness
of his countrymen, placed the canoe and everything in it "at
my orders," and made himself very agreeable. Our tolda
contained numerous boxes and packages of his and my own,
but still left plenty of room for us to sit or lie down comfortably; and in the cool of the morning and evening we stood
upon the plank at its mouth, or sat upon its top, enjoying the
fresh air and the cool prospect of dark waters around us. For
the first day or two we found no land, all the banks of the
river being flooded, but afterwards we had plenty of places on
which to go on shore and make our fire. Generally, as soon
after daylight as we could discover a convenient spot, we
landed and made coffee, into which we broke some biscuit and
put a piece of butter, which I soon found to be a very great
improvement in the absence of milk. About ten or eleven we
stopped again for breakfast—the principal meal for the Indians.
We now cooked a fowl, or some fish if we had caught any
during the night. About six we again landed to prepare
supper and coffee, which we sat sipping on the top of the
tolda, while we proceeded on our way, till eight or nine at
night, when the canoe was moored in a place where we could
hang up our hammocks on shore, and sleep comfortably till
four or five in the morning. Sometimes this was varied by
stopping for the night at six o'clock, and then we would start
again by midnight, or by one or two in the morning. We
would often make our stoppages at a cottage, where we could
buy a fowl or some eggs, or a bunch of bananas or some
oranges ; or at another time at a pretty opening in the forest,
where some would start off with a gun, to shoot a curassow or
a guan, and others would drop their line into the water, and

soon have some small but delicious fish to broil. Senhor L. was an old hand at canoe-travelling, and was always well provided with hooks and lines. Bait was generally carefully prepared during the day, and at night the lines would be thrown in; and we were often rewarded with a fine pirahíba of twenty or thirty pounds weight, which made us a breakfast and supper for the next day.

A little above Barra the river spreads out into great bays on each side, so as to be from six to ten miles wide; and here, when there is much wind, a heavy sea rises, which is very dangerous for small canoes. Above this the river again narrows to about a mile and a half, and soon afterwards branches out into diverging channels, with islands of every size between them. For several hundred miles after this the two banks of the river can never be seen at once: they are probably from ten to twenty-five miles apart. Some of the islands are of great size, reaching to thirty or forty miles in length, and with others often intervening between them and the shore.

On the second and third day after we left Barra, there were high, picturesque, gravelly banks to the river. A little further on, a few isolated rocks appear, and at the little village of Ayrão, which we reached in a week, there were broken ledges of sandstone rock of rather a crystalline texture. A little lower we had passed points of a soft sandstone, worn into caves and fantastic hollows by the action of the water. Further on, at Pedreiro, the rock was perfectly crystalline; while a little further still, at the mouth of the Rio Branco, a real granitic rock appears.

At Pedreiro we stayed for the night with a friend of Senhor L.'s, where the news of the city was discussed, and the prices of fish, salsaparilha, piassaba, etc., communicated. The next day we passed some picturesque granite rocks opposite the mouth of the Rio Branco, where again the two shores of the river are seen at one view. On a little island there are some curious Indian picture-writings, being representations of numerous animals and men, roughly picked out of the hard granite. I made careful drawings of these at the time, and took specimens of the rock.

The next day we reached Carvoeiro, a village desolate and half deserted, as are all those on the Rio Negro. We found only two families inhabiting it, a blacksmith, and a Brazilian, who bore the title of Capitão Vasconcellos, a good-humoured, civil man, who treated us very well the day we remained with him.  For dinner we had turtle, with silver knives and forks, but our table was a mat on the ground.  In the afternoon the Capitão got drunk with his old friend Senhor L., and then became very violent, and abused him as a vile, unworthy, skulking Portuguese villain, and used many more epithets, of which the language has a copious store.  Senhor L., who prides himself on never getting intoxicated, took it very coolly, and the next morning the Capitão expressed his heartfelt contrition, vowed eternal friendship, and regretted much that he should have given the "estrangeiro" so much reason to think ill of his countrymen.

Proceeding on our journey, we entered on a labyrinth of small islands, so flooded that they appeared like masses of bushes growing out of the water.  Though Senhor L. is well acquainted with the river, we here almost lost our way, and met another canoe which had quite done so.  As it was late, we stayed at a point of dry land for the night, and hung our hammocks under the trees.  The next day we called at the house of a man who owed Senhor L. some money, and who paid him in turtles, eight or nine of which we embarked.

The two shores of the river had only been seen for a moment.  Again we plunged into a sea of islands, and channels opening among them often stretched out to the horizon.  Sometimes a distant shore continued for days unbroken, but was at last found to be but a far-stretching island.  All was now again alluvial soil, and we sometimes had a difficulty in finding dry land to cook our meals on.  In a few days more we reached Barcellos, once the capital of the Rio Negro, but now depopulated and almost deserted.  On the shore lie several blocks of marble, brought from Portugal for some public buildings which were never erected.  The lines of the old streets are now paths through a jungle, where orange and other fruit-trees are mingled with cassias and tall tropical weeds.  The houses that remain are mostly ruinous mud-huts, with here and there one more neatly finished and white-washed.

We called on an old Italian, who has the reputation of being rich, but a great miser.  He was, however, merry enough.  He gave us coffee sweetened with molasses, and pressed us to stay

their insect prey over the stream, and amused us with
rapid evolutions; the tree-frogs commenced their mournful
, a few lingering parrots would cross the river to their
and the guarhibas fill the air with their howling voices.
at length the dews of evening fell thick upon us, I would
beneath the tolda, while Senhor L., wrapping himself
heet, preferred taking his repose outside.

September 30th, just a month after we had left Barra,
ain saw the opposite side of the river, and crossed over
it is about four miles wide. The next day we reached
where the granitic rocks commence, and I was delighted
p out of the canoe on to a fine sloping table of granite,
quartz-veins running across it in various directions. From
point the river became more picturesque. Small rocky
ls abounded, and fine granite beaches were frequent, offer-
delightful places to take our picnic meals. Fish too
ne yet more abundant, and we were seldom without this
y.

the 3rd of October we reached a sitio, where resided a
breed Brazilian named João Cordeiro (John Lamb), who
friend of Senhor L. as well as a customer. We stayed
two days, while a good part of the cargo of the canoe was
out for Senhor João to choose what he liked best.
, for the second time since we left Barra, we saw a few
, and had milk to our coffee. I amused myself by walking
e forest and catching some insects, of which I found many
species. At length, the gay cottons and gauzes, the beads
cutlery, wines and spirits, sugar and butter, having been
ted, we went on our way, Senhor João promising to get
ty of piassaba, salsa, and other products, ready to pay
or L. by the time he next sent to the city.
he following day we reached St. Isabel, a miserable village
grown with weeds and thickets, and having at this time but
gle inhabitant, a Portuguese, with whom we took a cup of
e, sweetening it, however, with our own sugar, as he had no
luxury He was one of the many decent sort of men
drag on a miserable existence here, putting up with hard-
s and deprivations which in a civilised community would
only the result of the most utter poverty.
n the 8th we reached Castanheiro, and stayed a day with
her Portuguese, one of the richest traders on the river.

ON THE RIO NEGRO.

PLATE V.

breakfast with him,—which me
house filled with cables, anch
johns.   We had silver forks an
a tablecloth, and raw spirits an
fare placed upon it.   He, howe
to take to the canoe.

In a day or two more we p
called Cabuqueno.   About Barc
pretty little palm growing at the
*Mauritia*, which was afterwards
were now more plentiful than i
and several species occurred
often sent two men in a small ca
ing, and they would by ten o'c
sufficient for our breakfast and
a great interest in the beauty an
whenever I could, made accurate
them.   Many are of a most exc
thing I have tasted in England,
salt waters ; and many species ha
water they are boiled in a rich
drop of this is wasted, but, with
all consumed, with as much re
delicate soup.   Our tolda was
generally being from 95° to 100° i
the temperature was about 75°,
being 85° and feeling quite warm
the water would be about 86°, an
from its contrast with the heated a

We had altogether very fine we
or at least four or five times in a
or storm, which came on suddenly
and often thunder and rain, but p
or two, leaving the atmosphere be
great luxury of this river is the abse
instead of being the signal for
brought us the pleasantest part of
the top of the tolda, enjoying the
sipping a cup of coffee—our greate
sunset faded rapidly away and th
above us.   At this quiet hour the

hunt
their
chant
nests
Wher
turn
in a

Or
we ag
wher
a par
to st
with
this
islan
ing
beca
luxu

O
half-
was
here
take
Her
cow
in t
new
and
sele
plen
Sen

T
ove
a si
coff
suc
wh
shi
be

an

PLATE VI.

A VILLAGE ON THE RIO NEGRO.

He owed his wealth principally to having steadily refused to take goods on credit, which is the curse of this country : he thus was always his own master, instead of being the slave of the Barra and Pará merchants, and could buy in the cheapest and sell in the dearest market.   With economy and a character for closeness, he had accumulated some five or six thousand pounds, which went on rapidly increasing, as in this country living costs a man nothing, unless he drinks or gambles.   He trades with the Indians, takes the product in his own canoe to Pará, buys the articles he knows are most saleable, and gets a profit of about a hundred per cent. on all the business he does. It may give some insight into the state of this country to know that, though this man is distinguished from almost all other traders by his strict integrity and fairness, which all allow, yet he is seldom spoken well of, because he does not enter into the extravagance and debauchery which it is thought he can well afford.

A little further on we passed some more curious Indian picture-writings on a granite rock, of which I took a sketch. On the 11th we reached Wanawacá, the seat of a Brazilian from Pernambuco, banished to the Rio Negro for joining in some insurrection.   I had heard the most horrible stories of this man's crimes.   He had murdered the Indians, carried away their wives and daughters, and committed barbarities that are too disgusting to mention.   Yet, as I had a letter of introduction to him, and he was a friend of Senhor L., we went to call upon him.   I found him a mild, quiet, polite, white-haired old gentleman, who received us with great civility, gave us a very good breakfast, and conversed in an unusually rational manner.   When we had gone, Senhor L. asked me if I was not surprised to see such a mild-looking man.   " But," said he, " these soft-spoken ones are always the worst.   He is a regular hypocrite, and he will stick at nothing.   Among his friends he will boast of his crimes, and he declares there is nothing that he will not do for his own pleasure or profit."

The next day we stayed at another village, São Jozé, where we were to leave our little vessel, and proceed in two smaller ones, as the stream was now so rapid that we could not make much way, and the Falls a little higher up were quite impass-able for our larger canoe.   Here we stayed two days, unloading and loading.   I found plenty to do capturing the butterflies, several rare species of which were abundant on the hot rocks by the river's side.  At length all was right, and we proceeded on our way in two heavily-laden canoes, and rather cramped for room compared to what we had been before.  We had several little rapids to pass, round projecting points of rock, where the Indians had to jump into the water and push the canoe past the difficulty.  In two days more we reached the village of São Pedro, where Senhor L. borrowed another canoe, much better and more convenient, so that we had again half a day's delay.  The owner was a young Brazilian trader, a very hospitable and civil fellow, with whom we spent a pleasant evening.  He and Senhor L. were old cronies, and began talking in a language I could not understand, though I knew it was some kind of Portuguese.  I soon, however, found out what it was, and Senhor L. afterwards told me that he had learnt it when a boy at school.  It consisted in adding to every syllable another, rhyming with it, but beginning with p; thus to say, "Venha ca" (come here), he would say, "Venpenhapa capa," or if in English "Comepum herepere;" and this, when spoken rapidly, is quite unintelligible to a person not used to it.  This Senhor was a bit of a musician, and amused us with some simple tunes on the guitar, almost the only instrument used in this part of the country.

Leaving this place, we passed the mouth of the small river Curicuriarí, from which we had a fine view of the Serras of the same name.  These are the finest mountains I had yet seen, being irregular conical masses of granite about three thousand feet high.  They are much jagged and peaked, clothed with forest in all the sloping parts, but with numerous bare precipices, on which shine huge white veins and masses of quartz, putting me in mind of what must be the appearance of the snow-capped Andes.  Lower down, near St. Isabel, we had passed several conical peaks, but none more than a thousand feet high : these all rise abruptly from a perfectly level plain, and are not part of any connected range of hills.

On the same day, the 19th of October, we reached the celebrated Falls of the Rio Negro.  Small rocky islands and masses of bare rock now began to fill the river in every part.  The stream flowed rapidly round projecting points, and the main channel was full of foam and eddies.  We soon arrived at the commencement of the actual rapids.  Beds and ledges

of rock spread all across the river, while through the openings
between them the water rushed with terrific violence, forming
dangerous whirlpools and breakers below.   Here it was necessary to cross to the other side, in order to get up.   We dashed
into the current, were rapidly carried down, got among the
boiling waves, then passed suddenly into still water under
shelter of an island; whence starting again, we at length
reached the other side, about a mile across.   Here we found
ourselves at the foot of a great rush of water, and we all got
out upon the rocks, while the Indians, with a strong rope,
partly in the water, and partly on land, pulled the canoe up,
and we again proceeded.   As we went on we constantly
encountered fresh difficulties.   Sometimes we had to cross
into the middle of the stream, to avoid some impassable mass
of rocks ; at others, the canoe was dragged and pushed in
narrow channels, which hardly allowed it to pass.   The Indians,
all naked, with their trousers tied round their loins, plunged
about in the water like fishes.   Sometimes a projecting crag
had to be reached with the tow-rope.   An Indian takes it in
his hand, and leaps into the rapid current : he is carried down
·by its irresistible force.   Now he dives to the bottom, and
there swims and crawls along where the stream has less
power.   After two or three trials he reaches the rock, and tries
to mount upon it ; but it rises high and abruptly out of the
water, and after several efforts he falls back exhausted, and
floats down again to the canoe amid the mirth and laughter
of his comrades.   Another now tries, with the same result.
Then another plunges in without the rope, and thus unen-
cumbered mounts on the rock and gives a helping hand to his
companion ; and then all go to work, and we are pulled up past
the obstacle.

   But a little ahead of us is an extensive mass of rocks.   There
is no passage for the canoe, and we must cross to yonder islet
far in the middle of the stream, where, by the height of the
water, Senhor L. and the pilot judge we shall find a passage.
Every stone, even those under water, form eddies or returning
currents, where a canoe can rest in its passage.   Off we go, to
try to reach one of them.   In a moment we are in a stream
running like a mill-race.   " Pull away, boys ! " shouts Senhor
L.   We are falling swiftly down the river.   There is a strong
rapid carrying us, and we shall be dashed against those black

masses just rising above the foaming waters. "All right, boys!" cries Senhor L.; and just as we seemed in the greatest danger, the canoe wheels round in an eddy, and we are safe under the shelter of a rock. We are in still water, but close on each side of us it rages and bubbles, and we must cross again. Now the Indians are rested; and so off we go,—down drops the canoe,—again the men strain at their paddles,— again we are close on some foaming breakers: I see no escape, but in a moment we are in an eddy caused by a sunken mass above us; again we go on, and reach at length our object, a rocky island, round which we pull and push our canoe, and from the upper point cross to another, and so make a zigzag course, until, after some hours' hard work, we at length reach the bank, perhaps not fifty yards above the obstacle which had obliged us to leave it.

Thus we proceeded, till, reaching a good resting-place about five in the afternoon, we stayed for the night to rest the Indians well, against the further fatigues to be encountered the following day.

Most of the principal rapids and falls have names. There are the "Furnos" (ovens), "Tabocal" (bamboo), and many others. The next day we went on in a similar manner to the day before, along a most picturesque part of the river. The brilliant sun, the sparkling waters, the strange fantastic rocks, and broken woody islands, were a constant source of interest and enjoyment to me. Early in the afternoon we reached the village of São Gabriel, where are the principal falls. Here the river is narrower, and an island in the middle divides it into two channels, along each of which rolls a tremendous flood of water down an incline formed by submerged rocks. Below, the water boils up in great rolling breakers, and, a little further down, forms dangerous eddies and whirlpools. Here we could only pass by unloading the canoe almost entirely, and then pulling it up amidst the foaming watér as near as possible to the shore. This done, Senhor L. and myself dressed, and proceeded up the hill to the house of the Commandante, who must give permission before any one can pass above the fort. He was a friend of Senhor L., and I brought him a letter of introduction; so he was pretty civil, gave us some coffee, chatted of the news of the river and the city for an hour or two, and invited us to breakfast with him before we left the next morning.  We then went to the house of an old Portuguese trader, whom I had met in Barra, with whom we supped and spent the evening.

The next morning, after breakfasting with the Commandante, we proceeded on our way.  Above São Gabriel the rapids are perhaps more numerous than below.  We twisted about the river, round islands and from rock to rock, in a most complicated manner.  On a point where we stayed for the night I saw the first tree-fern I had yet met with, and looked on it with much pleasure, as an introduction to a new and interesting district: it was a small, thin-stemmed, elegant species, about eight or ten feet high.  At night, on the 22nd, we passed the last rapid, and now had smooth water before us for the rest of our journey.  We had thus been four days ascending these rapids, which are about thirty miles in length.  The next morning we entered the great and unknown river "Uaupés," from which there is another branch into the Rio Negro, forming a delta at its mouth.  During our voyage I had heard much of this river from Senhor L., who was an old trader up it, and well acquainted with the numerous tribes of uncivilised Indians which inhabit its banks, and with the countless cataracts and rapids which render its navigation so dangerous and toilsome.  Above the Uaupés the Rio Negro was calm and placid, about a mile, or sometimes two to three miles wide, and its waters blacker than ever.

On the 24th of October, early in the morning, we reached the little village of Nossa Senhora da Guía, where Senhor L. resided, and where he invited me to remain with him as long as I felt disposed.

The village is situated on high ground sloping down suddenly to the river.  It consists of a row of thatched mud-huts, some of them whitewashed, others the colour of the native earth.  Immediately behind are some patches of low sandy ground, covered with a shrubby vegetation, and beyond is the virgin forest.  Senhor L.'s house had wooden doors, and shutters to the windows, as had also one or two others.  In fact, Guía was once a very populous and decent village, though now as poor and miserable as all the others of the Rio Negro.  Going up to the house I was introduced to Senhor L.'s family, which consisted of two grown-up daughters, two young ones, and a little boy of eight years old.  A good-looking "mamelúca," or half-breed woman, of about thirty, was introduced as the "mother of his younger children." Senhor L. had informed me during the voyage that he did not patronise marriage, and thought everybody a great fool who did. He had illustrated the advantages of keeping oneself free of such ties by informing me that the mother of his two elder daughters having grown old, and being unable to bring them up properly or teach them Portuguese, he had turned her out of doors, and got a younger and more civilised person in her place. The poor woman had since died of jealousy, or "passion," as he termed it. When young, she had nursed him during an eighteen months' illness and saved his life; but he seemed to think he had performed a duty in turning her away,—for, said he, "She was an Indian, and could only speak her own language, and, so long as she was with them, my children would never learn Portuguese."

The whole family welcomed him in a very cold and timid manner, coming up and asking his blessing as if they had parted from him the evening before, instead of three months since. We then had some coffee and breakfast; after which the canoe was unloaded, and a little house just opposite his, which happened to be unoccupied, was swept out for me. My boxes were placed in it, my hammock hung up, and I soon made myself comfortable in my new quarters, and then walked out to look about me.

In the village were about a dozen houses belonging to Indians, all of whom had their sitios, or country-houses, at from a few hours' to some days' distance up or down the river, or on some of the small tributary streams. They only inhabit the village at times of festas, or on the arrival of a merchant like Senhor L., when they bring any produce they may have to dispose of or, if they have none, get what goods they can on credit, with the promise of payment at some future time.

There were now several families in the village to welcome their sons and husbands, who had formed our crew; and for some days there was a general drinking and dancing from morning to night. During this time, I took my gun into the woods, in order to kill a few birds. Immediately behind the house were some fruit-trees, to which many chatterers and other pretty birds resorted, and I managed to shoot some every day. Insects were very scarce in the forest; but on the river-side there were often to be found rare butterflies, though not in sufficient abundance to give me much occupation. In a few days, Senhor L. got a couple of Indians to come and hunt for me, and I hoped then to have plenty of birds. They used the gravatána, or blow-pipe, a tube ten to fifteen feet in length, through which they blow small arrows with such force and precision, that they will kill birds or other game as far off, and with as much certainty, as with a gun. The arrows are all poisoned, so that a very small wound is sufficient to bring down a large bird. I soon found that my Indians had come at Senhor L.'s bidding, but did not much like their task ; and they frequently returned without any birds, telling me they could not find any, when I had very good reason to believe they had spent the day at some neighbouring sitio. At other times, after a day in the forest, they would bring a little worthless bird, which can be found around every cottage. As they had to go a great distance in search of good birds, I had no hold upon them, and was obliged to take what they brought me, and be contented. It was a great annoyance here, that there were no good paths in the forest, so that I could not go far myself, and in the immediate vicinity of the village there is little to be obtained.

I found it more easy to procure fishes, and was much pleased by being frequently able to add to my collection of drawings. The smaller species I also preserved in spirits. The electrical eel is common in all the streams here ; it is caught with a hook, or in weirs, and is eaten, though not much esteemed. When the water gets low, and leaves pools among the rocks, many fish are caught by poisoning the waters with a root called "timbo." The mouths of the small streams are also staked across, and large quantities of all kinds are obtained. The fish thus caught are very good when fresh, but putrefy sooner than those caught in weirs or hooked.

Not being able to do much here, I determined to take a trip up a small stream to a place where, on a lonely granite mountain, the "Cocks of the Rock" are found. An Indian, who could speak a little Portuguese, having come from a village near it, I agreed to return with him. Senhor L. lent me a small canoe ; and my two hunters, one of whom lived there, accompanied me. I took with me plenty of ammunition, a great box for my birds, some salt, hooks, mirrors, knives, etc., for the Indians, and left Guía early one morning. Just below the village we turned into the river Isanna, a fine stream, about half a mile wide, and in the afternoon reached the mouth of the small river Cobati (fish), on the south side, which we entered.   We had hitherto seen the banks clothed with thick virgin forest, and here and there were some low hills covered entirely with lofty trees.   Now the country became very bushy and scrubby ; in parts sandy and almost open ; perfectly flat, and apparently inundated at the high floods. The water was of a more inky blackness ; and the little stream, not more than fifty yards wide, flowed with a rapid current, and turned and doubled in a manner that made our progress both difficult and tedious.   At night we stopped at a little piece of open sandy ground, where we drove stakes in the earth to hang our hammocks.   The next morning at daybreak we continued our journey.   The whole day long we wound about, the stream keeping up exactly the same bleak character as before ;—not a tree of any size visible, and the vegetation of a most monotonous and dreary character,   At night we stayed near a lake, where the Indians caught some fine fish, and we made a good supper.   The next day we wound about more than ever ; often, after an hour's hard rowing, returning to within fifty yards of a point we had started from.   At length, however, early in the afternoon, the aspect of the country suddenly changed ; lofty trees sprang up on the banks, the characteristic creepers hung in festoons over them ; moss-covered rocks appeared ; and from the river gradually rose up a slope of luxuriant virgin forest, whose varied shades of green and glistening foliage were most grateful to the eye and the imagination, after the dull, monotonous vegetation of the previous days.

In half an hour more we were at the village, which consisted of five or six miserable little huts imbedded in the forest. Here I was introduced to my conductor's house.   It contained two rooms, with a floor of earth, and smoky thatch overhead. There were three doors, but no windows.   Near one of these I placed my bird-box, to serve as a table, and on the other side swung my hammock.   We then took a little walk to look about us.   Paths led to the different cottages, in which were large families of naked children, and their almost naked parents.   Most of the houses had no walls, but were mere thatched sheds supported on posts, and with sometimes a smal room enclosed with a palm-leaf fence, to make a sleeping apartment. There were several young boys here of from ten to fifteen years of age, who were my constant attendants when I went into the forest. None of them could speak a single word of Portuguese, so I had to make use of my slender stock of Lingoa Geral. But Indian boys are not great talkers, and a few monosyllables would generally suffice for our communications. One or two of them had blow-pipes, and shot numbers of small birds for me, while others would creep along by my side and silently point out birds, or small animals, before I could catch sight of them. When I fired, and, as was often the case, the bird flew away wounded, and then fell far off in the forest, they would bound away after it, and seldom search in vain. Even a little humming-bird, falling in a dense thicket of creepers and dead leaves, which I should have given up looking for in despair, was always found by them.

One day I accompanied the Indian with whom I lived into the forest, to get stems for a blow-pipe. We went, about a mile off, to a place where numerous small palms were growing: they were the *Iriartea setigera* of Martius, from ten to fifteen feet high, and varying from the thickness of one's finger to two inches in diameter. They appear jointed outside, from the scars of the fallen leaves, but within have a soft pith, which, when cleared out, leaves a smooth, polished bore. My companion selected several of the straightest he could find, both of the smallest and largest diameter. These stems were carefully dried in the house, the pith cleared out with a long rod made of the wood of another palm, and the bore rubbed clean and polished with a little bunch of roots of a tree-fern, pulled backwards and forwards through it. Two stems are selected of such a size, that the smaller can be pushed inside the larger; this is done, so that any curve in the one may counteract that in the other; a conical wooden mouthpiece is then fitted on to one end, and sometimes the whole is spirally bound with the smooth, black, shining bark of a creeper. Arrows are made of the spinous processes of the Patawá (*Œnocarpus Batawa*) pointed, and anointed with poison, and with a little conical tuft of tree cotton (the silky covering of the seeds of a *Bombax*) at the other end, to fill up exactly, but not tightly, the bore of the tube: these arrows are carried in a wicker quiver, well covered with pitch at the lower part, so that it can be inverted in wet weather to keep the arrows dry. The blow-pipe, or gravatána, is the principal weapon here. Every Indian has one, and seldom goes into the forest, or on the rivers, without it.

I soon found that the Cocks of the Rock, to obtain which was my chief object in coming here, were not to be found near the village. Their principal resort was the Serra de Cobáti, or mountain before mentioned, situated some ten or twelve miles off in the forest, where I was informed they were very abundant. I accordingly made arrangements for a trip to the Serra, with the intention of staying there a week. By the promise of good payment for every "Gallo" they killed for me, I persuaded almost the whole male population of the village to accompany me. As our path was through a dense forest for ten miles, we could not load ourselves with much baggage : every man had to carry his gravatána, bow and arrows, *rédé,* and some farinha ; which, with salt, was all the provisions we took, trusting to the forest for our meat ; and I even gave up my daily and only luxury of coffee.

We started off, thirteen in number, along a tolerable path. In about an hour we came to a mandiocca-field and a house, the last on the road to the Serra. Here we waited a short time, took some "mingau," or gruel, made of green plantains, and got a volunteer to join our company. I was much struck with an old woman whose whole body was one mass of close deep wrinkles, and whose hair was white, a sure sign of very great age in an Indian ; from information I obtained, I believe she was more than a hundred years old. There was also a young "mamelúca," very fair and handsome, and of a particularly intelligent expression of countenance, very rarely seen in that mixed race. The moment I saw her I had little doubt of her being a person of whom I had heard Senhor L. speak as the daughter of the celebrated German naturalist, Dr. Natterer, by an Indian woman. I afterwards saw her at Guía, and ascertained that my supposition was correct. She was about seventeen years of age, was married to an Indian, and had several children. She was a fine specimen of the noble race produced by the mixture of the Saxon and Indian blood.

Proceeding onwards, we came to another recently-cleared mandiocca-field. Here the path was quite obliterated, and we had to cross over it as we could. Imagine the trees of a virgin forest cut down so as to fall across each other in every conceivable direction. After lying a few months they are burnt; the fire, however, only consumes the leaves and fine twigs and branches; all the rest remains entire, but blackened and charred. The mandiocca is then planted without any further preparation; and it was across such a field that we, all heavily laden, had to find our way. Now climbing on the top of some huge trunk, now walking over a shaking branch or creeping among a confused thicket of charcoal, few journeys require more equanimity of temper than one across an Amazonian clearing.

Passing this, we got into the forest. At first the path was tolerable; soon, however, it was a mere track a few inches wide, winding among thorny creepers, and over deep beds of decaying leaves. Gigantic buttress trees, tall fluted stems, strange palms, and elegant tree-ferns were abundant on every side, and many persons may suppose that our walk must necessarily have been a delightful one; but there were many disagreeables. Hard roots rose up in ridges along our path, swamp and mud alternated with quartz pebbles and rotten leaves; and as I floundered along in the barefooted enjoyment of these, some overhanging bough would knock the cap from my head or the gun from my hand; or the hooked spines of the climbing palms would catch in my shirt-sleeves, and oblige me either to halt and deliberately unhook myself, or leave a portion of my unlucky garment behind. The Indians were all naked, or, if they had a shirt or trousers, carried them in a bundle on their heads, and I have no doubt looked upon me as a good illustration of the uselessness and bad conse quences of wearing clothes upon a forest journey.

After four or five hours' hard walking, at a pace which would not have been bad upon clear level ground, we came to a small stream of clear water, which had its source in the Serra to which we were going. Here we waited a few moments to rest and drink, while doing which we heard a strange rush and distant grunt in the forest. The Indians started up, all excitement and animation: "Tyeassú!" (wild hogs) they cried, seizing their bows and arrows, tightening the strings, and grasping their long knives. I cocked my gun, dropped in a bullet, and hoped to get a shot at a "porco;" but being afraid, if I went with them, of losing myself in the forest, I waited with the boys in hopes the game would pass near me. After a little time we heard a rushing and fearful gnashing of teeth, which made me stand anxiously expecting the animals to appear; but the sound went further off, and died away at length in the distance.

The party now appeared, and said that there was a large herd of fine pigs, but that they had got away. They, however, directed the boys to go on with me to the Serra, and they would go again after the herd. We went on accordingly over very rough, uneven ground, now climbing up steep ascents over rotting trunks of fallen trees, now descending into gullies, till at length we reached a curious rock—a huge table twenty or thirty feet in diameter, supported on two points only, and forming an excellent cave; round the outer edge we could stand upright under it, but towards the centre the roof was so low that one could only lie down. The top of this singular rock was nearly flat, and completely covered with forest-trees, and it at first seemed as if their weight must overbalance it from its two small supports; but the roots of the trees, not finding nourishment enough from the little earth on the top of the rock, ran along it to the edge, and there dropped down vertically and penetrated among the broken fragments below, thus forming a series of columns of various sizes supporting the table all round its outer edge. Here, the boys said, was to be our abode during our stay, though I did not perceive any water near it. Through the trees we could see the mountain a quarter or half a mile from us,—a bare, perpendicular mass of granite, rising abruptly from the forest to a height of several hundred feet.

We had hung up our *rédés* and waited about half an hour, when three Indians of our party made their appearance, staggering under the weight of a fine hog they had killed, and had slung on a strong pole. I then found the boys had mistaken our station, which was some distance further on, at the very foot of the Serra, and close to a running stream of water, where was a large roomy cave formed by an immense overhanging rock. Over our heads was growing a forest, and the roots again hung down over the edge, forming a sort of screen to our cave, and the stronger ones serving for posts to hang our redes. Our luggage was soon unpacked, our *rédés* hung, a fire lighted, and the pig taken down to the brook, which ran at the lower end of the cave, to be skinned and prepared for cooking.

The animal was very like a domestic pig, but with a higher back, coarser and longer bristles, and a most penetrating odour. This I found proceeded from a gland situated on the back, about six inches above the root of the tail: it was a swelling, with a large pore in the centre, from which exuded an oily matter, producing a most intense and unbearable pigsty smell, of which the domestic animal can convey but a faint idea. The first operation of the Indians was to cut out this part completely, and the skin and flesh for some inches all round it, and throw the piece away. If this were not done, they say, the "pitiú" (*catinga*, Port.), or bad smell, would render all the meat uneatable. The animal was then skinned, cut up into pieces, some of which were put into an earthen pot to stew, while the legs and shoulders were kept to smoke over the fire till they were thoroughly dry, as they can thus be preserved several weeks without salt.

The greater number of the party had not yet arrived, so we ate our suppers, expecting to see them soon after sunset. However, as they did not appear, we made up our fires, put the meat on the "moqueen," or smoking stage, and turned comfortably into our *rédés*. The next morning, while we were preparing breakfast, they all arrived, with the produce of their hunting expedition. They had killed three hogs, but as it was late and they were a long way off, they encamped for the night, cut up the animals, and partially smoked all the prime pieces, which they now brought with them carefully packed up in palmleaves. The party had no bows and arrows, but had killed the game with their blow-pipes, and little poisoned arrows about ten inches long.

After breakfast was over we prepared for an attack upon the "Gallos." We divided into three parties, going in different directions. The party which I accompanied went to ascend the Serra itself as far as practicable. We started out at the back of our cave, which was, as I have stated, formed by the base of the mountain itself. We immediately commenced the ascent up rocky gorges, over huge fragments, and through gloomy caverns, all mixed together in the most extraordinary confusion. Sometimes we had to climb up precipices by roots and creepers, then to crawl over a surface formed by angular rocks, varying from the size of a wheelbarrow to that of a house.   I could not have imagined that what at a distance appeared so insignificant, could have presented such a gigantic and rugged scene.   All the time we kept a sharp look-out, but saw no birds.   At length, however, an old Indian caught hold of my arm, and whispering gently, " Gallo ! " pointed into a dense thicket.   After looking intently a little while, I caught a glimpse of the magnificent bird sitting amidst the gloom, shining out like a mass of brilliant flame.   I took a step to get a clear view of it, and raised my gun, when it took alarm and flew off before I had time to fire.   We followed, and soon it was again pointed out to me.   This time I had better luck, fired with a steady aim, and brought it down.   The Indians rushed forward, but it had fallen into a deep gully between steep rocks, and a considerable circuit had to be made to get it.   In a few minutes, however, it was brought to me, and I was lost in admiration of the dazzling brilliancy of its soft downy feathers.   Not a spot of blood was visible, not a feather was ruffled, and the soft, warm, flexible body set off the fresh swelling plumage in a manner which no stuffed specimen can approach.   After some time, not finding any more gallos, most of the party set off on an excursion up a more impracticable portion of the rock, leaving two boys with me till they returned. We soon got tired of waiting, and as the boys made me understand that they knew the path back to our cave, I determined to return.   We descended deep chasms in the rocks, climbed up steep precipices, descended again and again, and passed through caverns with huge masses of rocks piled above our heads.   Still we seemed not to get out of the mountain, but fresh ridges rose before us, and more fearful fissures were to be passed.   We toiled on, now climbing by roots and creepers up perpendicular walls, now creeping along a narrow ledge, with a yawning chasm on each side of us.   I could not have imagined such serrated rocks to exist.   It appeared as if a steep mountain-side had been cut and hacked by some gigantic force · into fissures and ravines, from fifty to a hundred feet deep.   My gun was a most inconvenient load when climbing up these steep and slippery places, and I did it much damage by striking its muzzle against the hard granite rock.   At length we appeared to have got into the very heart of the mountain : no outlet was visible, and through the dense forest and matted underwood, with which every part of these rocks were covered, we could only see an interminable succession of ridges, and chasms, and gigantic blocks of stone, with no visible termination. As it was evident the boys had lost their way, I resolved to turn back. It was a weary task. I was already fatigued enough, and the prospect of another climb over these fearful ridges, and hazardous descent into those gloomy chasms, was by no means agreeable. However, we persevered, one boy taking my gun ; and after about an hour's hard work we got back to the place whence we had started, and found the rest of the party expecting us. We then went down by the proper

path, which they told me was the only known way of ascending and descending the mountain, and by which we soon arrived at our cave.

The accompanying sketch gives a section of this mountain, as near as I can make it out. The extraordinary jaggedness of the rocks is not at all exaggerated, and is the more surprising when you get into it, because from a distance it appears one smooth forest-covered hill, of very inconsiderable height, and of a gradual slope. Besides the great caverns and ridges shown above, the surfaces of each precipice are serrated in a most extraordinary manner, forming deep sloping gutters, cut out of the smooth face of the rock, or sometimes vertical channels, with angular edges, such as might be supposed to be formed were the granite in a plastic state forced up against hard angular masses.

On reaching the cave I immediately skinned my prize before it was dark, and we then got our supper. No more "gallos" were brought in that day. The fires were made up, the pork put to smoke over them, and around me were thirteen naked Indians, talking in unknown tongues. Two only could speak a little Portuguese, and with them I conversed, answering their various questions about where iron came from, and how calico was made, and if paper grew in my country, and if we had much mandiocca and plantains ; and they were greatly astonished to hear that all were white men there, and could not imagine how white men could work, or how there could be a country without forest. They would ask strange questions about where the wind came from, and the rain, and how the sun and moon got back to their places again after disappearing from us ; and when I had tried to satisfy them on these points, they would tell me forest tales of jaguars and pumas, and of the fierce wild hogs, and of the dreadful curupurí, the demon of the woods, and of the wild man with a long tail, found far in the centre of the forest. They told me also a curious tale about the tapir, which, however, others have assured me is not true.

The tapir, they say, has a peculiar fancy for dropping his dung only in the water, and they never find it except in brooks and springs, though it is so large and abundant that it could not be overlooked in the forest. If there is no water to be found, the animal makes a rough basket of leaves and carries it to the nearest stream, and there deposits it. The Indians' tale goes, that one tapir met another in the forest with a basket in his mouth. "What have you in your basket ? " said the one. "Fruit," answered the other. "Let me have some," said the first. "I won't," said the other ; upon which the first tapir pulled the basket from the other's mouth, broke it open, and on seeing the contents both turned tail, quite ashamed of themselves, ran away in opposite directions, and never came near the spot again all their lives.

With such conversation we passed the time till we fell asleep. We rose with the earliest dawn, for the naked Indian feels the chill morning air, and gets up early to renew his fire, and make some mingau to warm himself. Having no coffee, I had to put up also with "mingau" (farinha gruel), and we then all started off again in search of game. This time I took the forest, having had enough of the Serra, and the two boys came with me for guides and companions. After wandering about a good way we found some fine curassow-birds high up in lofty trees, and succeeded in shooting one. This, with a large jacamar, was all we could find, so we returned to the cave, skinned the jacamar, and put the "mutun" (curassow-bird) on the fire for breakfast.

In the afternoon the other parties returned unsuccessful, one only bringing in a gallo. The next day nothing at all was met with, and it was therefore agreed to move our camp to a spot some miles off on the other side of the Serra, where was a feeding-place of the gallos. We accordingly started ; and if our former path was bad enough, this was detestable. It was principally through second-growth woods, which are much thicker than the virgin forest, full of prickly plants, entangled creepers, and alternations of soft mud and quartz pebbles under foot. As our farinha was getting low, we had sent half our party home, to bring such a supply as would enable us to remain a week in our new camp.

On reaching the place we found a pleasant open glade and low woods, where there had formerly been a small Indian settlement. It was much more airy and agreeable than our cave, so closely surrounded by the tall dense forest that scarcely a straggling ray of sunshine could enter. Here were numerous trees of a species of *Melastoma*, bearing purple berries, of which the gallos and many other birds are very fond. There was a little shed, just large enough to hang my hammock under ; this we repaired and thatched, and made our head-quarters, where I soon established myself comfortably. We had not been here long before we heard the shrill cry of a gallo near us. All immediately started off, and I soon had the pleasure of again seeing this living flame darting among the foliage. My gun, however, had been wetted in walking so far through the dripping underwood, and missed fire. In the evening two fine birds were brought in,—a very satisfactory commencement. The next evening the party who had gone to the village returned with farinha, salt, and a few mammee apples, which were very refreshing.

We stayed here four days longer, with various success :

some days we had not a bird; others, plenty of game, and one or two gallos. What with monkeys, guans, and mutuns, we had pretty good fare in the meat way. One day I went out alone, and by patiently watching under a fruit-tree, in a drenching shower, was rewarded by obtaining another beautiful gallo. Two were brought in alive: one of them I killed and skinned at once, knowing the great risk of attempting to keep them alive; the other was kept by the Indian who caught it, but a few weeks afterwards it died. They are caught by snares at certain places, where the males assemble to play. These places are on rocks, or roots of trees, and are worn quite smooth and clean. Two or three males meet and perform a kind of dance, walking and jigging up and down. The females and young are never seen at these places, so that you are sure of catching only full-grown fine-plumaged males. I am not aware of any other bird that has this singular habit. On the last day of our stay, we were rather short of provisions. The Indians supped well off a young alligator they had caught in a brook near; but the musky odour was so strong that I could not stomach it, and, after getting down a bit of the tail, finished my supper with mingau.

The next day we returned home to the little village. With twelve hunters, nine days in the forest, I had obtained twelve gallos, two of which I had shot myself; I had, besides, two fine trogons, several little blue-capped manakins, and some curious barbets, and ant-thrushes.

At the village I spent nearly a fortnight more, getting together a good many small birds, but nothing very rare. I shot a specimen of the curious bald-headed brown crow (*Gymnocephalus calvus*), which, though common in Cayenne, is very rare in the Rio Negro district; nobody, in fact, but the Indians, had ever seen the bird, and they regarded it as my greatest curiosity. I also skinned a black agouti, and made drawings of many curious fish.

The Padre having come to Guía, most of the Indians returned with me to attend the festa, and get their children baptized. When we arrived, however, we found that he had left for the villages higher up, and was to call on his return. I now wished to set off as soon as possible for the Upper Rio Negro, in Venezuela; but of course no Indian could be got to go with me till the Padre returned, and I was obliged to wait patiently and idly at Guia. For days I would go out into the forest, and not get a bird worth skinning; insects were equally scarce. The forest was gloomy, damp, and silent as death. Every other day was wet, and almost every afternoon there was a thunderstorm : and on these dull days and weary evenings, I had no resource but the oft-told tales of Senhor L., and the hackneyed conversation on buying and selling calico, on digging salsa, and cutting piassaba.

At length, however, the Padré, Frei Jozé, arrived with Senhor Tenente Filisberto, the Commandante of Marabitanas. Frei Jozé dos Santos Innocentos was a tall, thin, prematurely old man, thoroughly worn out by every kind of debauchery, his hands crippled, and his body ulcerated; yet he still delighted in recounting the feats of his youth, and was celebrated as the most original and amusing story-teller in the province of Pará. He was carried up the hill, from the river-side, in a hammock; and took a couple of days to rest, before he commenced his ecclesiastical operations. I often went with Senhor L. to visit him, and was always much amused with his inexhaustible fund of anecdotes : he seemed to know everybody and everything in the Province, and had always something humorous to tell about them. His stories were, most of them, disgustingly coarse; but so cleverly told, in such quaint and expressive language, and with such amusing imitations of voice and manner, that they were irresistibly ludicrous. There is always, too, a particular charm in hearing good anecdotes in a foreign language. The point is the more interesting, from the obscure method of arriving at it; and the knowledge you acquire of the various modes of using the peculiar idioms of the language, causes a pleasure quite distinct from that of the story itself. Frei Jozé never repeated a story twice in the week he was with us; and Senhor L., who has known him for years, says he had never before heard many of the anecdotes he now related. He had been a soldier, then a friar in a convent, and afterwards a parish priest: he told tales of his convent life, just like what we read in Chaucer of their doings in his time. Don Juan was an innocent compared with Frei Jozé; but he told us he had a great respect for his cloth, and never did anything disreputable—*during the day !*

At length the baptisms took place : there were some fifteen or twenty Indian children of all ages, to undergo the operation at once. There are seven or eight distinct processes in the Roman Catholic baptism, well calculated to attract the attention of the Indians : there is water and holy oil,—and spittle rubbed on the eyes,—and crosses on the eyes, nose, mouth, and body, —and kneeling and prayers in between, which all bear sufficient resemblance to the complicated operations of their own "pagés" (conjurors), to make them think they have got something very good, in return for the shilling they pay for the ceremony.

The next day there were a few weddings, the ceremony of which is very like our own. After it was over, Frei Jozé gave the newly married people a very good and practical homily on the duties of the married state, which might have done some good, had the parties to whom it was addressed understood it; which, as it was in Portuguese, they did not. He at all times strenuously exhorted the Indians to get married, and thus save their souls,—and fill his pocket. The only two white men, besides myself, were, however, bad examples,—for they were not, nor would be married, though they both had large families ; which the Padré got over by saying, "Never mind what these white people do, they will all go to purgatory, but don't you be such fools as to go too !" at which Senhor L. and the Commandante laughed heartily, and the poor Indians looked much astonished.

# CHAPTER IX.

## JAVITA.

Leave Guía—Marabitánas—Serra de Cocoí—Enter Venezuela—São
Carlos—Pass the Cassiquiare—Antonio Dias—Indian Shipbuilders
—Feather-work—Maróa and Pimichín—A Black Jaguar—Poisonous
Serpents—Fishing—Walk to Javíta—Residence there—Indian Road-
makers—Language and Customs—A Description of Javíta—Run-
away Indians—Collections at Javíta—Return to Tómo—A Domestic
Broil—Marabitánas, and its Inhabitants—Reach Guía.

WHEN at length our visitors were gone, I commenced
arrangements for my voyage further up the country.

Senhor L. lent me a canoe, and I had four Indians to go
with me, only one of whom, an old man named Augustinho,
could speak a little broken Portuguese. I took with me my
watch, sextant, and compass, insect- and bird-boxes, gun and
ammunition, with salt, beads, fish-hooks, calico, and coarse
cotton cloth for the Indians. My men all had their gravatánas
and quivers of poisoned arrows, a pair of trousers, shirt,
paddle, knife, tinder-box, and *rédé*, which comprise the whole
assortment of an Indian's baggage.

On the 27th of January, 1851, we left Guía, paddling up
against the stream. The canoe had been fresh caulked, but
still I found it leaking so much, as to keep me constantly
baling ; and in the afternoon, when we stayed for dinner, I made
an examination, and found out the cause of the leakage. The
cargo was heavy and was supported on a little stage, or floor,
resting upon cross-bearers in the bottom of the canoe ; the
ends of these bearers had been carelessly placed just on a seam,
so that the whole weight of the cargo tended to force out the
plank, and thus produce the leak. I was accordingly obliged
to unload the boat entirely, and replace the bearers in a better
position, after which I was glad to find the leak much
diminished.

On the 28th, in the afternoon, we arrived at the little village of Mabé, which we reached in very good time, for the inhabitants had just returned from a fishing expedition : they had procured a great quantity of fish by poisoning an igaripé near, and I purchased enough for our supper and breakfast.   I found several which I had not seen before; among them, a most curious little species allied to *Centrarcus,* called the butterfly fish, from the extraordinary development of its fins, and pretty banded markings.

On the 29th, about noon, we passed the mouth of the river Xié, a black-water stream of moderate size and no great length.   There is little trade up it, and the Indians inhabiting it are uncivilised and almost unknown.

On the 30th we came in sight of the Serras of the Cababurís, and the long row of hills called Pirapucó (the long fish) : they consist of lofty and isolated granite peaks, like those generally found in this district.   The next day we reached Marabitánas, the frontier fort of Brazil : there is now only the remnant of a mud entrenchment, and a small detachment of soldiers.   As the Commandante was not there, we did not stay, except to purchase a few plantains.

On the 1st of February we reached the Serra of Cocoí, which marks the boundary between Brazil and Venezuela.   This is a granite rock, very precipitous and forming nearly a square frustum of a prism, about a thousand feet high.   It rises at once out of the forest plain, and is itself, on the summit and the less precipitous portions, covered with thick wood.   Here the piums, or little biting flies, swarm and made us very uncomfortable for the rest of the day.   We had now beautiful weather, and in the evening slept on a fine granite beach very comfortably.   The next night we stayed at a rock on which we found some curious figures engraven below high-water mark. Here having a clear horizon up the river to the north, I saw my old friend the pole-star, though I was only in 1° 20′ north latitude.   We had now every day fine rocky beaches, along which I often walked, while young Luiz would shoot fish for us with his bow and arrow.   He was very skilful, and always had his bow by his side, and as we approached a rock or shallow would fit his arrow and send it into some glittering acarrá or bright-coloured tucunaré.

At length, on the afternoon of the 4th of February, we

arrived at São Carlos, the principal Venezuelan village on the Rio Negro. This was the furthest point reached by Humboldt from an opposite direction, and I was therefore now entering upon ground gone over fifty years before by that illustrious traveller. At the landing-place I was agreeably surprised to see a young Portuguese I had met at Guia, and as he was going up the river to Tomo in a day or two, I agreed to wait and take him with me. I went with him to the house of the Commissario, got introduced, and commenced my acquaintance with the Spanish language. I was civilly received, and found myself in the midst of a party of loosely-dressed gentlemen, holding a conversation on things in general. I found some difficulty in making out anything, both from the peculiarity of accent and the number of new words constantly occurring; for though Spanish is very similar to Portuguese in the verbs, pronouns, and adjectives, the nouns are mostly different, and the accent and pronunciation peculiar.

We took our meals at the Commissario's table, and with every meal had coffee, which custom I rather liked. The next day I walked into the forest along the road to Soláno, a villageon the Cassiquiare. I found a dry, sandy soil, but with very few insects. The village of São Carlos is laid out with a large square, and parallel streets. The principal house, called the Convento, where the priests used to reside, is now occupied by the Commissario. The square is kept clean, the houses whitewashed, and altogether the village is much neater than those of Brazil. Every morning the bell rings for matins, and the young girls and boys assemble in the church and sing a few hymns; the same takes place in the evening; and on Sundays the church is always opened, and service performed by the Commissario and the Indians.

Soon after leaving the village we passed the mouth of the Cassiquiare, that singular stream which connects the Rio Negro with the Orinooko near the sources of both. It is a mixture of white and black water, and swarms with piuñs, which are abundant down to São Carlos; but on passing the mouth of the Cassiquiare they cease immediately, and up to the sources of the Rio Negro there is a freedom at least from this pest. In the evening we stayed at an Indian cottage, and bought a fine cabeçudo, or big-headed turtle, for a basin of salt: it furnished us with an excellent supper for eight persons, and even the next day we did not finish it all. The weather was now hot, and brilliantly fine, contrasting much with the constant rains of Guía ; and, marvellous to relate, the people here told us they had not had any rain for three months past. The effects were seen in the river, which was very low and still falling, and so full of rocks and shallows as to render it sometimes difficult for us to find a passage for our canoes.

After passing the village of São Miguel these difficulties increased, till we came to a place where the whole channel, a mile wide, appeared but one bed of rocks, with nowhere water enough for our canoe to pass, though eighteen inches would have sufficed. We went wandering about over this rocky plain in search of some opening, and after much difficulty succeeded in pushing and dragging our boat over the rocks. We passed by two or three " Caños," or channels leading to the Cassiquiare, up which many of the inhabitants were now going, to lay in a stock of fish and cabeçudos against the " tiempo del faminto " (time of famine), as the wet season is called, when but little fish and game are to be obtained.

On the 10th of February we reached Tómo, a village at the mouth of a stream of the same name. The inhabitants are all Indians, except one white man, a Portuguese, named Antonio Dias, of whom I had heard much at Barra. I found him in his shirt and trousers, covered with dust and perspiration, having just been assisting his men at their work at some canoes he was building. He received me kindly, with a strange mixture of Portuguese and Spanish, and got the " casa de nação," or stranger's house, a mere dirty shed, swept out for my accommodation for a few days. Like most of the white men in this neighbourhood, he is occupied entirely in building large canoes and schooners for the Rio Negro and Amazon trade. When finished, the hulls alone are taken down to Barra or to Pará, generally with a cargo of piassába or farinha, and there sold. He had now one on the stocks, of near two hundred tons burden ; but most of them are from thirty to a hundred tons. These large vessels have to be taken down the cataracts of the Rio Negro, which can only be done in the wet season, when the water is deep.

It seems astonishing how such large vessels can be constructed by persons entirely ignorant of the principles of naval architecture. They are altogether made by the Indians without drawing or design.   During the time when Brazil and Venezuela were under the Portuguese and Spanish governments, building-yards were established in several places where good timber was to be found, and the Indians were employed, under naval architects from Spain and Portugal, in the construction of vessels for the coast and inland trade.   When the independence of these countries took place, all such establishments were broken up, and a long succession of revolutions and disturbances occurred.   The Indians employed had, however, learnt an art they did not forget, but taught it to their children and countrymen.   By eye and hand alone they will form the framework and fit on the planks of fine little vessels of a hundred tons or more, with no other tools than axe, adze, and hammer.   Many a Portuguese, who has scarcely ever seen a boat except during his passage to Brazil, gets together half-a-dozen Indians with some old Indian carpenter at their head, buys a dozen axes and a few thousands of nails, and sets up as a shipbuilder.   The products of the Upper Rio Negro, principally piassába, pitch, and farinha, are bulky, and require large vessels to take them down, but their value in iron and cotton goods can be brought up again in a very small canoe.   Large vessels, too, cannot possibly return up the cataracts.   Those made on the Upper Rio Negro, therefore, never return there, and the small traders require a new one annually.   They are used below in the navigation of the Amazon, and of all its branches not obstructed by falls or rapids.   The vessels are made very cheaply and roughly, and seldom of the best timbers, which are difficult to obtain in sufficient quantity.   On an average these canoes do not last more than six or eight years,— many not more than two or three, though there are woods which will stand for thirty years perfectly sound.   Owing to these peculiar circumstances, there is a constant demand for these Spanish vessels, as they are called ; and the villages of São Carlos, Tiriquím, São Miguel, Tómo, and Maróa are entirely inhabited by builders of canoes.

While I was at Tómo the village was being cleaned, by scraping off the turf and weeds wherever they appeared within the limits of the houses.   The people show an instance of their peculiar delicacy in this work: they will not touch any spot on which there lies a piece of dung of a dog or any animal, or the body of any dead bird or reptile, but hoe carefully around it, and leave a little circular tuft of grass marking the spot where all such impurities exist. This is partly owing to a kind of superstition; but in many other ways they show a dislike to touch, however remotely, any offensive animal substance. This idea is carried so far as to lead them sometimes to neglect the sick in any offensive disease. It seems to be a kind of feeling very similar to that which exists in many animals, with regard to the sick and the dying.

Senhor Antonio Dias was rather notorious, even in this country of loose morals, for his patriarchal propensities, his harem consisting of a mother and daughter and two Indian girls, all of whom he keeps employed at feather-work, which they do with great skill,—Senhor Antonio himself, who has some taste in design, making out the patterns. The cocks of the rock, white herons, roseate spoonbills, golden jacamars, metallic trogons, and exquisite little seven-coloured tanagers, with many gay parrots, and other beautiful birds, offer an assortment of colours capable of producing the most exquisite effects. The work is principally applied to the borders or fringes of hammocks. The hammocks themselves are of finely netted palm-fibre string, dyed of red, yellow, green, and other brilliant colours. The fringes are about a foot deep, also finely netted, of the same material, and on these are stuck, with the milk of the cow-tree, sprays and stars and flowers of feather-work. In the best he puts in the centre the arms of Portugal or Brazil beautifully executed; and the whole, on a ground of the snowy white heron's feathers, has a very pleasing effect.

Senhor Antonio informed me, that, owing to the lowness of the water, I could not go on any further in my canoe, and must therefore get an Indian *obá*, of one piece of wood, to stand the scraping over the rocks up to Pimichin; so, on the 13th, I left Tómo with Senhor Antonio in his canoe, for Maroa, a village a few miles above, where I hoped to get an obá suited for the remainder of the journey. This was a large village, entirely inhabited by Indians, and with an Indian Commissario, who could read and write, and was quite fashionably dressed in patent-leather boots, trousers, and straps. I here got an obá, lent me by a Gallician trader, and took two Indians with me from the place to bring it back. Senhor Antonio returned to Tómo, and about three P.M. I started on my journey in my little tottering canoe.

About a mile above Maróa, we reached the entrance of the little river Pimichín, up which we were to ascend. At the very mouth was a rock filling up the channel, and we had great difficulty in passing. We then had deep water for some distance, but came again to rocks and reedy shallows, where our heavily-laden canoe was only got over by great exertions. At night we reached a fine sandy beach, where we stayed, but had not been fortunate enough to get any fish, so had nothing for supper but farinha mingau and a cup of coffee ; and I then hung my hammock under a little palm-leaf shed, that had been made by some former traveller.

Our breakfast was a repetition of our supper, and we again started onwards, but every half hour had to stop and partly unload our boat, and drag it over some impediment. In many places there was a smooth ledge of rock with only a little water trickling over it, or a series of steps forming minature cascades. The stream was now sunk in a little channel or ravine fifteen or twenty feet deep, and with an interminable succession of turnings and windings towards every point of the compass. At length, late in the evening, we reached the port of Pimichín, formerly a village, but now containing only two houses. We found an old shed without doors and with a leaky roof—the traveller's house—of which we took possession.

Our canoe being unloaded, I went to one of the cottages to forage, and found a Portuguese deserter, a very civil fellow, who gave me the only eatable thing he had in the house, which was a piece of smoke-dried fish, as hard as a board and as tough as leather. This I gave to the Indians, and got him to come and take a cup of coffee with me, which, though he had some coffee-trees around his house, was still quite a treat, as he had no sugar or molasses. From this place a road leads overland about ten miles through the forest to Javíta, a village on the Témi, a branch of the Atabapo, which flows into the Orinooko. Finding that I could get nothing to eat here, I could not remain, as I had at first intended, but was obliged to get my things all carried by road to Javíta, and determined to walk over the next day to see about getting men to do it. In the evening I took my gun, and strolled along the road a little way into the forest, at the place I had so long looked forward to reaching, and was rewarded by falling in with one of the lords of the soil, which I had long wished to encounter.

As I was walking quietly along I saw a large jet-black animal come out of the forest about twenty yards before me, which took me so much by surprise that I did not at first imagine what it was. As it moved slowly on, and its whole body and long curving tail came into full view in the middle of the road, I saw that it was a fine black jaguar. I involuntarily raised my gun to my shoulder, but remembering that both barrels were loaded with small shot, and that to fire would exasperate without killing him, I stood silently gazing. In the middle of the road he turned his head, and for an instant paused and gazed at me, but having, I suppose, other business of his own to attend to, walked steadily on, and disappeared in the thicket. As he advanced, I heard the scampering of small animals, and the whizzing flight of ground birds, clearing the path for their dreaded enemy.

This encounter pleased me much. I was too much surprised, and occupied too much with admiration, to feel fear. I had at length had a full view, in his native wilds, of the rarest variety of the most powerful and dangerous animal inhabiting the American continent. I was, however, by no means desirous of a second meeting, and, as it was near sunset, thought it most prudent to turn back towards the village.

The next morning I sent all my Indians to fish, and walked myself along the road to Javíta, and thus crossed the division between the basins of the Amazon and the Orinooko. The road is, generally speaking, level, consisting of a series of slight ascents and descents, nowhere probably varying more than fifty feet in elevation, and a great part of it being over swamps and marshes, where numerous small streams intersect it. At those places roughly squared trunks of trees are laid down longitudinally, forming narrow paths or bridges, over which passengers have to walk.

The road is about twenty or thirty feet wide, running nearly straight through a lofty forest. On the sides grow numbers of the Inajá palm (*Maximiliana regia*), the prickly Mauritia (*M. aculeata*) in the marshes, and that curious palm the Piassába, which produces the fibrous substance now used for making brooms and brushes in this country for street-sweeping and domestic purposes. This is the first and almost the only point where this curious tree can be seen, while following any regular road or navigation. From the mouth of the Padauarí (a branch of the Rio Negro about five hundred miles above Barra), it is found on several rivers, but never on the banks of the main stream itself. A great part of the population of the Upper Rio Negro is employed in obtaining the fibre for exportation; and I thus became acquainted with all the localities in which it is found. These are the rivers Padauarí, Jahá, and Darahá on the north bank of the Rio Negro, and the Marié and Xié on the south. The other two rivers, the Maravihá and Cababurís, on the north, have not a tree; neither have the Curicuriarí, Uaupés, and Isánna, on the south, though they flow between the Marié and the Xié, where it abounds. In the whole of the district about the Upper Rio Negro above São Carlos, and about the Atabapo and its branches, it is abundant, and just behind the village of Tómo was where I first saw it. It grows in moist places, and is about twenty or thirty feet high, with the leaves large, pinnate, shining, and very smooth and regular. The whole stem is covered with a thick coating of the fibres, hanging down like coarse hair, and growing from the bases of the leaves, which remain attached to the stem. Large parties of men, women, and children go into the forests to cut this fibre. It is extensively used in its native country for cables and small ropes for all the canoes and larger vessels on the Amazon. Humboldt alludes to this plant by the native Venezuelan name of Chíquichíqui, but does not appear to have seen it, though he passed along this road. I believe it to be a species of *Leopoldinia*, of which two other kinds occur in the Rio Negro and, like this tree, are found there only. I could not find it in flower or fruit, but took a sketch of its general appearance, and have called it *Leopoldinia Piassaba*, from its native name, in the greater part of the district which it inhabits.

On approaching the end of the road I came to a "rhossa," or cleared field, where I found a tall, stout Indian planting cassáva. He addressed me with "Buenos dias," and asked me where I was going, and if I wanted anything at the village, for that the Commissario was away, and he was the Capitão. I replied in the best Spanish I could muster up for the occasion, and we managed to understand each other pretty well. He was rather astonished when I told him I was going to stay at the village, and seemed very doubtful of my intentions. I informed him, however, that I was a "Naturalista," and wanted birds, insects, and other animals; and then he began to comprehend, and at last promised to send me some men the day after the next, to carry over my luggage. I accordingly turned back without going to the village, which was still nearly a mile off.

On my return to Pimichin I found that my Indians had had but little success in fishing, three or four small perch being all we could muster for supper. As we had the next day to spare, I sent them early to get some "timbo" to poison the water, and thus obtain some more fish. While they were gone, I amused myself with walking about the village, and taking notes of its peculiarities. Hanging up under the eaves of our shed was a dried head of a snake, which had been killed a short time before. It was a jararáca, a species of *Craspedocephalus*, and must have been of a formidable size, for its poison-fangs, four in number, were nearly an inch long. My friend the deserter informed me that there were plenty like it in the mass of weeds close to the house, and that at night they came out, so that it was necessary to keep a sharp watch in and about the house. The bite of such a one as this would be certain death.

At Tómo I had observed signs of stratified upheaved rocks close to the village. Here the flat granite pavement presented a curious appearance : it contained, imbedded in it, fragments of rock, of an angular shape, of sandstone crystallized and stratified, and of quartz. Up to São Carlos I had constantly registered the boiling-point of water with an accurate thermometer, made for the purpose, in order to ascertain the height above the level of the sea. There I had unfortunately broken it, before arriving at this most interesting point, the watershed between the Amazon and the Orinooko. I am, however, inclined to think that the height given by Humboldt for São Carlos is too great. He himself says it is doubtful, as his barometer had got an air-bubble in it, and was emptied and refilled by him, and before returning to the coast was broken, so as to render a comparison of its indications impossible. Under these circumstances, I think little weight can be attached to the observations. He gives, however, eight hundred and twelve feet as the height of São Carlos above the sea. My observations made a difference of 0·5° of Fahrenheit in the temperature of boiling water between Barra and São Carlos, which would give a height of two hundred and fifty feet, to which may be added fifty feet for the height of the station at which the observations were made at Barra, making three hundred feet. Now the height of Barra above the sea I cannot consider to be more than a hundred feet, for both my own observations and those of Mr. Spruce with the aneroid would make Barra lower than Pará, if the difference of pressure of the atmosphere was solely owing to height, the barometer appearing to stand regularly higher at Barra than at Pará,—a circumstance which shows the total inapplicability of that instrument to determine small heights at very great distances. I cannot therefore think that São Carlos is more than four hundred, or at the outside five hundred feet, above the level of the sea. Should, as I suspect, the mean pressure of the atmosphere in the interior and on the coasts of South America differ from other causes than the elevation, it will be a difficult point ever accurately to ascertain the levels of the interior of this great continent, for the distances are too vast and the forests too impenetrable to allow a line of levels to be carried across it.

When my Indians returned with the roots of timbo, we all set to work beating it on the rocks with hard pieces of wood, till we had reduced it to fibres. It was then placed in a small canoe, filled with water and clay, and well mixed and squeezed, till all the juice had come out of it. This being done, it was carried a little way up the stream, and gradually tilted in, and mixed with the water. It soon began to produce its effects : small fish jumped up out of the water, turned and twisted about on the surface, or even lay on their backs and sides. The Indians were in the stream with baskets, hooking out all that came in the way, and diving and swimming after any larger ones that appeared at all affected. In this way, we got in an hour or two a basketful of fish, mostly small ones, but containing many curious species I had not before met with. Numbers escaped, as we had no weir across the stream ; and the next day several were found entangled at the sides, and already putrefying. I now had plenty to do. I selected about half a dozen of the most novel and interesting species to describe and figure, and gave the rest to be cleaned and put in the pot, to provide us a rather better supper than we had had for some days past.

The next morning early our porters appeared, consisting of

one man and eight or ten women and girls. We accordingly made up loads for each of them. There was a basket of salt about a hundred pounds weight, four baskets of farinha, besides boxes, baskets, a jar of oil, a demijohn of molasses, a portable cupboard, and numerous other articles. The greater part of these were taken, in loads proportioned to the strength of the bearers, and two of my Indians accompanied them, and were to return in the evening, and then go with me the next day. Night came, however, and they did not appear ; but near midnight they came in, telling me that they could not keep up with the Javíta Indians, and night coming on while they were in the middle of the road, they had hid their burdens in the forest and returned. So the next morning they had to go off again to finish their journey, and I was obliged to wait till they came back, and was delayed another day before I could get all my things taken.

I occupied myself in the forest catching a few insects, which, however, were not very numerous. The following morning we had nothing for breakfast, so I sent the Indians off early to fish, with positive instructions to return by ten o'clock, in order that we might get to Javíta before night. They chose, however, to stay till past noon, and then came with two or three small fish, which did not give us a mouthful apiece. It was thus two o'clock before we started. I was pretty well loaded with gun, ammunition, insect-boxes, etc., but soon got on ahead, with one Indian boy, who could not understand a single word of Portuguese. About halfway I saw a fine mutun, a little way off the road, and went after it ; but I had only small shot in my gun, and wounded it, but did not bring it down. I still followed, and fired several times but without effect, and as it had suddenly got dark I was obliged to leave it. We had still some miles to go. The sun had set, so we pushed on quickly, my attendant keeping close at my heels. In the marshes and over the little streams we had now some difficulty in finding our way along the narrow trunks laid for bridges. I was barefoot, and every minute stepped on some projecting root or stone, or trod sideways upon something which almost dislocated my ankle. It was now pitch-dark : dull clouds could just be distinguished through the openings in the high arch of overhanging trees, but the road we were walking on was totally invisible. Jaguars I knew abounded here, deadly serpents were plentiful, and at every step I almost expected to feel a cold, gliding body under my feet, or deadly fangs in my leg. Through the darkness I gazed, expecting momentarily to encounter the glaring eyes of a jaguar, or to hear his low growl in the thicket. But to turn back or to stop were alike useless : I knew that we could not be very far from the village, and so pressed on, with a vague confidence that after all nothing disagreeable would happen, and that the next day I should only laugh at my fears overnight. Still the sharp fangs of the dried snake's head at Pimichin would come across my memory, and many a tale of the fierceness and cunning of the jaguar were not to be forgotten. At length we came to the clearing I had reached two days before, and I now knew that we had but a short distance to go. There were, however, several small streams to cross. Suddenly we would step into water, which we felt but could not see, and then had to find the narrow bridge crossing it. Of the length of the bridge, its height above the water, or the depth of the stream, we were entirely ignorant ; and to walk along a trunk four inches wide under such circumstances, was rather a nervous matter. We proceeded, placing one foot before the other, and balancing steadily, till we again felt ourselves on firm ground. On one or two occasions I lost my balance, but it was luckily only a foot or two to the ground and water below, though if it had been twenty it would have been all the same. Some half dozen of brooks and bridges like this had to be passed, and several little up and downs in the road, till at length, emerging from the pitchy shade upon an open space, we saw twinkling lights, which told us the village was before us.

In about a quarter of an hour more we reached it, and, knocking at a door, asked where the Commissario lived. We were directed to a house on the other side of the square, where an old man conducted us to the " Casa de nação" (a shed with a door), in which were all my goods. On asking him if he could furnish me something for supper, he gave us some smoked turtles' eggs and a piece of salt fish, and then left us. We soon made a fire with some sticks we found, roasted our fish, and made a supper with the eggs and some farinha ; I then hung up my hammock, and my companion lay on the ground by the side of the fire ; and I slept well, undisturbed by dreams of snakes or jaguars.

The next morning I called on the Commissario, for the old man I had seen the evening before was only a capitão. I found him in his house : he was an Indian who could read and write, but not differing in any other respect from the Indians of the place. He had on a shirt and a pair of short-legged trousers, but neither shoes nor stockings. I informed him why I had come there, showed him my Brazilian passport, and requested the use of the Convento (a house formerly occupied by the priests, but now kept for travellers) to live in. After a little demur, he gave me the key of the house, and so I said good-morning, and proceeded to take possession.

About the middle of the day, the Indians who had started with me the day before arrived ; they had been afraid to come on in the dark, so had encamped in the road. I now got the house swept out, and my things taken into it. It consisted of two small rooms, and a little verandah at the back ; the larger room contained a table, chair, and bench, and in the smaller I hung up my hammock. My porters then came to be paid for bringing over my goods. All wanted salt, and I gave them a basinful each and a few fish-hooks, for carrying a heavy load ten miles : this is about their regular payment.

I had now reached the furthest point in this direction that I had wished to attain. I had passed the boundary of the mighty Amazon valley, and was among the streams that go to swell another of the world's great waters—the Orinooko. A deficiency in all other parts of the Upper Amazon district was here supplied,—a road through the virgin forest, by which I could readily reach its recesses, and where I was more sure of obtaining the curious insects of so distant a region, as well as the birds and other animals which inhabit it ; so I determined to remain here at least a month, steadily at work. Every day I went myself along the road, and sent my Indians, some to fish in the little black river Temi, others with their gravatánas to seek for the splendid trogons, monkeys, and other curious birds and animals in the forest.

Unfortunately, however, for me, on the very night I reached the village it began to rain, and day after day cloudy and showery weather continued. For three months Javíta had enjoyed the most splendid summer weather, with a clear sky and hardly a shower. I had been wasting all this time in the rainy district of the cataracts of the Rio Negro. No one there could tell me that the seasons, at such a short distance, differed so completely, and the consequence was that I arrived at Javíta on the very last day of summer.

The winter or rainy season commenced early this year. The river kept rapidly rising. The Indians constantly assured me that it was too soon for the regular rains to commence,—that we should have fine weather again,—the river would fall, and the winter not set in for two or three weeks. However, such was not the case. Day after day the rain poured down; every afternoon or night was wet, and a little sunshine in the morning was the most we were favoured with. Insects consequently were much more scarce than they otherwise would have been, and the dampness of the atmosphere rendered it extremely difficult to dry and preserve those that I obtained. However, by perseverance I amassed a considerable number of specimens; and what gave me the greatest pleasure was, that I almost daily obtained some new species which the Lower Amazon and Rio Negro had not furnished me with. During the time I remained here (forty days), I procured at least forty species of butterflies quite new to me, besides a considerable collection of other orders; and I am sure that during the dry season Javíta would be a most productive station for any persevering entomologist. I never saw the great blue butterflies, *Morpho Menelaus, M. Helenor*, etc., so abundant as here. In certain places in the road I found them by dozens sitting on the ground or on twigs by the roadside, and could easily have captured a dozen or twenty a day if I had wanted them. In birds and mammalia I did not do much, for my Indians wanted to get back, and were lazy and would not hunt after them. During my walks in the forest, I myself saw wild-pigs, agoutis, coatis, monkeys, numerous beautiful trogons, and many other fine birds, as well as many kinds of serpents.

One day I had brought to me a curious little alligator of a rare species, with numerous ridges and conical tubercles (*Caiman gibbus*), which I skinned and stuffed, much to the amusement of the Indians, half a dozen of whom gazed intently at the operation.

Of fish, too, I obtained many new species, as my Indians were out fishing every day to provide our supper, and I generally had some to figure and describe in the afternoon. I formed a good collection of the smaller kinds in spirits. My drawings here

were made under great difficulties.  I generally returned from
the forest about three or four in the afternoon, and if I found
a new fish, had to set down immediately to figure it before
dark.  I was thus exposed to the pest of the sand-flies, which,
every afternoon, from four to six, swarm in millions, causing
by their bites on the face, ears, and hands, the most painful
irritation.  Often have I been obliged to start up from my seat,
dash down my pencil, and wave my hands about in the cool
air to get a little relief.  But the sun was getting low, and I
must return to my task, till, before I had finished, my hands
would be as rough and as red as a boiled lobster, and violently
inflamed.  Bathing them in cold water, however, and half an
hour's rest, would bring them to their natural state ; in which
respect the bite of this little insect is far preferable to that of
the mosquito, the piuḿ, or the mutúca, the effects of whose
bites are felt for days.

The village of Javíta is rather a large one, regularly laid out,
and contains about two hundred inhabitants : they are all
Indians of pure blood ; I did not see a white man, a mulatto,
or a half-breed among them.  Their principal occupation is in
cutting piassába in the neighbouring forests, and making cables
and cordage of it.  They are also the carriers of all goods
across the " Estrada de Javíta," and, being used to this service
from childhood, they will often take two loads a day ten miles
each way, with less fatigue than a man not accustomed to the
work can carry one.  When my Indians accompanied the
Javítanos the first time from Pimichin, they could not at all
keep up with them, but were, as I have related, obliged to stop
halfway.  They go along the road at a sort of run, stopping to
rest twice only for a few minutes each time.  They go over the
narrow bridges with the greatest certainty, often two together,
carrying heavy loads suspended from a pole between them.
Besides this, once or twice a year they will go in a body to
clean the road as far as the middle, where there is a cross
erected.  The inhabitants of Maróa, Tómo, and other villages
of the Rio Negro assemble to clean the other half.  One of
these cleanings occurred while I was there.  The whole village,
men, women, and children, turned out, the former carrying
axes and cutlasses, the latter bundles of switches to serve as
brooms.  They divided themselves into parties, going on to
different parts of the road, and then worked to meet each

other.  The men cut down all overhanging or fallen trees which obstructed the way, and cleared off all the brushwood and weeds which were growing up on the sides.  The women and girls and boys carried these away, and swept clean with their switch brooms all the dead leaves and twigs, till the whole looked quite neat and respectable.  To clear up a road five miles in length in this manner was no trifle, but they accomplished it easily and very thoroughly in two days.

A little while after the men again turned out, to make new bridges in several places where they had become decayed.  This was rather a laborious task.  Large trees had to be cut down, often some distance from the spot; they were then roughly squared or flattened on top and bottom, and with cords of withes and creepers, and with numerous long sticks and logs placed beneath for rollers, were dragged by twenty or thirty men to the spot, placed in a proper position over the marsh or stream, propped and wedged securely, and the upper surface roughed with the axe to make the footing more sure.  In this way eight or ten of these bridges were made in a few days, and the whole road put in complete order.  This work is done by order of the Commissario Geral at São Fernando, without any kind of payment, or even rations, and with the greatest cheerfulness and good humour.

The men of Javíta when at work wear only the " tanga," in other respects being entirely naked.  The women wear usually a large wrapping dress passing over the left shoulder but leaving the right arm perfectly free, and hanging loosely over their whole person.  On Sundays and festivals they have well-made cotton gowns, and the men a shirt and trousers.  Here exists the same custom as at São Carlos, of the girls and boys assembling morning and evening at the church to sing a hymn or psalm.  The village is kept remarkably clean and free from weeds by regular weekly hoeings and weedings, to which the people are called by the Capitãos, who are the executive officers under the Commissario.

My evenings were very dull, having few to converse with, and no books.  Now and then I would talk a little with the Commissario, but our stock of topics was soon exhausted.  One or two evenings I went to their festas, when they had made a quantity of " xirac "—the caxirí of the Brazilian Indians —and were very merry.  They had a number of peculiar monotonous dances, accompanied by strange figures and con-tortions. The young girls generally came neatly dressed, their glossy hair beautifully plaited, and with gay ribbons or flowers to set it off. The moment the xirac is finished the party breaks up, as they do not seem to think it possible to dance without it : sometimes they make enough to last two or three days. Their dances appear quite national, but they have appa-rently left off paint, as I saw very little used.

The language spoken by these people is called the Maniva or Baniwa, but it differs considerably from the Baniwa of the Rio Negro, and is not so harsh and guttural. At Tómo and Maróa another language is spoken, quite distinct from this, but still called the Baniwa ; a little further down, at São Carlos, the Barré is used ; so that almost every village has its language. Here the men and old women all speak Spanish tolerably, there having formerly been priests living at the Convento, who instructed them. The younger women and the boys and girls, not having had this advantage, speak only the native tongue ; but many of them can understand a little Spanish. I found considerable difficulty in making myself intelligible here. The white men, who are called "rationáles" (rationals), could understand my mixed Portuguese and Spanish very well, but the Indians, knowing but little Spanish themselves, cannot of course comprehend any deviations from the ordinary method of speaking. I found it necessary, therefore, to keep my Spanish by itself, as they could better understand a little and good, than a great deal of explanation in the mixed tongue.

Some of my dull and dreary evenings I occupied in writing a description of the village and its inhabitants, in what may probably be very dreary blank verse ; but as it shows my ideas and thoughts at the time, I may as well give it the reader in place of the more sober and matter-of-fact view of the matter I should probably take now. I give it as I wrote it, in a state of excited indignation against civilised life in general, got up to relieve the monotony of my situation, and not altogether as my views when writing in London in 1853.

A DESCRIPTION OF JAVÍTA.

"'Tis where the streams divide, to swell the floods
Of the two mighty rivers of our globe ;
Where gushing brooklets in their narrow beds

Lie hid, o'ershadow'd by th' eternal woods,
And trickle onwards,—these to increase the wave
Of turbid Orinooko ; those, by a longer course
In the Black River's isle-strewn bed, flow down
To mighty Amazon, the river-king,
And, mingled with his all-engulfing stream,
Go to do battle with proud Ocean's self,
And drive him back even from his own domain.
There is an Indian village ; all around,
The dark, eternal, boundless forest spreads
Its varied foliage.   Stately palm-trees rise
On every side, and numerous trees unknown
Save by strange names uncouth to English ears.
Here I dwelt awhile  the one white man
Among perhaps two hundred living souls.
They pass a peaceful and contented life,
These black-hair'd, red-skinn'd, handsome, half-wild men.
Directed by the sons of Old Castile,
They keep their village and their houses clean ;
And on the eve before the Sabbath-day
Assemble all at summons of a bell,
To sweep within and all around their church,
In which next morn they meet, all neatly dress'd,
To pray as they've been taught unto their God.
It was a pleasing sight, that Sabbath morn,
Reminding me of distant, dear-loved home.
On one side knelt the men, their simple dress
A shirt and trousers of coarse cotton cloth :
On the other side were women and young girls,
Their glossy tresses braided with much taste,
And on their necks all wore a kerchief gay,
And some a knot of riband in their hair.
How like they look'd, save in their dusky skin,
To a fair group of English village maids !
Yet far superior in their graceful forms ;
For their free growth no straps or bands impede,
But simple food, free air, and daily baths
And exercise, give all that Nature asks
To mould a beautiful and healthy frame.

  " Each day some labour calls them.   Now they go
To fell the forest's pride, or in canoe
With hook, and spear, and arrow, to catch fish ;
Or seek the various products of the wood,
To make their baskets or their hanging beds.
The women dig the mandiocca root,
And with much labour make of it their bread.
These plant the young shoots in the fertile earth—
Earth all untill'd, to which the plough, or spade,
Or rake, or harrow, are alike unknown.

The young girls carry water on their heads
In well-formed pitchers, just like Cambrian maids;
And all each morn and eve wash in the stream,
And sport like mermaids in the sparkling wave.

   " The village is laid out with taste and skill :
In the midst a spacious square, where stands the church,
And narrow streets diverging all around.
Between the houses, filling up each space,
The broad, green-leaved, luxuriant plantain grows,
Bearing huge bunches of most wholesome fruit;
The orange too is there, and grateful lime ;
The Inga pendent hangs its yard-long pods
(Whose flowers attract the fairy humming-birds);
The guava, and the juicy, sweet cashew,
And a most graceful palm, which bears a fruit
In bright red clusters, much esteem'd for food ;
And there are many more which Indians
Esteem, and which have only Indian names.
Th chouses are of posts fill'd up with mud,
Smooth'd, and wash'd over with a pure white clay;
A palm-tree's spreading leaves supply a thatch
Impervious to the winter's storms and rain.
No nail secures the beams or rafters, all
Is from the forest, whose lithe, pendent cords
Bind them into a firm enduring mass.
From the tough fibre of a fan-palm's leaf
They twist a cord to make their hammock-bed,
Their bow-string, line, and net for catching fish.
Their food is simple—fish and cassava-bread,
With various fruits, and sometimes forest game,
All season'd with hot, pungent, fiery peppers.
Sauces and seasonings too, and drinks they have,
Made from the mandiocca's poisonous juice ;
And but one foreign luxury, which is salt.
Salt here is money : daily they bring to me
Cassava cakes, or fish, or ripe bananas,
Or birds or insects, fowls or turtles' eggs,
And still they ask for salt.   Two teacups-full
Buy a large basket of cassava cakes,
A great bunch of bananas, or a fowl.

   "One day they made a festa, and, just like
Our villagers at home, they drank much beer,
(Beer made from roasted mandiocca cakes,)
Call'd here "shirac," by others "caxirí,"
But just like beer in flavour and effect ;
And then they talked much, shouted and sang,
And men and maids all danced in a ring
With much delight, like children at their play.

For music they've small drums and reed-made fifes,
And vocal chants, monotonous and shrill,
To which they'll dance for hours without fatigue.
The children of small growth are naked, and
The boys and men wear but a narrow cloth.
How I delight to see those naked boys!
Their well-form'd limbs, their bright, smooth, red-brown skin,
And every motion full of grace and health;
And as they run, and race, and shout, and leap,
Or swim and dive beneath the rapid stream,
Or, all bareheaded in the noonday sun,
Creep stealthily, with blowpipe or with bow,
To shoot small birds or swiftly gliding fish,
I pity English boys; their active limbs
Cramp'd and confined in tightly-fitting clothes;
Their toes distorted by the shoemaker,
Their foreheads aching under heavy hats,
And all their frame by luxury enervate.
But how much more I pity English maids,
Their waist, and chest, and bosom all confined
By that vile torturing instrument called stays!

"And thus these people pass their simple lives.
They are a peaceful race; few serious crimes
Are known among them; they nor rob nor murder,
And all the complicated villanies
Of man called civilised are here unknown.
Yet think not I would place, as some would do,
The civilised below the savage man;
Or wish that we could retrograde, and live
As did our forefathers ere Cæsar came.
'Tis true the miseries, the wants and woes,
The poverty, the crimes, the broken hearts,
The intense mental agonies that lead
Some men to self-destruction, some
To end their days within a madhouse cell,
The thousand curses that gold brings upon us,
The long death-struggle for the means to live,—
All these the savage knows and suffers not.
But then the joys, the pleasures and delights,
That the well-cultivated mind enjoys;
The appreciation of the beautiful
In nature and in art; the boundless range
Of pleasure and of knowledge books afford;
The constant change of incident and scene
That makes us live a life in every year;—
All these the savage knows not and enjoys not.
Still we may ask, 'Does stern necessity
Compel that this great good must co-exist
For ever with that monstrous mass of ill?

Must millions suffer these dread miseries,
While but a few enjoy the grateful fruits?'
For are there not, confined in our dense towns,
And scattered over our most fertile fields,
Millions of men who live a lower life—
Lower in physical and moral health—
Than the Red Indian of these trackless wilds?
Have we not thousands too who live a life
More low, through eager longing after gold,—
Whose thoughts, from morn to night, from night to morn,
Are—how to get more gold?
What know such men of intellectual joys?
They've but one joy—the joy of getting gold.
In nature's wondrous charms they've no delight,
The one thing beautiful for them is—gold.
Thoughts of the great of old which books contain,
The poet's and the historian's fervid page,
Or all the wonders science brings to light,
For them exist not.   They've no time to spend
In such amusements : 'Time,' say they, 'is gold.'
And if they hear of some immortal deed,
Some noble sacrifice of power or fortune
To save a friend or spotless reputation,—
A deed that moistens sympathetic eyes,
And makes us proud we have such fellow-men,—
They say, 'Who make such sacrifice are fools,
For what is life without one's hard-earn'd gold?'
Rather than live a man like one of these,
I'd be an Indian here, and live content
To fish, and hunt, and paddle my canoe,
And see my children grow, like young wild fawns,
In health of body and in peace of mind,
Rich without wealth, and happy without gold!"

JAVÍTA, *March,* 1851.                                        A. W.

I had gone on here in my regular routine some time, when one morning, on getting up, I found none of the Indians, and no fire in the verandah.   Thinking they had gone out early to hunt or fish, as they sometimes did, I lit the fire and got my breakfast, but still no sign of any of them.   Looking about, I found that their hammocks, knives, an earthen pan, and a few other articles, were all gone, and that nothing was left in the house but what was my own.   I was now convinced that they had run away in the night, and left me to get on as I could.   They had been rather uneasy for some days past, asking me when I meant to go back.   They did not like being among people whose language they could not speak, and had

been lately using up an enormous quantity of farinha, hoping
when they had finished the last basket that I should be unable
to purchase any more in the village, and should therefore be
obliged to return. The day before I had just bought a fresh
basket, and the sight of that appears to have supplied the last
stimulus necessary to decide the question, and make them fly
from the strange land and still stranger white man, who spent
all his time in catching insects, and wasting good caxaça by
putting fish and snakes into it. However, there was now
nothing to be done, so I took my insect-net, locked up my
house, put the key (an Indian-made wooden one) in my pocket,
and started off for the forest.

I had luckily, a short time before, bought a fine Venezuelan
cheese and some dried beef, so that, with plenty of cassava-
bread and plantains, I could get on very well. In the evening
some of my usual visitors among the Indians dropped in, and
were rather surprised to see me lighting my fire and preparing
my dinner ; and on my explaining the circumstances to them,
they exclaimed that my Indians were "mala gente" (bad
fellows), and intimated that they had always thought them no
better than they should be. I got some of the boys to fetch
me water from the river, and to bring me in a stock of fuel,
and then, with coffee and cheese, roasted plantains and cassava-
bread, I lived luxuriously. My coffee, however, was just
finished, and in a day or two I had none. This I could hardly
put up with without a struggle, so I went down to the cottage
of an old Indian who could speak a little Spanish, and begged
him, "por amor de Dios,' to get me some coffee from a small
plantation he had. There were some ripe berries on the trees,
the sun was shining out, and he promised to set his little girl
to work immediately. This was about ten in the morning.
I went into the forest, and by four returned, and found that
my coffee was ready. It had been gathered, the pulp washed
off, dried in the sun (the longest part of the business), husked,
roasted, and pounded in a mortar ; and in half an hour more
I enjoyed one of the most delicious cups of coffee I have ever
tasted.

As I wanted to remain a fortnight longer, I tried to persuade
one of the brown damsels of the village to come and make my
fire and cook for me; but, strange to say, not one would
venture, though in the other villages of the Rio Negro I might

at any moment have had my choice of half a dozen; and I was forced to be my own cook and housemaid for the rest of my stay in Javíta.

There was now in the village an old Indian trader who had come from Medina, a town at the foot of the Andes, near Bogotá, and from him and some other Indians I obtained much information relative to that part of the country, and the character of the streams that flow from the mountains down to the Orinooko. He informed me that he had ascended by the river Muco, which enters the Orinooko above the Falls of Maypures, and by which he had reached a point within twenty miles of the upper waters of the Meta, opposite Medina. The river Muco had no falls or obstructions to navigation, and all the upper part of its course flowed through an open country, and had fine sandy beaches; so that between this river and the Guaviare is the termination of the great forest of the Amazon valley.

The weather was now terribly wet. For successive days and nights rain was incessant, and a few hours of sunshine was a rarity. Insects were few, and those I procured it was almost impossible to dry. In the drying box they got destroyed by mould, and if placed in the open air and exposed to the sun minute flies laid eggs upon them, and they were soon eaten up by maggots. The only way I could preserve them was to hang them up some time every evening and morning over my fire. I now began to regret more than ever my loss of the fine season, as I was convinced that I could have reaped a splendid harvest. I had, too, just began to initiate the Indian boys into catching beetles for me, and was accumulating a very nice collection. Every evening three or four would come in with their treasures in pieces of bamboo, or carefully tied up in leaves. I purchased all they brought, giving a fish-hook each; and among many common I generally found some curious and rare species. *Coleoptera*, generally so scarce in the forest districts of the Amazon and Rio Negro, seemed here to become more abundant, owing perhaps to our approach to the margins of the great forest, and the plains of the Orinooko.

I prepared to leave Javíta with much regret. Although, considering the season, I had done well, I knew that had I been earlier I might have done much better. In April I had arranged to go up the unexplored Uaupés with Senhor L., and even the prospect of his conversation was agreeable after the weary solitude I was exposed to here.

I would, however, strongly recommend Javíta to any naturalist wishing for a good unexplored locality in South America It is easily reached from the West Indies to Angostura, and thence up the Orinooko and Atabápo. A pound's worth of fish-hooks, and five pounds laid out in salt, beads, and calico, will pay all expenses there for six months. The traveller should arrive in September, and can then stay till March, and will have the full benefit of the whole of the dry season. The insects alone would well repay any one; the fishes are also abundant, and very new and interesting ; and, as my collections were lost on the voyage home, they would have all the advantage of novelty.

On the 31st of March I left Javíta, the Commissario having sent five or six Indians to carry my luggage, four of whom were to proceed with me to Tómo. The Indians of São Carlos, Tómo, and Maróa had been repairing their part of the road, and were returning home, so some of them agreed to go with me in the place of the Javítanos. They had found in the forest a number of the harlequin beetles (*Acrocinus longimanus*), which they offered me, carefully wrapped up in leaves ; I bought five for a few fish-hooks each. On arriving at Pimichin the little river presented a very different appearance from what it had when I last saw it. It was now brim-full, and the water almost reached up to our shed, which had before been forty yards off, up a steep rocky bank. Before my men ran away I had sent two of them to Tómo to bring my canoe to Pimichin, the river having risen enough to allow it to come up, and I now found it here. They had taken a canoe belonging to Antonio Dias, who had passed Javíta a few days before on his way to São Fernando, so that when he returned he had to borrow another to go home in.

We descended the little river rapidly, and now saw the extraordinary number of bends in it. I took the bearings of thirty with the compass, but then there came on a tremendous storm of wind and rain right in our faces, which rendered it quite impossible to see ahead. Before this had cleared off night came on, so that the remainder of the bends and doubles of the Pimichin river must still remain in obscurity. The country it flows through appears to be a flat sandy tract, covered with a low scrubby vegetation, very like that of the river Cobáti, up which I ascended to the Serra to obtain the cocks of the rock.

It was night when we reached Maróa, and we were nearly passing the village without seeing it. We went to the " casa de nação," rather a better kind of shed than usual, and, making a good fire, passed a comfortable night. The next morning I called on Senhor Carlos Bueno (Charles Good), the dandy Indian Commissario, and did a little business with him. I bought a lot of Indian baskets, gravatánas, quivers, and ururí or curarí poison, and in return gave him some fish-hooks and calico, and, having breakfasted with him, went on to Tómo.

Senhor Antonio Dias was not there, having gone to São Carlos, so I determined to wait a few days for his return, as he had promised to send men with me to Guia. I took up my abode with Senhor Domingos, who was busy superintending the completion of the large vessel before mentioned, in order to get it launched with the high water, which was now within a foot or two of its bottom. I amused myself walking about the campo with my gun, and succeeded in shooting one of the beautiful little black-headed parrots, which have the most brillant green plumage, crimson under-wings, and yellow cheeks; they are only found in these districts, and are rather difficult to obtain. I also got some curious fish to figure,— in particular two large species of *Gymnotus*, of the group which are not electric.

The Indians had a festa while I was here. They made abundance of " shirac," and kept up their dancing for thirty hours. The principal peculiarity of it was that they mixed up their civilised dress and their Indian decorations in a most extraordinary manner. They all wore clean trousers and white or striped shirts; but they had also feather-plumes, bead neck-laces, and painted faces, which made altogether a rather queer mixture. They also carried theirh ammocks like scarfs over their shoulders, and had generally hollow cylinders in their hands, used to beat upon the ground in time to the dancing. Others had lances, bows, and wands, ornamented with feathers, producing as they danced in the moonlight a singular and wild appearance.

Senhor Antonio Dias delayed his return, and rather a scene

in his domestic circle took place in consequence. As might be expected, the ladies did not agree very well together. The elder one in particular was very jealous of the Indian girls, and took every opportunity of ill-treating them, and now that the master was absent went, I suppose, to greater lengths than usual ; and the consequence was, one of the girls ran away. This was an unexpected *dénouement*, and they were in a great state of alarm, for the girl was a particular favourite of Senhor Antonio's, and if he returned before she came back he was not likely to be very delicate in showing his displeasure. The girl had gone off in a canoe with a child about a year old ; the night had been stormy and wet, but that sort of thing will not stop an Indian. Messengers were sent after her, but she was not to be found ; and then the old lady and her daughter went off themselves in a tremendous rain, but with no better success. One resource more, however, remained, and they resolved to apply to the Saints. Senhor Domingos was sent to bring the image of St. Antonio from the church. This saint is supposed to have especial power over things lost, but the manner of securing his influence is rather singular :—the poor saint is tied round tightly with a cord and laid on his back on the floor, and it is believed that in order to obtain deliverance from such durance vile he will cause the lost sheep to return. Thus was the unfortunate St. Antony of Tómo now treated, and laid ignominiously on the earthen floor all night, but without effect ; he was obstinate, and nothing was heard of the wanderer. More inquiries were made, but with no result, till two days afterwards Senhor Antonio himself returned accompanied by the girl. She had hid herself in a sitio a short distance from the village, waited for Senhor Antonio's passing, and then joined him, and told her own story first ; and so the remainder of the harem got some hard words, and I am inclined to think some hard blows too.

Before leaving Tómo, I purchased a pair of the beautiful feather-work borders, before alluded to, for which I paid £3 in silver dollars. Five Indians were procured to go with me, and at the same time take another small canoe, in which to bring back several articles that Senhor Antonio was much in want of. We paid the men between us, before going, with calicoes and cotton cloth, worth in England about twopence a yard, but here valued at 2s. 6d., and soap, beads, knives, and axes, in the same proportion.  On the way, I got these Tómo Indians to give me a vocabulary of their language, which differs from that of the villages above and below them.  We paddled by day, and floated down by night; and as the current was now tremendous, we got on so quickly, that in three days we reached Marabitanas, a distance which had taken us nine in going up.

Here I stayed a week with the Commandante, who had invited me when at Guia.  I, however, did little in the collecting way : there were no paths in the forest, and no insects, and very few birds worth shooting.  I obtained some very curious half-spiny rodent animals, and a pretty white-marked bird, allied to the starlings, which appears here only once a year in flocks, and is called " Ciucí uera " (the star-bird).

The inhabitants of Marabitanas are celebrated for their festas : their lives are spent, half at their festas, and the other half in preparing for them.  They consume immense quantities of raw spirit, distilled from cane-juice and from the mandiocca : at a festa which took place while I was here, there was about a hogshead of strong spirit consumed, all drunk raw.  In every house, where the dancing takes place, there are three or four persons constantly going round with a bottle and glass, and no one is expected ever to refuse ; they keep on the whole night, and the moment you have tasted one glass, another succeeds, and you must at least take a sip of it.  The Indians empty the glass every time ; and this continues for two or three days.  When all is finished, the inhabitants return to their sitios, and commence the preparation of a fresh lot of spirit for the next occasion.

About a fortnight before each festa—which is always on a Saint's day of the Roman Catholic Church—a party of ten or a dozen of the inhabitants go round, in a canoe, to all the sitios and Indian villages within fifty or a hundred miles, carrying the image of the saint, flags, and music.  They are entertained at every house, the saint is kissed, and presents are made for the feast ; one gives a fowl, another some eggs or a bunch of plantains, another a few coppers.  The live animals are frequently promised beforehand for a particular saint ; and often, when I have wanted to buy some provisions, I have been assured that " that is St. John's pig," or that " those fowls belong to the Holy Ghost."

Bidding adieu to the Commandante, Senhor Tenente Antonio Filisberto Correio de Araujo, who had treated me with the greatest kindness and hospitality, I proceeded on to Guia, where I arrived about the end of April, hoping to find Senhor L. ready, soon to start for the river Uaupés ; but I was again doomed to delay, for a canoe which had been sent to Barra had not yet returned, and we could not start till it came. It was now due, but as it was manned by Indians, only who had no particular interest in hurrying back, it might very well be a month longer. And so it proved, for it did not arrive till the end of May. All that time I could do but little ; the season was now very wet, and Guia was a poor locality. Fishes were my principal resource, as Senhor L. had a fisherman out every day, to procure us our suppers, and I always had the day's sport brought to me first, to select any species I had not yet seen. In this way I constantly got new kinds, and became more than ever impressed with the extraordinary variety and abundance of the inhabitants of these rivers. I had now figured and described a hundred and sixty species from the Rio Negro alone ; I had besides seen many others ; and fresh varieties still occurred as abundantly as ever in every new locality. I am convinced that the number of species in the Rio Negro and its tributaries alone would be found to amount to five or six hundred. But the Amazon has most of its fishes peculiar to itself, and so have all its numerous tributaries, especially in their upper waters ; so that the number of distinct kinds inhabiting the whole basin of the Amazon must be immense.

# CHAPTER X.

## FIRST ASCENT OF THE RIVER UAUPÉS.

Rapid Current—An Indian Malocca—The Inmates—A Festival—Paint
and Ornaments—Illness—São Jeronymo—Passing the Cataracts—
Jauarité—The Tushaúa Calistro—Singular Palm—Birds—Cheap
Provisions—Edible Ants, and Earthworms—A Grand Dance—Feather
Ornaments—The Snake-dance—The Capí—A State Cigar—Ananá-
rapicóma—Fish—Chegoes—Pass down the Falls—Tame Birds—
Orchids—Piuñs—Eating Dirt—Poisoning—Return to Guia—Manoel
Joaquim—Annoying Delays.

AT length the long-looked-for canoe arrived, and we immediately made preparations for our voyage. Fish-hooks and
knives and beads were looked out to suit the customers we
were going among, and from whom Senhor L. hoped to obtain
farinha and sarsaparilla: and I, fish, insects, birds, and all
sorts of bows, arrows, blowpipes, baskets, and other Indian
curiosities.

On the 3rd of June, at six in the morning, we started. The
weather had cleared up a few days before, and was now very
fine. We had only two Indians with us, the same who had
run away from Javíta, and who had been paid their wages
beforehand, so we now made them work it out. Those who
had just returned from Barra were not willing to go out again
immediately, but we hoped to get plenty on entering the
Uaupés. The same afternoon we reached São Joaquim, at
the mouth of that river; but as there were no men there, we
were obliged to go on, and then commenced our real difficulties,
for we had to encounter the powerful current of the over-
flowing stream. At first some bays, in which there were
counter-currents, favoured us; but in more exposed parts, the
waters rushed along with such violence, that our two paddles
could not possibly move the canoe.

We could only get on by pulling the bushes and creepers and tree-branches which line the margin of the river, now that almost all the adjacent lands were more or less flooded. The next day we cut long hooked poles, by which we could pull and push ourselves along at all difficult points, with more advantage. Sometimes, for miles together, we had to proceed thus,—getting the canoe filled, and ourselves covered, with stinging and biting ants of fifty different species, each producing its own peculiar effect, from a gentle tickle to an acute sting; and which, getting entangled in our hair and beards, and creeping over all parts of our bodies under our clothes, were not the most agreeable companions. Sometimes, too, we would encounter swarms of wasps, whose nests were concealed among the leaves, and who always make a most furious attack upon intruders. The naked bodies of the Indians offered no defence against their stings, and they several times suffered while we escaped. Nor are these the only inconveniences attending an up-stream voyage in the time of high flood, for all the river-banks being overflowed, it is only at some rocky point which still keeps above water that a fire can be made; and as these are few and far between, we frequently had to pass the whole day on farinha and water, with a piece of cold fish or a pacova, if we were so lucky as to have any. All these points, or sleeping places, are well known to the traders in the river, so that whenever we reached one, at whatever hour of the day or night, we stopped to make our coffee and rest a little, knowing that we should only get to another haven after eight or ten hours of hard pulling and paddling.

On the second day we found a small "Sucurujú" (*Eunectes murinus*), about a yard long, sunning itself on a bush over the water; one of our Indians shot it with an arrow, and when we stayed for the night roasted it for supper. I tasted a piece, and found it excessively tough and glutinous, but without any disagreeable flavour; and well stewed, it would, I have no doubt, be very good. Having stopped at a sitio we purchased a fowl, which, boiled with rice, made us an excellent supper.

On the 7th we entered a narrow winding channel, branching from the north bank of the river, and in about an hour reached a "malocca," or native Indian lodge, the first we had encountered. It was a large, substantial building, near a hundred feet long, by about forty wide and thirty high, very strongly constructed of round, smooth, barked timbers, and thatched with the fan-shaped leaves of the Caraná palm.  One end was square, with a gable, the other circular ; and the eaves, hanging over the low walls, reached nearly to the ground.  In the middle was a broad aisle, formed by the two rows of the principal columns supporting the roof, and between these and the sides were other rows of smaller and shorter timbers ; the whole of them were firmly connected by longitudinal and transverse beams at the top, supporting the rafters, and were all bound together with much symmetry by sipós.

Projecting inwards from the walls on each side were short partitions of palm-thatch, exactly similar in arrangement to the boxes in a London eating-house, or those of a theatre.  Each of these is the private apartment of a separate family, who thus live in a sort of patriarchal community.  In the side aisles are the farinha ovens, tipitís for squeezing the mandiocca, huge pans and earthen vessels for making caxirí, and other large articles, which appear to be in common ; while in every separate apartment are the small pans, stools, baskets, redes, water-pots, weapons, and ornaments of the occupants.  The centre aisle remains unoccupied, and forms a fine walk through the house.  At the circular end is a cross partition or railing about five feet high, cutting off rather more than the semicircle, but with a wide opening in the centre : this forms the residence of the chief or head of the malocca, with his wives and children ; the more distant relations residing in the other part of the house.  The door at the gable end is very wide and lofty, that at the circular end is smaller, and these are the only apertures to admit light and air.  The upper part of the gable is loosely covered with palm-leaves hung vertically, through which the smoke of the numerous wood fires slowly percolates, giving, however, in its passage a jetty lustre to the whole of the upper part of the roof.

On entering this house, I was delighted to find myself at length in the presence of the true denizens of the forest.  An old and a young man and two women were the only occupiers, the rest being out on their various pursuits.  The women were absolutely naked ; but on the entrance of the " brancos " they slipped on a petticoat, with which in these lower parts of the river they are generally provided but never use except on such occasions. Their hair was but moderately long, and they were without any ornament but strongly knitted garters, tightly laced immediately below the knee.

It was the men, however, who presented the most novel appearance, as different from all the half-civilised races among whom I had been so long living, as they could be if I had been suddenly transported to another quarter of the globe. Their hair was carefully parted in the middle, combed behind the ears, and tied behind in a long tail reaching a yard down the back. The hair of this tail was firmly bound with a long cord formed of monkeys' hair, very soft and pliable. On the top of the head was stuck a comb, ingeniously constructed of palm-wood and grass, and ornamented with little tufts of toucans' rump feathers at each end ; and the ears were pierced, and a small piece of straw stuck in the hole ; altogether giving a most feminine appearance to the face, increased by the total absence of beard or whiskers, and by the hair of the eyebrows being almost entirely plucked out. A small strip of "tururí" (the inner bark of a tree) passed between the legs, and secured to a string round the waist, with a pair of knitted garters, constituted their simple dress.

The young man was lazily swinging in a maqueira, but disappeared soon after we entered ; the elder one was engaged making one of the flat hollow baskets, a manufacture peculiar to this district. He continued quietly at his occupation, answering the questions Senhor L. put to him about the rest of the inhabitants in a very imperfect " Lingoa Geral," which language is comparatively little known in this river, and that only in the lower and more frequented parts. As we wanted to procure one or two men to go with us, we determined to stay here for the night. We succeeded in purchasing for a few fish-hooks some fresh fish, which another Indian brought in : and then prepared our dinner and coffee, and brought our maqueiras up to the house, hanging them in the middle aisle, to pass the night there. About dusk many more Indians, male and female, arrived ; fires were lighted in the several compartments, pots put on with fish or game for supper, and fresh mandiocca cakes made. I now saw several of the men with their most peculiar and valued ornament—a cylindrical, opaque, white stone, looking like marble, but which is really quartz imperfectly crystallized. These stones are from four to eight inches long, and about an inch in diameter.   They are ground round, and flat at the ends, a work of great labour, and are each pierced with a hole at one end, through which a string is inserted, to suspend it round the neck.   It appears almost incredible that they should make this hole in so hard a substance without any iron instrument for the purpose.   What they are said to use is the pointed flexible leaf-shoot of the large wild plantain, triturating with fine sand and a little water ; and I have no doubt it is, as it is said to be, a labour of years.   Yet it must take a much longer time to pierce that which the Tushaúa wears as the symbol of his authority, for it is generally of the largest size, and is worn transversely across the breast, for which purpose the hole is bored lengthways from one end to the other, an operation which I was informed sometimes occupies two lives.   The stones themselves are procured from a great distance up the river, probably from near its sources at the base of the Andes ; they are therefore highly valued, and it is seldom the owners can be induced to part with them, the chiefs scarcely ever.   I here purchased a club of hard red wood for a small mirror, a comb for half-a-dozen small fish-hooks, and some other trifling articles.

A portion only of the inhabitants arrived that night, as when traders come they are afraid of being compelled to go with them, and so hide themselves.   Many of the worst characters in the Rio Negro come to trade in this river, force the Indians, by threats of shooting them, into their canoes, and sometimes even do not scruple to carry their threats into execution, they being here quite out of reach of even that minute portion of the law which still struggles for existence in the Rio Negro.

We passed the night in the malocca, surrounded by the naked Indians hanging round their fires, which sent a fitful light up into the dark smoke-filled roof.   A torrent of rain poured without, and I could not help admiring the degree of sociality and comfort in numerous families thus living together in patriarchal harmony.   The next morning Senhor L. succeeded in persuading one Indian to earn a "saía" (petticoat) for his wife, and embark with us, and so we bade adieu to Assaí Paraná (Assaí river).   On lifting up the mat covering of our canoe, I found lying comfortably coiled up on the top of my box a fine young boa, of a species of which I possessed two live specimens at Guía : he had probably fallen in unperceived during our passage among the bushes on the river-side. In the afternoon we reached another village, also situated up a narrow igaripé, and consisting of a house and two maloccas at some distance from it. The inhabitants had gone to a neighbouring village, where there was caxirí and dancing, and two women only were left behind with some children. About these houses were several parrots, macaws, and curassow-birds, which all these Indians breed in great numbers. The next day we reached Anandrapicóma, or "Pine-apple Point," the village where the dance was taking place. It consisted of several small houses besides the large malocca, many of the Indians who have been with traders to the Rio Negro imitating them in using separate dwellings.

On entering the great malocca a most extraordinary and novel scene presented itself. Some two hundred men, women, and children were scattered about the house, lying in the maqueiras, squatting on the ground, or sitting on the small painted stools, which are made only by the inhabitants of this river. Almost all were naked and painted, and wearing their various feathers and other ornaments. Some were walking or conversing, and others were dancing, or playing small fifes and whistles. The regular festa had been broken up that morning; the chiefs and principal men had put off their feather head-dresses, but as caxirí still remained, the young men and women continued dancing. They were painted over their whole bodies in regular patterns of a diamond or diagonal character, with black, red, and yellow colours; the former, a purple or blue black, predominating. The face was ornamented in various styles, generally with bright red in bold stripes or spots, a large quantity of the colour being applied to each ear, and running down on the sides of the cheeks and neck, producing a very fearful and sanguinary appearance. The grass in the ears was now decorated with a little tuft of white downy feathers, and some in addition had three little strings of beads from a hole pierced in the lower lip. All wore the garters, which were now generally painted yellow. Most of the young women who danced had besides a small apron of beads of about eight inches by six inches, arranged in diagonal patterns with much taste; besides this, the paint on their naked bodies was their only ornament; they had not even the comb in their hair, which the men are never without.

The men and boys appropriated all the ornaments, thus reversing the custom of civilised countries and imitating nature, who invariably decorates the male sex with the most brilliant colours and most remarkable ornaments.  On the head all wore a coronet of bright red and yellow toucans' feathers, set in a circlet of plaited straw.  The comb in the hair was ornamented with feathers, and frequently a bunch of white heron's plumes attached to it fell gracefully down the back. Round the neck or over one shoulder were large necklaces of many folds of white or red beads, as well as the white cylindrical stone hung on the middle of a string of some black shining seeds.

The ends of the monkey-hair cords which tied the hair were ornamented with little plumes, and from the arm hung a bunch of curiously-shaped seeds, ornamented with bright coloured feathers attached by strings of monkeys' hair.  Round the waist was one of their most valued ornaments, possessed by comparatively few,—the girdle of onças' teeth.  And lastly, tied round the ankles were large bunches of a curious hard fruit, which produce a rattling sound in the dance.  In their hands some carried a bow and a bundle of curabís, or war-arrows; others a murucú, or spear of hard polished wood, or an oval painted gourd, filled with small stones and attached to a handle, which, being shaken at regular intervals in the dance, produced a rattling accompaniment to the leg ornaments and the song.

The wild and strange appearance of these handsome, naked, painted Indians, with their curious ornaments and weapons, the stamp and song and rattle which accompanies the dance, the hum of conversation in a strange language, the music of fifes and flutes and other instruments of reed, bone, and turtles' shells, the large calabashes of caxirí constantly carried about, and the great smoke-blackened gloomy house, produced an effect to which no description can do justice, and of which the sight of half-a-dozen Indians going through their dances for show, gives but a very faint idea.

I stayed looking on a considerable time, highly delighted at such an opportunity of seeing these interesting people in their most characteristic festivals.  I was myself a great object of admiration, principally on account of my spectacles, which they saw for the first time and could not at all understand.

A hundred bright pairs of eyes were continually directed on me from all sides, and I was doubtless the great subject of conversation. An old man brought me three ripe pine-apples, for which I gave him half-a-dozen small hooks, and he was very well contented.

Senhor L. was conversing with many of the Indians, with whom he was well acquainted, and was arranging with one to go up a branch of the river, several days' journey, to purchase some salsa and farinha for him. I succeeded in buying a beautiful ornamented murucú, the principal insignia of the Tushaúa, or chief. He was very loth to part with it, and I had to give an axe and a large knife, of which he was much in want. I also bought two cigar-holders, about two feet long, in which a gigantic cigar is placed and handed round on these occasions. The next morning, after making our payments for the articles we had purchased, we went to bid our adieus to the chief. A small company who had come from some distance were taking their leave at the same time, going round the great house in Indian file, and speaking in a muttering tone to each head of a family. First came the old men bearing lances and shields of strong wicker-work, then the younger ones with their bows and arrows, and lastly the old and young women carrying their infants and the few household utensils they had brought with them. At these festivals drink alone is provided, in immense quantities, each party bringing a little mandiocca-cake or fish for its consumption, which, while the caxirí lasts, is very little. The paint on their bodies is very durable, for though they never miss washing two or three times a day, it lasts a week or a fortnight before it quite disappears.

Leaving Ananárapicóma, we arrived the same evening at Mandii Paraná, where there was also a malocca, which, owing to the great rise of the river, could only be reached by wading up to the middle through the flooded forest. I accordingly stayed to superintend the making of a fire, which the soaking rain we had had all the afternoon rendered a somewhat difficult matter, while Senhor L. went with an Indian to the house to arrange some "negocio" and obtain fish for supper. We stayed here for the night, and the next morning the Indians came down in a body to the canoe, and made some purchases of fish-hooks, beads, mirrors, cloth for trousers, etc., of Senhor

L., to be paid in farinha, fowls, and other articles on our return. I also ordered a small canoe as a specimen, and some sieves and fire-fanners, which I paid for in similar trifles ; for these Indians are so accustomed to receive payment before-hand, that without doing so you cannot depend upon their making anything. The next day, the 12th of June, we reached São Jeronymo, situated about a mile below the first and most dangerous of the Falls of the Uaupés.

For the last five days I had been very ill with dysentery and continual pains in the stomach, brought on, I believe, by eating rather incautiously of the fat and delicious fish, the white Pirahiba or Laulau, three or four times consecutively without vegetable food. Here the symptoms became rather aggravated, and though not at all inclined to despond in sickness, yet as I knew this disease to be a very fatal one in tropical climates, and I had no medicines or even proper food of any kind, I certainly did begin to be a little alarmed. The worst of it was that I was continually hungry, but could not eat or drink the smallest possible quantity of anything without pains of the stomach and bowels immediately succeeding, which lasted several hours. The diarrhœa too was continual, with evacuations of slime and blood, which my diet of the last few days, of tapioca-gruel and coffee, seemed rather to have increased.

I remained here most of the day in my maqueira, but in the afternoon some fish were brought in, and finding among them a couple of new species, I set to work figuring them, determined to let no opportunity pass of increasing my collections. This village has no malocca, but a number of small houses ; having been founded by the Portuguese before the Independence. It is pleasantly situated on the sloping bank of the river, which is about half a mile wide, with rather high land opposite, and a view up to the narrow channel, where the waters are bounding and foaming and leaping high in the air with the violence of the fall, or more properly rapid.

There was a young Brazilian "negociante" and his wife residing in this village, and as he was also about ascending the river to fetch farinha, we agreed to go together. The next morning we accordingly started, proceeding along the shore to near the fall, where we crossed among boiling foam and whirling eddies, and entered into a small igaripé, where the canoe was entirely unloaded, all the cargo carried along a rugged path through the forest, and the canoe taken round a projecting point, where the violence of the current and the heaving waves of the fall render it impossible for anything but a small empty obá to pass, and even that with great difficulty,

The path terminated at a narrow channel, through which a part of the river in the wet season flows, but which in the summer is completely dry. Were it not for this stream, the passage of the rapids in the wet season would be quite impossible; for though the actual fall of the water is trifling, its violence is inconceivable. The average width of the river may be stated at near three times that of the Thames at London; and it is in the wet season very deep and rapid. At the fall it is enclosed in a narrow sloping rocky gorge, about the width of the middle arch of London Bridge, or even less. I need say no more to prove the impossibility of ascending such a channel. There are immense whirlpools which engulf large canoes. The waters roll like ocean waves, and leap up at intervals, forty or fifty feet into the air, as if great subaqueous explosions were taking place.

Presently the Indians appeared with our canoe, and, assisted by a dozen more who came to help us, pulled it up through the shallows, where the water was less violent. Then came another difficult point; and we plunged again into the forest with half the Indians carrying our cargo, while the remainder went with the canoe. There were several other dangerous places, and two more disembarkations and land carriages, the last for a considerable distance. Above the main fall the river is suddenly widened out into a kind of a lake, filled with rocky islands, among which are a confusion of minor falls and rapids. However, having plenty of Indians to assist us, we passed all these dangers by a little after midday, and reached a malocca, where we stayed for the afternoon repairing the wear and tear of the palm-mats and toldas, and cleaning our canoe and arranging our cargo, ready to start the next morning.

In two days more we reached another village, called Jukeíra Picóma, or Salt Point, where we stayed a day. I was well satisfied to find myself here considerably better, owing, I believe, to my having tried fasting as a last resource: for two

days I had only taken a little farinha gruel once in the twenty-
four hours.  In a day and a half from Jukeíra we reached
Jauarité, a village situated just below the caxoeira of the same
name, the second great rapid on the Uaupés.  Here we had
determined to stay some days and then return, as the caxoeira
is very dangerous to pass, and above it the river, for many
days' journey, is a succession of rapids and strong currents,
which render the voyage up at this season in the highest
degree tedious and disagreeable.  We accordingly disembarked
our cargo into a house, or rather shed, near the shore, made
for the accommodation of traders, which we cleaned and took
possession of, and felt ourselves quite comfortable after the
annoyances we had been exposed to in reaching this place.
We then walked up to the malocca, to pay a visit to the
Tushaúa.  This house was a noble building of its kind, being
one hundred and fifteen feet long, seventy-five wide, and about
twenty-five feet high, the roof and upper timbers being black
as jet with the smokes of many years.  There were besides
about a dozen private cottages, forming a small village.  Scattered around were immense numbers of the Pupunha Palm
(*Guilielma speciosa*), the fruit of which forms an important
part of the food of these people during the season; it was now
just beginning to ripen.  The Tushaúa was rather a respect-
able-looking man, the possessor of a pair of trousers and a
shirt, which he puts on in honour of white visitors.  Senhor
L., however, says he is one of the greatest rogues on the river,
and will not trust him, as he does most of the other Indians,
with goods beforehand.  He rejoices in the name of Calistro,
and pleased me much by his benevolent countenance and
quiet dignified manner.  He is said to be the possessor of
great riches in the way of oncas' teeth and feathers, the result
of his wars upon the Macús and other tribes of the tributary
rivers; but these he will not show to the whites, for fear of
being made to sell them.  Behind the malocca I was pleased
to see a fine broad path, leading into the forest to the several
mandiocca rhossas.  The next morning early I went with my
net to explore it, and found it promise pretty well for insects,
considering the season.  I was greatly delighted at meeting in
it the lovely clear-winged butterfly allied to the *Esmeralda*,
that I had taken so sparingly at Javíta; and I also took a
specimen of another of the same genus, quite new to me.  A

A STREAM IN THE FOREST.

PLATE VII.

plain-coloured *Acræa*, that I had first met with at Jukeíra, was
here also very abundant.

In a hollow near a small stream that crossed the path I
found growing the singular palm called "Paxiúba barriguda"
(the big-bellied paxiuba). It is a fine, tall, rather slender tree,
with a head of very elegant curled leaves. At the base of the
stem is a conical mass of air-roots, five or six feet high, more
or less developed in all the species of this genus. But the
peculiar character from which it derives its name is, that the
stem at rather more than halfway up swells suddenly out to
double its former thickness or more, and after a short distance
again contracts, and continues cylindrical to the top. It is
only by seeing great numbers of these trees, all with this
character more or less palpable, that one can believe it is not
an accidental circumstance in the individual tree, instead of
being truly characteristic of the species. It is the *Iriartea
ventricosa* of Martius.

I tried here to procure some hunters and fishermen, but
was not very successful. I had a few fish brought me, and
now and then a bird. A curious bird, called anambé, was
flying in flocks about the pupunha palms, and after much
trouble I succeeded in shooting one, and it proved, as I had
anticipated, quite different from the *Gymnoderus nudicollis*,
which is a species much resembling it in its flight, and common
in all parts of the Rio Negro. I went after them several times,
but could not succeed in shooting another; for though they
take but short flights, they remain at rest scarcely an instant.
About the houses here were several trumpeters, curassow-birds,
and those beautiful parrots, the anacás (*Derotypus accipitrinus*),
which all wander and fly about at perfect liberty, but being
bred from the nest, always return to be fed. The Uaupés
Indians take much delight, and are very successful, in breeding
birds and animals of all kinds.

We stayed here a week, and I went daily into the forest
when the weather was not very wet, and generally obtained
something interesting. I frequently met parties of women and
boys, going to and returning from the rhossas. Sometimes
they would run into the thicket till I had passed; at other
times they would merely stand on one side of the path, with a
kind of bashful fear at encountering a white man while in that
state of complete nudity, which they know is strange to us.

When about the houses in the village however, or coming to fill their water-pots or bathe in the river close to our habitation, they were quite unembarrassed, being, like Eve, " naked and not ashamed." Though some were too fat, most of them had splendid figures, and many of them were very pretty. Before daylight in the morning all were astir, and came to the river to wash. It is the chilliest hour of the twenty-four, and when we were wrapping our sheet or blanket more closely around us, we could hear the plunges and splashings of these early bathers. Rain or wind is all alike to them : their morning bath is never dispensed with.

Fish were here very scarce, and we were obliged to live almost entirely on fowls, which, though very nice when well roasted and with the accompaniment of ham and gravy, are rather tasteless simply boiled or stewed, with no variation in the cookery, and without vegetables. I had now got so thoroughly into the life of this part of the country, that, like everybody else here, I preferred fish to every other article of food. One never tires of it; and I must again repeat that I believe there are fish here superior to any in the world. Our fowls cost us about a penny each, paid in fish-hooks or salt, so that they are not such expensive food as they would be at home. In fact, if a person buys his hooks, salt, and other things in Pará, where they are about half the price they are at Barra, the price of a fowl will not exceed a halfpenny; and fish, pacovas, and other eatables that the country produces, in the same proportion. A basket of farinha, that will last one person very well a month, will cost about threepence; so that with a small expenditure a man may obtain enough to live on. The Indians here made their mandiocca bread very differently from, and very superior to, those of the adjacent rivers. The greater part is tapioca, which they mix with a small quantity of the prepared mandiocca-root, and form a white, gelatinous, granular cake, which with a little use is very agreeable, and is much sought after by all the white traders on the river. Farinha they scarcely ever eat themselves, but make it only to sell; and as they extract the tapioca, which is the pure glutinous portion of the root, to make their own bread, they mix the refuse with a little fresh mandiocca to make farinha, which is thus of a very poor quality ; yet such is the state of agriculture on the Rio Negro, that the city of Barra depends in a great measure upon this refuse food of the Indians, and several thousand alqueires are purchased, and most of it sent there, annually.

The principal food of these Indians is fish, and when they have neither this nor any game, they boil a quantity of peppers, in which they dip their bread. At several places where we stopped this was offered to our men, who ate with a relish the intensely burning mess. Yams and sweet potatoes are also abundant, and with pacovas form a large item in their stock of eatables. Then they have the delicious drinks made from the fruits of the assaí, baccába, and patawá palms, as well as several other fruits.

The large saúbas and white ants are an occasional luxury, and when nothing else is to be had in the wet season they eat large earth-worms, which, when the lands in which they live are flooded, ascend trees, and take up their abode in the hollow leaves of a species of *Tillandsia*, where they are often found accumulated by thousands. Nor is it only hunger that makes them eat these worms, for they sometimes boil them with their fish to give it an extra relish.

They consume great quantities of mandiocca in making caxirí for their festas, which are continually taking place. As I had not seen a regular dance, Senhor L. asked the Tushaúa to make some caxirí and invite his friends and vassals to dance, for the white stranger to see. He readily consented, and, as we were to leave in two or three days, immediately sent round a messenger to the houses of the Indians near, to make known the day and request the honour of their company. As the notice was so short, it was only those in the immediate neighbourhood who could be summoned.

On the appointed day numerous preparations were taking place. The young girls came repeatedly to fill their pitchers at the river early in the morning, to complete the preparation of the caxirí. In the forenoon they were busy weeding all round the malocca, and sprinkling water, and sweeping within it. The women were bringing in dry wood for the fires, and the young men were scattered about in groups, plaiting straw coronets or arranging some other parts of their ornaments. In the afternoon, as I came from the forest, I found several engaged in the operation of painting, which others had already completed. The women had painted themselves or each other, and presented a neat pattern in black and red all over their bodies, some circles and curved lines occurring on their hips and breasts, while on their faces round spots of a bright vermilion seemed to be the prevailing fashion. The juice of a fruit which stains of a fine purplish-black is often poured on the back of the head and neck, and, trickling all down the back, produces what they, no doubt, consider a very elegant dishabille. These spotted beauties were now engaged in performing the same operation for their husbands and sweet-hearts, some standing, others sitting, and directing the fair artists how to dispose the lines and tints to their liking.

We prepared our supper rather early, and about sunset, just as we had finished, a messenger came to notify to us that the dance had begun, and that the Tushaúa had sent to request our company. We accordingly at once proceeded to the malocca, and entering the private apartment at the circular end, were politely received by the Tushaúa, who was dressed in his shirt and trousers only, and requested us to be seated in maqueiras. After a few minutes' conversation I turned to look at the dancing, which was taking place in the body of the house, in a large clear space round the two central columns. A party of about fifteen or twenty middle-aged men were dancing; they formed a semicircle, each with his left hand on his neighbour's right shoulder. They were all completely furnished with their feather ornaments, and I now saw for the first time the head-dress, or acangatára, which they value highly. This consists of a coronet of red and yellow feathers disposed in regular rows, and firmly attached to a strong woven or plaited band. The feathers are entirely from the shoulders of the great red macaw, but they are not those that the bird naturally possesses, for these Indians have a curious art by which they change the colours of the feathers of many birds.

They pluck out those they wish to paint, and in the fresh wound inoculate with the milky secretion from the skin of a small frog or toad. When the feathers grow again they are of a brilliant yellow or orange colour, without any mixture of blue or green, as in the natural state of the bird; and on the new plumage being again plucked out, it is said always to come of the same colour without any fresh operation. The feathers are renewed but slowly, and it requires a great number of them to make a coronet, so we see the reason why the owner esteems it so highly, and only in the greatest necessity will part with it.

Attached to the comb on the top of the head is a fine broad plume of the tail-coverts of the white egret, or more rarely of the under tail-coverts of the great harpy eagle. These are large, snowy white, loose and downy, and are almost equal in beauty to a plume of white ostrich feathers. The Indians keep these noble birds in great open houses or cages, feeding them with fowls (of which they will consume two a day), solely for the sake of these feathers; but as the birds are rare, and the young with difficulty secured, the ornament is one that few possess. From the ends of the comb cords of monkeys' hair, decorated with small feathers, hang down the back, and in the ears are the little downy plumes, forming altogether a most imposing and elegant head-dress. All these dancers had also the cylindrical stone of large size, the necklace of white beads, the girdle of onças' teeth, the garters, and ankle-rattles. A very few had besides a most curious ornament, the nature of which completely puzzled me : it was either a necklace or a circlet round the forehead, according to the quantity pos- sessed, and consisted of small curiously curved pieces of a white colour with a delicate rosy tinge, and appearing like shell or enamel. They say they procure them from the Indians of the Japurá and other rivers, and that they are very expensive, three or four pieces only costing an axe. They appear to me more like portions of the lip of a large shell cut into perfectly regular pieces than anything else, but so regular in size and shape, as to make me doubt again that they can be shell, or that Indians can form them.

In their hands each held a lance, or bundle of arrows, or the painted calabash-rattle. The dance consisted simply of a regular sideway step, carrying the performers round and round in a circle; the simultaneous stamping of the feet, the rattle and clash of the leg ornaments and calabashes, and a chant of a few words repeated in a deep tone, producing a very martial and animated effect. At certain intervals the young women joined in, each one taking her place between two men, whom she clasped with each arm round the waist, her head bending forward beneath the outstretched arm above, which, as the women were all of low stature, did not much interfere with their movements. They kept their places for one or two rounds, and then, at a signal of some sort, all left and retired to their seat on stools or on the ground, till the time should come for them again to take their places.   The greater part of them wore the " tanga," or small apron of beads, but some were perfectly naked.   Several wore large cylindrical copper earrings, so polished as to appear like gold.   These and the garters formed their only ornaments,—necklaces, bracelets, and feathers being entirely monopolised by the men.   The paint with which they decorate their whole bodies has a very neat effect, and gives them almost the appearance of being dressed, and as such they seem to regard it ; and however much those who have not witnessed this strange scene may be disposed to differ from me, I must record my opinion that there is far more immodesty in the transparent and flesh-coloured garments of our stage-dancers, than in the perfect nudity of these daughters of the forest.

In the open space outside the house, a party of young men and boys, who did not possess the full costume, were dancing in the same manner.   They soon, however, began what may be called the snake dance.   They had made two huge artificial snakes of twigs and bushes bound together with sipós, from thirty to forty feet long and about a foot in diameter, with a head of a bundle of leaves of the Umboöba (*Cecropia*), painted with bright red colour, making altogether a very formidable-looking reptile.   They divided themselves into two parties of twelve or fifteen each, and lifting the snakes on their shoulders, began dancing.

In the dance they imitated the undulations of the serpent, raising the head and twisting the tail.   They kept advancing and retreating, keeping parallel to each other, and every time coming nearer to the principal door of the house.   At length they brought the heads of the snakes into the very door, but still retreated several times.   Those within had now concluded their first dance, and after several more approaches, in came the snakes with a sudden rush, and, parting, went one on the right side and one on the left.   They still continued the advancing and retreating step, till at length, each having tra-versed a semicircle, they met face to face.   Here the two snakes seemed inclined to fight, and it was only after many retreatings and brandishings of the head and tail, that they could muster resolution to rush past each other.   After one or two more rounds, they passed out to the outside of the house, and the dance, which had apparently much pleased all the spectators, was concluded.

During all this time caxirí was being abundantly supplied, three men being constantly employed carrying it to the guests. They came one behind the other down the middle of the house, with a large calabash-full in each hand, half stooping down, with a kind of running dance, and making a curious whirring, humming noise : on reaching the door they parted on each side, distributing their calabashes to whoever wished to drink. In a minute or two they were all empty, and the cup-bearers returned to fill them, bringing them every time with the same peculiar forms, which evidently constitute the etiquette of the caxirí-servers. As each of the calabashes holds at least two quarts, the quantity drunk during a whole night that this process is going on must be very great.

Presently the Capí was introduced, an account of which I had had from Senhor L. An old man comes forward with a large newly-painted earthen pot, which he sets down in the middle of the house. He then squats behind it, stirs it about, and takes out two small calabashes-full, which he holds up in each hand. After a moment's pause, two Indians advance with bows and arrows or lances in their hands. Each takes the proffered cup and drinks, makes a wry face, for it is intensely bitter, and stands motionless perhaps half a minute. They then with a start twang their bows, shake their lances, stamp their feet, and return to their seats. The little bowls are again filled, and two others succeed them, with a similar result. Some, however, become more excited, run furiously, lance in hand, as if they would kill an enemy, shout and stamp savagely, and look very warlike and terrible, and then, like the others, return quietly to their places. Most of these receive a hum or shake of applause from the spectators, which is also given at times during the dances.

The house at this time contained at least three hundred men, women, and children ; a continual murmuring conversation was kept up, and fifty little fifes and flutes were constantly playing, each on its own account, producing a not very harmo-nious medley. After dark a large fire was lighted in the middle of the house, and as it blazed up brightly at intervals, illumi-nating the painted and feather-dressed dancers and the numerous strange groups in every variety of posture scattered about the great house, I longed for a skilful painter to do justice to a scene so novel, picturesque, and interesting.

A number of fires were also made outside the house, and the young men and boys amused themselves by jumping over them when flaming furiously, an operation which, with their naked bodies, appeared somewhat hazardous. Having been now looking on about three hours, we went to bid adieu to the Tushaúa, previous to retiring to our house, as I did not feel much inclined to stay with them all night. We found him with a few visitors, smoking, which on these occasions is performed in a very ceremonious manner. The cigar is eight or ten inches long and an inch in diameter, made of tobacco pounded and dried, and enclosed in a cylinder made of a large leaf spirally twisted. It is placed in a cigar-holder about two feet long, like a great two-pronged fork. The bottom is pointed, so that when not in use it can be stuck in the ground. This cigar was offered to us, and Senhor L. took a few whiffs for us both, as he is a confirmed smoker. The caxirí was exceedingly good (although the mandiocca-cake of which it is made is chewed by a parcel of old women), and I much pleased the lady of the Tushaúa by emptying the calabash she offered me, and pronouncing it to be " purángareté" (excellent). We then said " Eré" (adieu), and groped our way down the rough path to our river-side house, to be sung to sleep by the hoarse murmur of the cataract. The next morning the dance was still going on, but, as the caxirí was nearly finished, it terminated about nine o'clock, and the various guests took their leave.

During the dance, Bernardo, an Indian of São Jeronymo, arrived from the Rio Apaporis. Senhor L. had sent a message to him by his son (who had come with us) to procure some Indian boys and girls for him, and he now came to talk over the business. The procuring consists in making an attack on some malocca of another nation, and capturing all that do not escape or are not killed. Senhor L. has frequently been on these expeditions, and has had some narrow escapes from lances and poisoned arrows. At Ananárapicóma there was an Indian dreadfully scarred all over one shoulder and part of his back, the effects of a discharge of B.B. shot which Senhor L. had given him, just as he was in the act of turning with his bow and arrow : they are now excellent friends, and do business

together.  The "negociantes" and authorities in Barra and
Pará, ask the traders among the Indians to procure a boy or
girl for them, well knowing the only manner in which they can
be obtained; in fact, the Government in some degree authorise
the practice.  There is something to be said too in its favour,
for the Indians make war on each other,—principally the
natives of the margin of the river on those in the more distant
igaripés,—for the sake of their weapons and ornaments, and
for revenge of any injury, real or imaginary, and then kill all
they can, reserving only some young girls for their wives.  The
hope of selling them to the traders, however, induces them to
spare many who would otherwise be murdered.  These are
brought up to some degree of civilisation (though I much doubt
if they are better or happier than in their native forests), and
though at times ill-treated, they are free, and can leave their
masters whenever they like, which, however, they seldom do
when taken very young.  Senhor L. had been requested by
two parties at Barra—one the Delegarde de Policia—to furnish
them each with an Indian girl, and as this man was an old
hand at the business, he was now agreeing with him, furnishing him with powder and shot—for he had a gun—and giving
him some goods, to pay other Indians for assisting him, and to
do a little business at the same time if he had the opportunity.
He was to return at the furthest in a fortnight, and we were to
wait for him in São Jeronymo.

The Tushaúa came to pay us a visit almost every day, to
talk a little, and sometimes drink a cup of coffee.  His wife
and some of his daughters, who possessed a "saía," also often
came, bringing us pacovas, mandiocca-cake, and other things,
for which they always expected to be paid.  We bought here a
good number of stools and baskets, which cost five or six
hooks each; also fowls, parrots, trumpeters, and some other
tame birds.  When we first arrived, almost the whole body of
the inhabitants came to visit us, requesting to see what we had
brought to sell; accordingly we spread out our whole stock of
fish-hooks, knives, axes, mirrors, beads, arrow-heads, cottons
and calicoes, which they handled and admired in unintelligible
languages, for about two hours.  It is necessary to make this ex-
position in every village, as they will bring nothing to sell unless they first know that you have what they want in exchange.

Two days after the dance we bade adieu to Jauarité, and by

midday reached Jukeíra, where we had determined to spend another week. There was no regular house here for the accommodation of travellers, so we had to take possession of an unoccupied shed, which the Tushaúa had prepared for us, and where we soon found we were exposed to a pest abundant in all Indians' houses, the "bichos do pé," or chegoes. Nor was this all, for the blood-sucking bats were abundant, and the very first night bit Senhor L., as well as his little boy, who in the morning presented a ghastly sight, both legs being thickly smeared and blotched with blood. There was only one bite on the toe, but the blood flows plentifully, and as the boy was very restless at night, he had managed to produce the sanguinary effect I have mentioned. Several of the Indians were also bitten, but I escaped by always well wrapping my feet in my blanket.

The paths in the forest here were not so good as those at Jauarité, and produced me very few insects; the Indians, however, were rather better in bringing me birds and fish. I obtained some very pretty little tanagers, and several new fish. In one lot of small fish brought to me in a calabash were seven different species, five of which were quite new to me. A species of *Chalceus*, called Jatuarána, was abundant here, and most delicious eating, almost, if not quite, equal to the Waracú, but like it very full of forked spines, which require practice and delicate handling to extract, or they may produce dangerous effects. Several Indians of the Coveu nation, from considerably higher up the river, were staying here. They are distinguished by the ear-lobe being pierced with so large a hole as to be plugged with a piece of wood the size of a common bottle-cork. When we entered their house they set before us, on the ground, smoked fish and madiocca-cake, which Senhor L. informs me is the general custom higher up the river, where the Indians have not lost any of their primitive customs by intercourse with the whites. Senhor L. had bought a quantity of "coroá" (the fibres of a species of *Bromelia*, very like flax), and he set these and several other Indians to twist it into thread, which they do by rolling it on their breasts, and form a fine well-twisted two-strand string, of which fine maqueiras are netted. Each one in two or three days produced a ball of string of a quarter of a pound weight, and they were well satisfied with a small basin of salt or half-a-dozen hooks in payment.

On one or two days of bright sunshine, a beautiful *Papilio* came about the house, settling on the ground in moist places : I succeeded in taking two specimens ; it is allied to *P. Thoas*, and will probably prove a new species. This was my only capture worth mentioning at Jukeíra. I had seen the same species at Jauarité, but could not take a specimen. I purchased one of the red macaws painted as I have mentioned above. Senhor L. was here quite a martyr to the chegoes, frequently extracting ten or a dozen in a day, which made his feet so full of holes and wounds as to render walking painful, as I had experienced at Cobáti and Javíta. I, however, escaped pretty well, seldom having to take out more than two or three at a time, partly I believe owing to my being a good deal in the forest and to my always wearing slippers in the house. When a person has only one or two now and then, it is a trifling affair, and one is apt to think, as I for a long time did, that the dread of chegoes was quite unnecessary, and the accounts of their persecutions much exaggerated. Let any one, however, who still thinks so, take a trip into this part of the country, and live a month in an Indian's house, and he will be thoroughly undeceived.

After staying here six days, finding little to be done, we proceeded on our downward passage to São Jeronymo. On the second day, in the morning, we reached Urubuquárra, the malocca of Bernardo, situated just above the falls. There is a path from this place through the forest, about three miles, to the village ; and as there were no Indians here to assist us in passing the falls, we set ours to work, carrying part of the cargo along it. In the afternoon Bernardo's son, who had returned before us with a canoe-load of farinha, came in, and we arranged to pass the falls the next morning. The river had risen considerably since we ascended, and had now reached a higher point than had been known for several years, and the rapids were proportionally more dangerous. I therefore preferred going through the forest, carrying with me two small boxes, containing the insects I had collected, and my drawings of fish,—the loss of which would have been irreparable. The morning was fine, and I had a pleasant walk, though the path was very rugged in places, with steep descents and ascents at the crossing of several small brooks. Arrived at São Jeronymo, I waited for Senhor L., at the house of Senhor Augustinho, the young Brazilian before mentioned, who had returned from Jauarité before us, with upwards of a hundred alqueires of farinha. About midday a tremendous storm of wind and rain came on, and in the afternoon Senhor L. arrived with the canoe, thoroughly soaked; and informed me that they had had a most dangerous passage, a portion of the path where the cargo had to be carried through the forest being breast-deep in water; and at some of the points, the violence of the current was so great that they narrowly escaped being carried down to the great fall, and dashed to pieces on the rocks.

Here was a good house for travellers, (though without doors,) and we took possession and settled ourselves for a week or ten days' stay. We nearly filled the house with farinha, pitch, baskets, stools, earthen pots and pans, maqueiras, etc.; we had also near a hundred fowls, which had been brought crammed into two huge square baskets, and were now much pleased to be set at liberty,—as well as a large collection of tame birds, parrots, macaws, paroquets, etc., which kept up a continual cawing and crying, not always very agreeable. All these birds were loose, flying about the village, but returning generally to be fed. The trumpeters and curassow-birds wandered about the houses of the Indians, and sometimes did not make their appearance for several days; but being brought up from the nest, or even sometimes from the egg, there was little danger of their escaping to the forest. We had nine pretty little black-headed parrots, which every night would go of their own accord into a basket prepared for them to sleep in.

From what I had seen on this river, there is no place equal to it for procuring a fine collection of live birds and animals; and this, together with the desire to see more of a country so interesting and so completely unknown, induced me, after mature deliberation, to give up for the present my intended journey to the Andes, and to substitute another voyage up the river Uaupés, at least to the Jurupari (Devil) cataract, the "*ultima Thule*" of most of the traders, and about a month's voyage up from its mouth. Several traders who had arrived at São Jeronymo on the way up, as well as the more intelligent Indians, assured me that in the upper districts there are many birds and animals not met with below. But what above all attracted me, was the information that a white species of the celebrated umbrella-chatterer was to be found there. The information on this point from several parties was so positive that, though much inclined to doubt the existence of such a bird at all, I could not rest satisfied without one more trial, as, even if I did not find it, I had little doubt of obtaining many new species to reward me. The worst of it was, that I must go to Barra and return—a voyage of fifteen hundred miles— which was very disagreeable. But there was no remedy, for I had a considerable lot of miscellaneous collections here and at Guia, as well as what I left at Barra, which must be packed and sent off to England, or they might be destroyed by damp and insects. Besides which I could not undertake a voyage on this wild river for several months, without being well supplied with necessaries, and articles for barter with the Indians, which could only be obtained at Barra ; moreover, the best season for ascending would not arrive for two or three months, so that I could do scarcely anything if I remained here. The months of November, December, January, and February, are the "vasante," or low water, and then is the summer-season, when the river presents a totally different and a much more agreeable aspect, being everywhere bordered with fine sandy or rocky beaches, on which one can eat and sleep with comfort at any hour. Fish are then much more abundant ; turtles of a new species are said to be found on the sands, in the upper part of the river, and to lay abundance of eggs ; the delicious fruit of the baccába and patawá palms are then ripe, and birds and insects of all kinds more easily procurable. These four months I hoped, therefore, to spend there, so as to be able to descend to Barra, and thence to Pará, in time to return to England by July or August, with a numerous and valuable collection of live animals. It was on account of these, principally, that I determined to return to England a year before the time I had fixed upon, as it was impossible to send them without personal care and attendance.

And so, having once made up my mind to this course, with what delight I thought upon the sweets of home ! What a paradise did that distant land seem to me ! How I thought of the many simple pleasures, so long absent,—the green fields, the pleasant woods, the flowery paths, the neat gardens,—all so unknown here ! What visions of the fireside did I conjure up, of the social tea-table, with familiar faces around it !

What a luxury seemed simple bread and butter!—and to think that, perhaps in one short year, I might be in the midst of all this! There was a pleasure in the mere thought, that made me leap over the long months, the weary hours, the troubles and annoyances of tedious journeys, that had first to be endured. I passed hours in solitary walks thinking of home; and never did I in former years long to be away in this tropic-land, with half the earnestness with which I now looked forward to returning back again.

Our stay at São Jeronymo was prolonged by the non-appearance of Bernardo. Insects were not so plentiful even as at Jauarité; but I generally found something in my walks, and obtained two fine species of *Satyridæ* quite new to me. In a little patch of open bushy campo, which occurs about a mile back from the village, I was delighted to find abundance of orchids. I had never seen so many collected in one place; it was a complete natural orchid-house. In an hour's ramble, I noticed about thirty different species;—some, minute plants scarcely larger than mosses, and one large semi-terrestrial species, which grew in clumps eight or ten feet high. There were but few in flower, and most of them were very small, though pretty. One day, however, I was much delighted to come suddenly upon a magnificent flower: growing out of a rotten stem of a tree, just level with my eye, was a bunch of five or six blossoms, which were three inches in diameter, nearly round, and varying from a pale delicate straw-colour to a rich deep yellow, on the basal portion of the labellum. How exquisitely beautiful did it appear in that wild, sandy, barren spot! A day or two afterwards I found another handsome species, the flowers of which, unlike those of most of the family, were of very short duration, opening in the morning, and lasting but a single day. The sight of these determined me to try and send some to England, as from such a distant and unexplored locality there would probably be many new species. I accordingly began bringing a few home every day, and, packing them in empty farinha-baskets, placed them under a rough stage, with some plantain-leaves to defend them from the heat of the sun, till we should be ready to embark. I was rather doubtful of the result, as they could not arrive in England before the winter, which might be injurious; but on my next voyage, I looked forward to bringing a larger collection of these beautiful and interesting plants, as they would then arrive in a good season of the year.

São Jeronymo is celebrated for its abundance of fish, but at this season they are in all places difficult to take. However, we had on most days enough for breakfast and supper, and scarcely a day passed but I had some new and strange kinds to add to my collection. The small fishes of these rivers are in wonderful variety, and the large proportion of the species here, different from those I had observed in the Rio Negro, led me to hope that in the upper parts of the river I should find them almost entirely new.

Here we were tolerably free from chegoes, but had another plague, far worse, because more continual. We had suffered more or less from piums in all parts of the river, but here they were in such countless myriads, as to render it almost impossible to sit down during the day. It was most extraordinary that previously to this year they had never been known in the river. Senhor L. and the Indians all agreed that a pium had hitherto been a rarity, and now they were as plentiful as in their very worst haunts. Having long discarded the use of stockings in these " altitudes," and not anticipating any such pest, I did not bring a pair, which would have been useful to defend my feet and ankles in the house, as the pium, unlike the mosquito, does not penetrate any covering, however thin.

As it was, the torments I suffered when skinning a bird or drawing a fish, can scarcely be imagined by the unexperienced. My feet were so thickly covered with the little blood-spots produced by their bites, as to be of a dark purplish-red colour, and much swelled and inflamed. My hands suffered similarly, but in a less degree, being more constantly in motion. The only means of taking a little rest in the day, was by wrapping up hands and feet in a blanket. The Indians close their houses, as these insects do not bite in the dark, but ours having no door, we could not resort to this expedient. Whence these pests could thus suddenly appear in such vast numbers is a mystery which I am quite unable to explain.

When we had been here about a week, some Indians who had been sent to Guia with a small cargo of farinha, returned and brought us news of two deaths, which had taken place in the village since we had left. One was of Jozé, a little Indian boy in Senhor L.'s house, who had killed himself by eating dirt,—a very common and destructive habit among Indians and half-breeds in the houses of the whites. All means had been tried to cure him of the habit he had been physicked and whipped, and confined · indoors, but when no other opportunity offered he would find a plentiful supply in the mud-walls of the house. The symptoms produced were swelling of the whole body, face, and limbs, so that he could with difficulty walk, and not having so much care taken of him after we left, he ate his fill and died.

The other was an old Indian, the Juiz of the festa of St. Antonio, which took place shortly after we left. He was poisoned with caxirí, into which had been put the juice of a root which produces the most dreadful effects : the tongue and throat swell, putrefy, and rot away, and the same effects seem to take place in the stomach and intestines, till, in two or three days, the patient dies in great agony. The poisoner was not known, but it was suspected to be a young woman, sister of an Indian who died in the village a short time before, and whose death they imagined to be caused by charms or witchcraft ; and the present murder was probably in revenge for this supposed injury. Coroners' inquests are here unknown, and the poor old man was buried, and nothing more thought about the matter ; perhaps, however, his friends may resort to the same means to repay the suspected parties.

A few days afterwards a boy died in São Jeronymo, and for several hours a great crying and wailing was made over the body. His maqueira, and bow and arrows, were burnt in a fire made at the back of the house, within which, according to the universal custom of these Indians, he was buried, and the mother continued her mournful wailing for several days.

The only additions I made to my collections during the time I stayed here, were a prehensile-tailed ant-eater, and one of the small nocturnal monkeys called " Juruparí Macaco," or Devil Monkey, a species very closely allied to that called " Iá," which inhabits the Solimões. After waiting anxiously a fortnight, Bernado made his appearance with three of his wives and a host of children : he had been unsuccessful in his projected attack, the parties having obtained notice of his motions and absconded. He had taken every precaution, by entering in a different river from that in which the attack was to be made, and penetrating through the forest; but his movements were, no doubt, thought suspicious, and it was considered safer to get out of his way; he was, however, confident of succeeding next time in another place, where he thought he could arrive unawares.

Having now no further cause for delay, we loaded our canoes, and the next morning left São Jeronymo, on our return to Guia, where we arrived on the morning of the 24th, having been absent on our trip fifty days.

The most important event that had occurred in the village was the arrival from Barra of Manoel Joaquim, a half-breed Brazilian, some time resident at Guia. This man was a specimen of the class of white men found in the Rio Negro. He had been a soldier, and had been engaged in some of the numerous revolutions which had taken place in Brazil. It was said he had murdered his wife, and for that, or some other crimes, had been banished to the Rio Negro, instead of being hung, as he deserved. Here he was accustomed to threaten and shoot at the Indians, to take their daughters and wives from them, and to beat the Indian woman who lived with him, so that she was obliged to hide for days in the forest. The people of Guia declared he had murdered two Indian girls, and had committed many other horrible crimes. He had formerly been friendly with Senhor L., but, a year or two ago, had quarrelled with him, and had attempted to set fire to his house; he had also attempted to shoot an old Mulatto soldier, who was friendly with Senhor L. For these and other crimes, the Subdelegarde de Policia of the district had indicted him, and after taking the depositions of the Indians and of Senhor L. against him, had wished to send him prisoner to Barra, but could not do so, because he had no force at his command. He therefore applied to the Commandante of Marabitánas, who was at Guia at the time; but he was Manoel Joaquim's "compadre," and took his part, and would not send him as a prisoner, but let him go in his own canoe, accompanied by two soldiers, bearing a recommendation from the Commandante in his favour.

This had happened shortly before we left for the Uaupés; and now we found that Manoel Joaquim had returned in great triumph—firing salutes and sending up rockets at every village he passed through. He had gone on to Marabitánas; but in a day or two more returned, and brought me some letters and papers from Barra. There also came a letter to Senhor L. from the Delegarde de Policia in Barra, saying, that Manoel Joaquim had presented himself, and that he (the Delegarde) had asked him if he came a prisoner ; that he replied, " No ; he came to attend to his own business." " Well, then," said the Delegarde, "as you have not been incommoded by this indictment, it is better to treat these slanders and quarrels with disdain ; " and said he to Senhor L., " I would advise you to do the same." And so ended the attempt to punish a man who, if one-half the crimes imputed to him were true, ought, by the laws of Brazil, to have been hung, or imprisoned for life. The poor Subdelegarde, it seems, through pure ignorance, committed some informalities, and this was the reason why Manoel Joaquim so easily and gloriously escaped.

The best of it is that there is a special officer in Barra and in every other city, called the " Promotor Publico," whose sole duty it is to see that all the other officers of justice and of police do their duty, so that no criminal may escape or injustice be done, by the laxity or connivance of any of these parties. Yet, with all this, nothing is easier in the Rio Negro, than for any person possessed of friends or money, to defeat the ends of justice.

I now found another unavoidable delay in my projected voyage to Barra. A canoe that was making for me was not yet ready, and I did not know where to obtain one sufficiently capacious to take all my luggage and collections : but, a few days after, a Spaniard, or Venezuelano, arrived at Guia with a canoe for Manoel Joaquim ; and as he was to return by Mara-bitánas, I took the opportunity of writing to the Commandante, asking the loan of his igarité, for the voyage to Barra and back. He very kindly consented, and in about a week I received it ; but I was as badly off as ever, for a canoe without men was of no use ; and the Indians, fearing the results of Manoel Joaquim's return, had all left Guia, and retired to their sitios in distant igaripés, and in the most inaccessible depths of the forest. The Commandante had sent orders to two Indians to go with me, but these were not sufficient to descend the falls with safety ; so, as Senhor L. was about to remove to São Joaquim, at the mouth of the Uaupés, I agreed to go with him, and try and procure more men there. My Indians took nearly a fortnight to prepare the canoe with new toldas—about two days work; but then, though I was in a hurry, they were not.

Senhor L. had not a single man left with him, and had to take his canoe down himself, and bring back Indians to assist him to remove his goods and his family, when we went all together to São Joaquim, where he intended to reside some time. I now thought I should be able to leave immediately, but found it not such an easy matter, for every Indian I applied to had some business of his own to attend to, before he could possibly go with me to Barra. One said, his house was very much out of repair, and he must first mend it; another had appointed a dance to take place in a week or two, and when that was over, he was at my service; so I still had to wait a little longer, and try the Brazilian remedy for all such annoyances—" paciencia."

# CHAPTER XI.

## ON THE RIO NEGRO.

Difficulties of Starting—Descending the Falls—Catching an Alligator
—Tame Parrots—A Fortnight in Barra—Frei Jozé's Diplomacy—
Pickling a Cow-Fish—A River Storm—Brazilian Veracity—Wanawáca
—Productiveness of the Country—A Large Snake—São Gabriel—
São Joaquim—Fever and Ague.

At length, on the 1st of September, after another week's delay,
having succeeded in procuring two more Indians and a pilot, I left
on my long-desired voyage. One Indian I could only persuade
to go, by sending four others to assist him for three days in
clearing his mandiocca rhossa, without doing which he would
not leave. My canoe went fully loaded, as I took a quantity
of farinha and miscellaneous goods for Senhor L., and I had
some little fear of the passage of the falls, which was not
diminished by my pilot's being completely stupefied with his
parting libations of caxirí. He was also rather fearful, saying,
that the canoe was overloaded, and that he did not know the
channel well below São Gabriel; and that from there to Camanaú
I must get another pilot.

The rapids, before arriving at São Gabriel, are not very
dangerous, and much to my satisfaction we arrived there in
safety, about four in the afternoon. We there partially unloaded, to pass the narrow channel at the Fort, which was also
accomplished with safety; though not without danger at one
point, where the canoe got out of the proper course, and the
waves dashed in rather fearfully. I then succeeded in agreeing
with a good pilot to take us down the next morning, and was
much relieved by his informing me, that, the river being very
full, the falls were not dangerous, and the canoe would pass
with perfect safety without more unloading. I therefore will-

ingly paid him what he asked, four milreis (about nine shillings) ; and the next morning, having got the canoe properly reloaded, we bade adieu to the Commandante, and in two hours had passed safely down to Camanaú.

The navigation of these falls is of a character quite distinct from anything in our part of the world. A person looking at the river sees only a rapid current, a few eddies, swells, and small breakers, in which there appears nothing very formidable. When, however, you are in the midst of them, you are quite bewildered with the conflicting motions of the waters. Whirling and boiling eddies, which burst up from the bottom at intervals, as if from some subaqueous explosion, with short cross-waves, and smooth intervening patches, almost make one giddy. On one side of the canoe there is often a strong down-current ; while, on the other, it flows in an opposite direction. Now there is a cross stream at the bows, and a diagonal one at the stern, with a foaming Scylla on one side and a whirling Charybdis on the other. All depends upon the pilot, who, well acquainted with every sunken rock and dangerous whirl-pool, steers clear of all perils,—now directing the crew to pull hard, now to slacken, as circumstances require, and skilfully preparing the canoe to receive the impetus of the cross currents that he sees ahead. I imagine that the neighbourhood of the arches of Old London Bridge, at certain states of the tide, must have presented on a small scale somewhat similar dangers. When the river is low, the descent is more perilous ; for, though the force of the waters is not so great, they are so crammed with rocks in all stages of submersion, that to avoid them becomes a work requiring the greatest knowledge and care on the part of the pilot. Having passed these much-dreaded rapids, we proceeded pleasantly to São Jozé, where I stayed a day, to take out part of Senhor's L.'s cargo, and reload the canoe properly for the voyage to Barra.

In the afternoon, a fine specimen of one of the smaller species of alligator, or Jacaré, was brought in, and preparations were made to cut it up for supper. I, however, immediately determined to skin it, and requested to be allowed to do so, promising to get out the tail and body, for culinary purposes, in a very short time. After about an hour's hard work, I extracted the most meaty part of the tail, which is considered the best ; and in another hour delivered up the body, leaving the head and legs to be cleaned the next day in the canoe. The animal was nearly six feet long, and the scales of the belly could only be cut by heavy blows with a hammer on a large knife. It was caught with a line, to which was attached, by the middle, a short strong pointed stick baited with fish ; when swallowed, the stick remains firmly fixed across the stomach of the animal. The flesh has a very strong but rather agreeable odour, like guavas or some musky fruit, and is much esteemed by Indians and many whites ; but it requires to be young, fat, and well dressed, to form, in my opinion, a palatable meal. I had plenty of work the next day, cleaning the head and limbs, and these furnished a supply of meat for my Indians' supper.

I called at the sitio of Senhor Chagas, whom I had met at Guia, and from him I again received the most positive information of the existence, on the river Uaupés, of a white umbrella-bird, having himself seen a specimen, which one of his Indians had killed.

On the 6th I reached the sitio of Senhor João Cordeiro, the Subdelegarde, where I stopped to breakfast ; and arranged with him to remain a few days at his house, on my return voyage, in order to skin and prepare the skeleton of a cow-fish, which he promised to procure for me, as they are very abundant in the river Urubaxí, which enters the Rio Negro just above his house, and where he, every year, takes great numbers with the net and harpoon. At breakfast we had some of the meat,— preserved, by being boiled or fried in its own oil ; it is then put into large pots, and will keep many months. On taking my leave, he sent me a plate of the meat, and some sausages for my voyage.

I here finished stuffing my Jacaré, and was obliged to borrow a drill to make the holes to sew up the skin. I had no box to put it in, and no room for it in the canoe, so I tied it on a board, and had a palm-leaf mat made to cover it from rain, on the top of the tolda. Senhor João told us to visit his " cacoarie," or fish-weir, on our way down, and take what we found in it. We did so, and of fish only got one,—a curious mailed species, quite new to me, and which gave me an afternoon's work to figure and describe. There were also five small red-headed turtles, which were very acceptable, and furnished us with dinner for several days.

We proceeded pleasantly on our voyage, sometimes with rain

and sometimes with sunshine, and often obliged to make a
supper of farinha and water, on account of there being no land
on which to make a fire; but to all these inconveniences I was
by this time well inured, and thought nothing of what, a year
before, was a very great hardship. At the different sitios
where I called, I often received orders for Barra; for everybody
whom I had once seen was, on a second encounter, an old
friend, and would take a friend's privilege. One requested me
to bring him a pot of turtle oil,—another, a garafão of wine;
the Delegarde wanted a couple of cats, and his clerk a couple
of ivory small-tooth combs; another required gimlets, and
another, again, a guitar. For all these articles I received not
a vintem of payment, but was promised the money certain on
my return, or an equivalent in coffee or tobacco, or some
other article current in the Rio Negro. To many persons,
with whom I had never spoken, I was nevertheless well known,
and addressed by name; and these would often hint that such
and such an article they were much in want of, and, without
directly requesting me to get it for them, would intimate that
if I should bring it, they would be happy to purchase it of me.

The only live animals I had with me were a couple of parrots,
which were a never-failing source of amusement. One was a
little "Marianna," or Macaí of the Indians, a small black-
headed, white-breasted, orange-neck and thighed parrot; the
other, an Anacá, a most beautiful bird, banded on the breast
and belly with blue and red, and the back of the neck and
head covered with long bright red feathers margined with
blue, which it would elevate when angry, forming a handsome crest somewhat similar to that of the harpy eagle; its
ornithological name is *Derotypus accipitrinus*, the hawk-headed
parrot. There was a remarkable difference in the characters of
these birds. The Anacá was of a rather solemn, morose, and
irritable disposition; while the Mariánna was a lively little
creature, inquisitive as a monkey, and playful as a kitten. It
was never quiet, running over the whole canoe, climbing into
every crack and cranny, diving into all the baskets, pans, and
pots it could discover, and tasting everything they contained.
It was a most omnivorous feeder, eating rice, farinha, every kind
of fruit, fish, meat, and vegetable, and drinking coffee too as well
as myself; and as soon as it saw me with basin in hand, would
climb up to the edge, and not be quiet without having a share,

which it would lick up with the greatest satisfaction, stopping now and then, and looking knowingly round, as much as to say, "This coffee is very good," and then sipping again with increased gusto.  The bird evidently liked the true flavour of the coffee, and not that of the sugar, for it would climb up to the edge of the coffee-pot, and hanging on the rim plunge boldly down till only its little tail appeared above, and then drink the coffee-grounds for five minutes together.  The Indians in the canoe delighted to imitate its pretty clear whistle, making it reply and stare about, in a vain search after its companions.  Whenever we landed to cook, the Marianna was one of the first on shore, —not with any view to an escape, but merely to climb up some bush or tree and whistle enjoyment of its elevated position, for as soon as eating commenced, it came down for a share of fish or coffee.  The more sober Anacá would generally remain quietly in the canoe, till, lured by the cries and whistles of its lively little companion, it would venture out to join it ; for, notwithstanding their difference of disposition, they were great friends, and would sit for hours side by side, scratching each other's heads, or playing together just like a cat and a kitten ; the Marianna sometimes so exasperating the Anacá by scratches and peckings, and by jumping down upon it, that a regular fight would ensue, which, however, soon terminated, when they would return to their former state of brotherhood. I intended them as presents to two friends in Barra, but was almost sorry to part them.

On the 15th of September, exactly a fortnight after leaving São Joaquim, we arrived safely at Barra.  The whitened houses and open situation of the city appeared quite charming, after being so long accustomed to the mud-walled, forest-buried villages of Rio Negro.  I found that my friend Mr. Spruce was in the city, being a prisoner there, as I had been at Guia, for want of men.  He occupied a house, made classic to the Naturalist by having been the abode of Dr. Natterer, where he kindly accommodated me during my stay, which I intended should be as short as possible.

Bad news was awaiting me from Pará.  Letters, dated more than three months back, from my correspondent, Mr. Miller, informed me of the dangerous illness of my brother, who had been attacked by yellow fever ; and when the canoe left, which brought the letter, was exhibiting such symptoms as

left little hope of his recovery. The only additional information brought since, was that the *Princess Victoria*, with a
valuable cargo, had been lost entering Pará; and that the consequent excitement and anxiety of Mr. Miller, had led to an
attack of brain fever, which had terminated in his death. From
no one could I obtain a word of information about my brother,
and so remained in a state of the greatest suspense. Had he
recovered, he would himself, of course, have written; but, on
the other hand, it was strange that none of the English residents in Pará had sent me a line to inform me of his death,
had it occurred.

I was a fortnight in Barra, busily occupied buying and selling, and arranging and packing my miscellaneous collections.
I had to make insect-boxes and packing-cases, the only carpenter in the place having taken it into his head to leave a
good business, and, like everybody else, go trading about the
rivers.

In the evening, and at all spare moments, we luxuriated in
the enjoyments of rational conversation,—to me, at least, the
greatest, and here the rarest of pleasures. Mr. Spruce, as well
as myself, much wished that we could ascend together; but
my canoe was too small to accommodate us both, and my men
were too few for his, loaded, as it would be, with our combined
cargoes. No men were to be obtained at Barra for love or
money. Even the authorities, when they require to make
some journey on official business, are obliged, frequently, to
beg men of Senhor Henrique or some other negociante. To
such a state is this fine country reduced by Brazilian misrule
and immorality!

Just as I was about to start, the Subdelegarde sent to inform
me I must take a passport, an annoyance I had quite forgotten.
However, there was no remedy, as the clerk does not like to
lose his fee of a " crusado." I had first to get paper stamped
(and the Stamp-office was not open), and then to go the other
end of the city to where the clerk lived, to get the passport.
As everything was on board and all ready, this was a great
bore, and Senhor Henrique advised me to go without a passport, and he would send it after me. As I knew the Subdelegarde would not send after me to fetch me back, I took his
advice and started. Mr. Spruce came with me for a day's trip,
taking a couple of boys and a montaría to return in. We had

a fine wind, which took us across the great bays above Barra ; and about four in the afternoon we landed on a sandy beach, near which were a couple of cottages.  Here Mr. S. found some handsome new flowering shrubs and trees, and I obtained five specimens of a small fish, a pacú new to me, so we both had work till supper-time ; after which meal we hung our redes under the bushes as we best could, and passed an agreeable night.  The next morning we bade each other farewell ; Mr. S. returning to Barra, and I pursuing my voyage up the river. On arriving at a sitio, where I had on the way down left my montaría in order that it might not be stolen in Barra, I found my precaution had been of no avail, as it had been stolen a few days before by an Indian of the Rio Branco.  He had had his own canoe taken from him near that place, by a man going to the Solimões, who tried to compel the owner to go also, and so, in self-defence, the Indian took mine to pursue his journey. I had no remedy, so we went on, trusting to buy a montaría somewhere shortly.  We had several strong " trovoádos," which were rather dangerous, owing to my canoe being very much loaded.  One came on with great violence from the other side of the river, raising tremendous waves, which would have driven us on shore and broken our boat all to pieces, had there not luckily been some bushes in the water, to which we fastened prow and poop, and remained tossing and rolling about more than an hour, baling out the water as fast as it came in, and in constant fear of shipping a sea that would send us to the bottom.

The same evening I overtook Frei Jozé, who was on a pastoral and trading visit to Pedreiro.  We stayed at the same place to sleep, and I went to converse a little with him in his canoe, which was large and commodious.  Our conversation turning on the prevalence of the small-pox in Pará, he related an anecdote of his own diplomatic powers with respect to that dreadful disease, on which he appeared to pride himself considerably.

" When I was in Bolivia," said he, " there were several nations of very warlike Indians, who plundered and murdered travellers on the way to Stª. Cruz.  The President sent the soldiers after them, and spent much money in powder and ball, but with very little effect.  The small-pox was in the city at the time, and the clothes of all who died of it were ordered to be burnt, to prevent infection.   One day conversing with his Excellency about the Indians, I put him up to a much cheaper way than powder and ball for exterminating them.   " Instead of burning the clothes," said I, "just order them to be put in the way of the Indians : they are sure to take possession of them, and they'll die off like wildfire.   He followed my advice, and in a few months there was no more heard of the depredations of the Indians.   Four or five nations were totally destroyed." "For," added he, "the bixiga plays the devil among the Indians."   I could hardly help a shudder at this cool account of such a cold-blooded massacre, but said nothing, consoling myself with the idea that it was probably one of the ingenious fabrications of Frei Jozé's fertile brain ; though it showed that he would look upon the reality as a very politic and laudable action.

At Pedreiro I bought a couple of fine turtles, and stayed half a day to kill and cook one.   It was very fat, so we fried almost all the meat and put it in a large pot with the oil, as it keeps a long time, and, boiled up with a little rice, makes an excellent dinner when fish are not to be had.   The insides, all of which are eatable, together with the meat adhering to the upper and lower shell, and some of the eggs (of which there were near two hundred) were sufficient for all the crew for two days.   At Carvoeiro I stayed a day to get my guns mended, some large hooks made, and the tolda (which the Indians had made very badly in Barra) repaired.   Senhor Vasconcellos gave me a curious flat-headed species of river-tortoise I had not before met with ; he had kept it in a small pond two years, having brought it from the lower Amazon.   Here I had strong symptoms of fever, and expected I was going to have an attack of the much-dreaded ' seizãos,' for which Carvoeiro is a noted locality.   Looking after the arrangement of the canoe in the hot sun did not do me much good ; and shortly after leaving, I found myself quite knocked up, with headache, pains in the back and limbs, and violent fever.   I had commenced operations that morning by taking some purgative medicine, and the next day I began taking doses of quinine, drinking plentifully cream-of-tartar water, though I was so weak and apathetic that at times I could hardly muster resolution to move myself to prepare them.   It is at such times that one feels the want of a friend or attendant ; for of course it is impossible to get the Indians to do these little things without so much explanation and showing as would require more exertion than doing them oneself.  By dint, however, of another purge, an emetic, washing and bathing, and quinine three times a day, I succeeded in subduing the fever ; and in about four days had only a little weakness left, which in a day or two more quite passed away.  All this time the Indians went on with the canoe as they liked ; for during two days and nights I hardly cared if we sank or swam.  While in that apathetic state I was constantly half-thinking, half-dreaming, of all my past life and future hopes, and that they were perhaps all doomed to end here on the Rio Negro.  And then I thought of the dark uncertainty of the fate of my brother Herbert, and of my only remaining brother in California, who might perhaps ere this have fallen a victim to the cholera, which according to the latest accounts was raging there.  But with returning health these gloomy thoughts passed away, and I again went on, rejoicing in this my last voyage, and looking forward with firm hope to home, sweet home !  I, however, made an inward vow never to travel again in such wild, unpeopled districts without some civilised companion or attendant.

I had intended to skin the remaining turtle on the voyage and had bought a large packing-case to put it in ; but not having room in the canoe, it had been secured edgeways, and one of its feet being squeezed had begun to putrefy, so we were obliged to kill it at once and add the meaty parts to our stock of " mixira " (as meat perserved in oil is called), for the voyage.

We continued our progress with a most tedious slowness, though without accident, till we arrived on the 29th of October at the sitio of João Cordeiro, the Subdelegarde, where I intended staying some days, to preserve the skin and skeleton of a cow-fish.  I found here an old friend, Senhor Jozé de Azevedos, who had visited us at Guia, now ill with ague, from which he had been suffering severely for several days, having violent attacks of vomiting and dysentery.  As usual, he was quite without any proper remedies, and even such simple ones as cooling drinks during the fever were shunned as poison ; hot broths, or caxaça and peppers, being here considered the appropriate medicines.  With the help of a few sudorifics and purgatives, and cooling drinks and baths, with quinine between the fits, he soon got better,—much to his astonishment, as he was almost afraid to submit himself to the treatment I recommended.

I spent a whole week here, for the fishermen were unsuccessful, and for five days no Peixe boi appeared. I, however, had plenty to do, as I skinned a small turtle and a " matamatá (*Chelys Matamata*), that Senhor João gave me. This is an extraordinary river-tortoise, with a deeply-keeled and tubercled shell, and a huge flat broad head and neck, garnished with curious lobed fleshy appendages; the nostrils are prolonged into a tube,—giving the animal altogether a most singular appearance. Some of our Indians went every day to fish, and I several times sent the net, and thus procured many new species to figure and describe, which kept me pretty constantly at work, the intervals being filled up by visits to my patient, eating water-melons, and drinking coffee. This is a fine locality for fish, and as far as they are concerned I should have liked to stay a month or two, as there were many curious and interesting species to be found here, which I had not yet obtained.

At length one morning the Peixi boi we had been so long expecting, arrived. It had been caught the night before, with a net, in a lake at some distance. It was a nearly full-grown male, seven feet long and five in circumference. By the help of a long pole and cords four Indians carried it to a shed, where it was laid on a bed of palm-leaves, and two or three men set to work skinning it; I myself operating on the paddles and the head, where the greatest delicacy is required, which the Indians are not accustomed to. After the skin was got off, a second operation was gone through, to take away the layer of fat beneath it, with which to fry the meat I intended to preserve; the inside was then taken out, and the principal mass of meat at once obtained from the belly, back, and sides of the tail. This was all handed over to Senhor João, who undertook to prepare it for me; his men being used to the work, from having some scores to operate upon every year. My Indians then cut away the remaining meat from the ribs, head, and arms for their own saucepans, and in a very short time left the skeleton tolerably bare. All this time I was at work myself at the paddles, and looking on to see that no bones were injured or carried away. I separated the skeleton into convenient pieces for entering into the barrel, cleaned out the spinal marrow, cleared off some more of the meat, and having sprinkled it over with salt, put it with the skin into the barrel to drain for the night, and left the Indians to make a good supper, and stuff themselves till contented. The next day, after arranging the skin and the bones afresh, I with some trouble fastened in the head of the barrel, when I found the brine that was in it oozing out in every direction, and soon discovered that the cask was riddled by little wood-boring beetles. The holes seemed innumerable, but I immediately set to work with two of my Indians, stopping them up with little wooden pegs. We were occupied at this some hours, and had pegged up I don't know how many hundred holes, till we could not by the closest examination discover any more. A huge pan of brine had been made by dissolving salt in boiling water, and as some of it was now cool I commenced filling with a funnel; when instantly, notwithstanding all our labour, out trickled the liquid by a dozen unperceived holes, most of them situated close to, or beneath the hoops. These last could not be plugged, so I pushed in tow and rag under the hoops, to be afterwards pitched over. With the filling and plugging we were occupied all day; holes constantly appearing in fresh places and obstinately refusing to be stopped. Nothing would adhere to the wet surface, so the upper part of the cask had to be dried, covered with pitch, then with cloth, and then again well pitched over. Then rolling over the barrel, another leaky portion was brought to the top, and treated in the same manner. After great labour, all seemed complete, yet numerous little streams still appeared; but as they were very small, and their sources quite undiscoverable, I left them in despair, trusting that the salt or the swelling of the wood would stop them. By the time I got the cask carried up to the house and deposited in charge of Senhor João till my return, it was dusk; and so finished two most disagreeable days' work with the Peixe boi. Senhor João had prepared me a pot of meat and sausages preserved in the oil, which I embarked, and got all ready to leave the next morning, as I had now been delayed a week of most valuable time. I left him also a box containing four species of turtles, which I had stuffed either here or on my voyage.

Continuing our journey, nothing particular occurred but several storms of rain and wind, accompanied with thunder, which sometimes retarded us, and sometimes helped us on. Many of them were complete hurricanes, the wind shifting round suddenly, through every point of the compass ; so that, if our little canoe had not been well ballasted with her cargo of salt and iron, she would have capsized. Once, in particular, at about four in the morning, we experienced one of these storms in a wide part of the river, where the waves raised were very great, and tossed us about violently. A sudden shift of the wind took our sail aback, and we had great difficulty in getting it in. The rain was driving thickly against us, and rendered it bitterly cold ; our montaria, which was towed astern, got water-logged,—plunged, and dashed against the canoe,—tore out its benches, and lost its paddles. I gave orders to cast it loose, thinking it impossible to save it ; but the Indians thought otherwise, for one of them plunged in after it, and succeeded in guiding it to the shore, where we also with much difficulty arrived, and managed to fasten our bows to some bushes, and get a rope out from our stern to a tree growing in the water, so as to prevent the canoe from getting broadside to the waves, which rolled in furiously, keeping one of our men constantly baling out water ; and thus we waited for daylight. I then gave the men a cup of caxaça each ; and when the sea had subsided sufficiently to allow of rowing, we continued our passage. These storms are the only things that make travelling here disagreeable : they are very frequent, but each succeeding one, instead of reconciling me to them, made me more fearful than before. It is by no means an uncommon thing for canoes to be swamped by them, or dashed to pieces on the sands ; and the Rio Negro has such a disagreeable notoriety for the suddenness and fury of its trovoádos, that many persons will never put up a sail when there is a sign of one approaching, but seek some safe port, to wait till it has passed.

On the 12th of November I reached the sitio of Senhor Chágas, where I stopped for the night : he gave me some letters to take up to São Gabriel, and just as I was going, requested me, as a favour, to tell everybody that I had not found him at his sitio, but that he was gone to the "mato" to get salsa. As I was on familiar terms with him, I told him that really I was very sorry I could not oblige him, but that, as I was not accustomed to lying, I should be found out immediately if I attempted it : he, however, insisted that I might surely try, and I should soon learn to lie as well as the best of them. So I told him at once, that in my country a liar was considered as bad as a thief; at which he seemed rather astonished. I gave him a short account of the pillory, as a proof of how much our ancestors detested lying and perjury, which much edified him, and he called his son (a nice boy of twelve or fourteen, just returned from school), to hear and profit by the example; showing, I think, that the people here are perfectly aware of the moral enormity of the practice, but that constant habit and universal custom, and above all, that false politeness which renders them unable verbally to deny anything, has rendered it almost a necessary evil. Any native of the country would have instantly agreed to Senhor Chágas's request, and would then have told every one of it up the river, always begging them not to say he told them,—thus telling a lie for themselves instead of for Senhor Chágas.

The next morning I reached Wanawáca, the sitio of Manoel Jacinto, and stayed to breakfast with him, luxuriating in milk with my coffee, and " coalhado," or curdled milk, pine-apple, and pacovas with cheese,—luxuries which, though every one might have, are seldom met with in the Rio Negro. His sitio is, perhaps, the prettiest on the river ; and this, simply because there is an open space of grass around the house, with some forest and fruit-trees scattered about it, affording shade for the cattle and sheep, and a most agreeable relief to the eye, long fatigued with eternal forest.

When I consider the excessively small amount of labour required in this country, to convert the virgin forest into green meadows and fertile plantations, I almost long to come over with half-a-dozen friends, disposed to work, and enjoy the country; and show the inhabitants how soon an earthly paradise might be created, which they had never even conceived capable of existing.

It is a vulgar error, copied and repeated from one book to another, that in the tropics the luxuriance of the vegetation overpowers the efforts of man. Just the reverse is the case : nature and the climate are nowhere so favourable to the labourer, and I fearlessly assert, that here, the "primeval" forest can be converted into rich pasture and meadow land, into cultivated fields, gardens, and orchards, containing every variety of produce, with half the labour, and, what is of more importance, in less than half the time than would be required at home, even though there we had clear, instead of forest ground to commence upon. It is true that ground once rudely cleared, in the manner of the country, by merely cutting down the wood and burning it as it lies, will, if left to itself, in a single year, be covered with a dense shrubby vegetation ; but if the ground is cultivated and roughly weeded, the trunks and stumps will have so rotted in two or three years, as to render their complete removal an easy matter, and then a fine crop of grass succeeds ; and, with cattle upon it, no more care is required, as no shrubby vegetation again appears. Then, whatever fruit-trees are planted will reach a large size in five or six years, and many of them give fruit in two or three. Coffee and cacao both produce abundantly with the mimimum of attention ; orange and other fruit-trees never receive any attention, but, if pruned, would no doubt yield fruit of a superior quality, in greater quantity. Pine-apples, melons, and water-melons are planted, and when ripe the fruit is gathered, there being no intermediate process whatever. Indian corn and rice are treated nearly in the same manner. Onions, beans, and many other vegetables, thrive luxuriantly. The ground is never turned up, and manure never applied ; if both were done, it is probable that the labour would be richly repaid. Cattle, sheep, goats, and pigs may be kept to any extent ; nobody ever gives them anything to eat, and they always do well. Poultry of all kinds thrive. Molasses may be easily made in any quantity, for cane put into the ground grows, and gives no trouble ; and I do not see why the domestic process used in the United States for making maple-sugar should not be applied here. Now, I unhesitatingly affirm, that two or three families, containing half-a-dozen working and industrious men and boys, and being able to bring a capital in goods of fifty pounds, might, in three years, find themselves in the possession of all I have mentioned. Supposing them to get used to the mandiocca and Indian-corn bread, they would, with the exception of clothing, have no one necessary or luxury to purchase : they would be abundantly supplied with pork, beef and mutton, poultry, eggs, butter, milk and cheese, coffee and cacao, molasses and sugar, delicious fish, turtles and turtles' eggs, and a great variety of game, would furnish their table with constant variety, while vegetables would not be wanting, and fruits, both cultivated and wild, in superfluous abundance, and of a quality that none but the wealthy of our land can afford. Oranges and lemons, figs and grapes, melons and water-melons, jack-fruits, custard-apples, pine-apples, cashews, alligator pears, and mammee apples are some of the commonest, whilst numerous palm and other forest fruits furnish delicious drinks, which everybody soon gets very fond of. Both animal and vegetable oils can be procured in abundance for light and cooking. And then, having provided for the body, what lovely gardens and shady walks might not be made! How easy to construct a natural orchid-house, beneath a clump of forest-trees, and collect the most beautiful species found in the neighbourhood! What elegant avenues of palms might be formed! What lovely climbers abound, to train over arbours, or up the walls of the house!

In the whole Amazon, no such thing as neatness or cultivation has ever been tried. Walks, and avenues, and gardens have never been made; but I can imagine how much beauty and variety might be called into existence from the gloomy monotony of the forest.

"England! my heart is truly thine,—my loved, my native earth!"

But the idea of the glorious life which might be led here, free from all the money-matter cares and annoyances of civilisation, makes me sometimes doubt, if it would not be wiser to bid thee adieu for ever, and come and live a life of ease and plenty in the Rio Negro.

This district is superior to any other part of the Amazon, and perhaps any other part of Brazil, in having a climate free from long droughts. In fact, the variableness of rain and sunshine, all the year round, is as great as in England itself; but it is this very thing which produces a perennial verdure. There are parts of the Rio Negro where the turtle, the peixe boi, and all sorts of fish abound; advantages, for which many persons endure the tormenting " carapanás " of the Solimões, but which can be had here without any insect torment, and with a far superior climate for agricultural purposes.

AN INDIAN VILLAGE ON THE RIO NEGRO.

PLATE VIII.

All cultivated products of the soil are so scarce that they meet with a ready sale at good prices, not only in the city of Barra, but also to passing traders, who have no time or means for cultivating them themselves. Tobacco, coffee, molasses, cotton, castor-oil, rice, maize, eggs, poultry, salt-meat, and fish, all kinds of oils, cheese, and butter, can always be sold,—the supply being invariably below the demand,—and, besides providing clothing and other extras, which in this climate are a mere trifle, might be made to produce a handsome profit. To do all this requires some experience and some industry ; but not a tithe of either which are necessary to get a bare living at home.

Leaving this pleasant place about midday, we proceeded slowly on. One of my best Indians fell ill of fever and ague ; and, a few days after, another was attacked. It was in vain attempting, at any sitio or village, to get men to help me on the rest of my voyage; no offer of extra wages would induce them to leave their houses ; all had some excuse of occupation or illness, so we were forced to creep on as well as we could. Two days below the Falls I bought a smaller canoe of a Portuguese trader, to ascend the Úaupés, and moved my cargo into it, leaving that of Senhor Lima with the other canoe, to be sent for afterwards. At Camanaú, I with much difficulty, and some delay, procured a pilot and another Indian, to go with me to São Gabriel. There, after another day's delay, I found two Indians, who agreed to go as far as São Joaquim ; and after keeping me waiting three or four hours beyond the time appointed, absconded at night from the sitio where we slept, having been previously paid double wages for the whole distance. Here, however, I was lucky enough to get three more in place of the two rogues ; but as another of my Indians had now fallen ill, we still had few enough for passing the numerous rapids and rocks with which the river is obstructed.

One day we found, coiled up on the bank, a large Sucurujú, the first large snake I had met with, and as I was very anxious to secure it, to preserve the skin, I loaded my gun, and telling **my Indians** not to let it escape, fired. It remained motionless some time, as if stunned *by* the shock, and then slowly began to uncoil, turning its head down towards the water, but evidently so much injured as to be unable to move its body on land. In vain I cried to the Indians to secure it :

the pilot had been severely bitten by one some time before, and was afraid; and so, instead of obeying me, they kept striking it with a thick stick, which only hastened its descent down the bank into the water, where, sinking to the bottom among dead trees, it was quite out of our power. As near as I could judge, the snake was fifteen or twenty feet long, and as thick as my thigh. At São Gabriel I saw also, on the rocks, asleep, one of the most deadly serpents of South America, the Surucucú (*Lachesis mutus*). It is very handsomely marked with rich umber-brown, and armed with terrific poison-fangs, two on each side; it is much dreaded, as its bite is said to be incurable.

On leaving São Gabriel I was again attacked with fever, and on arriving at São Joaquim I was completely laid up. My Indians took the opportunity to steal a quantity of the caxaça I had brought for preserving the fishes, and anything else they could lay their hands on; so I was glad, on the occasion of a slight remission of the fever, to pay their wages and send them off. After a few days, the violence of the fever abated, and I thought I was going to get over it very easily; but such was not the case, for every alternate day I experienced a great depression, with disinclination to motion: this always followed a feverish night, in which I could not sleep. The next night I invariably slept well perspiring profusely, and, the succeeding day, was able to move about, and had a little appetite. The weakness and fever, however, increased, till I was again confined to my *rédé*,—could eat nothing, and was so torpid and helpless, that Senhor L., who attended me, did not expect me to live. I could not speak intelligibly, and had not strength to write, or even to turn over in my hammock. A few days after this, I was attacked with severe ague, which recurred every two days. I took quinine for some time without any apparent effect, till, after nearly a fortnight, the fits ceased, and I only suffered from extreme emaciation and weakness. In a few days, however, the fits of ague returned, and now came every day. Their visits, thus frequent, were by no means agreeable; as, what with the succeeding fever and perspiration, which lasted from before noon till night, I had little quiet repose. In this state I remained till the beginning of February, the ague continuing, but with diminished force; and though with an increasing appetite, and eating heartily,

yet gaining so little strength, that I could with difficulty stand
alone, or walk across the room with the assistance of two
sticks.   The ague, however, now left me, and in another week,
as I could walk with a stick down to the river-side, I went to
São Gabriel, to see Mr. Spruce, who had arrived there, and
had kindly been to see me a short time before.   I purchased
some wine and biscuits of the Commandante, and then
returned to São Joaquim, determined, though the wet season
was now again beginning, to set off for the Upper Uaupés, as
soon as I could procure men, and get my canoe ready.

# CHAPTER XII.

## THE CATARACTS OF THE UAUPÉS.

Start for the Uaupés—São Jeronymo and Jauarité—Indians run Away—
Numerous Cataracts—Reach Carurú—Difficult Passage—Painted
Malocca—Devil Music—More Falls—Ocokí—Curious Rocks—Reach
Uarucapurí—Cobeu Indians—Reach Mucúra—An Indian's House
and Family—Height above the Sea—Tenente Jesuino—Return to
Uarucapurí—Indian Prisoners—Voyage to Jauarité—Correcting the
Calendar—Delay at São Jeronymo.

AT length, on the 16th of February, two months and twenty-three
days after my arrival at São Joaquim, I left on my voyage up
the Uaupés. I was still so weak that I had great difficulty
in getting in and out of the canoe ; but I thought I should be
as well there as confined in the house ; and as I now longed
more than ever to return home, I wished first to make this
voyage, and get a few living birds and animals to take with me.
I had seven Uaupés Indians that Senhor L. had brought from
São Jeronymo, in order to take me up the river. Three more,
who had already received payment for the voyage, did not
appear ; and, though they knew very well the time of my
leaving, had fixed on that very day to give a feast of fish and
caxirí. Antonio, my former pilot to Barra, was one. I met
him coming to the village from his sitio, and he flatly refused
to come with me, unless I waited some days more for him ; I
therefore made him send his Macu boy, João, instead, to go
and return, and so pay for what both owed. This he did, and
we went on our way rejoicing, for Antonio was what they call
an Indian " ladino," or crafty ; he could speak Portuguese, and,
strongly suspecting him of being an expert thief, I was not
sorry to be without his company.

On Saturday evening, the 21st, we arrived at São Jeronymo,
where I was cordially received by Senhor Augustinho. The

next day was occupied in paying my men, and sending for
Bernardo to conduct my canoe up the falls, and get me more
Indians for the voyage.

On Monday he arrived, and I let him take the canoe, but
did not go with him, as, for some days past, the ague had again
attacked me, and this was the day of the fit; so I sent the two
guardas, my head men, who could speak Portuguese, to take
charge of the canoe and cargo, and remained myself till the
next day.   In the evening a small trader arrived from above,
very tipsy, and an Indian informed Senhor Augustinho that it
was with my caxaça, which the men whom I had brought
specially to take charge of my cargo, had opened.   This I next
day found to be the case, as the seals had been broken, and
clumsily refastened with a burning stick.   These men were
half-civilised Indians, who came with me as hunters, to inter-
pret for me with the Indians and take charge of my goods, on
account of which I paid them extra wages.   They ate with me,
and did not row with the other Indians ; but the temptation of
being left alone for nearly a day, with a garafão of caxaça, was
too strong for them.   Of course I passed all over in silence,
appearing to be perfectly ignorant of what had taken place, as,
had I done otherwise, they would probably both have left me,
after having received the greater part of their payment beforehand, and I should have been unable to proceed on my
voyage.

With Bernardo's assistance, I soon got ten paddles in my
canoe ; and having paid most of them out of my stock of axes,
mirrors, knives, beads, etc., we went along very briskly to
Jauarité, where we arrived on the morning of the 28th.   I was
anxious to pass the caxoeira immediately, but was delayed,—
paying two Indians, who left me here, and procuring others ;
so my ague fit fell upon me before we left the village, and I
was very weak and feverish when we went to pass the falls.
We unloaded the whole of the cargo, which had to be carried
a considerable distance through the forest ; and even then,
pulling the canoe up the falls was a matter of great difficulty.
There are two falls, at some distance from each other, which
make the land-carriage very long.

We then re-embarked, when Bernardo coolly informed me
that he could go no further, after having received payment for
the whole voyage.  His brother, he said, should go in his

place; and when I returned, he would pay me what he owed me. So I was forced to make the best of it; but shortly after I found that his brother would only go to Jacaré caxoeira, and thus I was a second time deceived.

On starting, I missed João, and found that he had left us in the village, telling the guardas that he had only agreed with me to come so far, and they had never said a word to me about it till now, that it was too late. Antonio's debt therefore still remained unpaid, and was even increased by a knife which João had asked for, and I had given him, in order that he might go on the voyage satisfied.

The river now became full of rocks, to a degree to which even the rockiest part of the Rio Negro was a trifle. All were low, and would be covered at high-water, while numbers more remained below the surface, and we were continually striking against them. That afternoon we passed four more falls, the "Uacú" (a fruit), "Uacará" (Egret), "Mucúra" (Opossum), and "Japóna" (oven) caxoeiras. At Uacará there was a malocca of the same name; and at Japóna another, where we passed the night. All these rapids we ascended without unloading; but the Uacará was very bad, and occasioned us much trouble and delay. The next morning, when about to start, we found that another Indian was missing: he had absconded in the night, and it was useless attempting to seek him, though we knew he had gone to Uacará Malocca, where he wished to stay the day before, but where all knowledge of him would be denied and he well hidden, had we returned to fetch him. He was one who had received full payment, making three who had already gone away in my debt; a not very encouraging beginning for my voyage.

We passed the "Tyeassu" (Pig) caxoeira early, and then had a good stretch of quiet water till midday, when we reached the "Oomarie" (a fruit) caxoeira, where there is a sitio. Here we dined off a fine fresh Tucunaré, which an old man sold me; and I agreed with his son, by the temptation of an axe, to go with me. We pulled the canoe up this rapid without unloading, which is seldom done, except when the river is low, as it now was. The rest of the day we had quiet water, and stopped at a rock to make our supper and sleep.

*March 1st.*—We passed the "Macáco" (monkey) caxoeira early. The rocks here, and particularly about Oomarie caxoeira, were so full of parallel veins, as to give them the appearance of being stratified and thrown up nearly vertically; whereas they are granitic, and similar to those we had already seen. We then soon reached the "Irá" (Honey) and "Baccába" (a Palm) caxoeiras; at both of which there are figures or picture-writings on the rocks, which I stayed to sketch. In passing the latter rapid, we knocked off one of the false keels I had had put to the canoe previous to starting, to preserve the bottom in the centre, where it was worn very thin by being dragged over the rocks by its former owner. We therefore stopped at a sandbank, unloaded the canoe, and plugged up the nail-holes, which were letting in water very fast.

The next day we passed in succession the "Arára Mirí" (Little Macaw), "Tamaquerié" (Gecko), "Paroquet," "Japoó" (a bird), "Arára" (Macaw), "Tatú" (Armadillo), "Amána" (Rain), "Camóa" (?), "Yauti" (Tortoise); and, finally, about three P.M., arrived at "Carurú" (a water-plant) caxoeira. The last five of these, before arriving at Carurú, were exceedingly bad; the passage being generally in the middle of the river, among rocks, where the water rushes furiously. The falls were not more than three or four feet each; but, to pull a loaded canoe up these, against the foaming waters of a large river, was a matter of the greatest difficulty for my dozen Indians, their only resting-place being often breast-deep in water, where it was a matter of wonder that they could stand against the current, much less exert any force to pull the canoe. At Arára fall, the usual passage is over the dry rock, and we unloaded for that purpose; but all the efforts of the Indians could not get the heavy canoe up the steep and rugged ascent which was the only pathway. Again and again they exerted themselves, but to no purpose; and I was just sending by an old man, who was passing in a small canoe, to Carurú for assistance, when he suggested that by getting a long sipó (the general cable in these rivers) we might obtair a good purchase, to pull the canoe up the margin of the fall, which we had previously tried without success. We accordingly did so, and by great exertions the difficulty was passed,—much to my satisfaction, as sending to Carurú would have occasioned a great and very annoying delay.

The river from Jauarité may be said to average about a

third of a mile wide, but the bends and turns are innumerable ; and at every rapid it almost always spreads out into such deep bays, and is divided into channels by so many rocks and islands, as to make one sometimes think that the water is suddenly flowing back in a direction contrary to that it had previously been taking.  Carurú caxoeira itself is greater than any we had yet seen,—rushing amongst huge rocks down a descent of perhaps fifteen or twenty feet.  The only way of passing this, was to pull the canoe over the dry rock, which rose considerably above the level of the water, and was rather rugged, being interrupted in places by breaks or steps two or three feet high.  The canoe was accordingly unloaded, quantities of poles and branches cut and laid in the path to prevent the bottom being much injured by the rocks, and a messenger sent to the village on the other side of the river to request the Tushaúa to come with plenty of men to our assistance.  He soon arrived with eleven Indians, and all hands set to work pushing the canoe, or pulling at the sipós ; and even then, the strength of five-and-twenty persons could only move it by steps, and with great difficulty.  However, it was at length passed, and we then proceeded to the village, where the Tushaúa lent us a house.

The canoe was so weak in the bottom in one place, that I was fearful of some accident in my descent, so I determined to stay here two or three days, to cut out the weak part and put in a strong board.  I now also saw that this canoe was much too heavy to proceed further up the river, as at many of the falls there was no assistance to be obtained, even in places as difficult to pass as Carurú ; so I opened negotiations to purchase a very large " obá " of the Tushaúa, which, before leaving, I effected for an axe, a shirt and trousers, two cutlasses, and some beads.   We were delayed here five entire days, owing to the difficulty of finding a tree of good wood sufficiently large to give a board of twelve or fourteen inches wide ; and at last I was obliged to be content with two narrow boards, clumsily inserted, rather than be exposed to more delay.

There was a large malocca here, and a considerable number of houses.  The front of the malocca was painted very taste-fully in diamonds and circles, with red, yellow, white, and black.  On the rocks were a series of strange figures, of which I took a sketch.  The Indians were of the " Ananás " or Pine-

apple tribe; I bought some dresses and feather ornaments of
them; and fish, mandiocca-cakes, etc., were brought me in
considerable quantities, the articles most coveted in return
being fish-hooks and red beads, of both of which I had a large
stock.   Just below the fall, the river is not more than two or
three hundred yards wide; while above, it is half a mile, and
contains several large islands.

The large black pacu was abundant here, and, with other
small fish, was generally brought us in sufficient quantity to
prevent our recurring to fowls, which are considered by the
traders to be the most ordinary fare a man can live on.   I
now ate for the first time the curious river-weed, called carurú,
that grows on the rocks.   We tried it as a salad, and also
boiled with fish; and both ways it was excellent;—boiled, it
much resembled spinach.

Here, too, I first saw and heard the "Juriparí," or Devil-
music of the Indians.   One evening there was a caxirí-drinking;
and a little before dusk a sound as of trombones and bassoons
was heard coming on the river towards the village, and
presently appeared eight Indians, each playing on a great
bassoon-looking instrument.   They had four pairs, of different
sizes, and produced a wild and pleasing sound.   They blew
them all together, tolerably in concert, to a simple tune, and
showed more taste for music than I had yet seen displayed
among these people.   The instruments are made of bark
spirally twisted, and with a mouthpiece of leaves.

In the evening I went to the malocca, and found two old
men playing on the largest of the instruments.   They waved
them about in a singular · manner, vertically and sideways,
accompanied by corresponding contortions of the body, and
played a long while in a regular tune, accompanying each other
very correctly.   From the moment the music was first heard,
not a female, old or young, was to be seen; for it is one of the
strangest superstitions of the Uaupés Indians, that they consider it so dangerous for a woman ever to see one of these
instruments, that having done so is punished with death,
generally by poison.   Even should the view be perfectly
accidental, or should there be only a suspicion that the pro-
scribed articles have been seen, no mercy is shown; and it is
said that fathers have been the executioners of their own
daughters, and husbands of their wives, when such has been

the case. I was of course anxious to purchase articles to which such curious customs belong, and spoke to the Tushaúa on the subject. He at length promised to sell them me on my return, stipulating that they were to be embarked at some distance from the village, that there might be no danger of their being seen by the women.

On the morning previous to that on which we were to leave, two more of our Indians who had received full payment on starting, were discovered to have left us. They had taken possession of a canoe, and absconded in the night; leaving me no remedy, but the chance of finding them in their houses on my return, and the still more remote chance of their having anything to pay me with.

The Indians here have but little characteristic distinction from those below. The women wear more beads around their necks and arms. The lower lip is often pierced, and two or three little strings of white beads inserted; but as the nations are so mixed by inter-marriages, this custom is probably derived from the Tucanos. Some of the women and children wore two garters, one above the ankle and one below the knee— swelling out the calf enormously, which they consider a very great beauty. I did not see here so many long tails of hair; most of the men having probably been to the Rio Negro with some trader, and thence worn their hair like Christians; or perhaps because the last Tushaúa was a "homen muito civilizado" (a very well-bred person).

After four days' delay, we at length started, with a comparatively small complement of Indians, but with some extra men to assist us in passing several caxoeiras, which occur near at hand. These are the "Piréwa" (Wound), "Uacorouá" (Goat-sucker), "Maniwára" (White Ant), "Matapí" (Fish-trap), "Amána" (Rain), "Tapíracúnga" (Tapir's head), "Tapíra eura" (Tapir's mouth), and "Jacaré" (Alligator). Three of these were very bad, the canoe having to be unloaded entirely, and pulled over the dry and uneven rocks. The last was the highest; the river rushing furiously about twenty feet down a rugged slope of rock. The loading and unloading of the canoe three or four times in the course of as many hours, is a great annoyance. Baskets of farinha and salt, of mandiocca-cakes and pacovas, are strewn about. Panellas are often broken; and when there comes a shower of rain, everything has to be heaped together in a hurry,—palm-leaves cut, and the more perishable articles covered; but boxes, *rédés*, and numerous other articles are sure to be wetted, rendering us very uncomfortable when again hastily tumbled into the over-crowded canoe.   If I had birds or insects out drying, they were sure to be overturned, or blown by the wind, or wetted by the rain, and the same fate was shared by my note-books and papers.   Articles in boxes, unless packed tight, were shaken and rumpled by not being carried evenly; so that it was an excellent lesson in patience, to bear all with philosophical serenity.   We had passed all these falls by midday; and at night slept on a rock, where there was a small rapid and a house without inhabitants.

On the 8th we had tolerably quiet water, with only two small rapids, the "Taiéna" (Child), and "Paroquet" caxoeiras. On the 9th, in the morning, we reached the "Pacu" fall, and then had a quiet stream, though full of rocks, till the afternoon, when we passed the "Macucú" (a tree), "Anacás" (Pine-apple), and "Uacú" (a fruit) caxoeiras; all very bad and difficult ones.   We had left Carurú with very little farinha, as none was to be had there, and we had seen no inhabited sitios where any could be purchased; so our Indians were now on short allowance of "beijú," which they had brought with them. Of a passing Indian I bought a basket of Ocokí, and some fish.   The Ocokí is a large pear-shaped fruit, with a hard thick outer skin of almost a woody texture, then a small quantity of very sweet pulpy matter, and within a large black oval stone. The pulp is very luscious, but is so acrid as to make the mouth and throat sore, if more than two or three are eaten.   When, however, the juice is boiled it loses this property; and when made into mingau with tapioca, is exceedingly palatable and very highly esteemed in the Upper Rio Negro, where it is abundant.   It takes at least a peck of fruit to give one small panella of mingau.

On the next day, the 10th, in the afternoon, the Indians all suddenly sprang like otters into the water, swam to the shore, and disappeared in the forest.   "Ocokí," was the answer to my inquiries as to the cause of their sudden disappearance; and I soon found they had discovered an ocokí-tree, and were load-ing themselves with the fruit to satisfy the cravings of hunger, for an Indian's throat and mouth seem invulnerable to all those scarifying substances which act upon civilised man.   The tree is one of the loftiest in the forest, but the fruit falls as soon as ripe, and its hard woody coating preserves it from injury. Baskets, shirts, trousers, etc., were soon filled with the fruit and emptied into the canoe ; and I made each of the Indians bring a small basketful for me ; so that we had " mingau de ocokí " for three succeeding mornings.

The rocks from Carurú often present a scoriaceous appearance, as if the granite had been remelted.   Sometimes they are a mass of burnt fragments, sometimes a honeycombed rock with a shining surface.   In some places there are enclosed fragments of a finer-grained rock, apparently sandstone, and numerous veins and dykes, which often cross each other in three or four sets.   The rocks are, in many places, so broken and cleft vertically, as to appear stratified and thrown up on end.   The rounded form and concentric arrangement, observed in the Rio Negro, is here also constantly met with.   The interstices of the rounded and angular masses of rock are often filled with a curious volcanic substance, which outwardly resembles pitch, but consists of scoriæ, sand, clays, etc., variously cemented together.

On the 10th we passed the " Tapioca," " Tucáno " (Toucan), " Tucunaré " (a fish), " Uaracú pinimi " (a fish), and " Tyeassú " (Pig) caxoeiras.   The first was very bad, and both difficult and dangerous to pass ; it consisted of many distinct falls among huge masses of rock.   At one place the canoe remained stuck fast, amidst foaming waters, on the very edge of a fall, for nearly an hour ; all the efforts of the Indians could not move it forward.   They heaved it over from one side to the other, but with no effect ; till I began to despair of getting out of the difficulty before night.   At last the canoe suddenly moved on, with apparently not so much force as had been before applied to it ; but my Indians, being of several nations, did not understand any common language, and it was impossible to get them to act in concert, or obey any leader.   It was probably some chance combination of forces, that at last extricated us from our unpleasant situation.   At this fall, on the rocks, were very numerous figures, or picture-writings, and I stopped to make drawings of them ; of which I had by this time a rather extensive collection.

The next three falls were small rapids ; but the last, which we reached late in the evening, was fearful. The river makes a sudden bend, and is confined in a very narrow channel, which is one confused mass of rocks of every size and shape, piled on one another, and heaped up in the greatest possible confusion. Every stone which rises above high-water mark is covered with vegetation; and among the whole the river rushes and foams, so as to make the task of pilot one of no ordinary difficulty. Just as it was getting dark, we passed out of these gloomy narrows into a wider and more cheerful part of the river, and stayed at a rock to sup and sleep.

On the 11th, early, we reached Uarucapurí, where are a village and several maloccas. The first which we entered was inhabited by people of the Cobeu nation. There were about a dozen handsome men, all clean-limbed and well painted, with armlets and necklaces of white beads, and with the ears plugged with a piece of wood the size of a common bottle-cork, to the end of which was glued a piece of porcelain presenting a white shining surface. We agreed with these men to help to pass our canoe up the falls, and then proceeded on our walk through the village. My old friend Senhor Chagas was here, and with him I breakfasted off a fine pirahíba which his men had caught that morning, and which was the first I had eaten since my illness.

With some difficulty I succeeded in buying two or three baskets of farinha; and being anxious to get to my journey's end, which was now near at hand, about midday we proceeded. Our pilot and his son left us, and we had now only six paddles; but four or five additional men came with us to pass the remaining caxoeiras, which were near. Close to the village we passed the "Cururú" (a toad), and "Murucututú" (an owl) falls, both rather bad; and, soon after, arrived at the "Uacoroúa" (Goatsucker), the last great fall on the river below the "Jurupari," which is many days further up. Here the river is precipitated over a nearly vertical rock, about ten feet high, and much broken in places. The canoe had to be entirely unloaded, and then pulled up over the rocks on the margin of the fall, a matter of considerable difficulty. To add to our discomfort, a shower of rain came on while the canoe was passing; and the Indians, as usual, having scattered the cargo about in great confusion, it had to be huddled together and covered with mats and palm-leaves, till the shower, which was luckily a short one, passed over.  Loading again and proceeding onwards, we passed three small rapids, the "Tatu" (Armadillo), "Ocokí" (a fruit), and "Pir_anterá_" (a fish) caxoeiras; and our additional Indians here left us, with their payment of fish-hooks and arrow-heads, as we now had only smooth water before us.  In the afternoon we passed a malocca, where one of the Indians wished to land to see his friends; and as we did not stay, at night he took his departure, and we saw no more of him.

Early the next morning we reached Mucúra, where two young Brazilians, whom I had met with below, were residing, trading for salsa.  I was now in the country of the painted turtle and the white umbrella-bird, and I determined to make a stay of at least a fortnight, to try and obtain these much-desired rarities.

Messrs. Nicoláu and Bellarmine were both out, and their little palm-leaf huts were evidently quite inadequate to my accommodation.  The only other house was a small Indian malocca, also made entirely of "palha;" and I agreed with the owner to let me have half of it, giving him a small knife and mirror in payment, with which he was well contented.  We accordingly cleared and swept out our part of the house, unloaded and arranged our things, and I then sent my guardas to a malocca, in which there were said to be plenty of Indians, to see if they had any farinha or pacovas to dispose of; and also to let them know that I would purchase birds, or fish, or any other animals they could obtain for me.  The men were all out; but the same afternoon they came in great force to see the "Branco," and make an attack on my fish-hooks and beads, bringing me fish, pacovas, farinha, and mandiocca-cake, for all of which one of these two articles was asked in exchange.

I was now settled at the limit of my expedition, for I could not think of going a week further up only to see Juruparí caxoeira,—wasting the little time I had to rest, before again descending.  We had made a favourable voyage, without any serious accident, up a river perhaps unsurpassed for the difficulties and dangers of its navigation.  We had passed fifty caxoeiras, great and small; some mere rapids, others furious cataracts, and some nearly perpendicular falls.  About twenty were rapids, up which, by the help of a long sipó attached to the canoe, instead of a rope, we were pulled without much difficulty.  About eighteen were very bad and dangerous, requiring the canoe to be partially unloaded where practicable, and all the exertions of my Indians, often with additional assistance, to pass; and twelve were so high and furious as to require the canoe to be entirely unloaded, and either pulled over the dry and often very precipitous rocks, or with almost equal difficulty up the margin of the fall. At Carurú, as I have said, four-and-twenty men were scarcely able to pull my empty canoe over the rock, though plentifully strewn with branches and bushes, to smooth the asperities which would otherwise much damage the bottom: this was the reason why I purchased the Tushaúa's smaller obá, to proceed; and it was well I did, or I might otherwise have had to return without ever reaching the locality I had at length attained.

The next day, the 13th, I was employed drawing some new fish brought me the preceding evening. My hunters went out and brought me nothing but a common hawk. In the afternoon, the father and brother of the Indian I had found in the house, arrived, with their wives and families; so now, with my six Indians and two hunters, we were pretty full; some of them, however, slept in a shed, and we were as comfortably accommodated as could be expected. The wives of the father and two sons were perfectly naked, and were, moreover, apparently quite unconscious of the fact. The old woman possessed a "saía," or petticoat, which she sometimes put on, and seemed then almost as much ashamed of herself as civilised people would be if they took theirs off. So powerful is the effect of education and habit!

Having been told by Senhor Chagas that there was an excellent hunter in the Codiarí, a river which enters from the north a short distance above Mucúra, I sent Philippe, one of my guardas, to try and engage him, and also to buy all the living birds and animals he could meet with. The following day he returned, bringing with him one "Maçaco barrigudo" (*Lagothrix Humboldtii*), and a couple of parrots. On most days I had a new fish or two to figure, but birds and insects were very scarce. This day Senhor Nicoláu returned. On my first arrival I had been told that he had a "tataruga pintata" (painted turtle) for me, but that he would give it me himself on his arrival; so I did not meddle with it, though my Indians saw it in a "corrál," in a small stream near the house. On arriving, he sent to fetch it, but found it had escaped, though it had been seen in its cage on the preceding day. I thus lost perhaps my only chance of obtaining a much-desired and probably undescribed river turtle, as the time of egg-laying was past, and they had now retired into the lakes, and become very scarce and difficult to be met with.

As my Indians were here doing nothing, I sent three of them with Sebastião up the Codiarí, with beads, hooks, mirrors, etc., to buy monkeys, parrots, or whatever else they could meet with, as well as some farinha, which I did not wish to be in want of again. I sent them with instructions to go for five or six days, in order to reach the last stitio, and purchase all that was to be had. In two days, however, they returned, having been no further than Philippe had gone, Sebastião saying that his companions would not go on. He brought me some parrots and small birds, bows, bird-skins, and more farinha than my canoe would carry, all purchased very dearly, judging by the remnant of articles brought back.

Being now in a part of the country that no European traveller had ever before visited, I exceedingly regretted my want of instruments to determine the latitude, longitude, and height above the sea. The two last I had no means whatever of ascertaining, having broken my boiling-point thermometer, and lost my smaller one, without having been able to replace either. I once thought of sealing up a flask of air, by accurately weighing which on my return, the density of air at that particular time would be obtained, and the height at which a barometer would have stood might be deduced. But, besides that this would only give a result equal to that of a single barometer observation, there were insuperable difficulties in the way of sealing up the bottle, for whether sealing-wax or pitch were used, or even should the bottle be hermetically sealed, heat must be applied, and at the moment of application would, of course, rarefy the air within the bottle, and so produce in such a delicate operation very erroneous results. My observations, however, on the heights of the falls we passed, would give their sum as about two hundred and fifty feet ; now if we add fifty for the fall of the river between them, we shall obtain three hundred feet, as the probable height of the point I reached above the mouth of the river ; and, as I have every reason to believe that that is not five hundred feet above the sea, we shall obtain eight hundred feet as the probable limit of the height of the river above the sea-level, at the point I reached. Nothing, however, can accurately determine this fact, but a series of barometer or " boiling-point " observations ; and to determine this height above the next great fall, and ascertain the true course and sources of this little-known but interesting and important river, would be an object worth the danger and expense of the voyage.

There is said to be a week's smooth water above this place, to the Juruparí caxoeira, which is higher than any below it ; and above this no other fall has been found, though traders have been ten or fifteen days up. They say the river still keeps as wide or wider than below,—that the water is as " white," or muddy, as that of the Solimões,—that many trees, birds, and fish peculiar to the Solimões are there found,—that the Indians have Spanish knives, ponchos, and coins,—and relate that, higher up, there are extensive " campos," with cattle, and men on horseback. All these interesting particulars seem to show that the river has its sources in the great plains which extend to the base of the Andes, somewhere near where the sources of the Guaviare are placed in most maps ; but the latter river, from all the information I can obtain, is much smaller, and has a much shorter course. Having only a pocket surveying sextant, without any means of viewing two objects much differing in brilliancy, I endeavoured to obtain the latitude as accurately as I could, first by means of the zenith-distance at noon, obtained by a plumb-line and image of the sun, formed by a lens of about fifteen inches focus ; and afterwards, by the meridian altitude of a star, obtained on a calm night, by reflection in a cuya of water. I took much care to ensure an accurate result, and have every reason to believe that the mean of the two observations will not be more than two or three minutes from the truth.

My expectations of finding rare and handsome birds here were quite disappointed. My hunter and Senhor Nicoláu killed a few umbrella-birds of the Rio Negro species ; but of the white bird such contradictory statements were given,—many knowing nothing whatever about it, others saying that it was sometimes, but very rarely seen,—that I am inclined to think it is a mere white variety, such as occurs at times with our blackbirds and starlings at home, and as are sometimes found among the curassow-birds and agoutis. Another bird,

which I had been long searching for, the " anambé de catinga,"
a species of *Cyanurus*, was here shot ; and before leaving, I
obtained four or five specimens of it, and as many of the
commoner black-headed species.   One or two small birds, new
to me, were also obtained ; and these, with two or three scarce
butterflies, and about a dozen new species of fish, composed
my natural-history collections in this remote and unvisited
district.   This was entirely owing, however, to my unfortunate
and unforeseen illness, for birds in great variety had been very
abundant, but the time of the fruit was now over ; fish and
turtles, too, were in extraordinary plenty at the commencement
of the fall of the river, two months back ; and during that
period, constituting the short summer in these districts, while I
lay half dead at São Joaquim, insects were doubtless more
numerous.

But as there was now no remedy I made myself as contented
as I could, and endeavoured at least to complete my collection
of the arms, implements, and ornaments of the natives.   The
Indians here were mostly "Cobeus," and I obtained several of
their peculiar ornaments and dresses, to add to my collection.
I also took advantage of the visit of a Tushaúa, or chief, who
well understood the Lingoa Geral, to obtain a vocabulary of
their language.

Just as I was about to leave on my voyage down, I received a
note from Senhor Chagas, requesting, in the name of Tenente
Jesuino, the loan of my canoe, to ascend higher up the river ;
which, as the time of his stay was very uncertain, I was
obliged to refuse.   This Tenente, an ignorant half-breed, was
sent by the new Barra government to bring all the Tushaúas,
or chiefs, of the Uaupés and Isanna rivers to Barra, to receive
diplomas and presents.   An Indian, sent by him, had arrived at
Carurú caxoeira, and wished to buy the obá of the Tushaúa,
after I had paid for and got possession of it, and even had the
impudence to request me to give it back again, in order that
he might purchase or borrow it ; and my refusal was, of course,
quite sufficient seriously to offend the said Tenente.

On the 25th, having been just a fortnight at Mucúra, I left,
much disappointed with regard to the collections I had made
there.   The same day I reached Uarucapurí, whence I could
not proceed without a pilot, as the falls below are very
dangerous.   There was hardly a male in the village, Messrs.

Jesuino and Chagas having taken all with them up the river, to assist in an attack on an Indian tribe, the " Carapanás," where they hoped to get a lot of women, boys, and children, to take as presents to Barra.   There was scarcely anything to be had to eat : fish were not to be caught, though we sent our Indians out every day ; and though fowls were abundant, their owners were out, and those in charge of them would not sell them. At length, after four days, I succeeded in persuading the son of the Tushaúa to go with me as pilot to Jauarité, he not being able to resist the knives, beads, and mirror, which I spread out before him.

I had collected scarcely anything in this place, but a single specimen of the beautiful and rare topaz-throated hummer (*Trochilus pyra*) and a new butterfly of the genus *Callithea*. I heard of the handsome bronze Jacana being found here, but my hunters searched for it in vain.

On the morning after we left, we saw a fine deer on a sand-bank near us, so I sent Manoel into the forest to get behind it, while we remained quietly watching from the canoe.   After walking about the beach a short time, it took to the water to cross the river, when we followed in pursuit ; and, notwith-standing its turnings and doublings, soon came up,—when the poor animal was despatched by a blow on the head, and pulled into the canoe.   The Indians then went briskly on, rejoicing in the certainty of a dinner for the next day or two, in which I heartily joined them.   At Tapioca caxoeira we stayed two hours, to cook and salt the deer, and descended the fall without any accident.

On April 1st we passed a host of falls, shooting most of them amidst fearful waves and roaring breakers, and arrived safely at Carurú, where the Tushaúa gave us his house ; for, having two canoes, we were obliged to wait to get more Indians.   I was still too weak to go out into the forest ; and, besides, had my live stock to attend to, which now consisted of four monkeys, about a dozen parrots, and six or eight small birds.   It was a constant trouble to get food for them in sufficient variety, and to prevent them from escaping.   Most of the birds are brought up without being confined, and if placed in a cage, attempt constantly to get out, and refuse food till they die ; if, on the other hand, they are loose, they wander about to the Indians' houses, or into the forest, and are often lost. I here had two new toldas made to my canoes, but all attempts to hire men were fruitless. Fowls and fish were tolerably abundant, so we were better off than at Uarucapurí.

On the 4th, in the afternoon, Senhors Jesuino and Chagas arrived with a whole fleet of canoes, and upwards of twenty prisoners, all, but one, women and children. Seven men and one woman had been killed; the rest of the men escaped; but only one of the attacking party was killed. The man was kept bound, and the women and children well guarded, and every morning and evening they were all taken down to the river to bathe. At night there was abundance of caxirí and caxaça drunk in honour of the new-comers, and all the inhabitants assembled in the great house. I spoke to Jesuino about obtaining some Indians for me, which he promised to do. Next morning, however, his first act was to summon my pilot, and scold him for coming with me at all,—frightening the poor fellow so, that he immediately went off with his father down the river. Before he had left, however, having been told by my guardas what was going on, I applied to Jesuino about the matter, when he denied having said anything to the pilot, but refused to call him back, or make him fulfil his engagement with me. Soon after Jesuino left, having first sent five Indians to take me to Jauarité; so I started immediately after him. The men, however, had had instructions to go with me only a short distance, and then leave me where I could not procure any more; and about noon, much to my surprise, they got into a little obá, and intimated their intention to return, saying that they had only been told to come so far. I had overtaken Jesuino at this place, and now appealed to him; but though the men would have immediately obeyed an order from him he refused to give it, telling me that he had put them in my canoe, and now I must arrange with them as well as I could. I accordingly told the Indians, that if they came on with me to Jauarité, I would pay them well, but that, if they left me at this place, they should not have a single fish-hook; but they knew very well what Senhor Jesuino wanted, so without another word they paddled off, leaving me to get on as I could. I had now only one man and one boy in each canoe, to pass rapids which required six or eight good paddles to shoot with safety; but staying here was useless, so we went on,—drifting down the stream after Senhor Jesuino, who, no doubt, rejoiced in the idea that I should probably lose my canoes, if not my life, in the caxoeiras, and thought himself well revenged on the stranger who had dared to buy the canoe he had wanted to purchase.

In the afternoon we passed a caxoeira with considerable danger, and then, luckily, persuaded some Indians at a sitio to come with us to Jauarité. In the afternoon I stayed at several houses, purchasing fowls, parrots, bows and arrows and feathers ; and at one of them I found my runaway pilot, and made him give me two baskets of farinha, instead of the payment he had received for the voyage from Carurú to Jauarité. At the last caxoeira, close to Jauarité, we were very near losing our canoe, which was let down by a rope, I remaining in it ; but just in passing, it got twisted broadside, and the water rushing up from the bottom, had the curious effect of pushing it up against the fall, where it remained a considerable time completely on one side, and appearing as if every minute it would turn over. However, at last it was got out, and we reached the village, much to the surprise of Senhor Jesuino, who had arrived there but a few hours before us. My friend Senhor Augustinho, of São Jeronymo, was also there, and I spent the evening pleasantly with them.

I found that we differed in our calculations of the date, there being a day's difference in our reckonings of the day of the week and the day of the month. As I had been three months up the river, it was to be supposed I was wrong ; yet as I had kept a regular diary all the voyage, I could not at all make out how I had erred. This, however, is a common thing in these remote districts. When two parties meet, one going up and the other coming down the river, the first inquiry of the latter, after the usual compliments, is, " What day is it with you ? " and it not unfrequently happens, that there are three parties present, all of whom make it different days ; and then there is a comparison of authorities, and a determination of past Saints' days, in order to settle the correction of the disputed calendar. When at Caturú caxoeira, we had found that Messrs. Jesuino and Chagas differed from us on this important particular ; but as they had been some time out, we thought they might have erred as well as ourselves. Now, however, that Senhor Augustinho, who had recently come from

São Gabriel, whence he had brought the correct date, agreed with them, there was no withstanding such authority.   A minute examination of my diary was made, and it was then found that on our first stay at Carurú we had reckoned our delay there as five days instead of six.   The Indians generally keep accounts of the time very accurately on a voyage, by cutting notches on a stick, as boys do at school on the approach of the holidays.   In our case, however, even they were most of them wrong, for some of them agreed with me, while others made a day in advance, and others again a day behind us, so that we got completely confused.   Sometmies the traders residing at the Indian villages pass many months, without seeing a person from any civilised part, and get two or three days out in their reckonings.   Even in more populous places, where all the inhabitants depend on the priest or the commandante, errors have been made, and Sundays and Saints' days have been desecrated, while Mondays and common days have been observed in their place, much to the horror of all good Catholics.

The next morning I took a turn round the village,—bought some paroquets and parrots, and some feather ornaments and small pots, of the Tushaúa ; and then, having nothing to keep me at Jauarité, and having vainly endeavoured to get some Indians to go with me, I left for São Jeronymo.   On arriving at the first great fall of Pinupinú, we found only one Indian, and were obliged to send to the village for more.   That afternoon they did not cnoose to come, and we lost a beautiful day.   The next morning, as was to be expected, commenced a soaking rain ; but as the Indians arrived we went on, and about noon, the rain clearing off a little, we passed the fall of Panoré, and arrived safely at the village of São Jeronymo.   Here we disembarked, and unloaded our canoes, taking possession of the doorless " casa da nação," and made up our minds to remain quietly till we should get men to go down the river.

The same afternoon Jesuino arrived, and the next morning left,—kindly inquiring when I intended to proceed, and saying, he had spoken with the Tushaúa to get me Indians.   In two days, however, the Tushaúa also left for Barra, without giving me a single Indian, notwithstanding the promises and threats I had alternately employed.

The two Indians who had remained with me now left, and the two boys who had come from São Joaquim ran away, leaving me alone in my glory, with my two "guardas" and two canoes.  In vain I showed my axes, knives, beads, mirrors, and cloth, to every passing Indian ; not one could be induced to go with me, and I might probably have remained prisoner there for months, had not Senhor Victorino, the "Juiz de Paz," arrived, and also Bernado, my old pilot, who had left me at Jauarité, and had now been down to São Joaquim.  Between them, after a delay of several more days, some Indians were persuaded to receive payment to go with me as far as Castanheiro, where I hoped to get Capitão Ricardo to order them on to Barra.

## CHAPTER XIII.

### SÃO JERONYMO TO THE DOWNS.

Voyage down the Rio Negro—Arrive at Barra—Obtaining a Passport—
State of the City—Portuguese and Brazilian Enterprise—System of
Credit—Trade—Immorality, and its Causes—Leave Barra—A Storm
on the Amazon—Sarsaparilla—A Tale about Death—Pará—The
Yellow Fever—Sail for England—Ship takes Fire—Ten Days in
the Boats—Get picked up—Heavy Gales—Short of Provisions—
Storm in the Channel—Arrive at Deal.

AT length, on the 23rd of April, I bade adieu, with much
pleasure, to São Jeronymo. I stopped at several places to
buy beiju, fish, pacovas, and any parrots I could meet with.
My Indians went several times, early in the morning, to the
gapó to catch frogs, which they obtained in great numbers,
stringing them on a sipó, and, boiling them entire, entrails
and all, devoured them with much gusto. The frogs are
mottled of various colours, have dilated toes, and are called
Juí.

On the 26th we reached São Joaquim, where I stayed a
day, to make some cages for my birds, and embark the things
I had left with Senhor Lima.

On the 28th I went on to São Gabriel, and paid my respects
to the new Commandante, and then enjoyed a little conversation with my friend Mr. Spruce. Several of my birds died
or were lost here, and at São Joaquim. A little black monkey
killed and devoured two which had escaped from their cages,
and one of my most valuable and beautiful parrots (a single
specimen) was lost in passing the falls. I had left São
Joaquim with fifty-two live animals (monkeys, parrots, etc.),
which, in a small canoe, were no little trouble and annoyance.

I was lucky enough to get the Commandante to send a
soldier with me in charge of the Correio, or post, and thus

ensured my passage to Barra without further delays, a point on which I had been rather uneasy.  Leaving São Gabriel I stayed for the night at the house of Senhor Victoríno, of whom I bought several green parrots, and a beautiful "anacá," or purple and red-necked crested parrot, in place of the one which had gone overboard while passing the falls at São Gabriel.  The following day I reached the house of Senhor Palheta, and thought myself fortunate to purchase of him another anacá for seven shillings ; but the very next morning it died from cold, having flown into the river, and become completely chilled before it could be rescued.

On the 2nd of May I arrived at the sitio of my old friend Senhor Chagas, who made me breakfast with him, and sold me some farinha, coffee, and a lot of guinea-fowls' eggs ; and embraced me with great affection at parting, wishing me every happiness.  The same night I reached Castanheiro, where I particularly wished to get a pilot, to take me down the east bank of the river, for the purpose of making a sketch-survey of that side, and ascertaining the width of this extraordinary stream.  Senhor Ricardo, who is the Capitão dos Trabalha-dores, immediately gave me an order to embark a man, whose house I should pass the next day, and who, he said, was per-fectly acquainted with that side of the river.  After breakfast-ing with him the next morning, I left, well satisfied to have a prospect of accomplishing this long-cherished scheme.  On arriving at the house, however, it was empty, and there was no sign of it having been inhabited for some weeks, so that I had to give up all hopes of completing my project.

I applied again to the Subdelegarde, João Cordeiro, whose house I reached the next day, and also to the lieutenant of Senhor Ricardo, but without effect ; all making the usual reply, " Não ha gente nenhum aqui " (there is not a single person about there) ; so I was reluctantly compelled to proceed down the river by the same course which I had already traversed three times, as, by attempting to go on the other route without a pilot, I might lose my way, and not get to Barra for a month.

The fever and ague now attacked me again, and I passed several days very uncomfortably.  We had almost constant rains ; and to attend to my numerous birds and animals was a great annoyance, owing to the crowded state of the canoe, and the impossibility of properly cleaning them during the rain.

Some died almost every day, and I often wished I had had nothing whatever to do with them, though, having once taken them in hand, I determined to persevere.

On the 8th I reached Barcellos, and here I was annoyed by having to give an account of what I had in my canoes, and pay duty, the new Government of Barra not allowing anything to escape without contributing its share.

On the 11th we passed the mouth of the Rio Branco, and I noticed for the first time the peculiar colour of the water, which is a very pale yellow-olive, almost milky, very different from, and much whiter than, the waters of the Amazon, and making its name of the "White River" very appropriate. In the dry season the waters are much clearer.

In the morning I reached Pedreiro, and purchased a turtle, which we stopped to cook, a short distance below the village ; it was a very large and fat one, and we fried the greater part of the meat in fat for the rest of the voyage. At a sitio, in the evening, I bought two parrots, and the next morning, at Ayrão, five more ; and in the afternoon, at another sitio, a blue macaw, a monkey, a toucan, and a pigeon. At night we had a storm of rain and wind, and for a long time beat about in the middle of the river, tossed by the waves, without being able to find the shore.

On the 15th we reached "Ai purusá," where I bought some fish and maize. Here was lying a fine harpy eagle, which Senhor Bagatta had shot the day before, and, having plucked out some of the wing-feathers, had left it to rot ; I thus just missed, by a day, getting a specimen of this bird, which I so much desired, and which I had never been able to procure during a four years' residence in the country. We had plenty more rain every night, making the journey very disagreeable ; and at length, on the 17th, reached Barra do Rio Negro, now the capital of the new Province of Amazonas.

I was here kindly received by my friend Henrique Antony ; and I spent all the day in searching for some house or lodging, which was very hard to be procured, every house being occupied, and rents having much risen, from the influx of strangers and traders consequent on the arrival of the new Government. However, by the evening I succeeded in getting a small mud-floored, leaky-roofed room, which I was glad to hire, as I did not know how long I might be obliged to remain in Barra, before I could obtain a passage to Pará. The next morning I could not disembark my things till the new Custom-house opened, at nine o'clock; when I had to pay duties on every article, even on my bird-skins, insects, stuffed alligators, etc., and so it was night before I got everything on shore. The next day I paid off my Indians, and settled myself to wait patiently and attend to my menagerie, till I could get a passage to Pará.

For three weeks I had been nearly lame, with a sore and inflamed toe, into which the chegoes had burrowed under the nail, and rendered wearing a shoe, or walking, exceedingly painful; having been compelled to move about the last few days, it had inflamed and swelled, and I was now therefore glad to remain quietly at home, and by poultices and plaisters endeavour to cure it. During the short time the Indians had remained in charge of my canoe, while I was looking after a house, they had lost three of my birds; but I soon found I had quite enough left to keep me constantly employed attending to them. My parrots, in particular, of which I had more than twenty, would persist in wandering about into the street, and I lost several of my best, which were, no doubt, safely domiciled in some of the adjoining houses. I was much annoyed, too, by persons constantly coming to me, to sell them parrots or monkeys; and my repeated assurances, that I myself wanted to buy more, did not in the least check the pertinacity of my would-be customers.

The city was now full of fashionably-dressed young men, who received the public money for services they did not know how to perform. Many of them could not fill up a few dozen words in a printed form without making blunders, or in a shorter time than two or three hours; their contemplations seeming scarcely to rise beyond their polished-leather boots and gold watch-chains. As it was necessary to get a passport, I presented myself at the office of the " Chef de Policia," for the purpose; but was told that I must first advertise my intention of leaving in the newspaper. I accordingly did so, and about a week after went again. I was now requested to bring a formal application in writing, to have a passport granted me: I returned, and prepared one, and the next day went with it; now the Chef was engaged, and he must sign the requisition before anything else could be done. I called again the next day, and now that the requisition was signed, I had a blank form given me to go and get stamped in another office, in a distant part of the city. Off I had to go,—get the stamp, which took two clerks to sign, and paid my eight vintems for it; armed with this, I returned to the police-office, and now, to my surprise, the passport was actually made out and given me; and on paying another twelve vintems (sixpence), I was at liberty to leave Barra whenever I could; for as to leaving it whenever I pleased, that was out of the question.

The city of Barra, the capital of the Province and the residence of the President, was now in a very miserable condition. No vessel had arrived from Pará for five months, and all supplies were exhausted. Flour had been long since finished, consequently there was no bread; neither was there biscuit, butter, sugar, cheese, wine, nor vinegar; molasses even, to sweeten our coffee, was very scarce; and the spirit of the country (caxaça) was so nearly exhausted, that it could only be obtained retail, and in the smallest quantities: everybody was reduced to farinha and fish, with beef twice a week, and turtle about as often. This state of destitution was owing to there having been a vessel lost a month before, near Barra, which was coming from Pará; and at this time of the year, when the river is full, and the winds adverse, the passage frequently takes from seventy days to three months,—having to be performed almost entirely by warping with a rope sent ahead in a canoe, against the powerful current of the Amazon. It may therefore be well imagined that Barra was not the most agreeable place in the world to reside in, when, joined to the total absence of amusement and society which universally prevails there, the want of the common necessaries of life had also to be endured.

Several vessels were leaving for Pará, but all were so completely filled as not to have room for me or my baggage; and I had to wait in patience for the arrival of a small canoe from the Solimões, in which Senhor Henrique guaranteed me a passage to Pará.

Before proceeding with my journey, I will note the few observations that occur to me on the character and customs of the inhabitants of this fine country. I of course speak solely of the province of Pará, and it is probable that to the rest of Brazil my remarks may not in the least apply; so different in every respect is this part of the Empire from the more southern and better-known portion. There is, perhaps, no country in the world so capable of yielding a large return for agricultural labour, and yet so little cultivated ; none where the earth will produce such a variety of valuable productions, and where they are so totally neglected ; none where the facilities for internal communication are so great, or where it is more difficult or tedious to get from place to place ; none which so much possesses all the natural requisites for an immense trade with all the world, and where commerce is so limited and insignificant.

This may well excite some wonder, when we remember that the white inhabitants of this country are the Portuguese and their descendants,—the nation which a few centuries ago took the lead in all great discoveries and commercial enterprises,— which spread its colonies over the whole world, and exhibited the most chivalric spirit of enterprise in overcoming the dangers of navigation in unknown seas, and of opening a commercial intercourse with barbarous or uncivilised nations.

But yet, as far as I myself have been able to observe, their national character has not changed. The Portuguese, and their descendants, exhibit here the same perseverance, the same endurance of every hardship, and the same wandering spirit, which led and still leads them to penetrate into the most desolate and uncivilised regions in pursuit of commerce and in search of gold. But they exhibit also a distaste for agricultural and mechanical labour, which appears to have been ever a part of their national character, and which has caused them to sink to their present low condition in the scale of nations, in whatever part of the world they may be found. When their colonies were flourishing in every quarter of the globe, and their ships brought luxuries for the supply of half the civilised world, a great part of their population found occupation in trade, in the distribution of that wealth which set in a constant stream from America, Asia, and Africa, to their shores ; but now that this stream has been diverted into other channels by the energy of the Saxon races, the surplus population, averse from agriculture, and unable to find a support in the diminished trade of the country, swarm to Brazil, in the hope that wealth may be found there, in a manner more congenial to their tastes.

Thus we find the province of Pará overrun with traders, the

greater part of whom deserve no better name than pedlars, only they carry their goods in a canoe instead of upon their backs. As their distaste for agriculture, or perhaps rather their passionate love of trade, allows scarcely any of them to settle, or produce anything for others to trade in, their only resource is in the indigenous inhabitants of the country ; and as these are also very little given to cultivation except to procure the mere necessaries of life, it results that the only articles of commerce are the natural productions of the country, to catch or collect which requires an irregular and wandering life, better suited to an Indian's habits than the settled and continued exertions of agriculture. These products are principally dried fish, and oil from the turtles' eggs and cow-fish, for the inland trade ; and sarsaparilla, piassaba, india-rubber, Brazil-nuts, balsam of capivi, and cacao, for the exports. Though the coffee-plant and sugar-cane grow everywhere almost spontaneously, yet coffee and sugar have to be imported from other parts of Brazil for home consumption. Beef is everywhere bad, principally because there are no good pastures near the towns where cattle brought from a distance can be fattened, and no one thinks of making them, though it might easily be done. Vegetables are also very scarce and dear, and so are all fruits, except such as the orange and banana, which once planted only require the produce to be gathered when ripe ; fowls in Pará are 3*s.* 6*d.* each, and sugar as dear as in England. And all this because nobody will make it his business to supply any one of these articles ! There is a kind of gambling excitement in trade which outshines all the steady profits of labour, and regular mechanics are constantly leaving their business to get a few goods on credit and wander about the country trading.

There is, I should think, no country where such a universal and insecure system of credit prevails as here. There is hardly a trader, great or small, in the country, that can be said to have any capital of his own. The merchants in Pará, who have foreign correspondents, have goods out on credit ; they sell on credit to the smaller merchants or shopkeepers of Pará ; these again supply on credit the negociantes in the country towns. From these last the traders up the different rivers get their supplies also on credit. These traders give small parcels of goods to half-civilised Indians, or to any one who will take them, to go among the wild Indian tribes and buy up their produce. They, however, have to give credit to the Indians, who will not work till they have been paid six months beforehand; and so they are paid for sarsaparilla or oil, which is still in the forest or the lake. And at every step of this credit there is not the slightest security; and robbery, waste, and a profuse squandering away of the property of others, is of constant occurrence. To cover all these chances of loss, the profits are proportionably great at every step, and the consumer often has to pay two shillings a yard for calico worth twopence, and everything else in like proportion. It is these apparently enormous profits that lead mechanics and others into trade, as they do not consider the very small business that can be done in a given time, owing to the poverty of the country and the enormous number of traders in proportion to the purchasers. It seems a very nice and easy way of getting a living, to sell goods at double the price you pay for them, and then again to sell the produce you receive at double what you pay for it; but as the greater part of the small traders do not get rid of more than a hundred pounds' worth of goods in a year, and the expenses of Indians and canoes, their families and bad debts, wines and liquors, and the waste which always takes place where everything is obtained upon credit, are often double that sum, it is not to be wondered at that they are almost all of them constantly in debt to their correspondents, who, when they have once thus got a hold on them, do not allow them easily to get free.

It is this universal love of trade which leads, I think, to three great vices very prevalent here—drinking, gambling, and lying,—besides a whole host of trickeries, cheatings, and debaucheries of every description. The life of a river trader admits of little enjoyment to a man who has no intellectual resources; it is not therefore to be wondered at that the greater part of these men are more or less addicted to intoxication; and when they can supply themselves on credit with as much wine and spirits as they like, there is little inducement to break through the habit. A man who, if he had to pay ready money, would never think of drinking wine, when he can have it on credit takes twenty or thirty gallons with him in his canoe, which, as it has cost him nothing, is little valued, and he perhaps arrives at the end of his voyage without a drop.

In the towns in the interior every shop sells spirits, and numbers of persons are all day drinking, taking a glass at every place they go to, and, by this constant dramming, ruining their health perhaps more than by complete intoxication at more distant intervals. Gambling is almost universal in a greater or less degree, and is to be traced to that same desire to gain money by some easier road than labour, which leads so many into commerce; and the great number of traders, who have to get a living out of an amount of business which would not be properly sufficient for one-third the number, leads to the general use of trickery and lying of every degree, as fair means to be employed to entrap a new customer or to ruin a rival trader. Truth, in fact, in matters of business is so seldom made use of, that a lie seems to be preferred even when it can serve no purpose whatever, and where the person addressed must be perfectly aware of the falsehood of every asseveration made; but Portuguese politeness does not permit him by word or look to throw any doubt on his friend's veracity. I have been often amused to hear two parties endeavouring to cheat each other, by assertions which each party knew to be perfectly false, and yet pretended to receive as undoubted fact.

On the subjects of the most prevalent kind of immorality, it is impossible to enter, without mentioning facts too disgusting to be committed to paper. Vices of such a description as at home are never even alluded to, are here the subjects of common conversation, and boasted of as meritorious acts, and no opportunity is lost of putting the vilest construction upon every word or act of a neighbour.

Among the causes which tend to promote the growth of such wide-spread immorality, we may perhaps reckon the geographical position and political condition of the country, and the peculiar state of civilisation in which it now exists. To a native, a tropical climate certainly offers fewer pleasures, pursuits, and occupations than a temperate one. The heat in the dry, and the moisture in the rainy season do not admit of the outdoor exercise and amusements, in which the inhabitants of a temperate zone can almost constantly indulge. The short twilights afford but a few moments between the glare of the descending sun and the darkness of night. Nature itself, dressed in an eternal and almost unchangeable garb of verdure, presents but a monotonous scene to him who has beheld it from childhood.    In the interior of the country there is not a road or path out of the towns, along which a person can walk with comfort or pleasure ; all is dense forest, or more impassable clearings.    Here are no flower-bespangled meadows, no turfy glades, or smooth shady walks to tempt the lover of nature ; here are no dry gravelled roads, where, even in the intervals of rain, we may find healthy and agreeable exercise ; here are no field-side paths among golden corn or luxuriant clover.    Here are no long summer evenings, to wander in at leisure, and admire the slowly changing glories of the sunset ; nor long winter nights, with the blazing hearth, which, by drawing all the members of a family into close contact, promote a social intercourse and domestic enjoyment, which the inhabitants of a tropical clime can but faintly realise.

At length the canoe arrived in which I was to go to Pará, and I soon agreed for my passage, and set to work getting my things together.   I had a great number of cases and boxes, six large ones which I had left with Senhor Henrique the year before, being still in his possession, because the great men of Barra were afraid they might contain contraband articles, and would not let them pass.

I now got them embarked, by making a declaration of their contents, and paying a small duty on them.   Out of a hundred live animals which I had purchased or had had given to me, there now only remained thirty-four, consisting of five monkeys, two macaws, twenty parrots and paroquets of twelve different species, five small birds, a white-crested Brazilian pheasant, and a toucan.

On the 10th of June we left Barra, commencing our voyage very unfortunately for me ; for, on going on board, after bidding adieu to my friends, I missed my toucan, which had, no doubt, flown overboard, and not being noticed by any one, was drowned.   This bird I esteemed very highly, as he was full-grown and very tame, and I had great hopes of bringing him alive to England.

On the 13th we reached Villa Nova, at which place, being the last in the new Province, we had to disembark to show our passports, as if entering into another kingdom ; and not content with this, there is another station half a day further down, on the exact boundary-line, where all vessels have to stay a second time, and again present their papers, as if the great object of the Government were to make their regulations as annoying and expensive as possible. At Villa Nova I was glad to get some butter and biscuits ; quite a treat, after the scanty luxuries of Barra. Here, too, I met the kind priest, Padre Torquato, who had entertained us so hospitably on our ascent of the river. He received me with great kindness, and regretted I could not stay longer with him ; he gave me a curious animal, which I had heard of but never seen before, a forest-dog,—an animal somewhat resembling a fox, in its bushy tail and great taste for poultry, and apparently very tame and docile.

The next day we passed Obydos, the strong current of the river, now at its height, carrying us down with great rapidity ; and the succeeding night we had a tremendous storm, which blew and tossed our little vessel about in a very alarming manner. The owner of the canoe, an Indian, was much frightened ; he called upon the Virgin, and promised her several pounds of candles, if she would but save the canoe ; and, opening the door of the little cabin where I was sleeping, cried out in a most piteous voice, " Oh ! meu amigo, estamos perdidos " (Oh ! my friend, we are all lost). In vain I tried to comfort him with assurances that, as the vessel was new and strong, and not too heavily laden, there was no danger,—although the night was pitch dark, and the wind blew in the most fierce and furious gusts imaginable. We did not know whether we were in the middle of the river or near the side, and the only danger we were exposed to, was of our drifting ashore or running aground. After about an hour, however, the canoe came to a stop, without any shock whatever, and remained perfectly still, although the wind still blew. It was so dark that nothing was to be seen, and it was only by stretching his arm down over the side, that the master ascertained that we had drifted into one of the large compact beds of floating grass which, in many places, line the banks of the Amazon for hundreds of yards from the shore. Here, therefore, we were safely moored, and waited for the morning, sleeping comfortably, with the knowledge that we were out of all danger.

The next day, by noon, we reached the mouth of the Tapa-joz, and went in the montaria to Santarem, to make some purchases and visit my friends. I found old Captain Hislop ; but Mr. Bates, whom I most wished to see, had left a week before on an excursion up the Tapajoz. Having laid in a stock of sugar, vinegar, oil, biscuits, and fresh bread and meat, we proceeded on our journey, which we were anxious to complete as soon as possible.

On the 18th we passed Gurupá; and on the 19th entered the narrow channels which form the communication with the Pará river,—bidding adieu to the turbid mighty flood of the never-to-be-forgotten Amazon.

We here met a vessel from Pará, fifty days out, having made a much shorter distance than we, descending the river, had come in five.

On the 22nd we reached Breves, a neat little village with well-supplied shops, where I bought half a dozen of the pretty painted basins, for the manufacture of which the place is celebrated; we here also got some oranges, at six for a halfpenny.

The next day we stayed at a sitio built upon piles, for the whole country about here is covered at spring-tides. The master of the canoe had a lot of sarsaparilla to put up properly for the Pará market, and stayed a day to do it. The sarsaparilla is the root of a prickly, climbing plant, allied to our common black bryony; the roots are dug by the Indians, and tied up in bundles of various lengths and sizes; but, as it is a very light cargo, it is necessary to form it into packages of a convenient and uniform size and length, for closer stowage;— these are cylindrical, generally of sixteen pounds each, and are about three and a half feet long and five or six inches in diameter, cut square and even at the ends, and wound round closely from end to end with the long flexible roots of a species of *Pothos*, which, growing on the tops of lofty trees, hang down often a hundred feet or more, and, when the outer bark is scraped off, are universally used for this purpose. It was to do this binding we stayed here, the sarsa having been already done up in proper packages; and while the crew were busy about it, I occupied myself making some sketches of palms, which were yet wanting to complete my collection.

In two days more we reached the mouth of the Tocantíns, where there is a great bay,—so wide, that the further shore is not visible. As there are some dangerous sandbanks here, there is a pilot who takes canoes over, and we waited all day in order to start with the morning's tide, which is considered the most favourable for the passage. While here I got a few shells, and amused myself by talking with the pilot, his wife, and two very lively daughters. Our conversation turned upon the shortness and uncertainty of life ; which the old woman illustrated by a tale, which seemed to be another version of the "three warnings."

" A man and his wife were conversing together, and remarking on the unpleasantness of being subject to death. ' I should like to make friends with Death, some way,' said the man ; ' then perhaps he will not trouble me.' ' That you can easily do,' said his wife ; ' invite him to be padrinho (godfather) to our little boy, who is to be baptized next week ; you will then be able to talk to him on the subject, and he will surely not be able to refuse a slight favour to his " compadre." So he was invited accordingly, and came ; and after the ceremony and the feast were over, as he was going away, the man said to him, ' Compadre Death, as there are plenty of people in the world for you to take, I hope you will never come for me.' ' Really, Compadre,' replied Death, ' I cannot promise you that, for when God sends me for anybody I must go. However, I will do all I can, and I will at all events promise you a week's notice, that you may have time to prepare yourself.' Several years passed on, and Death at last came to pay them a visit. ' Good-evening, Compadre,' says he, ' I'm come on a disagreeable business : I have received orders to fetch you this day week, so I'm come to give you the notice I promised you.' ' Oh ! Compadre,' said the man, ' you're come very soon ; it's exceedingly inconvenient for me to go just now, I'm getting on very nicely, and shall be a rich man in a few years, if you will but let me alone : it's very unkind of you, Compadre ; I'm sure you can arrange it if you like, and take some one else instead of me.' ' Very sorry,' said Death, ' but it can't be done, nohow : I've got my orders, and I must obey them. Nobody ever gets off when the order's once given, and very few get so long a notice as I've been able to give you. However, I'll try all I can, and if I succeed, you won't see me this day week ; but I don't think there's any hope,—so good-bye.'

" When the day came, the man was in a great fright, for he did not expect to escape ; his wife, however, hit upon a plan, which they resolved to try. They had an old Negro man in the house, who used to be generally employed in the kitchen. They made him exchange clothes with his master, and sent him away out of the house ; the master then blacked his face, and made himself as much like the old nigger as he could. On the evening appointed Death came. 'Good-evening, Comadre,' said he ; 'where is my compadre?—I'm obliged to take him with me. 'Oh! Compadre,' said she, 'he didn't at all expect you, and is gone on some business into the village, and won't be back till late.' 'Now I'm in a pretty mess,' said Death ; 'I did not expect my compadre would have treated me so ; it's very ungentlemanly of him to get me into this scrape after all I've done for him. However, I must take somebody ;—who is there in the house?' The woman was rather alarmed at this question, for she expected he would immediately have started off to the village in search of her husband : however, she considered it best to be civil, so replied, 'There's only our old nigger, that's in the kitchen, getting supper ready. Sit down, Compadre, and take a bit, and then perhaps my husband will be in ; I'm very sorry he should give you so much trouble.' 'No, I can't stay,' said Death ; 'I've got a long way to go, and must take somebody, so let's see if the old nigger will do?' and he walked into the kitchen, where the man was pretending to be busily engaged over the fire. 'Well, if Compadre won't come, I suppose I must take the old nigger,' said Death ; and before the wife could speak a word, he stretched out his hand, and down fell her husband a corpse.

"So you see," said the old woman to me, "when a man's time is come he must go,: neither doctors nor anything else can stop him, and you can't cheat Death nohow." To which sentiment I did not think it worth while to make any objection.

About two days before had been St. John's day, when it is the custom to make bonfires and jump over and through them, which act is considered by the common people as an important religious ceremony. As we were talking about it, the old lady gravely asked if we knew that animals also passed through the fire? We replied that we were not aware of the fact; upon which she informed us that we might hereafter believe it, for that she had had ocular demonstration of it. "It was last year," said she, "on the day after St. John's, my son went out to hunt, and brought home a cotía and a pacá, and both of them were completely scorched all along the belly : they had evidently passed through the fire the night before." "But where do they get the fire from?" I asked. "Oh! God prepares it for them," said she; and on my hinting that fires were not often found in the forest unless lit by human hands, she at once silenced my objections by triumphantly asking me, "if anything was impossible with God?" at the same time observing that perhaps I was a Protestant, and did not believe in God or the Virgin. So I was obliged to give up the point; and though I assured her that Protestants did generally believe in God and went to church, she replied that she did not know, but had always heard to the contrary.

At length, on the 2nd of July, we reached Pará, where I was kindly received by my friend Mr. C., and was glad to learn that there was a vessel in port that would probably sail for London in about a week. Several times on the voyage down I had had fits of ague, and was still very weak and quite unable to make any exertion. The yellow fever, which the year before had cut off thousands of the inhabitants, still attacked new-comers, and scarcely a ship was in port but had a considerable portion of her crew in the hospital. The weather was beautiful; the summer or dry season was just commencing, vegetation was luxuriantly verdant, and the bright sky and clear fresh atmosphere seemed as if they could not harbour the fatal miasma which had crowded the cemetery with funeral crosses, and made every dwelling in the city a house of mourning. Once or twice I attempted to walk out into the forest, but the exertion generally brought on shiverings and sickness, so I thought it best to remain as quiet as possible till the time of my departure.

Since I had left the city it had been much improved. Avenues of almond and other trees had been formed along the road to Nazaré and round the Largo de Palacio; new roads and drives had been made, and some new buildings erected: in other respects the city was the same. The dirty, straggling, uncovered market, the carts of hacked beef, the loud chanting of the Negro porters, and the good-humoured smiling faces of the Indian and Negro girls selling their fruits and "doces," greeted me as of old. Fowls had risen in price from about 2*s.* to 3*s.* 6*d.*, and fruits and vegetables in about the same proportion; while in changing English money for Brazilian I now got about ten per cent. less than I used, and yet everybody complained of trade being very bad, and prices quite unremunerative. I heard many stories of miraculous cures of the yellow fever, when at its worst stage, and after the parties had been given up by the doctors. One had been cured by eating ices, another by drinking a bottle of wine; ices, in fact, had got into great favour as a fine tonic, and were taken daily by many persons as a most useful medicine.

I agreed for my passage in the brig *Helen*, two hundred and thirty-five tons, Captain John Turner, whose property she was; and on the morning of Monday, the 12th of July, we got aboard, and bade adieu to the white houses and waving palm-trees of Pará. Our cargo consisted of about a hundred and twenty tons of india-rubber, and a quantity of cocoa, arnotto, piassaba, and balsam of capivi. About two days after we left I had a slight attack of fever, and almost thought that I was still doomed to be cut off by the dread disease which had sent my brother and so many of my countrymen to graves upon a foreign shore. A little calomel and opening medicines, however, soon set me right again; but as I was very weak, and suffered much from sea-sickness, I spent most of my time in the cabin. For three weeks we had very light winds and fine weather, and on the 6th of August had reached about latitude 30° 30′ north, longitude 52° west.

On that morning, after breakfast, I was reading in the cabin, when the Captain came down and said to me, " I'm afraid the ship's on fire; come and see what you think of it," and proceeded to examine the lazaretto, or small hole under the floor where the provisions are kept, but no signs of fire were visible there. We then went on deck to the forepart of the ship, where we found a dense vapoury smoke issuing from the forecastle. The fore hatchway was immediately opened, and, the smoke issuing there also, the men were set to work clearing out part of the cargo. After throwing out some quantity without any symptom of approaching the seat of the fire, we opened the after hatchway; and here the smoke was much more dense, and in a very short time became so suffocating, that the men could not stay in the hold to throw out more cargo, so they were set to work pouring in water, while others proceeded to the cabin, and now found abundance of smoke issuing from the lazaretto, whence it entered through the joints of the bulkhead which separated it from the hold. Attempts were now made to break this bulkhead down; but the planks were so thick and the smoke so unbearable that it could not be effected, as no man could remain in the lazaretto to make more than a couple of blows. The cabin table was therefore removed, and a hole attempted to be cut in the cabin floor, so as to be able to pour water immediately on the seat of the fire, which appeared to be where the balsam was stowed. This took some time, owing to the suffocating smoke, which also continued to pour in dense volumes out of the hatchway. Seeing that there was now little chance of our being able to extinguish the fire, the Captain thought it prudent to secure our own safety, and called all hands to get out the boats, and such necessaries as we should want, in case of being obliged to take to them. The long-boat was stowed on deck, and of course required some time to get it afloat. The gig was hung on davits on the quarter, and was easily let down. All now were in great activity. Many little necessaries had to be hunted up from their hiding-places. The cook was sent for corks to plug the holes in the bottoms of the boats. Now no one knew where a rudder had been put away ; now the thowl-pins were missing. The oars had to be searched for, and spars to serve as masts, with proportionate sails, spare canvas, twine, cordage, tow-ropes, sail-needles, nails and tacks, carpenters' tools, etc. The Captain was looking after his chronometer, sextant, barometer, charts, compasses, and books of navigation ; the seamen were getting their clothes into huge canvas bags ; all were lugging about pilot-coats, blankets, south-westers, and oilskin coats and trousers ; and I went down into the cabin, now suffocatingly hot and full of smoke, to see what was worth saving. I got my watch and a small tin box containing some shirts and a couple of old note-books, with some drawings of plants and animals, and scrambled up with them on deck. Many clothes and a large portfolio of drawings and sketches remained in my berth ; but I did not care to venture down again, and in fact felt a kind of apathy about saving anything, that I can now hardly account for. On deck the crew were still busy at the boats ; two barrels of bread were got in, a lot of raw pork, some ham and cases of preserved meats, some wine and a large cask of water. The cask had to be lowered into the boat empty, for fear of any accident, and after being securely fixed in its place, filled with buckets from those on board.

The boats, having been so long drying in a tropical sun, were very leaky, and were now half full of water, and books, coats, blankets, shoes, pork, and cheese, in a confused mass were soaking in them.  It was necessary to put two men in each, to bale ; and everything necessary being now ready, the rest of the crew were called off again to pour water into the hatchways and cabin, from which rose volumes of thick yellow smoke.  Now, too, we could hear in the hold the balsam bubbling, like some great boiling caldron, which told of such intense heat, that we knew the flames must soon break out. And so it was, for in less than half an hour the fire burst through the cabin-floor into the berths, and consuming rapidly the dry pine-wood, soon flamed up through the skylight. There was now a scorching heat on the quarter-deck, and we saw that all hope was over, and that we must in a few minutes be driven by the terrible element to take refuge on the scarcely less dangerous one, which heaved and swelled its mighty billows a thousand miles on every side of us.  The Captain at length ordered all into the boats, and was himself the last to leave the vessel.  I had to get down over the stern by a rope into the boat, rising and falling and swaying about with the swell of the ocean ; and, being rather weak, rubbed the skin considerably off my fingers, and tumbled in among the miscellaneous articles already soaking there in the greatest confusion.  One sailor was baling with a bucket, and another with a mug ; but the water not seeming at all to diminish, but rather the contrary, I set to work helping them, and soon found the salt-water producing a most intense smarting and burning on my scarified fingers.

We now lay astern of the ship, to which we were moored, watching the progress of the fire.  The flames very soon caught the shrouds and sails, making a most magnificent conflagration up to the very peak, for the royals were set at the time.  Soon after, the fore rigging and sails also burnt, and flames were seen issuing from the fore hatchway, showing how rapidly the fire was spreading through the combustible cargo.  The vessel, having now no sails to steady her, rolled heavily, and the masts, no longer supported by the shrouds, bent and creaked, threatening to go overboard every minute. The main-mast went first, breaking off about twenty feet above the deck ; but the foremast stood for a long time, exciting our admiration and wonder, at the time it resisted the heavy rolls and lurches of the vessel; at last, being partly burned at the bottom, it went over, more than an hour after its companion. The decks were now a mass of fire, and the bulwarks partly burnt away. Many of the parrots, monkeys, and other animals we had on board, were already burnt or suffocated; but several had retreated to the bowsprit out of reach of the flames, appearing to wonder what was going on, and quite unconscious of the fate that awaited them. We tried to get some of them into the boats, by going as near as we could venture; but they did not seem at all aware of the danger they were in, and would not make any attempt to reach us. As the flames caught the base of the bowsprit, some of them ran back and jumped into the midst of the fire. Only one parrot escaped: he was sitting on a rope hanging from the bowsprit, and this burning above him let him fall into the water, where, after floating a little way, we picked him up.

Night was now coming on. The whole deck was a mass of fire, giving out an intense heat. We determined to stay by the vessel all night, as the light would attract any ship passing within a considerable distance of us. We had eaten nothing since the morning, and had had plenty to do and to think of, to prevent our being hungry; but now, as the evening air began to get cool and pleasant, we all found we had very good appetites, and supped well on biscuits and water.

We then had to make our arrangements for the night. Our mooring ropes had been burnt, and we were thus cast adrift from the ship, and were afraid of getting out of sight of it during the night, and so missing any vessel which might chance to be attracted by its light. A portion of the masts and rigging were floating near the ship, and to this we fastened our boats; but so many half-burnt spars and planks were floating about us, as to render our situation very perilous, for there was a heavy swell, and our boats might have been in an instant stove in by coming in contact with them.

We therefore cast loose again, and kept at a distance of a quarter or half a mile from the ship by rowing when requisite. We were incessantly baling the whole night. Ourselves and everything in the boats were thoroughly drenched, so we got little repose: if for an instant we dozed off into forgetfulness, we soon woke up again to the realities of our position, and to see the red glare which our burning vessel cast over us. It was now a magnificent spectacle, for the decks had completely burnt away, and as it heaved and rolled with the swell of the sea, presented its interior towards us filled with liquid flame,— a fiery furnace tossing restlessly upon the ocean.

At length morning came ; the dangers of the night were past, and with hopeful hearts we set up our little masts, and rigged our sails, and, bidding adieu to the still burning wreck of our ship, went gaily bounding along before a light east wind. And then pencils and books were hunted out, and our course and distance to Bermuda calculated ; and we found that this, the nearest point of land in the vast waste of waters round us, was at least seven hundred miles away. But still we went on full of hope, for the wind was fair, and we reckoned that, if it did not change, we might make a hundred miles a day, and so in seven days reach the longed-for haven.

As we had supped but scantily the night before, we had now good appetites, and got out our ham and pork, biscuit and wine and water, and made a very hearty meal, finding that even uncooked meat was not to be despised where no fire could be got to cook it with.

The day was fine and warm, and the floating seaweed, called gulf-weed, was pretty abundant. The boats still required almost incessant baling, and though we did not ship many seas, yet there was quite enough spray to keep us constantly wet. At night we got a rope fastened to the long-boat, for her to tow us, in order that we might not get separated ; but as we sailed pretty equally, we kept both sails up. We passed a tolerable night under the circumstances. The next day, the 8th, was fine, gulf-weed still floated plentifully by us, and there were numerous flying-fish, some of which fell into our boats, and others flew an immense distance over the waves. I now found my hands and face very much blistered by the sun, and exceedingly sore and painful. At night two boobies, large dusky sea-birds with very long wings, flew about us. During the night I saw several meteors, and in fact could not be in a better position for observing them, than lying on my back in a small boat in the middle of the Atlantic. We also saw a flock of small birds fly by, making a chirping noise ; the sailors did not know what they were.

The 9th was again fine and hot, and my blistered hands

were very painful. No ship appeared in sight, though we were crossing the track of the West India vessels. It was rather squally, and I passed a nervous, uncomfortable night; our boats did not, however, now leak so much, which was a great satisfaction.

The 10th was squally, and the wind veered to the south-west, so that we could not make our course for Bermuda, but were obliged to go to the north of it. The sea ran very high, and sudden gusts of wind would frequently heel us over in a manner very alarming to me. We had some heavy showers of rain, and should have liked to have caught some fresh water, but could not, as all our clothes and the sails were saturated with salt. Our position at noon was in latitude 31° 59' north, longitude 57° 22' west.

The 11th was still rough and squally. There was less gulf-weed now. The wind got still more to the westward, so that we were obliged to go nearly north. Our boats had now got swollen with the water, and leaked very little. This night I saw some more falling stars.

On the 12th the wind still kept foul, and we were getting quite out of the track of ships, and appeared to have but little chance of reaching Bermuda. The long-boat passed over some green water to-day, a sign of there being soundings, probably some rock at a moderate depth. Many dolphins swam about the boats; their colours when seen in the water are superb, the most gorgeous metallic hues of green, blue, and gold: I was never tired of admiring them.

On the 13th the wind was due west, blowing exactly from the point we wanted to go to. The day was very fine, and there were several stormy petrels, or Mother Cary's chickens, flying about us. We had now been a week in the boats, and were only halfway to the Islands, so we put all hands on short allowance of water before it was too late. The sun was very hot and oppressive, and we suffered much from thirst.

The 14th was calm, and we could not get on at all. The sun was scorching and we had no shelter, and were parched with thirst the whole day. Numerous dolphins and pilot-fish were about the boats. At night there was a very slight favour-able breeze, and as we had by this time got our clothes pretty dry we slept well.

On the 15th the wind again died away, and we had another

calm. The sea was full of minute *Medusæ*, called "blubber" by the sailors: some were mere whitish oval or spherical lumps, others were brown, and beautifully constructed like a little cap, swimming rapidly along by alternate contractions and expansions, and so expelling the water behind them. The day was very hot, and we suffered exceedingly from thirst. We were almost in despair about seeing a ship, or getting on to the Islands. At about 5 P.M., while taking our dinner, we saw the long-boat, which was at some distance from us, tack. "She must see a sail," said the captain, and looking round we saw a vessel coming nearly towards us, and only about five miles distant. We were saved!

The men joyfully drank the rest of their allowance of water, seized their oars, and pulled with hearty goodwill, and by seven o'clock we were alongside. The captain received us kindly on board. The men went first to the water-casks, and took long and hearty draughts, in which we joined them, and then enjoyed the almost forgotten luxury of tea. From having been so long cramped in the boats, I could hardly stand when I got on board.

That night I could not sleep. Home and all its pleasures seemed now within my grasp; and crowding thoughts, and hopes and fears, made me pass a more restless night than I should have done, had we still been in the boats, with diminished hopes of rescue. The ship was the *Jordeson*, Captain Venables, from Cuba, bound for London, with a cargo of mahogany, fustic, and other woods. We were picked up in latitude 32° 48' north, longitude 60° 27' west, being still about two hundred miles from Bermuda.

For several days afterwards we had fine weather and very light winds, and went creeping along about fifty miles a day. It was now, when the danger appeared past, that I began to feel fully the greatness of my loss. With what pleasure had I looked upon every rare and curious insect I had added to my collection! How many times, when almost overcome by the ague, had I crawled into the forest and been rewarded by some unknown and beautiful species! How many places, which no European foot but my own had trodden, would have been recalled to my memory by the rare birds and insects they had furnished to my collection! How many weary days and weeks had I passed, upheld only by the fond hope of bringing home many new and beautiful forms from those wild regions; every one of which would be endeared to me by the recollections they would call up,—which should prove that I had not wasted the advantages I had enjoyed, and would give me occupation and amusement for many years to come! And now everything was gone, and I had not one specimen to illustrate the unknown lands I had trod, or to call back the recollection of the wild scenes I had beheld! But such regrets I knew were vain, and I tried to think as little as possible about what might have been, and to occupy myself with the state of things which actually existed.

On the 22nd of August we saw three water-spouts, the first time I had beheld that curious phenomenon. I had much wished once to witness a storm at sea, and I was soon gratified.

Early in September we had a very heavy gale. The barometer had fallen nearly half an inch during the night; and in the morning it was blowing strong, and we had a good deal of canvas up when the captain began to shorten sail; but before it could be taken in, four or five sails were blown to pieces, and it took several hours to get the others properly stowed. By the afternoon we were driving along under double-reefed topsails. The sea was all in a foam, and dashed continually over us. By night a very heavy sea was up, and we rolled about fearfully, the water pouring completely over the bulwarks, deluging the decks, and making the old ship stagger like a drunken man. We passed an uncomfortable night, for a great sea broke into the cabin skylight and wetted us all, and the ship creaked and shook, and plunged so madly, that I feared something would give way, and we should go to the bottom after all; all night, too, the pumps were kept going, for she leaked tremendously, and it was noon the next day before she was got free of water. The wind had now abated, and we soon had fine weather again, and all hands were busy bending new sails and repairing the old ones.

We caught at different times several dolphins, which were not bad eating. I did not see so much to admire in the colours of the dying dolphin; they are not to be compared with the colours of the living fish seen in the blue transparent water.

We were now getting rather short of provisions, owing to

the increased number of mouths: our cheese and ham were finished,—then our peas gave out, and we had no more pea-soup,—next the butter came to an end, and we had to eat our biscuit dry,—our bread and pork, too, got very short, and we had to be put upon allowance. We then got some supplies from another ship; but our voyage was so much prolonged, and we had adverse winds and another heavy gale, so that we were again in want, finished our last piece of meat, and had to make some scanty dinners off biscuit and water. Again we were relieved with a little supply of pork and some molasses, and so managed pretty well.

We were in the Channel on the night of the 29th of September, when a violent gale occurred, that did great damage to the shipping, and caused the destruction of many vessels much more seaworthy than our own. The next morning we had four feet of water in the hold.

On the 1st of October the pilot came on board, and Captain Turner and myself landed at Deal, after an eighty days' voyage from Pará; thankful for having escaped so many dangers, and glad to tread once more on English ground.

## CHAPTER XIV.

### THE PHYSICAL GEOGRAPHY AND GEOLOGY OF THE AMAZON VALLEY.

THE basin of the Amazon surpasses in dimensions that of any other river in the world. It is entirely situated in the Tropics, on both sides of the Equator, and receives over its whole extent the most abundant rains. The body of fresh water emptied by it into the ocean, is therefore far greater than that of any other river; not only absolutely, but probably also relatively to its area, for as it is almost entirely covered by dense virgin forests, the heavy rains which penetrate them do not suffer so much evaporation as when they fall on the scorched Llanos of the Orinooko or the treeless Pampas of La Plata. For richness of vegetable productions and universal fertility of soil it is unequalled on the globe, and offers to our notice a natural region capable of supporting a greater population, and supplying it more completely with the necessaries and luxuries of life, than any other of equal extent. Of this wonderful district we will now describe the principal physical peculiarities.

From about 4° north latitude to 20° south, every stream that flows down the eastern slope of the Andes is a tributary of the Amazon. This is as if every river, from St. Petersburg to Madrid, united their waters into one mighty flood.

The Marañon, which is generally considered the main stream of the Amazon, deserves that title on several accounts. It rises to the westward of all the other great tributaries, and it receives all the waters which flow nearest to the Pacific, and most remote in a direct line from the mouth of the river. It flows for a considerable distance in the most westerly valley of the Andes, separated by one range only from the Pacific, and at the point where it breaks through the eastern chain of the

Andes, in 78° west longitude, is already a large river, on a meridian where all the other streams which can lay a claim to be considered the head-waters of the Amazon have as yet no existence. On going up the Amazon from its mouth, it is that branch on which you can keep longest in the general east and west direction of the river ; and if the actual length of its course is considered, it still keeps its place, for I find that there is not more than ten or twenty miles' difference between it and the Uaycali, reckoning to the most distant source of the latter ; and its course is at present so uncertain, that future surveys may increase or diminish it considerably.

These considerations, I think, decide the question as to the propriety of considering the Marañon as the true source of the Amazon. We find that from its origin in the Lake Lauricocha, to its mouth in longitude 50° west, in length, following the main curves, but disregarding the minuter windings, is 2,740 English miles.

Its extent, in a straight line from east to west, is about 2,050 miles ; and from north to south, its tributary streams cover a space of 1,720 miles.

The whole area of its basin, not including that of the Tocantíns, which I consider a distinct river, is 2,330,000 English square miles, or 1,760,000 nautical square miles. This is more than a third of all South America, and equal to two-thirds of all Europe. All western Europe could be placed in it without touching its boundaries, and it would even contain our whole Indian empire.

The numerous tributary streams of the Amazon, many of them equal to the largest rivers of Europe, differ remarkably in the colour of their waters, the character of the vegetation on their banks, and the animals that inhabit them. They may be divided into three groups,—the white-water rivers, the blue-water rivers, and the black-water rivers.

The main stream of the Amazon itself is a white-water river, this name being applied to those waters which are of a pale yellowish olive-colour. This colour does not seem to depend entirely on free earthy matter, but rather on some colouring material held in solution ; for in lakes and inlets, where the waters are undisturbed and can deposit all their sediment, they still retain the colour.

The waters of the Amazon continue of the same colour up

to the mouth of the Uaycali, when they become blue or transparent, and the white waters are extended up that branch.

This has been taken as an evidence of the Uaycáli being the main stream of the Amazon; but I cannot consider that it has anything to do with the question. It is evident that if equal quantities of clear and muddy water are mixed together, the result will differ very little from the latter in colour, and if the clear water is considerably more in quantity the resulting mixture will still be muddy. But the difference of colour between the white- and blue-water rivers, is evidently owing to the nature of the country they flow through: a rocky and sandy district will always have clear-water rivers; an alluvial or clayey one, will have yellow or olive-coloured streams. A river may therefore rise in a rocky district, and after some time flow through an alluvial basin, where the water will of course change its colour, quite independently of any tributaries which may enter it near the junctions of the two formations.

The Içá and Japurá have waters very similar in colour to the Amazon. The Rio Branco, a branch of the Rio Negro from the north, is remarkable for its peculiar colour: till I saw it, I had not believed it so well deserved its name. The Indians and traders had always told me that it was really white, much more so than the Amazon; and on descending the Rio Negro in 1852 I passed its mouth, and found that its waters were of a milky colour mixed with olive. It seemed as if it had a quantity of chalk in solution, and I have little doubt of there being on its banks considerable beds of the pure white clay which occurs in many parts of the Amazon, and which helps to give the waters their peculiar whiteness. The Madeira and Purús have also white waters in the wet season, when their powerful currents bring down the alluvial soil from their banks; but in the dry season they are a dark transparent brownish-olive.

All the rivers that rise in the mountains of Brazil have blue or clear water. The Tocantíns, the Xingú, and the Tapajóz, are the chief of this class. The Tocantins runs over volcanic and crystalline rocks in the lower parts of its course, and its waters are beautifully transparent; the tide, however, enters for some miles, and renders it turbid, as also the Xingú. The Tapajóz, which enters the Amazon about five hundred miles above Pará, is clear to its mouth, and forms a striking contrast to the yellow flood of that river.

It is above the Madeira that we first meet with the curious phenomenon of great rivers of black water. The Rio Negro is the largest and most celebrated of these. It rises in about 2° 30′ N. lat., and its waters are there much blacker than in the lower part of its course. All its upper tributaries, the smaller ones especially, are very dark, and, where they run over white sand, give it the appearance of gold, from the rich colour of the water, which, when deep, appears inky black. The small streams which rise in the same district, and flow into the Orinooko, are of the same dark colour. The Cassiquiare first pours in some white or olive-coloured water. Lower down, the Cababurís, Maravihá, and some smaller white-water streams help to dilute it, and then the Rio Branco adds its flood of milky water. Notwithstanding all this, the Rio Negro at its mouth still appears as black as ink; only in shallow water it is seen to be paler than it is up above, and the sands are not dyed of that pure golden tint so remarkable there.

On the south of the Amazon there are also some black-water streams—the Coary, the Teffe, the Juruá, and some others. The inhabitants have taken advantage of these, to escape from the plague of the mosquitoes, and the towns of Coary and Ega are places of refuge for the traveller on the Upper Amazon, those annoying insects being scarcely ever found on the black waters. The causes of the peculiar colour of these rivers are not, I think, very obscure; it appears to me to be produced by the solution of decaying leaves, roots, and other vegetable matter. In the virgin forests, in which most of these streams have their source, the little brooks and rivulets are half choked up with dead leaves and rotten branches, giving various brown tinges to the water. When these rivulets meet together and accumulate into a river, they of course have a deep brown hue, very similar to that of our bog or peat water, if there are no other circumstances to modify it. But if the streams flow through a district of soft alluvial clay, the colour will of course be modified, and the brown completely overpowered; and I think this will account for the anomalies observed, of streams in the same districts being of different colours. Those whose sources are pretty well known are seen to agree with this view. The Rio Negro, the Atabapo, the Isanna, and several other smaller rivers, have their sources and their whole course in the deep forest; they flow generally over clean granite rocks and beds of sand, and their streams are gentle, so as not to wear away the soft parts of their banks.

The Içá, Japurá, and Upper Amazon, on the contrary, flow through a long extent of alluvial country, and, having their sources on the slopes of the Andes, are much more liable to sudden floods, and by their greater velocity bring down a quantity of sediment.  In fact, it seems clear, that a thorough knowledge of the course of each river would enable us to trace the colour of its waters to the various peculiarities of the country through which it flows.

With the exception of the streams rising in the Andes, the boundaries of the Amazon basin, or the most distant sources of its tributaries on the north and south, are comparatively little elevated above the level of the sea.  The whole basin, with the exception of a very small portion, is one great plain of the most perfect and regular character.

The true altitude of the source in the Lake Lauricocha has not been ascertained.  At Tomependa Humboldt states it to be 1,320 feet above the sea: this is as near as possible 2,000 miles in a straight line from the mouth; so that the average rise is only eight inches in a mile.  But if we take the height at Tabatinga, on the boundary of Brazil, which, according to Spix and Martius is 670 feet, we shall find, the distance being about 1,400 miles, that the rise is only five and a half inches per mile.  If we had the height of Barra do Rio Negro accurately, we should no doubt find the rise to that point not more than two or three inches in a mile.  The distance is, in a straight line, about 700 miles, and we may therefore probably estimate the height at less than 200, and perhaps not more than 150 feet.

This height I am inclined to believe quite great enough, from some observations I made with an accurate thermometer, reading to tenths of a degree, on the temperature of boiling water.  This instrument I received from England, after leaving Pará.  The mean of five observations at Barra, some with river and some with rain-water, gave 212·5° as the temperature of boiling water; a remarkable result, showing that the barometer must stand there at more than thirty inches, and that unless it is, in the months of May and August, considerably more than that at the sea-level, Barra can be but very little elevated above the sea.

For the height of the country about the sources of the Rio Negro, Humboldt is our only authority. He gives 812 feet as the height of São Carlos ; he, however, states that the determination is uncertain, owing to an accident happening to the barometer ; I may, therefore, though with great diffidence, venture to doubt the result. The distance, in a straight line, from the mouth of the Rio Negro to São Carlos, is rather less than from the same point to Tabatinga, whose height is 670 feet. The current, however, from Tabatinga is much more rapid than down the Rio Negro, the lower part of which has so little fall, that in the month of January, when the Amazon begins to rise, the water enters the mouth of the Rio Negro, and renders that river stagnant for several hundred miles up. The falls of the Rio Negro I cannot consider to add more than fifty feet to the elevation, as above and below them the river is not very rapid. Thus, from this circumstance alone, we should be disposed to place São Carlos at a rather less elevation than Tabatinga, or at about 600 feet. My observations up the Rio Negro gave consistent results. At Castanheiro, about five hundred miles up, the temperature of boiling water was $212^\cdot4^\circ$, at the mouth of the Uaupés $212^\cdot2^\circ$, and at a point just below São Carlos, $212^\cdot0^\circ$. This would not give more than 250 feet for the height of São Carlos above Barra ; and, as we have estimated this at 200 feet above the sea, the height of São Carlos will become 450 feet, which I think will not be found far from the truth.

The velocity of the current varies with the width of the stream and the time of the year ; we have little accurate information on this subject. In a Brazilian work on the Province of Pará, the Madeira is stated to flow 2,970 braças, or about three and a half miles, an hour in the wet season. At Obidos I made an observation in the month of November, when the Amazon is at the lowest level, and found it four miles an hour ; but this by no means represents the current in the rainy season. On descending to Pará, in the month of June, 1852, I found that we often floated down about five miles an hour, and as the wind was strong directly up the river, it probably retarded us, rather than helped us on, our vessel not being rigged in the best manner.

Martius calculates that 500,000 cubic feet of water per second pass Obidos.  This agrees pretty well with my own calculations of the quantity in the dry season; when the river is full, it is probably much greater.  If we suppose, on a moderate calculation, that seventy-two inches, or six feet, of rain fall annually over the whole Amazon valley, it will amount to 1,500,000 cubic feet per second, the whole of which must either evaporate, or flow out of the mouth of the Amazon; so that if we increase the amount given by Martius by one half, to take in the lower part of the Amazon and to allow for the whole year, we shall have the evaporation as one half of the rain falling annually.

It is a fact which has been frequently stated, and which seems fully established, that the Amazon carries its fresh waters out into the ocean, which it discolours for a distance of a hundred and fifty miles from its mouth.  It is also generally stated that the tide flows up the river as far as Obidos, five hundred miles from the mouth.  These two statements appear irreconcilable, for it is not easy to understand how the tides can flow up to such a great distance, and yet no salt water enter the river.  But the fact appears to be, that the tide never does flow up the river at all.  The water of the Amazon rises, but during the flood as well as the ebb the current is running rapidly down.  This takes place even at the very mouth of the river, for at the island of Mexiana, exposed to the open sea, the water is always quite fresh, and is used for drinking all the year round.  But as salt water is heavier than fresh, it might flow up at the bottom, while the river continued to pour down above it; though it is difficult to conceive how this could take place to any extent without some salt water appearing at the margins.

The rising of the water so far up the river can easily be explained, and goes to prove also that the slope of the river up to where the tide has any influence cannot be great; for as the waters of the ocean rose, the river would of course be banked up, the velocity of its current still forcing its waters onward; but it is not easy to see how the stream could be thus elevated to a higher level than the waters of the ocean which caused the rise, and we should therefore suppose that at Obidos, where the tidal rise ceases to be felt, the river is just higher than the surface of the ocean at the highest spring-tides.

A somewhat similar phenomenon is seen at the mouth of the Tapajóz. Here, at the end of the dry season, there is but a small body of water, and the current is very sluggish. The Amazon, however, rises considerably with the tides, and its waters then become higher than those of the Tapajóz, and they therefore enter into that river and force it back; we then see the Amazon flowing rapidly down, at the same time that the Tapajóz is flowing up.

It seems to be still a disputed question among geographers, whether the Pará river is or is not a branch of the Amazon. From my own observation, I am decidedly of opinion that it is not: it appears to me to be merely the outlet of the Tocantíns and of numerous other small streams. The canal or channel of Tagipurú, which connects it with the Amazon, and by which all the trade between Pará and the interior is carried on, is one of a complete network of channels, along which the tide ebbs and flows, so as in a great measure to disguise the true direction and velocity of its current. It seems probable that not a drop of Amazon water finds its way by this channel into the Pará river, and I ground my opinion upon the following facts.

It is well known, that in a tidal river the ebb-tide will continue longer than the flood, because the stream of the river requires to be overcome, and thus delays the commencement of the flood, while it facilitates that of the ebb. This is very remarkable in all the smaller rivers about Pará. Taking this as our guide, we shall be able to ascertain which way the current in the Tagipurú sets, independently of the tide.

On my journey from Pará to the Amazon, our canoe could only proceed with the tide, having to wait moored to the bank while it was against us, so that we were of course anxious to find the time of our tedious stoppages diminished. Up to a certain point, we always had to wait more time than we were moving, showing that the current set against us and towards Pará; but after passing that point, where there was a bend, and several streams met, we had but a short time to wait, and a long ebb in our favour, showing that the current was with us or towards the Amazon, whereas it would evidently have been different had there been any permanent current flowing from the Amazon through the Tagipurú towards Pará.

I therefore look upon the Tagipurú as a channel formed by

the small streams between the Tocantíns and Xingú, meeting together about Melgáco, and flowing through a low swampy country in two directions, towards the Amazon, and towards the Pará river.

At high tides the water becomes brackish, even up to the city of Pará, and a few miles down is quite salt. The tide flows very rapidly past Pará, up all the adjacent streams, and as far as the middle of the Tagipurú channel; another proof that a very small portion, if any, of the Amazon water is there to oppose it.

The curious phenomenon of the bore, or "piroróco," in the rivers Guamá and Mojú, I have described and endeavoured to explain in my Journal, and need not now repeat the account of it. (See page 89.)

Our knowledge of the courses of most of the tributaries of the Amazon is very imperfect. The main stream is tolerably well laid down in the maps as far as regards its general course and the most important bends; the details, however, are very incorrect. The numerous islands and parallel channels,—the great lakes and offsets,—the deep bays,—and the varying widths of the stream, are quite unknown. Even the French survey from Pará to Obidos, the only one which can lay claim to detailed accuracy, gives no idea of the river, because only one channel is laid down. I obtained at Santarem a manuscript map of the lower part of the river, much more correct than any other I have seen. It was, with most of my other papers, lost on my voyage home; but I hope to be able to obtain another copy from the same party. The Madeira and the Rio Negro are the only other branches of the Amazon whose courses are at all accurately known, and the maps of them are very deficient in anything like detail. The other great rivers, the Xingu, the Tapajóz, the Purús, Coarí, Teffe, Juruá, Jutaí, Jabarí, Içá, Japurá, etc., though all inserted in our maps, are put in quite by guess, or from the vaguest information of the general direction of their course. Between the Tocantíns and the Madeira, and between the Madeira and the Uaycali, there are two tracts of country of five hundred thousand square miles each, or each twice as large as France, and as completely unexplored as the interior of Africa.

The Rio Negro is one of the most unknown in its characteristic features; although, as before stated, its general course is laid down with tolerable accuracy. I have narrated in my Journal how I was prevented from descending on the north side of it, and thus completing my survey of its course.

The most remarkable feature is the enormous width to which it spreads,—first, between Barra and the mouth of the Rio Branco, and from thence to near St. Isabel. In some places, I am convinced, it is between twenty and thirty miles wide, and, for a very great distance, fifteen to twenty. The sources of the rivers Uaupés, Isanna, Xié, Rio Negro, and Guaviare, are very incorrectly laid down. The Serra Tunuhy is generally represented as a chain of hills cutting off these rivers; it is, however, a group of isolated granite peaks, about two thousand feet high, situated on the north bank of the river Isanna, in about 1° north latitude and 70° west longitude. The river rises considerably beyond them, in a flat forest-country, and further west than the Rio Negro, for there is a path across to the Inirizá, a branch of the Guaviare which does not traverse any stream, so that the Rio Negro does not there exist.

My own journey up the Uaupés extended to near 72° west longitude. Five days further in a small canoe, or about a hundred miles, is the Jurupari caxoeira, the last fall on the river. Above that, traders have been twelve days' journey on a still, almost currentless river, which, by the colour of its water, and the aspect of its vegetation, resembles the Upper Amazon. For all this distance, which must reach very nearly to the base of the Andes, the river flows through virgin forest. But the Indians in the upper part say there are campos, or plains, and cattle, further up; and they possess Spanish knives and other articles, showing that they have communications with the civilised inhabitants of the country to the east of Bogotá.

I am therefore strongly inclined to believe that the rivers Ariarí and others, rising about a hundred miles south of Bogotá, are not, as shown in all our maps, the sources of the Guaviare, but of the Uaupés, and that the basin of the Amazon must therefore be here extended to within sixty miles of the city of Bogotá. This opinion is strengthened by information obtained from the Indians of Javíta, who annually ascend the Guaviare to fish in the dry season, and who state that the river is very small, and in its upper part, where some hills occur and the forest ends, it is not more than a hundred yards wide ; whereas the Uaupés, at the furthest point the traders have reached, is still a large river, from a quarter of a mile to a mile in width.

The Amazon and all its branches are subject, like most tropical rivers, to an annual rise and fall of great regularity. In the main stream, and in all the branches which flow from the Andes, the waters begin to rise in December or January, when the rains generally commence, and continue rising till June, when the fine weather has just set in. The time when the waters begin to fall is about the 21st of June,—seldom deviating more than a few days from this date. In branches which have their sources in a different direction, such as the Rio Negro, the time of rising does not coincide. On that river the rains do not commence steadily till February or March, when the river rises with very great rapidity, and generally is quite filled by June, and then begins to fall with the Amazon. It thus happens that in the months of January and February, when the Amazon is rising rapidly, the Rio Negro is still falling in its upper part ; the waters of the Amazon therefore flow into the mouth of the Rio Negro, causing that river to remain stagnant like a lake, or even occasionally to flow back towards its source. The total rise of the Amazon between high and low water mark has not been accurately ascertained, as it cannot be properly determined without a spirit-level ; it is, however, certainly not less than forty, and probably often fifty feet. If therefore we consider the enormous water surface raised fifty feet annually, we shall gain from another point of view an idea of the immense quantity of water falling annually in the Amazon valley. We cannot take the length of the Amazon with its main tributaries at less than ten thousand miles, and their average width about two miles ; so that there will be a surface of twenty thousand square miles of water, raised fifty feet every year. But it is not only this surface that is raised, for a great extent of land on the banks of all the rivers is flooded to a great depth at every time of high water. These flooded lands are called, in the language of the country, "gapó," and are one of the most singular features of the Amazon. Sometimes on one side, sometimes on both, to a distance of twenty or thirty miles from the main river, these gapós extend on the Amazon, and on portions of all its great branches. They are all covered with a dense virgin forest of lofty trees, whose stems are every year, during six months, from ten to forty feet under water.   In this flooded forest the Indians have paths for their canoes, cutting across from one river to another, which are much used, to avoid the strong current of the main stream.   From the mouth of the river Tapajoz to Coary, on the Solimões, a canoe can pass, without once entering the Amazon : the path lies across lakes, and among narrow inland channels, and through miles of dense flooded forest, crossing the Madeira, the Purus, and a hundred other smaller streams. All along, from the mouth of the Rio Negro to the mouth of the Içá, is an immense extent of gapó, and it reaches also far up into the interior ; for even near the sources of the Rio Negro, and on the upper waters of the Uaupés, are extensive tracts of land which are annually overflowed.

In the whole country around the mouth of the Amazon, round the great island of Marajó, and about the mouths of the Tocantíns and Xingú, the diurnal and semi-monthly tides are most felt, the annual rise and fall being almost lost.   Here the low lands are overflowed at all the spring-tides, or every fort-night, subjecting all vegetation to another peculiar set of circumstances.   Considerable tracts of land, still covered with vegetation, are so low, that they are flooded at every high water, and again vary the conditions of vegetable growth.

## GEOLOGY.

Fully to elucidate the Geology of the Amazon valley, requires much more time and research than I was able to devote to it. The area is so vast, and the whole country being covered with forests renders natural sections so comparatively scarce, that the few distant observations one person can make will lead to no definite conclusions.

It is remarkable that I was never able to find any fossil remains whatever,—not even a shell, or a fragment of fossil wood, or anything that could lead to a conjecture as to the state in which the valley existed at any former period.   We are thus unable to assign the geological age to which any of the various beds of rock belong.[*]

My notes, and a fine series of specimens of the rocks of the Rio

---

[*] The sandstone rocks of Montealegre have since been ascertained to be of cretaceous age.

Negro, were lost, and I have therefore very few materials to go upon.

Granite seems to be, in South America, more extensively developed than in any other part of the world. Darwin and Gardner found it in every part of the interior of Brazil, in La Plata, and Chile. Up the Xingú Prince Adalbert met with it. Over the whole of Venezuela and New Granada, it was found by Humboldt. It seems to form all the mountains in the interior of Guiana, and it was met with by myself over the whole of the upper part of the Rio Negro, and far up the Uaupés towards the Andes.

From what I could see of the granitic formation of the Upper Rio Negro, it appeared to be spread out in immense undulating areas, the hollows of which, being filled up with alluvial deposits, form those beds of earth and clay which occur, of various dimensions, everywhere in the midst of the granite formation. In these places grow the lofty virgin forests, while on the scantily covered granite rocks, and where beds of sand occur, are the more open catinga forests, so different in their aspect and peculiar in their vegetation. What strikes one most in this great formation, is its almost perfect flatness. There are no ranges of mountains, or even slightly elevated plateaus ; all is level, except the abrupt peaks that rise suddenly from the plain, to a height of from one hundred to three thousand feet. In the Upper Rio Negro these peaks are very numerous. The first is the Serra de Jacamí, a little above St. Isabel ; it rises immediately from the bank of the river, on the south side, to a height of about six hundred feet. Several others are scattered about, but the Serras de Curicuriarí are the most lofty. They consist of a group of three or four mountains, rising abruptly to the height of near three thousand feet ; towards their summits are immense precipices and jagged peaks. Higher up, on the same river, is another group of rather less height. On the Uaupés are numerous hills, some conical, others dome-shaped, but all keeping the same character of abrupt elevations, quite independent of the general profile of the country. About the falls of the river Uaupés there are small hills of granite, broken about in the greatest confusion. Great chasms or bowls occur, and slender pillars of rock rise above the surrounding forest like dead trunks of giant trees. Up the river Isanna, the Tunuhy mountains are a similar isolated

*a*. Fragments embedded in granite.    *b*. Granite with twisted veins.
*c*. Stratified rocks protruded through granite.

GRANITE ROCKS AND VEINS, ETC.

PLATE IX.

group. The Cocoí is a quadrangular or cubical mass, about a thousand feet in elevation, which forms the boundary between Brazil and Venezuela ; and behind it are the Pirapocó, and the serras of the Cababurís, which seem rather more extensive, and form something more like a connected range of hills.

But the great peculiarity of them all is, that the country does not perceptibly rise to their bases ; they spring up abruptly, as if elevated by some local isolated force. I ascended one of the smaller of these serras as far as practicable, and have recorded my impressions of it in my Journal. (See page 153.)

The isolation and abrupt protrusion of these mountains is not, however, altogether without parallel in the Andes itself. This mighty range, from all the information I can obtain, rises with almost equal abruptness from an apparently level plain. The Andes of Quito, and southward to the Amazon, is like a hugh rocky rampart, bounding the great plain which extends in one unbroken imperceptible slope from the Atlantic Ocean to its base. It is one of the grandest physical features of the earth,--this vast unbroken plain,—that mighty and precipitous mountain-range.

The granitic rocks of the Rio Negro in general contain very little mica ; in some places, however, that mineral is abundant, and exists in large plates. Veins of pure quartz are common, some of very great size ; and numerous veins or dykes of granite, of a different colour or texture. The direction of these is generally nearer east and west, than north and south.

Just below the falls of the Rio Negro are some coarse sand-stone rocks, apparently protruding through the granite, dipping at an angle of 60° or 70° south-south-west. (Plate IX. *c.*) Near the same place a large slab of granite rock exhibits quantities of curiously twisted or folded quartz veins (Plate IX. *b.*), which vary in size from a line to some inches in diameter, and are folded in a most minute and regular manner.

On an island in the river, near this place, are finely stratified crystalline rocks, dipping south from 70° to vertical, and sometimes waved and twisted.

The granite often exhibits a concentric arrangement of laminæ, particularly in the large dome-shaped masses in the bed of the river (Plate X. *a. c*), or in portions protruding from the ground (Plate X. *b*).   Near São Gabriel, and in the Uaupés, large masses of pure quartz rock occur, and the shining white precipices of the serras are owing, I have no doubt, to the same cause.   At Pimichin, near the source of the Rio Negro, the granite contains numerous fragments of stratified sandstone rock imbedded in it (Plate IX. *a*) ; I did not notice this so distinctly at any other locality.

High up the river Uaupés there is a very curious formation All along the river-banks there are irregular fragments of rocks, with their interstices filled up with a substance that looks exactly like pitch.   On examination, it is found to be a conglomerate of sand, clay, and scoriæ, sometimes very hard, but often rotten and easily breaking to pieces ; its position immediately suggests the idea of its having been liquid, for the fragments of rocks appear to have sunk in it.

Coarse volcanic scoriæ, with a vitreous surface, are found over a very wide area.   They occur at Caripé, near Pará,—above Baião, in the Tocantíns,—at the mouth of the Tapajóz,—at Villa Nova, on the Amazon,—above Barra, on the Rio Negro, and again up the Uaupés.   A small conical hill behind the town of Santarem, at the mouth of the Tapajóz, has all the appearance of being a volcanic cone.

The neighbourhood of Pará consists entirely of a coarse iron sandstone, which is probably a continuation of the rocks observed by Mr. Gardner at Maranham and in the Province of Piauhy, and which he considered to belong to the chalk formation.   Up the Tocantíns we found fine crystalline stratified rocks, coarse volcanic conglomerates, and fine-grained slates.   At the falls were metamorphic slates and other hard crystalline rocks ; many of these split into flat slabs, well adapted for building, or even for paving, instead of the stones now imported from Portugal into Pará.   In the serras of Montealegre, on the north bank of the Amazon, are a great variety of rocks,—coarse quartz conglomerates, fine crystalline sandstones, soft beds of yellow and red sandstones, and indurated clay rocks.   These beds are all nearly horizontal, but are much cleft and shattered vertically ; they are alternately hard and soft, and by their unequal decay have formed the hanging stones and curious cave described in my Journal.

The general impression produced by the examination of the country is, that here we see the last stage of a process that has

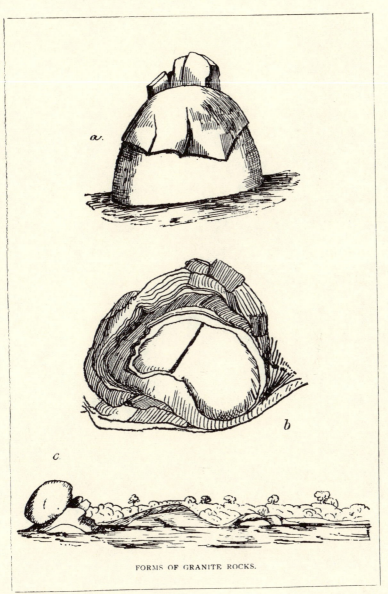

FORMS OF GRANITE ROCKS.

PLATE X.

been going on, during the whole period of the elevation of the Andes and the mountains of Brazil and Guiana, from the ocean. At the commencement of this period, the greater portion of the valleys of the Amazon, Orinooko, and La Plata must have formed a part of the ocean, separating the groups of islands (which those elevated lands formed on their first appearance) from each other. The sediment carried down into this sea by the rapid streams, running down the sides of these mountains, would tend to fill up and level the deeper and more irregular depressions, forming those large tracts of alluvial deposits we now find in the midst of the granite districts. At the same time volcanic forces were in operation, as shown by the isolated granite peaks which in many places rise out of the flat forest district, like islands from a sea of verdure, because their lower slopes, and the valleys between them, have been covered and filled up by the sedimentary deposits. This simultaneous action of the aqueous and volcanic forces, of submarine earthquakes and marine currents, shaking up, as it were, and levelling the mass of sedimentary matter brought down from the now increasing surface of dry land, is what has produced that marvellous regularity of surface, that gradual and imperceptible slope, which exists over such an immense area.*

At the point where the mountains of Guiana approach nearest to the chain of the Andes, the volcanic action appears to have been continued in the interval between them, throwing up the serras of Curicuriarí, Tunuhy, and the numerous smaller granite mountains of the Uaupés ; and it is here probably that dry land first appeared, connecting Guiana and New Granada, and forming that slightly elevated ridge which is now the watershed between the basins of the Amazon and Orinooko. The same thing occurs in the southern part of the continent, for it is where the mountains of Brazil, and the eastern range of the Bolivian Andes, stretch out to meet each other, that the sedimentary deposits in that part appear to have been first raised above the water, and thus to have determined the limits of the basin of the Amazon on the south. The Amazon valley would then have formed a great inland gulf or

---

* The isolated granite domes and pillars show that the whole area has been formerly covered with thick sedimentary rocks, which have been removed by denudation.

sea, about two thousand miles long and seven or eight hundred wide.

The rivers and mountain-torrents pouring into it on every side, would gradually fill up this great basin ; and the volcanic action still visible in the scoriæ of the Tocantíns and Tapajoz, and the shattered rocks of Montealegre, would all tend to the levelling of the vast area, and to determining the channels of the future rivers. This process, continuing for ages, would at length narrow this inland sea, almost within the limits of what is now gapó, or flooded land. Ridges, gradually elevated a few feet above the waters, would separate the tributary streams ; and then the eddies and currents would throw up sandbanks as they do now, and gradually define the limits of the river, as we now see it. And changes are yet going on. New islands are yearly forming in the stream, large tracts of flooded land are being perceptibly raised by the deposits upon them, and the numerous great lakes are becoming choked with aquatic plants, and filled up with sediment.

The large extent of flat land on the banks of the river will still continue to be flooded, till some renewed earthquakes raise it gradually above the waters ; during which time the stream will work for itself a wider and deeper bed, capable of containing its accumulated flood. In the course of ages per haps this might be produced by the action of the river itself, for at every annual inundation a deposit of sediment is formed, and these lands must therefore be rising, and would in time become permanently elevated above the highest rise of the river. This, however, would take a very long time, for as the banks rose, the river, unable to spread its waters over the adjoining country, would swell higher, and flow more rapidly than before, and so overflow a country elevated above the level of its former inundations.

The complete history of these changes,—the periods of elevation and of repose, the time when the dividing ridges first 'rose above the waters, and the comparative antiquity of the tributary streams,—cannot be ascertained till the country has been more thoroughly explored, and the organic remains, which must doubtless exist, be brought forward, to give us more accurate information respecting the birth and growth of the Amazon.

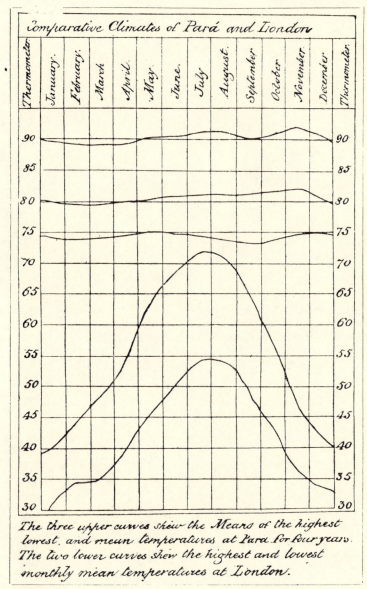

Comparative Climates of Pará and London

The three upper curves shew the Means of the highest
lowest, and mean temperatures at Pará for four years.
The two lower curves shew the highest and lowest
monthly mean temperatures at London.

PLATE XI.

## CLIMATE.

The climate of the Amazon valley seems remarkable for uniformity of temperature, and for a regular supply of moisture. There are, in most parts of it, six months' wet, and six months' dry season, neither of which are so severe as in some other tropical countries. From June to December is the dry, and from January to May the wet season. In the dry season there are a few occasional rains, especially about All Saints' day, in November; and during the wet season there are intervals of fine weather, and often bright mornings, and many days of gentle misty rain.

This is the general character of the climate over the whole of the main stream of the Amazon and its immediate neighbourhood. There are, however, remarkable deviations from this general routine, in particular localities. Pará itself is one of these exceptional places. Here the seasons are so modified, as to render the climate one of the most agreeable in the world. During the whole of the dry season, scarcely ever more than three days or a week passes without a slight thunderstorm and heavy shower, which comes on about four in the afternoon and by six has cleared off again, leaving the atmosphere delightfully pure and cool and all vegetable and animal life refreshed and invigorated. Had I only judged of the climate of Pará from my first residence of a year, I might be thought to have been impressed by the novelty of the tropical climate ; but on my return from a three years' sojourn on the Upper Amazon and Rio Negro, I was equally struck with the wonderful freshness and brilliancy of the atmosphere, and the balmy mildness of the evenings, which are certainly not equalled in any other part I have visited.

The wet season has not so many stormy and cloudy days as in other parts. Sunshine and rain alternate, and the days are comparatively bright and cheerful, even when rainy. Generally, the variation of the thermometer in any one day does not exceed 15° ; 75° being the lowest, and 90° the highest. The greatest variation in one day is not, I think, ever more than 20° ; and in four years, the lowest and highest temperatures were 70° and 95°, giving only an extreme variation of 25°. A more equable climate probably does not exist on the earth. (See Diagram, Plate XI.)

On the Guiana side of the Amazon, in the islands of Mexiana and Marajo, the seasons are more strongly marked than even higher up the river. In the dry season, for about three months, no rain ever falls; and in the wet it is almost continual.

But it is in the country about the falls of the Rio Negro that the most curious modification of the seasons occur. Here the regular tropical dry season has almost disappeared, and a constant alternation of showers and sunshine occurs, almost all the year round. In the months of June, July, August, and September, when the Amazonian summer is in all its glory, we have here only a little finer weather about June, and then rain again as much as ever; till, in January or February, when the wet season in the Amazon commences, there is generally here a month or two of fine warm weather. It is then that the river, which has been very slowly falling since July, empties rapidly, and in March is generally at its lowest ebb. In the beginning of April it suddenly begins to rise, and by the end of May has risen twenty feet, and then continues slowly rising till July, when it reaches its highest point, and begins to fall with the Amazon. The district of the greatest quantity of rain, or rather of the greatest number of rainy days, seems to be very limited, extending only from a little below the falls of São Gabriel to Marabitanas at the confines of Brazil, where the Pirapocó and Cocoí mountains, and the Serra of Tunuhy, seem to form a separation from the Venezuela district, where there is a more regular summer in the months of December, January, and February.

The water of the Rio Negro in the month of September did not vary in temperature more than two degrees. I unfortunately lost my thermometers, or had intended making a regular series of observations on the waters of the higher parts of the rivers I ascended.

'The extreme variation of the barometer at Pará for three years was only three-tenths of an inch (see diagram, Plate XII.). The mean height, with all the necessary corrections, would seem to be almost exactly thirty inches; I have, however, already given my reasons for believing that there is a considerable difference in the pressure of the atmosphere in the interior of the country. In the month of May some very cold days are said to occur annually on the Upper Amazon

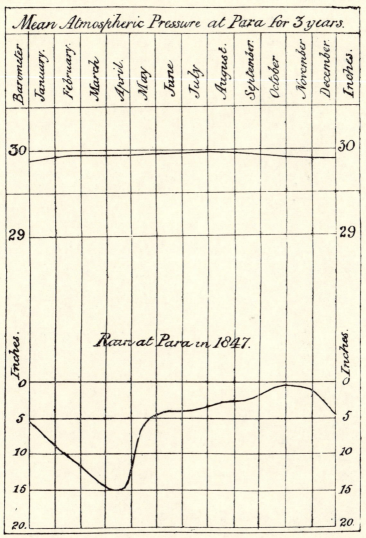

Mean Atmospheric Pressure at Para for 3 years.

Barometer | January. | February. | March | April. | May | June | July | August. | September. | October | November | December. | Inches.

30 — 30
29 — 29

Inches. — Inches.

Rain at Para in 1847.

0
5
10
15
20.

PLATE XII.

and Rio Negro ; but I never myself experienced anything of the kind worthy of notice. Many intelligent persons have assured me that the cold is sometimes so severe that the inhabitants suffer much, and, what is much more extraordinary, the fishes in the rivers die of it. Allowing this to be the fact, I am quite unable to account for it, as it is difficult to conceive that a diminution of temperature of five or ten degrees, which is as much as ever takes place, can produce any effect upon them.

I have an authentic account of hail having once fallen on the Upper Amazon, a remarkable occurrence at a place only three degrees south of the equator, and about two hundred feet above the level of the sea. The children were out at play, and brought it to their parents, astonished at a substance falling from the clouds quite new to them, and which was so remarkably cold. The person who told me was a Portuguese, and his information can be perfectly relied on.

# CHAPTER XV

## VEGETATION OF THE AMAZON VALLEY.

PERHAPS no country in the world contains such an amount of vegetable matter on its surface as the valley of the Amazon. Its entire extent, with the exception of some very small portions, is covered with one dense and lofty primeval forest, the most extensive and unbroken which exists upon the earth. It is the great feature of the country,—that which at once stamps it as a unique and peculiar region. It is not here as on the coasts of southern Brazil, or on the shores of the Pacific, where a few days' journey suffices to carry us beyond the forest district, and into the parched plains and rocky serras of the interior. Here we may travel for weeks and months inland, in any direction, and find scarcely an acre of ground unoccupied by trees. It is far up in the interior, where the great mass of this mighty forest is found; not on the lower part of the river, near the coast, as is generally supposed.

A line from the mouth of the river Parnaíba, in long. 41° 30' W., drawn due west towards Guayaquil, will cut the boundary of the great forest in long. 78° 30', and, for the whole distance of about 2,600 miles, will have passed through the centre of it, dividing it into two nearly equal portions.

For the first thousand miles, or as far as long. 56° W., the width of the forest from north to south is about four hundred miles; it then stretches out both to the north and south, so that in long. 67° W. it extends from 7° N., on the banks of the Orinoko, to 18° S., on the northern slope of the Andes of Bolivia, a distance of more than seventeen hundred miles. From a point about sixty miles south-east of Tabatinga, a circle may be drawn of 1,100 miles in diameter, the whole area of which will be virgin forest.

Along the Andes of Quito, from Pasto to Guancabamba, it reaches close up to the eastern base of the mountains, and even ascends their lower slopes. In the moderately elevated country between the river Huallaga and Marañon, the forest extends only over the eastern portion, commencing in the neighbourhood of Moyobamba. Further on, to the east of Cuzco and La Paz, it spreads high up on the slopes of the Bolivian Andes, and passing a little to the west of Santa Cruz de la Sierra, turns off to the north-east, crossing the Tapajóz and Xingú rivers somewhere about the middle of their course, and the Tocantíns not far above its junction with the Araguàya, and then passes over to the river Parnaíba, which it follows to its mouth.

The Island of Marajó, at the mouth of the Amazon, has its eastern half open plains, while in the western the forest commences. On the north of the Amazon, from its mouth to beyond Montealegre, are open plains; but opposite the mouth of the Tapajóz at Santarem, the forest begins, and appears to extend up to the Serras of Carumaní, on the Rio Branco, and thence stretches west, to join the wooded country on the eastern side of the Orinoko. West of that river, it commences south of the Vicháda, and, crossing over the upper waters of the Guaviáre and Uaupés, reach the Andes east of Pasto, where we commenced our survey.

The forests of no other part of the world are so extensive and unbroken as this. Those of Central Europe are trifling in comparison; nor in India are they very continuous or extensive; while the rest of Asia seems to be a country of thinly wooded plains, and steppes, and deserts. Africa contains some large forests, situated on the east and west coasts, and in the interior south of the equator; but the whole of them would bear but a small proportion to that of the Amazon. In North America alone is there anything approaching to it, where the whole country east of the Mississippi and about the great lakes, is, or has been, an almost uninterrupted extent of woodland.

In a general survey of the earth, we may therefore look upon the New World as pre-eminently the land of forests, contrasting strongly with the Old, where steppes and deserts are the most characteristic features.

The boundaries of the Amazonian forest have not hitherto

been ascertained with much accuracy. The open plains of Caguan have been supposed much more extensive than they really are; but I have very nearly determined their limits to the south and east, by the observations I made, and the information I obtained in my voyage up the Uaupés. Again, on the Uaycáli there is a district marked on the maps as the "Pampas del Sacramento," which has been supposed to be an open plain; but the banks of the Amazon up to the mouth of the Uaycáli are clothed with thick forest, and Messrs. Smyth and Lowe, who crossed the Pampa in two places, found no open plains; and from their observations and those of Lieut. Mawe we must extend the forest district up to near Moyabamba, west of the Huallaga, and to the foot of the mountains east of Pasco and Tarma. I was informed by a native of Ecuador, well acquainted with the country, that the Napo, Tigre, Pastaza, and the adjacent rivers all flow through dense forest, which extends up even to Baéza and Canélos and over all the lower slopes of the Andes. Tschudi informs us that the forest districts commence on all the north and east slopes of the Andes of Peru, near Huánta, and at Urubámba north of Cúzco. I have learnt from a gentleman, a native of La Paz, that immediately on crossing the Bolivian Andes from that city and from Oropéssa and Santa Cruz, you enter the great forests, which extend over all the tributaries of the Madeira. Traders up the Purús and all the southern branches of the Upper Amazon, neither meet with, nor hear accounts of, any open land, so that there is little doubt but that the extent here pointed out is one vast, ever-verdant, unbroken forest.

The forests of the Amazon are distinguished from those of most other countries, by the great variety of species of trees composing them. Instead of extensive tracts covered with pines, or oaks, or beeches, we scarcely ever see two individuals of the same species together, except in certain cases, principally among the Palms. A great extent of flooded land about the mouth of the Amazon, is covered with the Mirití Palms (*Mauritia flexuosa* and *M. vinifera*), and in many places the Assaí (*Euterpe edulis*) is almost equally abundant. Generally, however, the same species of tree is repeated only at distant intervals. On a road for ten miles through the forest near Pará, there are only two specimens of the Masserandúba, or Cow-tree, and all through the adjoining district they are equally scarce. On the Javíta road, on the Upper Rio Negro, I observed the same thing. On the Uaupés, I once sent my Indians into the forest to obtain a board of a particular kind of tree; they searched for three days, and found only a few young trees, none of them of sufficient size.

Certain kinds of hard woods are used on the Amazon and Rio Negro, for the construction of canoes and the schooners used in the navigation of the river. The difficulty of getting timber of any one kind for these vessels is so great, that they are often constructed of half-a-dozen different sorts of wood, and not always of the same colours or degrees of hardness. Trees producing fruit, or with medicinal properties, are often so widely scattered, that two or three only are found within a reasonable distance of a village, and supply the whole population. This peculiarity of distribution must prevent a great trade in timber for any particular purpose being carried on here. The india-rubber and Brazil-nut trees are not altogether exceptions to this rule, and the produce from them is collected over an immense extent of country, to which the innumerable lakes and streams offer a ready access.

The chief district from which india-rubber is procured, is in the country between Pará and the Xingú. On the Upper Amazon and the Rio Negro it is also found, but is not yet collected.

The Brazil-nuts, from the *Bertholletia excelsa,* are brought chiefly from the interior; the greater part from the country around the junction of the Rio Negro and Madeira with the Amazon rivers. This tree takes more than a whole year to produce and ripen its fruits. In the month of January I observed the trees loaded at the same time with flowers and ripe fruits, both of which were falling from the tree; from these flowers would be formed the nuts of the following year; so that they probably require eighteen months for their complete development from the bud. The fruits, which are nearly as hard and heavy as cannon-balls, fall with tremendous force from the height of a hundred feet, crashing through the branches and undergrowth, and snapping off large boughs which they happen to strike against. Persons are sometimes killed by them, and accidents are not unfrequent among the Indians engaged in gathering them.

The fruits are all procured as they fall from the tree. They are collected together in small heaps, where they are opened with an axe, an operation that requires some practice and skill, and the triangular nuts are taken out and carried to the canoes in baskets. Other trees of the same family (*Lecythideæ*) are very abundant, and are remarkable for their curious fruits, which have lids, and are shaped like pots or cups, whence they are called "pot-trees." Some of the smaller ones are called by the natives "cuyas de macaco,"—monkeys' calabashes.

The next most important vegetable product of the Amazon district, is the Salsaparilha, the roots of *Smilax syphilitica*, and perhaps of other allied species. This plant appears to occur over the whole forest-district of the Amazon, from Venezuela to Bolivia, and from the Lower Amazon to Peru. It is not generally found near the great rivers, but far in the interior, on the banks of the small streams, and on dry rocky ground. It is principally dug up by the Indians, often by the most uncivilised tribes, and is the means of carrying on a considerable trade with them.

The Brazilian nutmegs, produced by the *Nectandrum Puchury*, grow in the country between the Rio Negro and Japura.

The Cumarú, or Tonquin-beans, are very abundant on the Upper Rio Negro, and are also found near Santarem on the Amazon.

A highly odoriferous bark, called by the Portuguese "Cravo de Maranhño" (Cloves of Maranham), is produced by a small tree growing only on one or two small tributaries of the Rio Negro.

A peculiar transparent oil, with an odour of turpentine, called Sassafras by the Venezuelans, is abundantly obtained by tapping a tree, common on the Upper Rio Negro, whence it is exported to Barra, and used for mixing oil-colours. In the Lower Amazon, a bitter oil, called Andiróba, much used for lamps, is made from a forest fruit.

A whitish resin, with a strong camphorous smell, is produced very abundantly in the Rio Negro and the Amazon, and is commonly used as pitch for the canoes and all the larger vessels of the country; while the inner bark of young trees of the *Bertholletia excelsa*, or Brazil-nut tree, is used instead of oakum for caulking.

Among the forest-trees of the Amazon, the *Leguminosæ* are much the most abundant in species, and they also most attract attention from their curious bean-like fruits, often of extraordinary size or length. Some of the Ingás, and allied genera, have pods a yard long, and very slender; while others are short, and three or four inches wide. There are some curious fruits of this family, which grow on a stalk three to five feet long and very slender, appearing as if some one had suspended a number of pods from the branches by long strings.

The flowers of this family are among the most brilliant and conspicuous; and their often finely-cut pinnate foliage has a very elegant appearance.

The following is a list of the principal vegetable productions of commercial value in the Amazon forests :—

India-rubber, from the sap of the *Siphonia elastica.*
Brazil-nuts, the seeds of the *Bertholletia excelsa.*
Salsaparilha, the roots of *Smilax syphilitica.*
Tonquin-beans, the seeds of *Dipteryx odorata.*
Puxiri, the fruit of *Nectandrum Puchury.*
· Sassafras oil, tree not known.
Andiroba oil, from the fruit of an unknown tree.
Crajurú, a red colour prepared from the leaves of *Bignonia Chica.*
Pitch—exudes from a forest tree.
Cacao, the seeds of *Theobroma Cacao* and other species.
Cravo, from an unknown tree.
Canella, the bark of *Canella alba.*
Vanilla, the fruits of various species of *Vanilla.*
Guaraná, a preparation from a fruit, grated in water, to form an agreeable and medicinal drink.
Piassába, the fibres from the petioles of a palm, *Leopoldinia* n. s.
Balsam Capivi, from the *Copaifera officinalis.*
Silk cotton, from various species of *Bombax.*

In many parts of my Journal, I have expressed an opinion that travellers have exaggerated the beauty and brilliancy of tropical vegetation, and on a calm review of all I have seen in the districts I have visited, I must repeat it.

There is a grandeur and solemnity in the tropical forest, but little of beauty or brilliancy of colour. The huge buttress trees, the fissured trunks, the extraordinary air roots, the twisted and wrinkled climbers, and the elegant palms, are what strike the attention and fill the mind with admiration and surprise and awe. But all is gloomy and solemn, and one feels a relief on again seeing the blue sky, and feeling the scorching rays of the sun.

It is on the roadside and on the rivers' banks that we see all the beauty of the tropical vegetation. There we find a mass of bushes and shrubs and trees of every height, rising over one another, all exposed to the bright light and the fresh air ; and putting forth, within reach, their flowers and fruit, which, in the forest, only grow far up on the topmost branches. Bright flowers and green foliage combine their charms, and climbers with their flowery festoons cover over the bare and decaying stems. Yet, pick out the loveliest spots, where the most gorgeous flowers of the tropics expand their glowing petals, and for every scene of this kind, we may find another at home of equal beauty, and with an equal amount of brilliant colour.

Look at a field of buttercups and daisies,—a hill-side covered with gorse and broom,—a mountain rich with purple heather, --or a forest-glade, azure with a carpet of wild hyacinths, and they will bear a comparison with any scene the tropics can produce. I have never seen anything more glorious than an old crab-tree in full blossom ; and the horse-chesnut, lilac, and laburnum will vie with the choicest tropical trees and shrubs. In the tropical waters are no more beautiful plants than our white and yellow water-lilies, our irises, and flowering rush ; for I cannot consider the flower of the *Victoria regia* more beautiful than that of the *Nymphæa alba*, though it may be larger ; nor is it so abundant an ornament of the tropical waters as the latter is of ours.

But the question is not to be decided by a comparison of individual plants, or the effects they may produce in the landscape, but on the frequency with which they occur, and the proportion the brilliantly coloured bear to the inconspicuous plants. My friend Mr. R. Spruce, now investigating the botany of the Amazon and Rio Negro, assures me that by far the greater proportion of plants gathered by him have inconspicuous green or white flowers; and with regard to the frequency of their occurrence, it was not an uncommon thing for me to pass days travelling up the rivers, without seeing any striking flowering tree or shrub. This is partly owing to the flowers of most tropical trees being quickly deciduous : they no sooner open, than they begin to fall; the Melastomas in particular, generally burst into flower in the morning, and the next day are withered, and for twelve months the tree bears no more flowers. This will serve to explain why the tropical flowering trees and shrubs do not make so much show as might be expected.

From the accounts of eye-witnesses, I believe that the forests of the southern United States present a more gay and brilliant appearance than those of tropical America.

Humboldt, in his " Aspects of Nature," repeatedly remarks on the contrast between the steppes of Tartary and the llanos of the Orinooko. The former, in the temperate zone, are gay with the most brilliant flowers ; while the latter, in the tropics, produce little but grasses and sedges, and only few and inconspicuous flowering plants. Mr. Darwin mentions the brilliancy of the flowers adorning the plains of Monte Video, which, with the luxuriant thistles of the Pampas, seems hardly equalled in the campos of tropical Brazil, where, with some exceptions, the earth is brown and sterile. The countless beautiful geraniums and heaths of the Cape cease on entering the tropics, and we have no account of any plants equally striking and brilliant supplying their place.

What we may fairly allow of tropical vegetation is, that there is a much greater number of species, and a greater variety of forms, than in the temperate zones. Among this great variety occur, as we might reasonably expect, the most striking and brilliant flowers, and the most remarkable forms of stem and foliage. But there is no evidence to show that the proportion of species bearing brightly coloured, compared to those bearing inconspicuous flowers, is any greater in the tropics than in the temperate regions ; and with regard to individuals—which is, after all, what produces the effects of vegetation—it seems probable that there is a greater mass of brilliant colouring and picturesque beauty, produced by plants in the temperate, than in the tropical regions.

There are several reasons which lead us to this conclusion. In the tropics, a greater proportion of the surface is covered either with dense forests or with barren deserts, neither of which can exhibit many flowers. Social plants are less common in the tropics, and thus masses of colour are less frequently produced. Individual objects may be more brilliant and striking, but the general effect will not be so great, as that of a smaller number of less conspicuous plants, grouped together in masses of various colours, so strikingly displayed in the meadows and groves of the temperate regions.

The changing hues of autumn, and the tender green of spring, are particular beauties which are not seen in tropical regions, and which are quite unsurpassed by anything that exists there. The wide expanse of green meadows and rich pastures is also wanting ; and, however much individual objects may please and astonish, the effect of the distant landscape is decidedly superior in the temperate parts of the world.

The sensations of pleasure we experience on seeing natural objects, depends much upon association of ideas with their uses, their novelty, or their history. What causes the sensations we feel on gazing upon a waving field of golden corn ? Not, surely, the mere beauty of the sight, but the associations we connect with it. We look on it as a national blessing, as the staff of life, as the most precious produce of the soil ; and this makes it beautiful in our eyes.

So, in the tropics, the broad-leaved banána, beautiful in itself, becomes doubly so, when looked upon as producing a greater quantity of food in a given time, and on a limited space, than any other plant. We take it as a type of the luxuriance of the tropics,—we look at its broad leaves, the produce of six months' growth,—we think of its delicious and wholesome fruit : and all this is beauty, as we gaze upon it.

In the same manner, a field of sugar-cane or an extensive plantation of cotton produces similar sensations : we think of the thousands they will feed and clothe, and the thought clothes them with beauty.

Palms too are subject to the same influence. They are elegant and graceful in themselves ; they are almost all useful to man ; they are associated with the brightness and warmth of the tropics : and thus they acquire an additional interest, a new beauty.

To the naturalist everything in tne tropics acquires this kind of interest, for some reason or other. One plant is a tropical form, and he examines it with curiosity and delight. Another is allied to some well-known European species, and this too attracts his attention. The structure of some are unknown, and he is pleased to examine them. The locality of another is doubtful, and he feels a great pleasure in determining it. He is ever examining individual objects, and confounds his own interest in them, from a variety of causes, with the sensations produced by their beauty, and thus is led to give exaggerated descriptions of the luxuriance and splendour of the vegetation.

As most travellers are naturalists, this supposition will account for the ideas of the tropics generally obtained from a perusal of their works.

If I have come to a different conclusion, it is not that I am incapable of appreciating the splendours of tropical scenery, but because I believe that they are not of the kind usually represented, and that the scenery of our own land is, of its own kind, unsurpassed: there is nothing approaching it in the tropics, nor is the scenery of the tropics to be found with us. There,—singular forms of stems and climbers, gigantic leaves, elegant palms, and individual plants with brilliant flowers, are the characteristic features. Here,—an endless carpet of verdure, with masses of gay blossoms, the varying hues of the foliage, and the constant variety of plain and forest, meadow and woodland, more than individual objects, are what fill the beholder with delight.

## CHAPTER XVI

### *A.* MAMMALIA.

NOTWITHSTANDING the luxuriance of the vegetation, which might be supposed to afford sustenance, directly or indirectly, to every kind of animal life, the Amazon valley is remarkably deficient in large animals, and of Mammalia generally has a smaller number both of species and individuals, than any other part of the world of equal extent, except Australia. Three small species of deer, which occur but rarely, are the only representatives of the vast herds of countless species of deer and antelopes and buffaloes which swarm in Africa and Asia, and of the wild sheep and goats of Europe and North America. The tapir alone takes the place of the elephants and rhinoceroses of the Old World. Two or three species of large *Felidæ*, and two wild hogs, with the capybára and páca, comprise almost all its large game; and these are all thinly scattered over a great extent of country, and never occur in such large numbers as do the animals representing them in other parts of the world.

Those singular creatures, the sloths, the armadilloes, and the ant-anters, are very generally distributed, but only occur singly and sparingly. The small agoutis are perhaps rather more plentiful; but almost the only animals found in any numbers are the monkeys, which are abundant, both in species and individuals, and are the only mammalia that give some degree of life to these trackless forests, which seem peculiarly fitted for their development and increase.

I met with twenty-one species of these animals, some of which I had no opportunity of examining. Several others exist; but it is necessary to reside for some years in each locality, in order to meet with all the different kinds. I subjoin a list of the species, with the localities in which they were found.

MONKEYS FOUND ON THE AMAZON AND THE RIO NEGRO.

1. *Mycetes seniculus,* Geoff.; on the Rio Negro and the north bank of the Amazon.

2. *Mycetes caraya,* Gray; on the Upper Amazon

3. *Mycetes beelzebub,* Br. Mus.; Pará.

4. *Lagothrix Humboldtii,* Geoff.; Upper Amazon and west of Rio Negro.

5. *Ateles paniscus,* Geoff.; Guiana, north bank of Amazon and east of Rio Negro.

6. *Cebus apella,* Erxl. (?); Amazon and Rio Negro.

7. *Cebus gracilis,* Spix; Rio Negro and Upper Amazon.

8. *Callithrix sciureus,* Geoff.; the whole Amazon valley.

9. *Callithrix torquatus (amictus,* Geoff.); Upper Rio Negro.

10. *Callithrix personatus,* Geoff.; south bank of Upper Amazon.

11. *Nyctipithecus trivirgatus,* Humb.; Upper Rio Negro.

12. *Nyctipithecus felinus,* Spix; Upper Amazon.

13. *Pithecia irrorata (hirsuta,* Spix); south bank of Upper Amazon.

14. *Pithecia* ——, north of Upper Amazon.

15. *Brachiurus satanas,* Br. Mus.; Guiana, east bank of Rio Negro.

16. *Brachiurus oakary,* Spix; Upper Rio Negro.

17. *Brachiurus rubicundus,* Isid.; Upper Amazon.

18. *Brachiurus* ——, south side of Upper Amazon.

19. *Jacchus bicolor,* Spix; north of the Amazon and Rio Negro.

20. *Jacchus tamarin,* Br. Mus.; Pará.

21. *Jacchus* n.s., Upper Rio Negro.

Of the above, the first seven have prehensile tails, a character only found among the monkeys of America. The howlers, forming the genus *Mycetes,* are the largest and most powerful. They have a bony vessel situated beneath the chin, and a strong muscular apparatus in the throat, which assists in producing the loud rolling noise from which they derive their name, and which appears as if a great number of animals were crying in concert. This, however, is not the case ; a full-grown male alone makes the howling, which is generally heard at night, or on the approach of rain.

The annexed list of the other larger mammalia of the Amazon district, will serve to confirm the statement of the extreme poverty of these regions in that class of animals. Owing to the loss of my notes and specimens, many of the specific names are doubtful : such are marked thus— ?

*Phyllostoma hastatum.*—This is a common bat on the Amazon, and is, I believe, the one which does much injury to the horses and cattle by sucking their blood ; it also attacks men, when it has opportunity. The species of blood-sucking bats seem to be numerous in the interior. They do not inhabit houses, like many of the frugivorous bats, but enter at dusk through any aperture they may find. They generally attack the tip of the toe, or sometimes any other part of the body that may be exposed. I have myself been twice bitten, once on the toe, and the other time on the tip of the nose ; in neither case did I feel anything, but awoke after the operation was completed : in what way they effect it is still quite unknown. The wound is a small round hole, the bleeding of which it is very difficult to stop. It can hardly be a bite, as that would awake the sleeper ; it seems most probable that it is either a succession of gentle scratches with the sharp edge of the teeth, gradually wearing away the skin, or a triturating with the point of the tongue, till the same effect is produced. My brother was frequently bitten by them, and his opinion was, that the bat applied one of its long canine teeth to the part, and then flew round and round on that as a centre, till the tooth, acting as an awl, bored a small hole ; the wings of the bat serving, at the same time, to fan the patient into a deeper slumber. He several times awoke while the bat was at work, and though of course the creature immediately flew away, it was his impression that the operation was conducted in the manner above described. Many persons are particularly annoyed by bats, while others are free from their attacks. An old Mulatto at Guia, on the Upper Rio Negro, was bitten almost every night, and though there were frequently half-a-dozen other persons in the room, he would be the party favoured by their attentions. Once he came to us with a doleful countenance, telling us, he thought the bats meant to eat him up quite, for, having covered up his hands and feet in a blanket, they had descended beneath his hammock of open network, and, attacking the most prominent part of his person, had bitten him through a hole in his trousers! We could not help laughing at the catastrophe, but to him it was no laughing matter.

Senhor Brandão, of Manaquery, informed me that he had once an Indian girl in his house, who was much subject to the attacks of the bats. She was at length so much weakened by loss of blood, that fears were entertained of her life, if they continued their attacks; and it was found necessary to send her to a distance, where these bloodthirsty animals did not abound.

The wound made by them is very difficult to heal, especially in its usual locality—the tip of the great toe, as it generally renders a shoe unbearable for a day or two, and forces one to the conclusion that, after the first time, for the curiosity of the thing, to be bitten by a bat is very disagreeable. They will, however, very rarely enter a lighted room, and for this reason the practice of burning a lamp all night is almost universal.

*Tapirus Americanus.*—The Tapir is common over the whole Amazon district, but is nowhere very abundant. It feeds on leaves and a great many different kinds of fruits, and sometimes does much injury in the mandiocca-fields of the Indians. Its flesh is very good eating, and is considered very wholesome, and is even said to be a remedy for the ague. It is a very shy and timid animal, wandering about principally at night. When the Indian discovers a feeding-place, he builds a stage between two trees, about eight feet above the ground, and there stations himself soon after dusk, armed with a gun, or with his bow and arrow. Though such a heavy animal, the tapir steps as lightly as a cat, and can only be heard approaching by the gentle rustling of the bushes; the slightest sound or smell will alarm it, and the Indian lies still as death for hours, till the animal approaches sufficiently near to be shot, or until, scenting its enemy, it makes off in another direction. I have accompanied the Indians on these expeditions, but always without success.

*Coassus nemorivagus.*

*C. rufus.*—These are the small white and red deer of the

forests, found in all parts of the Amazon. They have very small unbranched horns.

*Mazama campestris ?*—The " Viado galera," or horned deer of the Rio Branco, is probably of this species. It has small branched horns, and inhabits the open plains, never the thick forests.

*Dicotyles taiaçu.* The smaller wild Hog. Taititú of the Indians.

*D. labiatus ?*—The larger species, called by the natives " Taiaçu."

There seems to be also a third species, of the same size as the last.

*Arctopithecus flaccidus ?* Preguiça real. Ai, (Lingoa Geral). The great Sloth.

*Bradypus torquatus.* Ai, (Lingoa Geral).—These and some other species of sloths are not uncommon. They feed entirely on leaves, preferring those of the *Cecropias.* They are frequently attacked by the harpy eagle, and are also eaten by the Indians.

*Myrmecophaga jubata.* Tamanduá assu, (Lingoa Geral). "The great Ant-eater."—This animal is rare, but widely distributed. During rain it turns its long bushy tail up over its back and stands still ; the Indians, when they meet with one, rustle the leaves, and it thinks rain is falling, and turning up its tail, they take the opportunity of killing it by a blow on the head with a stick. It feeds on the large termites, or white ants, tearing up with its powerful claws the earth and rotten wood in which their nests are made. The Indians positively assert that it sometimes kills the jaguar, embracing it and forcing in its enormous claws, till they mutually destroy each other. They also declare that these animals are all females, and believe that the male is the " curupíra," or demon of the forests: the peculiar organisation of the animal has probably led to this ,error. It lives entirely on the ground.

*Tamandua tetradactylus ?* The smaller Prehensile-tailed Ant-eater.—This animal is entirely arboreal, feeding on the tree termites ; it has no nest, and sleeps in a fork of a tree with its head bent under its body.

*Cyclothurus didactylus.* Tamanduái, (Lingoa Geral). The small Silky-haired Ant-eater,—is arboreal, and rather abundant. There is another species much smaller, and as white as cotton ; but it is rare, and I never met with it.

*Priodonta gigas?* Tatuassú, (Lingoa Geral). The great Armadillo.—Rather scarce.

*Tatusia septemcinctus?* Tatu, (Lingoa Geral).—This and another very small species are the most abundant in the Amazon district, but can seldom be procured except by hunting with dogs. All the kinds are eaten, and their flesh is very white and delicate.

*Didelphis* ——. Opossum. Mucúra, (LingoaGeral).—Several species are found. They frequent the neighbourhood of houses, and attack poultry. The young are carried in an abdominal pouch, like the kangaroos, and have their little prehensile tails twisted round that of the mother.

*Hydrochœrus capybara.* Capywára, (Lingoa Geral).—This animal is found on all the river-banks. It feeds on grass, and takes to the water and dives when pursued. It is sometimes eaten, but is not considered very good.

*Cœlogenis paca.* Páca. (Lingoa Geral).—This animal is generally abundant. It is nocturnal, and is much esteemed for its meat, which is the very best the country produces, being fat, delicate, and very tender.

*Dasyprocta nigricans,* Natt. Black Agouti. Cotía, (Lingoa Geral).—This species is found on the Rio Negro.

*D. punctata?* Yellow Agouti.—This is probably the common Amazon species.

*D. agouti?* Cotiwya, (Lingoa Geral).—A smaller species, very widely distributed. All are eaten, but the meat is rather dry and tasteless.

*Cercolabes prehensilis.* The Brazilian Porcupine.—This animal is scarce. It is eaten by the Indians.

*Echimys* ——. Several species of these curious, spinous, rat-like animals are found on the Upper Rio Negro.

*Cercoleptes caudivolvus.* The Potto.—It is a nocturnal animal, and inhabits the banks of the Upper Amazon.

*Nasua olivacea?* Coatí.—Two species, the "Coatí" and the "Coatí mondi" of the Indians, are found on the Amazon.

*Lontra Brasiliensis?* The Brazilian Otter,—is abundant on the Rio Negro.

*Galera barbara.* Irára, (Lingoa Geral). Teeth, I. $\frac{6}{6}$ C. $\frac{1-1}{1-1}$ M. $\frac{4-4}{4-4}$. This is a curious animal, somewhat allied to the bears. It lives in trees, and eats honey, whence probably its Indian name, —from Irá, in the Lingoa Geral, "honey."

*Vulpes* —— ? A wild dog, or fox, of the forests; it hunts in small packs; it is easily domesticated, but is very scarce.

*Leopardus concolor.* The Puma. In the Lingoa Geral, Sasurána, "the false deer," from its colour.

*L. onça.* The Jaguar. Jauarité, (Lingoa Geral).—"The Great Dog."

*L. onça,* var. *nigra.* The Black Jaguar. Jauarité pixuna, (Lingoa Geral). Tigre (Spaniards).

*L. pictus* and *L. griseus.* Tiger Cats. Maracajá, (Lingoa Geral).

The Jaguar, or onça, appears to approach very nearly in fierceness and strength to the tiger of India. Many persons are annually killed or wounded by these animals. When they can obtain other food they will seldom attack man. The Indians, however, assert that they often face a man boldly, springing forward till within a few feet of him, and then, if the man turns, they will attack him; the hunters will sometimes meet them thus face to face, and kill them with a cutlass. They also destroy them with the bow and arrow, for which purpose an old knife-blade is used for the head of the arrow; and they say it is necessary not to pull too strong a bow, or the arrow will pass completely through the body of the animal, and not do him so much injury as if it remains in the wound. For the same reason, in shooting with a gun, they use rough leaden cylinders instead of bullets, which make a larger and rougher wound, and do not pass so readily quite through the body. I heard of one case, of a jaguar entering an Indian's house, and attacking him in his hammock.

The jaguar, say the Indians, is the most cunning animal in the forest: he can imitate the voice of almost every bird and animal so exactly, as to draw them towards him: he fishes in the rivers, lashing the water with his tail to imitate falling fruit, and when the fish approach, hooks them up with his claws. He catches and eats turtles, and I have myself found the unbroken shells, which he has cleaned completely out with his paws; he even attacks the cow-fish in its own element, and an eye-witness assured me he had watched one dragging out of the water this bulky animal, weighing as much as a large ox.

A young Portuguese trader told me he had seen (what many persons had before assured me often happened) an onça feeding on a full-grown live alligator, tearing and eating its tail. On leaving off, and retiring a yard or two, the alligator would begin to move towards the water, when the onça would spring upon it, and again commence eating at the tail, during which time the alligator lay perfectly still. We had been observing a cat playing with a lizard, both behaving in exactly the same manner, the lizard only attempting to move when the cat for a moment left it; the cat would then immediately spring upon it again : and my informant assured me that he had seen the jaguar treating the alligator in exactly the same way.

The onça is particularly fond of dogs, and will carry them off in preference to any other animal. When one has been committing any depredations, it is a common thing to tie a dog to a tree at night, the howling of which attracts the onça, which comes to seize it, and is then shot by a person concealed for the purpose.

It is a general belief among the Indians and the white inhabitants of Brazil, that the onça has the power of fascination. Many accounts are given to prove this; among others, a person informed me, that he had seen an onça standing at the foot of a high tree, looking up into it : on the top was a guariba, or howling-monkey, looking down at the onça, and jumping about from side to side, crying piteously; the onça stood still; the monkey continued descending lower and lower on the branches, still uttering its cries, till at length it fell down at the very feet of the onça, which seized and devoured it. Many incidents of this kind are related by persons who have witnessed them; but whether they are exaggerated, or are altogether imaginary, it is difficult to decide. The belief in them, by persons best acquainted with the habits of the animal, is universal.

Of the smaller Tiger-cats, there are several kinds, but having lost my collection of skins, I cannot ascertain the species. The Puma is considered much less fierce than the jaguar, and is very little feared by the inhabitants. There are several varieties of the jaguar, distinguished by the Indians by different names. The black variety is rarer than the others, and is generally thought to be quite distinct; in some localities it is unknown, while in others it is as abundant as the ocellated variety.

Many small rodent animals—squirrels, rats, etc.—complete the terrestrial mammalia of the Amazon district.

The waters of the Amazon, up even to the base of the Andes, are inhabited by several species of true *Cetacea*, of which, however, we have as yet but very scanty information.

Two, if not more, species of Dolphins are common in every part of the Amazon, and in almost all of its tributaries. They are found above the falls of the Rio Negro, and in the Cassiquiare and Upper Orinooko. They vary in size and colour, and two of them have distinct Indian names.—Piraiowára (Fish-dog), and Tucuxí.

D'Orbigny mentions their being killed by the inhabitants of Bolivia to make oil. In the Lower Amazon and Rio Negro they are scarcely ever caught, and I was unable to obtain a specimen. The species described by D'Orbigny is probably distinct, as he mentions their being twenty feet long, whereas none I have seen could have exceeded six or seven.

Herbivorous *Cetacea* are also found in the Amazon; they are called by the Brazilians, Peixe boi, or cow-fish, and by the Indians, Juarouá.

It has not yet been ascertained, whether the cow-fish of the Amazon is the same as the *Manatus* of the West Indies and the coasts of Guiana, or a distinct species. All the accounts of the *Manatus Americanus* mention it as being twelve or fifteen feet long on the average, and sometimes reaching twenty. Those of the Amazon appear to average seven or eight feet only; of five or six specimens I have myself seen, none have exceeded this; Lieutenant Smyth saw one on the Upper Uaycáli, of the same size; and Condamine describes the one he saw as not being larger.

The inhabitants of the Amazon give accounts of three kinds, which they seem to consider distinct, one smaller, and one larger than the common kind, and differing also in the shape of the tail and fins, and in the colour.

The West Indian species is always described as having external nails on the edge of the fin, or fore-arm. This I never observed in the Amazon species; though in cutting the edge of the fin to take out the bones entire, I must have noticed them, had they been as prominent as they are usually described; neither does Lieutenant Smyth mention them, though he could hardly have overlooked so singular an external character.

I am therefore inclined to think that the Amazon possesses

one or two distinct species. Having carefully prepared a skin and skeleton of a fine male (which, with the rest of my collections, was lost on the voyage home), I did not describe it so minutely as I otherwise should have done, but have some notes, referring to male and female specimens, which I will now give :—

*Manatus* of the Amazon.
Peixe boi, of the Portuguese.
Vaca marina, of the Spaniards.
Juarouá, of the Indians' Lingoa Geral.

The mammæ of the female are two, one close to the base of each fin behind. The muzzle is blunt, fleshy, and covered with numerous stiff bristles ; the nostrils are on the upper part of it, and lunate. The lips, thick, fleshy, and bristly, and the tongue rough. The skin is lead-colour, with a few pinkish-white marblings on the belly ; others have the whole of the neck and fore-part of the body beneath cream-colour, and another spot of the same colour on the underside of the tail. The skin is entirely smooth, resembling india-rubber in appearance, and there are short hairs scattered over it, about an inch apart ; it is an inch thick on the back, and a quarter of an inch on the belly ; beneath it, is a layer of fat, of an inch or more in thickness, enveloping every part of the body, and furnishing from five to ten gallons of oil.

The total length of full-grown animals is seven feet. The intestines are very voluminous. The lungs are two feet long, and six or seven inches wide, very cellular, and when blown up, much resemble a Macintosh air-belt. The ribs are each nearly semicircular, arching back from the spine, so as to form a ridge or keel inside, and on the back there is a great depth of flesh. The bone is excessively hard and heavy, and can scarcely be broken. The dung resembles that of a horse.

The cow-fish feeds on grass on the margins of the rivers and lakes. It is captured either with the harpoon, or with strong nets, placed at the mouth of some lake, whence it comes at night to feed.

Though it has very small eyes, and minute pores for ears, its senses are very acute ; and the fishermen say there is no animal can hear, see, and smell better, or which requires greater skill and caution to capture. When caught, it is killed by driving a wooden plug up its nostrils. The Indian fills his canoe full of water, and sinks it beneath the body; he then bales out the water, and paddles home with a load which requires a dozen men to move on shore. The meat is very good, and both for it and for the oil the animal is much sought after. It ascends most of the tributaries of the Amazon, but does not pass the falls or rapids.

## *B.* BIRDS.

The birds of the Amazon district are so numerous and striking, that it is impossible here to do more than mention a few of the most interesting and beautiful, so as to give some general idea of the ornithology of the district.

Among the birds of prey, the most conspicuous are the King Vulture (*Sarcorhamphus papa*), and the Harpy Eagle (*Thrasaëtos harpyia*), both of which are found in the whole district of the lower Amazon. There is also a great variety of eagles, hawks, kites, and owls, and probably between twenty and thirty species may be obtained in the country around Pará.

Those two fine eagles, the *Spizaëtus ornatus* and the *Morphnus Guianensis*, inhabit the Upper Amazon.

Among the smaller perching-birds, the yellow-breasted tyrant shrikes immediately attract attention, perched upon dead trees in the open grounds. In the forests the curious notes of the bush-shrikes (*Thamnophilinæ*) are often heard, and the ever-recurring vociferous cries of the great grey tyrant-flycatcher (*Lipaugus simplex*).

Several pretty little tanagers are found about Pará; but the exquisite little seven-coloured tanager (*Calospiza tatao*), and the scarcely less beautiful scarlet and black one (*Rhamphocelis nigrogularis,*) do not occur till we reach the Rio Negro and the Upper Amazon.

The Chatterers form one of the most splendid families of birds, and we have on the Amazon some of the finest species, such as the *Cotinga cayana, C. cœrulea, Phœnicurus carnifex,* and *P. militaris,* which are found at Pará, and the *C. Pompadoura,* and *P nigrogularis* on the Upper Amazon and Rio Negro.

The hang-nest Orioles, species of *Cassicus*, are numerous, and by their brilliant plumage of yellow or red and black, and their curious pendulous nests, give a character to the ornithology of the country.

Woodpeckers, kingfishers, and splendid metallic jacamars and trogons, are numerous in species and individuals. But of all the families of birds that inhabit this country, the parrots and the toucans are perhaps the most characteristic; they abound in species and individuals, and are much more frequently seen than any other birds.

From Pará to the Rio Negro I met with sixteen species of toucans, the most curious and beautiful of which is the *Pteroglossus Beauharnasii*, or "curl-crested Araçari," whose glossy crest of horny black curls is unique among birds.

Of parrots and paroquets I found at least thirty distinct species, varying in size from the little *Psittaculus passerinus*, scarcely larger than a sparrow, to the magnificent crimson macaws. In ascending the Amazon, large flocks of parrots are seen, every morning and evening, crossing the river to their feeding- or resting-places; and however many there may be, they constantly fly in pairs, as do also the macaws,—while the noisy little paroquets associate indiscriminately in flocks, and fly from tree to tree with a rapidity which few birds can surpass.

Though humming-birds are almost entirely confined to tropical America, they appear to abound most in the hilly and mountainous districts, and those of the level forests of the Amazon are comparatively few and inconspicuous. The whole number of species I met with in the Lower Amazon and Rio Negro, does not exceed twenty, and few of them are very handsome. The beautiful little *Lophornis Gouldi*, found rarely at Pará, and the magnificent *Topaza pyra*, which is not uncommon on the Upper Rio Negro, are, however, exceptions, and will bear comparison with any species in this wonderful family.

Probably no country in the world contains a greater variety of birds than the Amazon valley. Though I did not collect them very assiduously, I obtained upwards of five hundred species, a greater number than can be found all over Europe; and I have little hesitation in saying that any one collecting industriously for five or six years might obtain near a thousand different kinds.

### *C.* Reptiles and Fishes.

Like all tropical countries the Amazon district abounds in reptiles, and contains many of the largest size and most singular structure. The lizards and serpents are particularly abundant, and among the latter are several very venomous species ; but the most remarkable are the boa and the anaconda, which reach an enormous size. The former inhabits the land, and though it is often found very large, yet the most authentic and trustworthy accounts of monstrous serpents refer to the latter, the *Eunectes murinus* of naturalists, which lives in or near the water. The Indians are aware of the generic distinction of these creatures, for while they call the former " Jiboa," the latter is the " Sucurujú."

The largest specimens I met with myself were not more than from fifteen to twenty feet long, but I have had several accounts of their having been killed, and measured, of a length of thirty-two feet. They have been seen very much larger, but, as may be supposed, are then very difficult to kill or secure, owing to their tenacity of life and their acquatic habits. It is an undisputed fact that they devour cattle and horses, and the general belief in the country is that they are sometimes from sixty to eighty feet long.*

Alligators of three or four distinct species abound in the Amazon, and in all its tributary streams. The smaller ones are eaten by the natives, the larger often devour them in return. In almost every village some persons may be seen maimed by these creatures, and many children are killed every year. The eggs of all the different kinds are eaten, though they have a very strong musky odour. The largest species

---

* As so few Europeans have seen these large serpents, and the very existence of any large enough to swallow a horse or ox is hardly credited, I append the following account by a competent scientific observer, the well-known botanical traveller Dr. Gardner. In his " Travels in Brazil," p. 356, he says :—

" In the marshes of this valley in the province of Goyaz, near Arrayas, the Boa Constrictor is often met with of considerable size; it is not uncommon throughout the whole province, particularly by the wooded margins of lakes, marshes, and streams. Sometimes they attain the enormous length of forty feet: the largest I ever saw was at this place, but it was not alive. Some weeks before our arrival at Safè, the favourite riding horse of Senhor Lagoriva, which had been put out to pasture not far

(*Jacare nigra*) reaches a length of fifteen, or rarely of twenty feet.

The most interesting and useful reptiles of the Amazon are, however, the various species of fresh-water turtles, which supply an abundance of wholesome food, and from whose eggs an excellent oil is made. The largest and most abundant of these is the Tataruga, or great turtle of the Amazon, the Jurará of the Indians. It grows to the length of three feet, and has an oval flattish shell of a dark colour and quite smooth ; it abounds in all parts of the Amazon, and in most places is the common food of the inhabitants.

In the month of September, as soon as the sandbanks begin to be uncovered, the females deposit their eggs, scraping hollows of a considerable depth, covering them over carefully, smoothing and beating down the sand, and then walking across and across the place in various directions for the purpose of concealment. There are such numbers of them, that some beaches are almost one mass of eggs beneath the surface, and here the Indians come to make oil. A canoe is filled with the eggs, which are all broken and mashed up together. The oil rises to the top, and is skimmed off and boiled, when it will keep, and is used both for light and for cooking. Millions of eggs are thus annually destroyed, and the turtles have already become scarce in consequence. There are some extensive beaches which yield two thousand pots of oil annually ; each pot contains five gallons, and requires about two thousand five hundred eggs, which would give five millions of eggs destroyed in one locality.

But of those that remain, a very small portion are able to reach maturity. When the young turtles issue from the egg, and run to the water, many enemies are awaiting them. Great

from the house, could not be found, although strict search was made for it all over the Fazenda. Shortly after this, one of his vaqueiros, in going through a wood by the side of a small river, saw an enormous Boa suspended in the fork of a tree which hung over the water ; it was dead, but had evidently been floated down alive by a recent flood, and being in an inert state it had not been able to extricate itself from the fork before the waters fell. It was dragged out to the open country by two horses, and was found to measure thirty-seven feet in length ; on opening it the bones of a horse in a somewhat broken condition, and the flesh in a half-digested state, were found within it, the bones of the head being uninjured ; from these circumstances we concluded that the Boa had devoured the horse entire."

alligators open their jaws and swallow them by hundreds; the jaguars from the forest come and feed upon them; eagles and buzzards, and the great wood ibises attend the feast; and when they have escaped all these, there are many ravenous fishes which seize them in the stream.

The Indians catch the full-grown turtles, either with the hook, net, or arrow. The last is the most ingenious method, and requires the most skill. The turtle never shows its back above water, only rising to breathe, which it does by protruding its nostrils almost imperceptibly above the surface; the Indian's keen eyes perceive this, even at a considerable distance; but an arrow shot obliquely would glance off the smooth flat shell, so he shoots up into the air with such accurate judgment, that the arrow falls nearly vertically upon the shell, which it penetrates, and remains securely fixed in the turtle's back. The head of the arrow fits loosely on to the shaft, and is connected with it by a long fine cord, carefully wound round it; as the turtle dives, they separate, the light shaft forming a float or buoy, which the Indian secures, and by the attached cord draws the prize up into his canoe. In this manner almost all the turtles sold in the cities have been procured, and the little square vertical hole of the arrow-head may generally be seen in the shell.

Besides the great tataruga (*Podocnemis expansa*), there are several smaller kinds, also much used for food. The Tracaxa (*Emys tracaxa*, Spix) and the Cabeçudo (*E. macrocephala*, Spix) have been described by the French naturalists, Duméril and Bibron, as one species, under the name of *Peltocephalus tracaxa;* but they are quite distinct, and though their characters are perhaps not easy to define, they could never be confounded by any one who had examined them in the living state. They are found too in different localities. The tracaxa is abundant in the Amazon, in the Orinooko, and in the Guaviare, all white-water rivers, and very scarce in the Rio Negro. The cabeçudo is very abundant in the Rio Negro and in the Atabapo, but is not found in the Guaviare or the Amazon, appearing to be confined to the black-water streams. I obtained ten distinct kinds of river tortoises, or *Chelydidæ*, and there are also two or three kinds of land-tortoises inhabiting the adjacent district.

As might be expected in the greatest river in the world, there is a corresponding abundance and variety of fish. They supply the Indians with the greater part of their animal food, and are at all times more plentiful, and easier to be obtained, than birds or game from the forest.

During my residence on the Rio Negro I carefully figured and described every species I met with ; and at the time I left fresh ones were every day occurring. The soft-finned fishes are much the most numerous, and comprise some of the best kinds of food. Of the *Siluridæ* I obtained fifty-one species, of *Serrasalmo* twenty-four, of *Chalceus* twenty-six, of *Gymnotus* ten, and of spinous-finned fishes (*Acanthopterygia*) forty-two. Of all kinds of fishes I found two hundred and five species in the Rio Negro alone, and these, I am sure, are but a small portion of what exist there. Being a black-water river, most of its fishes are different from those found in the Amazon. In fact, in every small river, and in different parts of the same river, distinct kinds are found. The greater part of those which inhabit the Upper Rio Negro are not found near its mouth, where there are many other kinds equally unknown in the clearer, darker, and probably colder waters of its higher branches. From the number of new fishes constantly found in every fresh locality and in every fisherman's basket, we may estimate that at least five hundred species exist in the Rio Negro and its tributary streams. The number in the whole valley of the Amazon it is impossible to estimate with any approach to accuracy.

## *D.* Insects.

To describe the countless tribes of insects that swarm in the dense forests of the Amazon would require volumes. In no country in the world is there more variety and beauty ; nowhere are there species of larger size or of more brilliant colours. Here are found the extraordinary harlequin-beetle, the gigantic *Prioni* and *Dynastes ;* but these are exceptions to the great mass of the *Coleoptera*, which, though in immense variety, are of small size and of little brilliancy of colour, offering a great contrast to the generally large-sized and gorgeous species of tropical Africa, India, and Australia. In the other orders the same rule holds good, except in the *Hymenoptera,* which contain many gigantic and handsome species. It is in the lovely butterflies that the Amazonian forests are unrivalled, whether we consider the endless variety of the species, their large size, or their gorgeous colours. South America is the richest part of the world in this group of insects, and the Amazon seems the richest part of South America. This continent is distinguished from every other by having a most extensive and peculiar family, the *Heliconiidæ*, of which not a single species is found in either Europe, Asia, Africa, or even North America (excepting Mexico). Another family, still more extensive, of exquisitely beautiful small butterflies, the *Erycinidæ*, is also almost peculiar to it, a few species only being found in tropical Asia and Africa. In both these peculiar families the Amazon is particularly rich, so that we may consider it as the headquarters of South America *Lepidoptera*.

Pará itself, for variety of species, is perhaps the best locality for diurnal *Lepidoptera;* six hundred distinct kinds may be obtained within a day's walk of the city. At Santarem I had increased my collection to seven hundred species, at Barra to eight hundred, and I should have brought home with me nine hundred species had my collections arrived in safety. Mr. Bates, who has paid more exclusive attention to insects, states that he has now obtained twelve hundred species,—a wonderful collection to be made by one person, in a country without any variation of climate or of physical features, and no part of it elevated five hundred feet above the level of the sea.

## *E*. Geographical Distribution of Animals.

There is no part of natural history more interesting or instructive than the study of the geographical distribution of animals.

It is well known that countries possessing a climate and soil very similar, may differ almost entirely in their productions. Thus Europe and North America have scarcely an animal in common in the temperate zone; and South America contrasts equally with the opposite coast of Africa; while Australia differs almost entirely in its productions from districts under the same parallel of latitude in South Africa and South America. In all these cases there is a wide extent of sea separating the countries, which few animals can pass over; so that, supposing the animal productions to have been originally distinct, they could not well have become intermixed.

In each of these countries we find well-marked smaller districts, appearing to depend upon climate. The tropical and temperate parts of America and Africa have, generally speaking, distinct animals in each of them.

On a more minute acquaintance with the animals of any country, we shall find that they are broken up into yet smaller local groups, and that almost every district has peculiar animals found nowhere else. Great mountain-chains are found to separate countries possessing very distinct sets of animals. Those of the east and west of the Andes differ very remarkably. The Rocky Mountains also separate two distinct zoological districts ; California and Oregon on the one side, possessing plants, birds, and insects, not found in any part of North America east of that range.

But there must be many other kinds of boundaries besides these, which, independently of climate, limit the range of animals. Places not more than fifty or a hundred miles apart often have species of insects and birds at the one, which are not found at the other. There must be some boundary which determines the range of each species ; some external peculiarity to mark the line which each one does not pass.

These boundaries do not always form a barrier to the progress of the animal, for many birds have a limited range, in a country where there is nothing to prevent them flying in every direction,—as in the case of the nightingale, which is quite unknown in some of our western counties. Rivers generally do not determine the distribution of species, because, when small, there are few animals which cannot pass them ; but in very large rivers the case is different, and they will, it is believed, be found to be the limits, determining the range of many animals of all orders.

With regard to the Amazon, and its larger tributaries, I have ascertained this to be the case, and shall here mention the facts which tend to prove it.

On the north side of the Amazon, and the east of the Rio Negro, are found the following three species of monkeys, *Ateles paniscus, Brachiurus satanas*, and *Jacchus bicolor*. These are all found close up to the margins of the Rio Negro and Amazon, but never on the opposite banks of either river ; nor am I able to ascertain that either of them have ever been found in any other part of South America than Cayenne or Guiana, and the eastern part of Venezuela, a district which is bounded on the south and west by the Amazon and Rio Negro.

The species of *Pithecia*, No. 14 of my list, is found on the west side of the Rio Negro for several hundred miles, from its mouth up to the river Curicuriarí, but never on the east side, neither is it known on the south side of the Upper Amazon, where it is replaced by an allied species, the *P. irrorata* (*P. hirsuta*, Spix), which, though abundant there, is never found on the north bank. These facts are, I think, sufficient to prove that these rivers do accurately limit the range of some species, and in the cases just mentioned, the evidence is the more satisfactory, because monkeys are animals so well known to the native hunters, they are so much sought after for food, and all their haunts are so thoroughly searched, and the localities for the separate kinds are so often the subject of communication from one hunter to another, that it is quite impossible that any well-known species can exist in a particular district, unknown to men whose lives are occupied in forming an acquaintance with the various tenants of the forests.

On the south side of the Lower Amazon, in the neighbourhood of Pará, are found two monkeys, *Mycetes beelzebub* and *Jacchus tamarin*, which do not pass the river to the north. I have never heard of monkeys swimming over any river, so that this kind of boundary might be expected to be more definite in their case than in that of other quadrupeds, most of which readily take to the water.

Towards their sources, rivers do not form a boundary between distinct species ; but those found there, though ranging on both sides of the stream, do not often extend down to the mouth.

Thus on the Upper Rio Negro and its branches are found the *Callithrix torquatus, Nyctipithecus trivirgatus*, and *Jacchus* (No. 21), none of which inhabit the Lower Rio Negro or Amazon ; they are probably confined to the granitic districts which extend from Guiana across the sources of the Rio Negro towards the Andes.

Among birds it cannot be expected that we should find many proofs of rivers limiting their range ; but there is one very remarkable instance of a genus, the three known species of which are separated by rivers, namely, the three species of genus *Psophia, P. crepitans* (Linn.), *P. viridis* (Spix), and *P. leucoptera* (Spix). The *P. crepitans* is the common trumpeter of Guiana; it extends into the interior all over the country, beyond the sources of the Rio Negro and Orinooko, towards the Andes, and down to the Amazon, both east and west of the Rio Negro, but is never found on the south side of the Amazon.

The *P. viridis* is found in the forests of Pará, at Villa Nova, on the south bank of the Amazon, and up to the Madeira, where it is found at Borba, on the east bank.

The *P. leucoptera*, a most beautiful white-backed species, is found also on the south bank of the Amazon, at São Paulo, at Ega, at Coarí, and opposite the mouth of the Rio Negro, but not east of the Madeira, where the green-backed species commences. These birds are all great favourites in the houses of the Brazilians, and all three may sometimes be seen domesticated at Barra, where they are brought by the traders from the different districts in which they are found. They are inhabitants of the dense forests, and scarcely ever fly; so that we see the reason why the rivers should so sharply divide the species, which, spreading towards each other from different directions, might otherwise become intermingled. It is not improbable that, if the two Brazilian species extend as far as the sources of the Madeira, they may be found inhabiting the same district.

Of the smaller perching-birds and insects, which doubtless would have afforded many interesting facts corroborative of those already mentioned, I have nothing to say, as my extensive collection of specimens from the Rio Negro and Upper Amazon, all ticketed for my own use, have been lost; and of course in such a question as this, the exact determination of species is everything.

The two beautiful butterflies, *Callithea sapphira* and *C. Leprieuri*, which were originally found, the former in Brazil, and the latter in Guiana, have been taken by myself on the opposite banks of the Amazon, within a few miles of each other, but neither of them on both sides of that river.

Mr. Bates has since discovered another species, named after himself, on the south side of the Amazon; and a fourth, distinct from either of them, was found by me high up in one of the north-western tributaries of the Rio Negro, so that it seems probable that distinct species of this genus inhabit the opposite shores of the Amazon.

The cock of the rock, *Rupicola crocea*, is, on the other hand, an example of a bird having its range defined by a geological formation, and by the physical character of the country. Its range extends in a curving line along the centre of the mountainous district of Guiana, across the sources of the Rio Negro and Orinooko, towards the Andes; it is thus entirely comprised in the granite formation, and in that part of it where there are numerous peaks and rocks, in which the birds make their nests.

Whether it actually reaches the Andes, or occurs in the same district with the allied *R. Peruviana*, is not known, but personal information obtained in the districts it inhabits, shows that it is confined to the narrow tract I have mentioned, between 1° south and 6° north latitude, and from the mountains of Cayenne to the Andes, south of Bogotá.

Another bird appears bounded by a geological formation. The common red-backed parrot, *Psittacus festivus*, is found all over the Lower Amazon, but, on ascending the Rio Negro, has its northern limit about St. Isabel, or just where the alluvial country ends and the granite commences; it also extends up the Japura, but does not pass over to the Uaupés, which is all in the granite district.

The fine blue macaw (*Ara hyacinthina*) inhabits the borders of the hilly country south of the Amazon, from the sea-coast probably up to the Madeira. Below Santarem, it is sometimes found close up to the banks of the Amazon, but is said never to cross that river. Its head-quarters are the upper waters of the Tocantíns, Xingú, and Tapajoz rivers.

As another instance of a bird not crossing the Amazon, I may mention the beautiful curl-crested Araçarí (*Pteroglossus Beauharnaisii*), which is found on the south side of the Upper Amazon, opposite the Rio Negro, and at Coarí and Ega, but has never been seen on the north side. The green Jacamar of Guiana also (*Galbula viridis*) occurs all along the north bank of the Amazon, but is not found on the south, where it is replaced by the *G. cyanocollis* and *G. maculicauda*, both of which occur in the neighbourhood of Pará.

# CHAPTER XVII.

## ON THE ABORIGINES OF THE AMAZON.

COMPARING the accounts given by other travellers with my own obervations, the Indians of the Amazon valley appear to be much superior, both physically and intellectually, to those of South Brazil and of most other parts of South America; they more closely resemble the intelligent and noble races inhabiting the western prairies of North America. This view is confirmed by Prince Adalbert of Prussia, who first saw the uncivilised Indians of South Brazil, and afterwards those of the Amazon; and records his surprise and admiration at the vast superiority of the latter in strength and beauty of body, and in gentleness of disposition.

I have myself had opportunities of observing the Aborigines of the interior, in places where they retain all their native customs and peculiarities. These truly uncivilised Indians are seen by few travellers, and can only be found by going far beyond the dwellings of white men, and out of the ordinary track of trade. In the neighbourhood of civilisation the Indian loses many of his peculiar customs,—changes his mode of life, his house, his costume, and his language,—becomes imbued with the prejudices of civilisation, and adopts the forms and ceremonies of the Roman Catholic religion. In this state he is a different being from the true denizen of the forests, and it may be doubted, where his civilisation goes no further than this, if he is not a degenerate and degraded one; but it is in this state alone that he is met with by most travellers in Brazil, on the banks of the Amazon, in Venezuela, and in Peru.

I do not remember a single circumstance in my travels so striking and new, or that so well fulfilled all previous expectations, as my first view of the real uncivilised inhabitants of the river Uaupés.  Though I had been already three years in the country, and had seen Indians of almost every shade of colour and every degree of civilisation, I felt that I was as much in the midst of something new and startling, as if I had been instantaneously transported to a distant and unknown country.

The Indians of the Amazon and its tributaries are of a countless variety of tribes and nations ; all of whom have peculiar languages and customs, and many of them some distinct physical characteristics.  Those now found in the city of Pará, and all about the country of the Lower Amazon, have long been civilised,—have lost their own language, and speak the Portuguese, and are known by the general name of Tapúyas, which is applied to all Indians, and seems to be a corruption of "Tupis," the name applied to the natives of the coast-districts, on the first settlement of the country.  These Indians are short, stout, and well made.  They learn all trades quickly and well, and are a quiet, good-natured, inoffensive people.  They form the crews of most of the Pará trading canoes.  Their main peculiarity consists in their short stature, which is more observable than in any other tribe I am acquainted with.  It may be as well, before proceeding further, to mention the general characteristics of the Amazon Indians, from which the particular tribes vary but very slightly.

They are, a skin of a coppery or brown colour of various shades, often nearly the tint of smooth Honduras mahogany, —jet-black straight hair, thick, and never curled,—black eyes, and very little or no beard.  With regard to their features, it is impossible to give any general characteristics.  In some the whole face is wide and rather flattened, but I never could discern an unusual obliquity of the eyes, or projection of the cheek-bones ; in many, of both sexes, the most perfect regularity of features exists, and there are numbers who in colour alone differ from a good-looking European.

Their figures are generally superb ; and I have never felt so much pleasure in gazing at the finest statue, as at these living illustrations of the beauty of the human form.  The development of the chest is such as I believe never exists in the best-formed European, exhibiting a splendid series of convex undulations, without a hollow 'n any part of it.

Some native tribes exist in the rivers Guamá, Capím, and Acarrá, just above the city of Pará, but I could learn little definite about them. High up the rivers Tocantíns and Araguáya, there are numerous tribes of tall well-formed Indians, some of whom I have seen in Pará, where they arrive in canoes from the interior. Most of them have enormously elongated ears hanging down on their shoulders, produced probably by weights suspended from the lobe in youth. On the Xingú are many native tribes, some of whom were visited by Prince Adalbert. On the next river, the Tapajóz, dwell the Mundrucus, and they extend far into the interior, across to the Madeira and to the river Purús; they are a very numerous tribe, and portions of them are now civilised. The Máras, another of the populous tribes, are also partly civilised, about the mouths of the Madeira and Rio Negro; but in the interior, and up the river Purús, many yet live in a totally wild and savage state.

All along the banks of the main streams of the Amazon, Solimões, Madeira, and Rio Negro, live Indians of various races, in a semi-civilised state, and with their peculiar habits and languages in a great measure lost. Traces of these peculiarities are, however, still to be found, in the painted pottery manufactured at Breves, the elegant calabashes of Montealegre, the curious baskets of some tribes on the Rio Negro, and the calabashes of Ega, always painted in geometrical patterns.

Commencing near Santarem, and extending among all the half-civilised Indians of the Amazon, Rio Negro, and other rivers, the Lingoa Geral, or general Indian language, is spoken. Near the more populous towns and villages, it is used indiscriminately with the Portuguese; a little further, it is often the only language known; and far up in the interior it exists in common with the native language of the tribe to which the inhabitants belong. Thus on the Lower Amazon, all the Indians can speak both Portuguese and Lingoa Geral; on the Solimões and Rio Negro, Lingoa Geral alone is generally spoken; and in the interior, on the lakes and tributaries of the Solimoes, the Múra and Jurí tongues are in common use, with the Lingoa Geral as a means of communication with the traders. Near the sources of the Rio Negro, in Venezuela, the Barré and Baníwa languages are those used among the Indians themselves.

The Lingoa Geral is the Tupi, an Indian language found in the country by the Jesuits, and modified and extended by them for use among all the tribes included in their missions. It is now spread over all the interior of Brazil, and even extends into Peru and Venezuela, as well as Bolivia and Paraguay, and is the general vehicle of communication between the Brazilian traders and the Indians. It is a simple and euphonious language, and is often preferred by Europeans who get thoroughly used to it. I knew a Frenchman who had been twenty years in the Solimões, who always conversed with his wife and children in Lingoa Geral, and could speak it with more ease than either French or Portuguese; and, in many cases, I have seen Portuguese settlers whose children were unable to speak any other language.

I shall now proceed to give some account of the various tribes that still exist, in all their native integrity, among the trackless forests of the Purús, Rio Branco, Japurá, and the rivers Uaupés and Isánna, near the sources of the Rio Negro.

As I am best acquainted with the Indians of the river Uaupés, I shall first state all I know of them, and then point out the particulars in which other nations differ from them. The tribes which inhabit the Uaupés, as far as any of the traders ascend, and of which I can get any information, are the following :—

*Up the main stream.*

1. Queianás, at São Joaquim.
2. Tariánas, about São Jeronymo.
3. Ananás (Pine-apples), below Jauarité.
4. Cobeus, about Carurú caxoeira.
5. Piraiurú (Fish's mouth).
6. Pisá (Net).
7. Carapaná (Mosquito), Jurupuri caxoeira.
8. Tapüra (Tapir).
9. Uaracú (a Fish), above Jukeira Paraná.
10. Cohídias.
11. Tucundéra (an Ant).
12. Jacamí (Trumpeter).
13. Mirití (Mauritia Palm), Baccate Paraná.
14. Omáuas.

*On the river Tiquié.*

15. Macunás.
16. Taiassú (Pig Indians).
17. Tijúco (Mud Indians).

*On Japoó Paraná.*

18. Arapásso (Woodpeckers).

*On the river Apaporís.*

19. Tucános (Toucans).
20. Uacarrás (Herons).
21. Pirá (Fish).
22. Desannas.

*On the river Quiriri.*

23. Ipécas (Ducks).
24. Gi (Axe).
25. Coúa (Wasp).

*On the river Codaiarí.*

26. Corócoró (Green Ibis).
27. Bauhúnas.
28. Tatús (Armadillos).

*On Canísi Paraná.*

29. Tenimbúca (Ashes).

*Jukeíra Paraná).*

30. Mucúra (Opossum).

These tribes have almost all of them some peculiarities of language and customs, but they all go under the general name of " Uaupés," and distinguish themselves, as a body, from the inhabitants of other rivers. Hence the river is called " Rio dos Uaupés " (the River of the Uaupés), though the proper name of it is " Uacaiarí," and it is always so termed by the Indians.

The Uaupés are generally rather tall, five feet nine or ten inches being not an uncommon height, and they are very stout and well formed. Their hair is jet-black and straight, only turning grey with extreme old age.  The men do not cut their hair, but gather it behind into a long tail, bound round with cord, and hanging down to the middle of the back, and often to the thighs ; the hair of the women hangs loose down their backs, and is cut to a moderate length.  The men have very little beard, and that little they eradicate by pulling it out ; men and women also eradicate the hair of the eyebrows, the arm-pits, and the private parts.  The colour of the skin is a light, uniform, glossy reddish-brown.

They are an agricultural people, having a permanent abode, and cultivating mandiocca (*Jatropha Manihot*), sugar-cane (*Saccharum officinarum*), sweet potatoes (*Convolvulus Batatas*), carrá, or yam (*Dioscorea* sp.), pupunha palms (*Guilielma speciosa*), cocura (a fruit like grapes), pine-apples (*Ananassa sativa*), maize (*Zea Mays*), urucú or arnotto (*Bixa Orellana*), plantains and banánas (*Musa* sp.), abios (*Lucuma Caimito*), cashews (*Anacardium occidentale*), ingás (*Ingá* sp.), peppers (*Capsicum* sp.), tobacco (*Nicotiana Tabacum*), and plants for dyes and cordage.  All, even in the most remote districts, have now iron axes and knives, though the stone axes which they formerly used are still to be found among them.  The men cut down the trees and brushwood, which, after they have lain some months to dry, are burnt; and the mandiocca is then planted by the women, together with little patches of cane, sweet potatoes, and various fruits.  The women also dig up the mandiocca, and prepare from it the bread which is their main subsistence.  The roots are brought home from the field in large baskets called aturás, made of a climber, and only manufactured by these tribes; they are then washed and peeled, this last operation being generally performed with the teeth, after which they are grated on large wooden graters about three feet long and a foot wide, rather concave, and covered all over with small sharp pieces of quartz, inserted in a regular diagonal pattern.  These graters are an article of trade in all the Upper Amazon, as they are cheaper than the copper graters used in other parts of Brazil.  The pulp is placed to drain on a large sieve made of the bark of a water-plant.  It is then put into a long elastic cylinder made of the outer rind, or bark, of a climbing palm, a species of *Desmoncus :* this is filled with the half-dry pulp, and, being hung on a cross-beam between two posts, is stretched by a lever, on the further end of which the woman sits, and thus presses out the remaining liquid. These cylinders, called "tipitis," are also a considerable article of trade, and the Portuguese and Brazilians have not yet introduced any substitute for this rude Indian press. The pulp is then turned out, a dry compact mass, which is broken up, and the hard lumps and fibres picked out, when it is at once roasted on large flat ovens from four to six feet in diameter, with a sloping rim about six inches high. These ovens are well made, of clay mixed with the ashes of the bark of a tree called "caripé," and are supported on walls of mud about two feet high, with a large opening on one side, in which to make a fire of logs of wood. The mandiocca cakes, or "beijú," thus prepared, are sweet and agreeable to the taste ; but the Indians generally first soak the roots some days in water, which softens and ferments them, and gives the bread a sour taste, much relished by the natives, but not generally so agreeable to Europeans. The bread is made fresh every day, as when it gets cold and dry it is far less palatable. The women thus have plenty to do, for every other day at least they have to go to the field, often a mile or two distant, to fetch the root, and every day to grate, prepare, and bake the bread ; as it forms by far the greater part of their food, and they often pass days without eating anything else, especially when the men are engaged in clearing the forest. For the greater part of the year, however, the men go daily to fish, and at these times they have a good supply of this their favourite food. Meat and game they only eat occasionally ; they prefer jabutís, or land-tortoises, monkeys, inambus (*Tinamus* sp.), toucans, and the smaller species of wild pig (*Dicotyles torquatus*). But they will not eat the large wild pig (*D. labiatus*), the anta (*Tapirus Americanus*), or the white-rumped mutun (*Crax globicera?*). They consume great quantities of peppers (species of *Capsicum*), preferring the small red ones, which are of excessive pungency : when they have no fish, they boil several pounds of these peppers in a little water, and dip their bread into the fiery soup thus formed.

The poisonous juice expressed from the mandiocca root, when fermented and boiled in various ways, forms sauces and peculiarly flavoured drinks, of which they are very fond. In making their bread they have a peculiarity, not noticed among the neighbouring tribes, of extracting pure tapioca from the mandiocca, and, by mixing this with the ordinary pulp, forming a very superior cake.

They use plantains extensively, eating them as a fruit, and making a mingau, or gruel, by boiling and beating them into a pulp, which is a very agreeable food. From the fruits of the Baccába, Patawá, and Assai palms (*Œnocarpus Baccaba, Œ. Batawa, Euterpe oleracea* and allied species), they produce wholesome and nourishing drinks.

Besides these they make much use of sweet potatoes, yams, roasted corn, and many forest fruits, from all of which, and from mandiocca cakes, they make fermented drinks, which go under the general name of "caxirí." That made from the mandiocca is the most agreeable, and much resembles good table-beer. At their feasts and dances they consume immense quantities of it, and it does not seem to produce any bad effects. They also use, on these occasions, an intensely exciting preparation of the root of a climber,—it is called capí, and the manner of using it I have described in my Narrative (page 205).

The weapons of these Indians are bows and arrows, gravatánas, lances, clubs, and also small hand-nets, and rods and lines, for catching fish.

Their bows are of different kinds of hard elastic wood, well made, and from five to six feet long. The string is either of the "tucum" leaf fibre (*Astrocaryum vulgare*), or of the inner bark of trees called "tururi." The arrows are of various kinds, from five to seven feet long. The shaft is made of the flower-stalk of the arrow-grass (*Gynerium saccharinum*). In the war-arrows, or "curubís," the head is made of hard wood, carefully pointed, and by some tribes armed with the serrated spine of the ray-fish : it is thickly anointed with poison, and notched in two or three places so as to break off in the wound. Arrows for shooting fish are now almost always made with iron heads, sold by the traders, but many still use heads made of monkeys' bones, with a barb, to retain a hold of the fish : the iron heads are bent at an angle, so that the lower part projects and forms a barb, and are securely fastened on with twine and pitch. Lighter arrows are made for shooting birds and other small game, and these alone are feathered at the base. The feathers generally used are from the wings of the macaw, and, in putting them on, the Indian shows his knowledge of the principle which is applied in the spirally-grooved rifle-barrel : three feathers are used, and they are all secured spirally, so as to form a little screw on the base of the arrow, the effect of which of course must be, that the arrow revolves rapidly in its onward progress, and this no doubt tends to keep it in a direct course.

The gravatána and small poisoned arrows are made and used exactly as I have already described in my Narrative (page 147).

The small hand-nets used for catching fish are of two kinds, —a small ring-net, like a landing-net, and one spread between two slender sticks, just like the large folding-nets of entomologists : these are much used in the rapids, and among rocks and eddies, and numbers of fish are caught with them. They also use the rod and line, and consume an enormous quantity of hooks : there are probably not less than a hundred thousand fish-hooks sold every year in the river Uaupés ; yet there are still to be found among them many of their own hooks, ingeniously made of palm-spines. They have many other ways of catching fish : one is by a small cone of wicker, called a "matapí," which is placed in some little current in the gapó ; the larger end is entirely open, and it appears at first sight quite incapable of securing the fish, yet it catches great quantities, for when the fish get in they have no room to turn round, and cannot swim backwards, and three or four are often found jammed in the end of these little traps, with the scales and skin quite rubbed off their heads by their vain endeavours to proceed onwards. Other matapís are larger and more cylindrical, with a reversed conical mouth (as in our wire rat-traps), to prevent the return of the fish : these are often made of a very large size, and are placed in little forest-streams, and in narrow channels between rocks, where the fish, in passing up, must enter them. But the best method of procuring fish, and that which has been generally adopted by the Europeans in the country, is with the Cacoaries, or fish-weirs. These are principally used at high-water, when fish are scarce : they are formed at the margin of rivers, supported by strong posts, which are securely fixed at the time of low-water, when the place of the weir is quite dry ; to these posts is secured a high fence of split palm-stems, forming an entering angle, with a narrow opening into a fenced enclosure. Fish almost always travel against the stream, and generally abound more at the sides where the current is less rapid : they are guided by the side-wings of the weir into the narrow opening, from which they cannot find their way out. They are obtained by diving into the weir, and then catching them with the pisá (small net), or with the hand, or sticking them with a knife. In these cacoaries every kind of fish is caught, from the largest to the smallest, as well as river tortoises and turtles. The Indian generally feels about well with a rod before entering a cacoarí, to ascertain if it contains an electrical eel, in which case he gets it out first with a net. The Piránhas, species of *Serrasalmo*, are also rather dangerous, for I have seen an Indian boy return from the cacoary with his finger bitten off by one of them.

The " Geraú," is yet on a larger scale than the Cacoarí. It is used only in the cataracts, and is very similar to the eel-traps used at mills and sluices in England. It is a large wooden sieve, supported in the midst of a cataract, so that the full force of the water dashes through it. All the fish which are carried down by the violence of the current are here caught, and their numbers are often so great as to supply a whole village with food. At many of the falls on the Uaupés they make these geraús, which require the united exertions of the inhabitants to construct them ; huge timbers having to be planted in every crevice of the rocks, to withstand the strength of the torrent of water brought down by the winter's floods.

All the fish not used at the time are placed on a little platform of sticks over the fire, till they are so thoroughly dried and imbued with smoke, as to keep good any length of time. They are then used for voyages, and to sell to travellers, but, having no salt, are a very tasteless kind of food.

Salt is not so much sought after by these Indians as by many other tribes ; for they will generally prefer fish-hooks and beads in payment for any articles you may purchase of them. Peppers seem to serve them in place of salt. They do, however, extract from the fruits of the Inajá palm (*Maximiliana regia*) and the Jará palm (*Leopoldinia major*), and also from the Carurú (a species of *Lacis* very common on the rocks in the falls), a kind of flour which has a saline taste, and with which they season their food. The Carurú, indeed, has quite the smell of salt water, and is excellent eating, both boiled as a vegetable, or with oil and vinegar as a salad.

All the tribes of the Uaupés construct their dwellings after one plan, which is peculiar to them. Their houses are the abode of numerous families, sometimes of a whole tribe. The plan is a parallelogram, with a semicircle at one end. The dimensions of one at Jauarité were one hundred and fifteen feet in length, by seventy-five broad, and about thirty high. This house would hold about a dozen families, consisting of near a hundred individuals. In times of feasts and dances, three or four hundred are accommodated in them. The roof is supported on fine cylindrical columns, formed of the trunks of trees, and beautifully straight and smooth. In the centre a clear opening is left, twenty feet wide, and on the sides are little partitions of palm-leaf thatch, dividing off rooms for the separate families : here are kept the private household utensils, weapons, and ornaments ; while the rest of the space contains, on each side, the large ovens and gigantic pans for making caxirí, and, in the centre, a place for the children to play, and for their dances to take place. These houses are built with much labour and skill ; the main supporters, beams, rafters, and other parts, are straight, well proportioned to the strength required, and bound together with split creepers, in a manner that a sailor would admire. The thatch is of the leaf of some one of the numerous palms so well adapted to the purpose, and is laid on with great compactness and regularity. The side-walls, which are very low, are formed also of palm thatch, but so thick and so well bound together, that neither arrow nor bullet will penetrate them. At the gable-end is a large door-way, about six feet wide and eight or ten high : the door is a large palm-mat, hung from the top, supported by a pole during the day, and let down at night. At the semicircular end is a smaller door, which is the private entrance of the Tushaúa, or chief, to whom this part of the house exclusively belongs. The lower part of the gable-end, on each side of the entrance, is covered with the thick bark of a tree unrolled, and standing vertically. Above this is a loose hanging of palm-leaves, between the fissures of which the smoke from the numerous fires within finds an exit. In some cases this gable-end is much ornamented with symmetrical figures painted in colours, as at Carurú caxoeira.

The furniture consists principally of maqueiras, or hammocks, made of string, twisted from the fibres of the leaves of the *Mauritia flexuosa:* they are merely an open network of parallel threads, crossed by others at intervals of a foot; the loops at each end have a cord passed through them, by which they are hung up. The Uaupés make great quantities of string of this and other fibres, twisting it on their breasts or thighs, with great rapidity.

They have always in their houses a large supply of earthen pots, pans, pitchers, and cooking utensils, of various sizes, which they make of clay from the river and brooks, mixed with the ashes of the caripé bark, and baked in a temporary furnace. They have also great quantities of small saucer-shaped baskets, called "Balaios," which are much esteemed down the river, and are the subject of a considerable trade.

Two tribes in the lower part of the river, the Tariános and Tucános, make a curious little stool, cut from a solid block of wood, and neatly painted and varnished ; these, which take many days to finish, are sold for about a pennyworth of fish-hooks.

Their canoes are all made out of a single tree, hollowed and forced open by the cross-benches ; they are very thick in the middle, to resist the wear and tear they are exposed to among the rocks and rapids ; they are often forty feet long, but smaller ones are generally preferred. The paddles are about three feet long, with an oval blade, and are each cut out of one piece of wood.

These people are as free from the encumbrances of dress as it is possible to conceive. The men wear only a small piece of tururí passed between the legs, and twisted on to a string round the lions. Even such a costume as this is dispensed with by the women : they have no dress or covering whatever, but are entirely naked. This is the universal custom among the Uaupés Indians, from which, in a state of nature, they never depart. Paint, with these people, seems to be looked upon as a sufficient clothing ; they are never without it on some part of their bodies, but it is at their festivals that they exhibit all their art in thus decorating their persons : the colours they use are red, yellow, and black, and they dispose them generally in regular patterns, similar to those with which they ornament their stools, their canoes, and other articles of **furniture.**

They pour the juice of a tree, which stains a deep blue-black, on their heads, and let it run in streams all down their backs; and the red and yellow are often disposed in large round spots upon the cheeks and forehead.

The use of ornaments and trinkets of various kinds is almost confined to the men. The women wear a bracelet on the wrists, but none on the neck, and no comb in the hair; they have a garter below the knee, worn tight from infancy, for the purpose of swelling out the calf, which they consider a great beauty. While dancing in their festivals, the women wear a small tanga, or apron, made of beads, prettily arranged; it is only about six inches square, but is never worn at any other time, and immediately the dance is over, it is taken off.

The men, on the other hand, have the hair carefully parted and combed on each side, and tied in a queue behind. In the young men, it hangs in long locks down their necks, and, with the comb, which is invariably carried stuck in the top of the head, gives to them a most feminine appearance: this is increased by the large necklaces and bracelets of beads, and the careful extirpation of every symptom of beard. Taking these circumstances into consideration, I am strongly of opinion that the story of the Amazons has arisen from these feminine-looking warriors encountered by the early voyager. I am inclined to this opinion, from the effect they first produced on myself, when it was only by close examination I saw that they were men; and, were the front parts of their bodies and their breasts covered with shields, such as they always use, I am convinced any person seeing them for the first time would conclude they were women. We have only therefore to suppose that tribes having similar customs to those now living on the river Uaupés, inhabited the regions where the Amazons were reported to have been seen, and we have a rational explanation of what has so much puzzled all geographers. The only objection to this explanation is, that traditions are said to exist among the natives, of a nation of " women without husbands." Of this tradition, however, I was myself unable to obtain any trace, and I can easily imagine it entirely to have arisen from the suggestions and inquiries of Europeans themselves. When the story of the Amazons was first made known, it became of course a point with all future travellers to verify it, or if possible get a glimpse of these warlike ladies. The Indians must no doubt have been overwhelmed with questions and suggestions about them, and they, thinking that the white men must know best, would transmit to their descendants and families the idea that such a nation did exist in some distant part of the country. Succeeding travellers, finding traces of this idea among the Indians, would take it as a proof of the existence of the Amazons; instead of being merely the effect of a mistake at the first, which had been unknowingly spread among them by preceding travellers, seeking to obtain some evidence on the subject.

In my communications and inquiries among the Indians on various matters, I have always found the greatest caution necessary, to prevent one's arriving at wrong conclusions. They are always apt to affirm that which they see you wish to believe, and, when they do not at all comprehend your question, will unhesitatingly answer, "Yes." I have often in this manner obtained, as I thought, information, which persons better acquainted with the facts have assured me was quite erroneous. These observations, however, must only be taken to apply to those almost uncivilised nations who do not understand, at all clearly, any language in which you can communicate with them. I have always been able to rely on what is obtained from Indians speaking Portuguese readily, and I believe that much trustworthy information can be obtained from them. Such, however, is not the case with the wild tribes, who are totally incapable of understanding any connected sentence of the language in which they are addressed; and I fear the story of the Amazons must be placed with those of the wild man-monkeys, which Humboldt mentions and which tradition I also met with, and of the "curupíra," or demon of the woods, and "carbunculo," of the Upper Amazon and Peru; but of which superstitions we have no such satisfactory elucidation as I think has been now given of the warlike Amazons.

To return to our Uaupés Indians and their toilet. We find their daily costume enlivened with a few other ornaments; a circlet of parrots' tail-feathers is generally worn round the head, and the cylindrical white quartz-stone, already described in my Narrative (p. 191), is invariably carried on the breast, suspended from a necklace of black seeds.

At festivals and dances they decorate themselves with a complicated costume of feather head-dresses, cinctures, armlets, and leg ornaments, which I have sufficiently described in the account of their dances (p. 202).

We will now describe some peculiarities connected with their births, marriages, and deaths.

The women are generally delivered in the house, though sometimes in the forest. When a birth takes place in the house, everything is taken out of it, even the pans and pots, and bows and arrows, till the next day; the mother takes the child to the river and washes herself and it, and she generally remains in the house, not doing any work, for four or five days.

The children, more particularly the females, are restricted to a particular food : they are not allowed to eat the meat of any kind of game, nor of fish, except the very small bony kinds ; their food principally consisting of mandiocca-cake and fruits.

On the first signs of puberty in the girls, they have to undergo an ordeal. For a month previously, they are kept secluded in the house, and allowed only a small quantity of bread and water. All relatives and friends of the parents are then assembled, bringing, each of them, pieces of "sipó" (an elastic climber) ; the girl is then brought out, perfectly naked, into the midst of them, when each person present gives her five or six severe blows with the sipó across the back and breast, till she falls senseless, and it sometimes happens, dead. If she recovers, it is repeated four times, at intervals of six hours, and it is considered an offence to the parents not to strike hard. During this time numerous pots of all kinds of meat and fish have been prepared, when the sipós are dipped in them and given to her to lick, and she is then considered a woman, and allowed to eat anything, and is marriageable.

The boys undergo a somewhat similar ordeal, but not so severe ; which initiates them into manhood, and allows them to see the Juruparí music, which will be presently described.

Tattooing is very little practised by these Indians ; they all, however, have a row of circular punctures along the arm, and one tribe, the Tucános, are distinguished from the rest by three vertical blue lines on the chin ; and they also pierce the lower lip, through which they hang three little threads of white beads.

All the tribes bore their ears, and wear in them little pieces of grass, ornamented with feathers. The Cobeus alone expand the hole to so large a size, that a bottle-cork could be inserted : they ordinarily wear a plug of wood in it, but, on festas, insert a little bunch of arrows.

The men generally have but one wife, but there is no special limit, and many have two or three, and some of the chiefs more ; the elder one is never turned away, but remains the mistress of the house. They have no particular ceremony at their marriages, except that of always carrying away the girl by force, or making a show of doing so, even when she and her parents are quite willing. They do not often marry with re-lations, or even neighbours,—preferring those from a distance, or even from other tribes. When a young man wishes to have the daughter of another Indian, his father sends a message to say he will come with his son and relations to visit him. The girl's father guesses what it is for, and, if he is agreeable, makes preparations for a grand festival : it lasts, perhaps, two or three days, when the bridegroom's party suddenly seize the bride, and hurry her off to their canoes ; no attempt is made to pre-vent them, and she is then considered as married.

Some tribes, as the Uacarrás, have a trial of skill at shooting with the bow and arrow, and if the young man does not show himself a good marksman, the girl refuses him, on the ground that he will not be able to shoot fish and game enough for the family.

The dead are almost always buried in the houses, with their bracelets, tobacco-bag, and other trinkets upon them : they are buried the same day they die, the parents and relations keeping up a continual mourning and lamentation over the body, from the death to the time of interment ; a few days afterwards, a great quantity of caxirí is made, and all friends and relations invited to attend, to mourn for the dead, and to dance, sing, and cry to his memory. Some of the large houses have more than a hundred graves in them, but when the houses are small, and very full, the graves are made outside.

The Tariánas and Tucános, and some other tribes, about a month after the funeral, disinter the corpse, which is then much decomposed, and put it in a great pan, or oven, over the fire, till all the volatile parts are driven off with a most horrible odour, leaving only a black carbonaceous mass, which is pounded into a fine powder, and mixed in several large couchés (vats made of hollowed trees) of caxirí : this is drunk by the assembled company till all is finished ; they believe that thus the virtues of the deceased will be transmitted to the drinkers.

The Cobeus alone, in the Uaupés, are real cannibals : they eat those of other tribes whom they kill in battle, and even make war for the express purpose of procuring human flesh for food. When they have more than they can consume at once, they smoke-dry the flesh over the fire, and preserve it for food a long time. They burn their dead, and drink the ashes in caxirí, in the same manner as described above.

Every tribe and every " malocca " (as their houses are called) has its chief, or " Tushaúa," who has only a limited authority, principally in war, in making festivals, and in repairing the malocca and keeping the village clean, and in planting the mandiocca-fields ; he also treats with the traders, and supplies them with men to pursue their journeys. The succession of these chiefs is strictly hereditary in the male line, or through the female to her husband, who may be a stranger : their regular hereditary chief is never superseded, however stupid, dull, or cowardly he may be. They have very little law of any kind ; but what they have is of strict retaliation,—an eye for an eye and a tooth for a tooth ; and a murder is punished or revenged in the same manner and by the same weapon with which it was committed.

They have numerous " Pagés," a kind of priests, answering to the " medicine-men " of the North American Indians. These are believed to have great power : they cure all diseases by charms, applied by strong blowing and breathing upon the party to be cured, and by the singing of certain songs and incantations. They are also believed to have power to kill enemies, to bring or send away rain, to destroy dogs or game, to make the fish leave a river, and to afflict with various diseases. They are much consulted and believed in, and are well paid for their services. An Indian will give almost all his wealth to a pagé, when he is threatened with any real or imaginary danger.

They scarcely seem to think that death can occur naturally, always imputing it either to direct poisoning or the charms of some enemy, and, on this supposition, will proceed to revenge it. This they generally do by poisons, of which they have many which are most deadly in their effects : they are given at some festival in a bowl of caxirí, which it is good manners always to empty, so that the whole dose is sure to be taken. One of the poisons often used is most terrible in its effects, causing the tongue and throat, as well as the intestines, to putrefy and rot away, so that the sufferer lingers some days in the greatest agony : this is of course again retaliated, on perhaps the wrong party, and thus a long succession of murders may result from a mere groundless suspicion in the first instance.

I cannot make out that they have any belief that can be called a religion. They appear to have no definite idea of a God ; if asked who they think made the rivers, and the forests, and the sky, they will reply that they do not know, or sometimes that they suppose it was "Tupánau," a word that appears to answer to God, but of which they understand nothing. They have much more definite ideas of a bad spirit, "Juruparí," or Devil, whom they fear, and endeavour through their pagés to propitiate. When it thunders, they say the "Juruparí" is angry, and their idea of natural death is that the "Juruparí" kills them. At an eclipse they believe that this bad spirit is killing the moon, and they make all the noise they can to frighten him away.

One of their most singular superstitions is about the musical instruments they use at their festivals, which they call the Juruparí music. These consist of eight or sometimes twelve pipes, or trumpets, made of bamboos or palm-stems hollowed out, some with trumpet-shaped mouths of bark and with mouth-holes of clay and leaf. Each pair of instruments gives a distinct note, and they produce a rather agreeable concert, something resembling clarionets and bassoons. These instrument, however, are with them such a mystery that no woman must ever see them, on pain of death. They are always kept in sone igaripé, at a distance from the malocca, whence they are brought on particular occasions : when the sound of them is heard approaching, every woman retires into the woods, or into some adjoining shed, which they generally have near, and remains invisible till after the ceremony is over, when the instruments are taken away to their hiding-place, and the women come out of their concealment. Should any female be supposed to have seen them, either by accident or design, she is invaribly executed, generally by poison, and a father will not hesitate to sacrifice his daughter, or a husband his wife, on such an occasion.

They have many other prejudices with regard to women. They believe that if a woman, during her pregnancy, eats of any meat, any other animal partaking of it will suffer : if a domestic animal or tame bird, it will die ; if a dog, it will be for the future incapable of hunting ; and even a man will ever after be unable to shoot that particular kind of game. An Indian, who was one of my hunters, caught a fine cock of the rock, and gave it to his wife to feed, but the poor woman was obliged to live herself on cassava-bread and fruits, and abstain entirely from all animal food, peppers, and salt, which it was believed would cause the bird to die ; notwithstanding all precautions, however, the bird did die, and the woman got a beating from her husband, because he thought she had not been sufficiently rigid in her abstinence from the prohibited articles.

Most of these peculiar practices and superstitions are retained with much tenacity, even by those Indians who are nominally civilised and Christian, and many of them have been even adopted by the Europeans resident in the country : there are actually Portuguese in the Rio Negro who fear the power of the Indian pagés, and who fully believe and act on all the Indian superstitions respecting women.

The river Uaupés is the channel by which European manufactures find their way into the extensive and unknown regions between the Rio Guaviare on the one side, and the Japurá on the other. About a thousand pounds worth of goods enter the Uaupés yearly, mostly in axes, cutlasses, knives, fish-hooks, arrow-heads, salt, mirrors, beads, and a few cottons.

The articles given in exchange are salsaparilha, pitch, farinha, string, hammocks, and Indian stools, baskets, feather ornaments, and curiosities. The salsaparilha is by far the most valuable product, and is the only one exported. Great quantities of articles of European manufacture are exchanged by the Indians with those of remote districts, for the salsa which they give to the traders ; and thus numerous tribes, among whom no civilised man has ever yet penetrated, are well supplied with iron goods, and send the product of their labour to European markets.

In order to give some idea of the state of industry and the

arts among these people, I subjoin a list of articles which I collected when among them, to illustrate their manners, customs, and state of civilisation, but which were unfortunately all lost on my passage home.

LIST OF ARTICLES MANUFACTURED BY THE INDIANS
OF THE RIO DOS UAUPÉS.

*Household Furniture and Utensils.*

1. Hammocks, or maqueiras, of palm-fibre, of various materials, colours, and texture.
2. Small wooden stools, of various sizes, painted and varnished. (Plate XIV. *d.*)
3. Flat baskets of plaited bark, in regular patterns and of various colours.
4. Deeper baskets, called "Aturás." (Plate XIII. *d.*)
5. Calabashes and gourds, of various shapes and sizes.
6. Water-pitchers of earthenware.
7. Pans of earthenware for cooking.

*Articles used in the Manufacture of Mandiocca Bread.*

8. Mandiocca graters, of quartz fragments set in wood. (Plate XIII. *a.*)
9. Tipitis, or wicker elastic pressure cylinders.
10. Wicker sieves for straining the pulp.
11. Ovens for roasting cassava-bread and farinha. (Plate XIII. *b.*)
12. Plaited fans for blowing the fire and turning the cakes.

*Weapons used in War, Hunting, and Fishing.*

13. Bows of various woods and different sizes.
14. Quivers of curabís, or poisoned war-arrows.
15. Arrows with heads of monkey-bones.
16. Arrows, with iron heads, for shooting fish.
17. Gravatánas, or blow-tubes, from eight to fourteen feet long.
18. Wicker and wooden quivers, with poisoned arrows for them.
19. Small pots and calabashes, with the curarí or ururí poison.

*a*. Mandioca grater.   *b*. Oven.   *c*. Fire-place.   *d*. Basket.

INDIAN IMPLEMENTS AND DOMESTIC ARTICLES.

PLATE XIII.

20. Large carved clubs of hard wood.
21. Carved and feather ornamented lances.
22. Large circular shields of wicker-work.
23. Ditto, covered with tapir's skin.
24. Nets for fishing (Pisás).
25. Rod and line for fishing.
26. Palm-spine fish-hooks.
27. Small wicker traps for catching fish (Matapís).

### Musical Instruments.

28. A small drum.
29. Eight large trumpets, the Jurupari music.
30. Numerous fifes and flutes of reeds.
31. Fifes made of deer-bones.
31 a. Whistle of a deer's skull.
32. Vibrating instruments of tortise and turtle shells.

### Ornaments, Dress, and Miscellaneous.

33. About twenty distinct articles, forming the feather head-dress.
34. Combs of palm-wood, ornamented with feathers. (Plate XIV. a.)
35. Necklaces of seeds and beads.
36. Bored cylindrical quartz-stone.
37. Copper earrings, and wooden plugs for the ears.
38. Armlet of feathers, beads, seeds, etc.
39. Girdle of jaguars' teeth.
40. Numbers of cords, made of the "coroá" fibre, mixed with the hair of monkeys and jaguars,—making a soft elastic cord used for binding up the hair, and various purposes of ornament.
41. Painted aprons, or "tangas," made from the inner bark of a tree.
42. Women's bead tangas.
43. Rattles and ornaments for the legs.
44. Garters strongly knitted of "coroá."
45. Packages and carved calabashes, filled with a red pigment called "crajurú."
46. Large cloths of prepared bark.
47. Very large carved wooden forks for holding cigars. (Plate XIV. b.)

48. Large cigars used at festivals.
49. Spathes of the Bussu palm (*Manicaria saccifera*), used for preserving feather-ornaments, etc.
50. Square mats.
51. Painted earthen pot, used for holding the "capi" at festivals.
52. Small pot of dried peppers.
53. Rattles used in dancing, formed of calabashes, carved, and ornamented with small stones inside. (Plate XIV. *c.*) (Maracás.)
54. Painted dresses of prepared bark (tururí).
55. Balls of string, of various materials and degrees of fineness.
56. Bottle-shaped baskets, for preserving the edible ants.
57. Tinder-boxes of bambo carved, and filled with tinder from an ant's nest.
58. Small canoe hollowed from a tree.
59. Paddles used with ditto.
60. Triangular tool, used for making the small stools.
61. Pestles and mortars, used for pounding peppers and tobacco.
62. Bark bag, full of sammaúma, the silk-cotton of a *Bombax*, used for making blowing-arrows.
63. Chest of plaited palm-leaves, used for holding feather-ornaments.
64. Stone axes, used before the introduction of iron.
65. Clay cylinders, for supporting cooking utensils. (Plate XIII. *c.*) *

The Indians of the river Isánna are few in comparison with those of the Uaupés, the river not being so large or so productive of fish.

The tribes are named—
    Baníwas, or Manívas (Mandiocca).
    Arikénas.
    Bauatánas.
    Ciuçí (Stars).

* Specimens of Nos. 1, 2, 3, 9, 13, 14, 16, 17, 18, 21, 34, 36, 41, 47, 49, and 63, of this list, have been sent home by my friend R. Spruce, Esq., and may be seen in the very interesting Museum at the Royal Botanical Gardens, at Kew

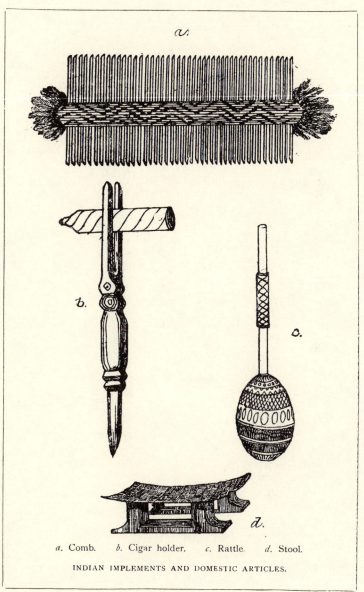

*a*. Comb.   *b*. Cigar holder.   *c*. Rattle.   *d*. Stool.

INDIAN IMPLEMENTS AND DOMESTIC ARTICLES.

PLATE XIV.

Coatí (the *Nasua coatimundi*).
Juruparí (Devils).
Ipéca (Ducks).
Papunauás, the name of a river, a tributary of the Guaviáre, but which has its sources close to the Isánna.

These tribes are much alike in all their customs, differing only in their languages ; as a whole, however, they offer remarkable points of difference from those of the river Uaupés.

In stature and appearance they are very similar, but they have rather more beard, and do not pull out the hair of the body and face, and they cut the hair of their head with a knife, or, wanting that, with a hard sharp grass. Thus, the absence of the long queue of hair forms a striking characteristic difference in their appearance.

In their dress they differ in the women always wearing a small tanga of turúri, instead of going perfectly naked, as among the Uaupés ; they also wear more necklaces and bracelets, and the men fewer, and the latter do not make use of so many feather-ornaments and decorations in their festivals.

Each family has a separate house, which is small, of a square shape, and possesses both a door and windows ; and the houses are collected together in little scattered villages. The Isánna Indians make small flat baskets like those of the Uaupés, but not the stools, nor the aturás, neither have they the white cylindrical stone which the others so much esteem. They marry one, two, or three wives, and prefer relations, marrying with cousins, uncles with nieces, and nephews with aunts, so that in a village all are connected. The men are more warlike and morose in their disposition than the Uaupés, by whom they are much feared. They bury their dead in their houses, and mourn for them a long time, but make no feast on the occasion. The Isánna Indians are said not to be nearly so numerous, nor to increase so rapidly, as the Uaupés; which may perhaps be owing to their marrying with relations, while the former prefer strangers.

The Arekaínas make war against other tribes, to obtain prisoners for food, like the Cobeus. In their superstitions and religious ideas they much resemble the Uaupés.

The Macás are one of the lowest and most uncivilised tribes of Indians in the Amazon district. They inhabit the forests and serras about the rivers Marié, Curicuriarí, and Urubaxí, and live a wandering life, having no houses and no fixed place of abode, and of course no clothing; they have little or no iron, and use the tusks of the wild pig to scrape and form their bows and arrows, and they make a most deadly kind of poison to anoint them. At night they sleep on a bundle of palm-leaves, or stick up a few leaves to make a shed if it rains, or sometimes, with "sipós," construct a rude hammock, which, however, serves only once. They eat all kinds of birds and fish, roasted or boiled in palm-spathes; and all sorts of wild fruits.

The Macás often attack the houses of other Indians situated in solitary places, and murder all the inhabitants; and they have even depopulated and caused the removal of several villages. All the other tribes of Indians catch them and keep them as slaves, and in most villages you will see some of them. They are distinguishable at once from the surrounding tribes by a wavy and almost curly hair, and by being rather lanky and ill-formed in their limbs: I am inclined, however, to think that this latter is partly owing to their mode of life, and the hardships and exposure they have to undergo; and some that I have seen in the houses of traders have been as well-formed and handsome as any of the other Indian tribes.

The Curetús are a nation inhabiting the country about the river Apaporís, between the Japurá and Uaupés. I met with some Indians of this tribe on the Rio Negro, and the only peculiarity I observed in them was, that their cheek-bones were rather more prominent than usual. From them, and from an Isánna Indian who had visited them, I obtained some information about their customs.

They wear their hair long like the Uaupés, and, like them, the women go entirely naked; and they paint their bodies, but do not tattoo. Their houses are large and circular, with walls of thatch, and a high conical capped roof, made like some chimney-pots, with the upper part overlapping, so as to let the smoke escape without allowing the rain to enter. They do not wander about, but reside in small permanent villages, governed by a chief, and are said to be long-lived and very peaceable, never quarrelling or making war with other nations. The men have but one wife. There are no pagés, or priests, among them, and they have no ideas of a superior Being. They cultivate mandiocca, maize, and other fruits, and use game more than fish for food. No civilised man has ever been among them, so they have no salt, and a very scanty supply of iron, and obtain fire by friction. It is said also that they differ from most other tribes in making no intoxicating drinks. Their language is full of harsh and aspirated sounds, and is somewhat allied to those of the Tucanos and Cobeus among the Uaupés.

In the lower part of the Japurá reside the "Uaenambeus," or Humming-bird Indians. I met with some of them in the Rio Negro, and obtained some information as to their customs and language. In most particulars they much resemble the last-mentioned tribe, particularly in their circular houses, their food, and mode of life. Like them they weave the fibres of the Tucúm palm-leaf (*Astrocaryum vulgare*) to make their hammocks, whereas the Uaupés and Isánna Indians always use the leaf of the Mirití (*Mauritia flexuosa*). They are distinguished from other tribes by a small blue mark on the upper lip. They have from one to four wives, and the women always wear a small apron of bark.

Closely allied to these are the Jurís of the Solimões, between the Içá and Japurá. A number of them have migrated to the Rio Negro, and become settled and partly civilised there. They are remarkable for a custom of tattooing in a circle (not in a square, as in a plate in Dr. Prichard's work) round the mouth, so as exactly to resemble the little black-mouthed squirrel-monkeys (*Callithrix sciureus*); from this cause they are often called the Juripixúnas (Black Juris), or by the Brazilians "Bocapreitos" (Black-mouths). From this strange errors have arisen: we find in some maps the note "Juries, curly-haired Negroes," whereas they are pure straight-haired Indians. They are good servants for canoe and agricultural work, and are the most skilful of all in the use of the gravatána, or blow-pipe.

In the same neighbourhood are Miránhas, who are cannibals; and the Ximánas and Cauxánas, who kill all their first-born children: in fact, between the Upper Amazon, the Guaviare, and the Andes, there is a region as large as England, whose inhabitants are entirely uncivilised and unknown.

On the south side of the Amazon also, between the Madeira and the Uaycáli, and extending to the Andes of Peru and Bolivia, is a still larger tract of unknown virgin forest, uninhabited by a single civilised man: here reside numerous nations of the native American race, known only by the reports of the border tribes, who form the communication between them and the traders of the great rivers.

One of the best-known and most regularly visited rivers of this great tract is the Purús, whose mouth is a short distance above the Rio Negro, but whose sources a three months' voyage does not reach. Of the Indians found on the banks of this river I have been able to get some information.

Five tribes are met with by the traders :—

1. Múras, from the mouth to sixteen days' voyage up.

2. Purupurús, from thence to about thirty days' voyage up.

3. Catauxís, in the district of the Purupurús, but in the igaripés and lakes inland.

4. Jamamarís, inland on the west bank.

5. Jubirís, on the river-banks above the Purupurús.

The Múras are rather a tall race, have a good deal of beard for Indians, and the hair of the head is slightly crisp and wavy. They used formerly to go naked, but now the men all wear trousers and shirts, and the women petticoats. Their houses are grouped together in small villages, and are scarcely ever more than a roof supported on posts ; very rarely do they take the trouble to build any walls. They make no hammocks, but hang up three bands of a bark called "invíra," on which they sleep ; but the more civilised now purchase of the traders hammocks made by other Indians. They practise scarcely any cultivation, except sometimes a little mandiocca, but generally live on wild fruits, and abundance of fish and game : their food is entirely produced by the river, consisting of the *Manatus*, or cow-fish, which is as good as beef, turtles, and various kinds of fish, all of which are in great abundance, so that the traders say there are no people who live so well as the Múras ; they have therefore no occasion for gravatánas, which they do not make, but have a great variety of bows and arrows and harpoons, and construct very good canoes. They now all cut their hair ; the old men have a large hole in their lower lip filled up with a piece of wood, but this custom is now disused. Each man has two or three wives, but there is no ceremony of marriage ; and they bury their dead sometimes in the house, but more commonly outside, and put all the goods of the deceased upon his grave. The women use necklaces and bracelets of beads, and the men tie the seeds of the india-rubber tree to their legs when they dance. Each village has a Tushaúa: the succession is hereditary, but the chief has very little power. They have pagés, whom they believe to have much skill, and are afraid of, and pay well. They were formerly very warlike, and made many attacks upon the Europeans, but are now much more peaceful; and are the most skilful of all Indians in shooting turtles and fish, and in catching the cow-fish. They still use their own language among themselves, though they also understand the Lingoa Geral. The white traders obtain from them salsaparilha, oil from turtles' eggs and the cow-fish, Brazil-nuts, and estopa, which is the bark of the young Brazil-nut tree (*Bertholletia excelsa*), used extensively for caulking canoes; and pay them in cotton goods, harpoon and arrow-heads, hooks, beads, knives, cutlasses, etc.

The next tribes, the Purupurús, are in many respects very peculiar, and differ remarkably in their habits from any other nation we have yet described. They call themselves Pamouirís, but are always called by the Brazilians Purupurús, a name also applied to a peculiar disease, with which they are almost all afflicted: this consists in the body being spotted and blotched with white, brown, or nearly black patches, of irregular size and shape, and having a very disagreeable appearance: when young, their skins are clear, but as they grow up, they invariably become more or less spotted. Other Indians are sometimes seen afflicted in this manner, and they are then said to have the Purupurú; though it does not appear whether the disease is called after the tribe of Indians who are most subject to it, or the Indians after the disease. Some say that the word is Portuguese, but this seems to be a mistake.

The Purupurús, men and women, go perfectly naked; and their houses are of the rudest construction, being semi-cylindrical, like those of our gipsies, and so small, as to be set up on the sandy beaches and carried away ih their canoes whenever they wish to move. These canoes are of the rudest construction, having a flat bottom and upright sides,—a mere square box, and quite unlike those of all other Indians. But what distinguishes them yet more from their neighbours is, that they use neither the gravatána, nor bow and arrows, but have an instrument called a "palheta," which is a piece of wood with a projection at the end, to secure the base of the arrow, the middle of which is held with the handle of the palheta in the hand, and thus thrown as from a sling : they have a surprising dexterity in the use of this weapon, and with it readily kill game, birds, and fish.

They grow a few fruits, such as yams and plantains, but seldom have any mandiocca, and they construct earthen pans to cook in.  They sleep in their houses on the sand of the prayas, making no hammocks or clothing of any kind ; they make no fires in their houses, which are too small, but are kept warm at night by the number of persons in them.  They bore large holes in the upper and lower lip, in the septum of the nose, and in the ears ; at their festivals they insert in these holes sticks, six or eight inches long; at other times they have only a short piece in, to keep them open.  In the wet season, when the prayas and banks of the river are all flooded, they construct rafts of trunks of trees bound together with creepers, and on them erect their huts, and live there till the waters fall again, when they guide their raft to the first sandy beach that appears.

Little is known of their domestic customs and superstitions.  The men have each but one wife ; the dead are buried in the sandy beaches ; and they are not known to have any pagés A few families only live together, in little movable villages, to each of which there is a Tushaúa.  They have, at times, dances and festivals, when they make intoxicating drinks from wild fruits, and amuse themselves with rude musical instruments, formed of reeds and bones.  They do not use salt, but prefer payment in fish-hooks, knives, beads, and farinha, for the salsaparilha and turtle-oil which they sell to the traders.

May not the curious disease, to which they are so subject, be produced by their habit of constantly sleeping naked on the sand, instead of in the comfortable, airy, and cleanly hammock, so universally used by almost every other tribe of Indians in this part of South America?

The Catauixis, though in the immediate neighbourhood of the last, are very different.  They have permanent houses, cultivate mandiocca, sleep in hammocks, and are clean-skinned.  They go naked like the last, but do not bore holes in their nose and lips ; they wear a ring of twisted hair on their arms and legs.  They use bows, arrows, and gravatánas, and make the ervadúra, or ururí poison.  Their canoes are made of the bark of a tree, taken off entire.  They eat principally forest game, tapirs, monkeys, and large birds; they are, however, cannibals, killing and eating any Indians of other tribes they can procure, and they preserve the meat, smoked and dried. Senhor Domingos, a Portuguese trader up the river Purús, informed me that he once met a party of them, who felt his belly and ribs, as a butcher would handle a sheep, and talked much to each other, apparently intimating that he was fat, and would be excellent eating.

Of the Jamamarís we have no authentic information, but that they much resemble the last in their manners and customs, and in their appearance.

The Jubirís are equally unknown ; they, however, most resemble the Purupurús in their habits and mode of life, and, like them, have their bodies spotted and mottled, though not to such a great extent.

In the country between the Tapajóz and the Madeira, among the labyrinth of lakes and channels of the great island of the Tupinambarános, reside the Mundrucús, the most warlike Indians of the Amazons. These are, I believe, the only perfectly tattooed nation in South America : the markings are extended all over the body ; they are produced by pricking with the spines of the pupunha palm, and rubbing in the soot from burning pitch to produce the indelible bluish tinge

They make their houses with mud walls, in regular villages. In each village they have a large building which serves as a kind of barrack, or fortress, where all the men sleep at night, armed with their bows and arrows, ready in case of alarm : this house is surrounded within with dried heads of their enemies : these heads they smoke and dry, so as to preserve all the features and the hair most perfectly. They make war every year with an adjoining tribe, the Parentintins, taking the women and children for slaves, and preserving the heads of the men. They make good canoes and hammocks. They live principally on forest-game, and are very agricultural, making quantities of farinha and growing many fruits. The men have each one wife, and each village its chief. Cravo or wild nutmegs, and farinha, are the principal articles of their trade ; and they receive in exchange cotton cloth, iron goods, salt, beads, etc.

In the Rio Branco are numerous tribes, and some of them are said to practise circumcision.

Others, near the sources of the Tapajóz, make the girls undergo the same cruel initiation as has been already described as common among the Uaupés and Isánna Indians.

On the north banks of the Rio Negro are many uncivilised tribes, very little known.

On the south banks, the Manaós were formerly a very numerous nation. It appears to have been from these tribes that the various accounts of imaginary wealth prevalent soon after the discovery of America were derived; the whole of them are now civilised, and their blood mingles with that of some of the best families in the Province of Pará; their language is said still to exist, and to be spoken by many old persons, but I was never fortunate enough to meet with any one understanding it.

One of the singular facts connected with these Indians of the Amazon valley, is the resemblance which exists between some of their customs, and those of nations most remote from them. The gravatána, or blow-pipe, reappears in the sumpitan of Borneo; the great houses of the Uaupés closely resemble those of the Dyaks of the same country; while many small baskets and bamboo-boxes, from Borneo and New Guinea, are so similar in their form and construction to those of the Amazon, that they would be supposed to belong to adjoining tribes. Then again the Mundrucús, like the Dyaks, take the heads of their enemies, smoke-dry them with equal care, preserving the skin and hair entire, and hang them up around their houses. In Australia the throwing-stick is used; and, on a remote branch of the Amazon, we see a tribe of Indians differing from all around them, in substituting for the bow a weapon only found in such a remote portion of the earth, among a people differing from them in almost every physical character.

It will be necessary to obtain much more information on this subject, before we can venture to decide whether such similarities show any remote connection between these nations, or are mere accidental coincidences, produced by the same wants, acting upon people subject to the same conditions of climate and in an equally low state of civilisation; and it offers additional matter for the wide-spreading speculations of the ethnographer.

The main feature in the personal character of the Indians

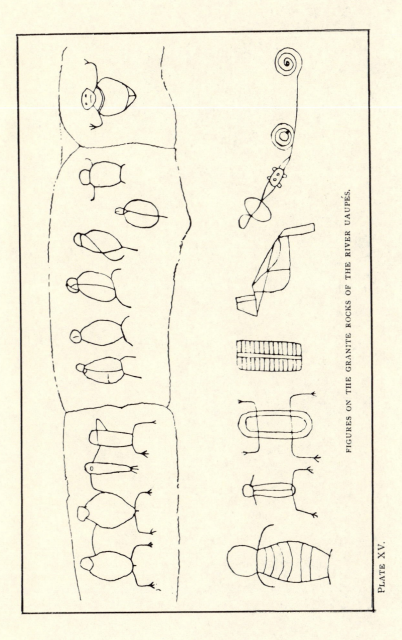

FIGURES ON THE GRANITE ROCKS OF THE RIVER UAUPÉS.

PLATE XV.

of this part of South America, is a degree of diffidence, bashfulness, or coldness, which affects all their actions. It is this that produces their quiet deliberation, their circuitous way of introducing a subject they have come to speak about, talking half an hour on different topics before mentioning it : owing to this feeling, they will run away if displeased rather than complain, and will never refuse to undertake what is asked them, even when they are unable or do not intend to perform it.

It is the same peculiarity which causes the men never to exhibit any feeling on meeting after a separation ; though they have, and show, a great affection for their children, whom they never part with ; nor can they be induced to do so, even for a short time. They scarcely ever quarrel among themselves, work hard, and submit willingly to authority. They are ingenious and skilful workmen, and readily adopt any customs of civilised life that may be introduced among them ; and they seem capable of being formed, by education and good government, into a peaceable and civilised community.

This change, however, will, perhaps, never take place : they are exposed to the influence of the refuse of Brazilian society, and will probably, before many years, be reduced to the condition of the other half-civilised Indians of the country, who seem to have lost the good qualities of savage life, and gained only the vices of civilisation.

# APPENDIX.

## ON AMAZONIAN PICTURE-WRITINGS.

As connected with the languages of these people, we may mention the curious figures on the rocks commonly known as picture-writings, which are found all over the Amazon district.

The first I saw was on the serras of Montealegre, as described in my Journal (p. 104). These differed from all I have since seen, in being painted or rubbed in with a red colour, and not cut or scratched as in most of the others I met with. They were high up on the mountain, at a considerable distance from any river.

The next I fell in with were on the banks of the Amazon, on rocks covered at high water just below the little village of Serpa. These figures are principally of the human face, and are roughly cut into the hard rock, blackened by the deposit which takes place in the waters of the Amazon, as in those of the Orinooko.

Again, at the mouth of the Rio Branco, on a little rocky island in the river, are numerous figures of men and animals of a large size scraped into the hard granitic rock. Near St. Isabel, S. Jozé, and Castanheiro, there are more of these figures, and I found others on the Upper Rio Negro in Venezuela. I took careful drawings of all of them,—which are unfortunately lost.

In the river Uaupés also these figures are very numerous, and of these I preserved my sketches. They contain rude representations of domestic utensils, canoes, animals, and

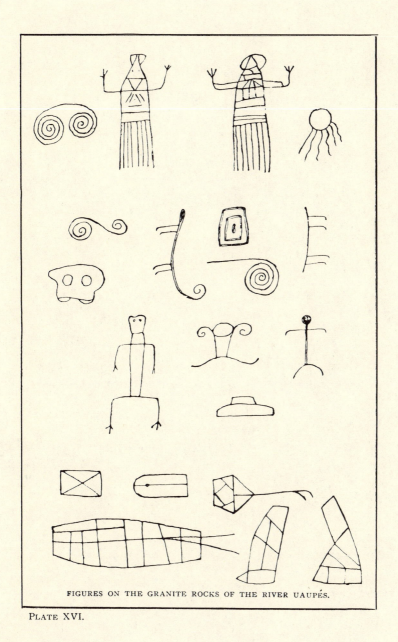

FIGURES ON THE GRANITE ROCKS OF THE RIVER UAUPÉS.

PLATE XVI.

human figures, as well as circles, squares, and other regular forms. They are all scraped on the excessively hard granitic rock. Some are entirely above and others below high-water mark, and many are quite covered with a growth of lichens, through which, however, they are still plainly visible. (Plates XV. and XVI.) Whether they had any signification to those who executed them, or were merely the first attempts of a rude art guided only by fancy, it is impossible now to say. It is, however, beyond a doubt that they are of some antiquity, and are never executed by the present race of Indians. Even among the most uncivilised tribes, where these figures are found, they have no idea whatever of their origin; and if asked, will say they do not know, or that they suppose the spirits did them. Many of the Portuguese and Brazilian traders will insist upon it that they are natural productions, or, to use their own expression, that "God made them;" and on any objection being made they triumphantly ask, "And could not God make them?" which of course settles the point. Most of them in fact are quite unable to see any difference between these figures and the natural marks and veins that frequently occur in the rocks.